T0200996

INTEGRAL METHODS IN LOW-FREQUENCY ELECTROMAGNETICS

INTEGRAL METHODS IN LOW-FREQUENCY ELECTROMAGNETICS

I. Doležel

Czech Technical University, Praha, Czech Republic

P. Karban

University of West Bohemia, Plzeň, Czech Republic

P. Šolin

University of Nevada, Reno, U.S.A.
Academy of Sciences of the Czech Republic, Praha, Czech Republic

A JOHN WILEY & SONS, INC., PUBLICATION

Library of Congress Cataloging-in-Publication Data:

Šolin, Pavel.
  Integral methods in low-frequency electromagnetics / Pavel Šolin, Ivo Doležel, Pavel Karban.
     p. cm.
  Includes bibliographical references.
  ISBN 978-0-470-19550-5 (cloth)
1. ELF electromagnetic fields—Mathematical models. 2. Integrals. I. Doležel, Ivo. II. Karban, Pavel,
1979– III. Title.

  QC665.E4S65 2009
  537—dc22   2009004205

Printed in the United States of America.

10 9 8 7 6 5 4 3 2 1

CONTENTS

LIST OF FIGURES

LIST OF TABLES

PREFACE

Nowadays, most standard problems in low-frequency electromagnetics are modeled via Maxwell's equations and solved by suitable finite element methods (FEMs). This partial differential equations (PDEs)-based approach is used in virtually all modern commercial codes (OPERA, MagNet, FLUX, and others), and its theoretical background can be found in numerous books and other references. Less frequently, finite difference methods (FDMs) are also used to solve PDE-based models–however, these methods are restricted to very simple geometries and lack the option of automatic adaptivity (mesh refinement aimed at the improvement of local resolution), and thus they are not real competitors to finite element methods.

Regardless of the quality of the numerical method used, the PDE-based approach has generic limitations that make it impractical for various important problem classes. These problems, typically, are not widely advertised in the literature since they hardly can be tackled by means of existing commercial or academic software. We can give the following examples:

- Multiscale problems involving geometrically incommensurable subdomains such as, for example, thin conductors of one-dimensional nature, coils built of such conductors, two-dimensional charged surfaces, and/or three-dimensional objects. In such situations, the application of FEMs is problematic due to meshing and other problems.

- The above-mentioned difficulties escalate if some parts of the computational arrangement are moving. Then the computational domain changes in time, and the need for frequent remeshing makes the application of FEMs impractical. In contrast to this, integral methods typically do not require meshing in all parts of the computational domain, such as in the air surrounding charged electrical objects, and thus they can handle motion naturally.

• Problems with uncertain geometries and/or uneasily implementable boundary conditions. As a simple example, let us mention the magnetic field of a time-variable current carrying massive conductor of an arbitrary cross section. In addition to the meshing problems mentioned above, the FEM requires either an appropriate choice of an artificial boundary at a sufficient distance from the solved system or the implementation of some suitable open-boundary technique. These problems are not present in integral models, as the boundary conditions are included in the kernel functions of the corresponding integrals.

Provided that the solved problems are linear and involve homogeneous media, the integral approach is able to avoid many difficulties of PDE-based methods. Historically, integral methods have been used much less frequently in computational electromagnetics compared to PDE-based models. For a long time PDE-based models have attracted more attention than the integral ones since the latter lead to large, fully populated (dense) matrices that are difficult to handle numerically. However, the situation in the domain is changing as progress is being made in the development of higher-order methods that lead to a significant reduction of the number of degrees of freedom, and thus the dense matrices become much smaller and easier to handle. The higher-order methods have a lot of computational potential that has not been explored yet.

The aim of our book is to summarize the current state-of-the-art knowledge on integral methods in low-frequency electromagnetics. It includes theory as well as a lot of examples, which we expect to be interesting for the electrical engineering community. We also expect that readers will appreciate our effort to present the field in a broader context of coupled problems with the dominance of electromagnetic fields, such as induction heating. All computations presented in the book are done by means of our own codes and a significant portion of our own original new results is included. At the end of the book we also discuss novel integral techniques of higher order of accuracy, which undoubtedly represent the future in this field.

We expect that this book will attract new attention to integral methods within the electrical engineering community.

I. DOLEZEL

P. KARBAN

P. SOLIN

Prague, Czech Republic, July 2008

ACKNOWLEDGMENTS

The work of the authors was sponsored partially by the Grant Agency of the Czech Republic (project No. 102/07/0496) and the Grant Agency of the Academy of Sciences of the Czech Republic (project No. IAA100760702).
    The authors also express very warm thanks to their families, without whose support the work on this book could never have been successfully finished.

CHAPTER 1

ELECTROMAGNETIC FIELDS AND THEIR BASIC CHARACTERISTICS

The aim of this introductory chapter is to revise the fundamental laws of electromagnetism and corresponding mathematical models. The analysis starts from Maxwell's equations in the differential and integral forms, constitutive relations, and discussion of the properties of various materials and media. Attention is also paid to the boundary conditions. Then we introduce potentials (suitable for description of fields with slow time variations) that are used for building the models of various kinds of fields (stationary, harmonic, or of general time evolution). The final part of this chapter is devoted to the energy of electromagnetic fields, forces acting on particular elements, and total power balance.

1.1 FUNDAMENTALS

Our considerations will be based on the macroscopic theory of electromagnetic fields working with a continuous model. This model is described by a system of equations for four vector quantities:

- electric field strength E,

- electric flux density D,

- magnetic field strength H,

- magnetic flux density B.

Integral Methods in Low-Frequency Electromagnetics. By I. Doležel, P. Karban, and P. Šolín.
Copyright © 2009 John Wiley & Sons, Inc.

The above quantities are generally functions of position vector r and time t, which can be expressed as $E = E(r,t)$, $D = D(r,t)$, $H = H(r,t)$, and $B = B(r,t)$. We will further accept that these quantities are continuous and continuously differentiable almost everywhere, except for sets of zero measure. Points at which the property of continuity is satisfied are called regular while the other points are called singular. The sets of singular points are represented, for example, by interfaces of media with different physical properties, along which the field vectors can change discontinuously.

Electromagnetic fields may be classified with respect to a number of various features and characteristics. We will present several typical viewpoints (but their list is far from being exhausted):

- field sources (electric charges , currents, permanent magnets),

- dimensionality (that is given by the lowest number of coordinates that fully describe the field distribution (1D, 2D, 3D)),

- boundedness (fields bounded in finite domains or open-boundary fields),

- time evolution of the field quantities (static or stationary fields, fields characterized by harmonic or periodic variation in time or quite general time dependencies),

- kinds of media (homogeneous or inhomogeneous, linear or nonlinear, isotropic or anisotropic, disperse or nondisperse),

- motion of sources or media and so on.

The behavior of macroscopic electromagnetic fields (no matter how they were produced and how complex they are) obeys Maxwell's equations supplemented with material relations. We will provide a brief review of the relevant theory whose elements can be found in a lot of classical and also modern references; see, for example, Refs. 1–12.

1.1.1 Maxwell's equations in integral form

Maxwell's equations in integral form in media unchanging in time read

$$\oint_C H \, ds = I + \frac{d\Psi}{dt}, \tag{1.1}$$

$$\oint_C E \, ds = -\frac{d\Phi}{dt}, \tag{1.2}$$

$$\oint_\Gamma D \, dS = Q, \tag{1.3}$$

$$\oint_\Gamma B \, dS = 0. \tag{1.4}$$

Equation (1.1) expresses the fact that the integral (as far as it exists) of magnetic field strength H along an arbitrary oriented closed loop C is equal to the total current passing through the loop. This current is given by the sum of conductive current I and displacement current $d\Psi/dt$, where Ψ represents the corresponding dielectric flux. The second equation (1.2) expresses a similar rule for the electric field strength; its integral along a loop of the same properties is given by the negative value of time variation of total magnetic flux passing through it. The following equation (1.3) states that the integral (as far as it exists) of electric flux density passing through any closed surface Γ is equal to the total charge Q (that represents the field source) in the corresponding volume. And finally, an analogous integral (1.4) of the magnetic flux density is equal to zero (magnetic field is divergence-free).

Even when Maxwell's equations in the integral form provide a good idea about the relations between field sources and field quantities, their usage for determination of the field distribution is possible only in a few selected cases characterized by linear properties and simple geometries.

1.1.2   Maxwell's equations in differential form

Our attention will be focused first on systems without any movement (positions of its active and passive parts are supposed to be permanent). In this case the application of Stokes theorem on (1.1) and (1.2) and Gauss' theorem on (1.3) and (1.4) leads to obtaining Maxwell's equations in the differential form:

$$\operatorname{curl} \boldsymbol{H} = \boldsymbol{J} + \frac{\partial \boldsymbol{D}}{\partial t}, \tag{1.5}$$

$$\operatorname{curl} \boldsymbol{E} = -\frac{\partial \boldsymbol{B}}{\partial t}, \tag{1.6}$$

$$\operatorname{div} \boldsymbol{D} = \varrho, \tag{1.7}$$

$$\operatorname{div} \boldsymbol{B} = 0. \tag{1.8}$$

Here $\boldsymbol{J}$ denotes the density of conductive currents (that may include both source currents and eddy currents) and ϱ the electric charge density. These equations hold exactly, however, only at the regular points of the domain, while on interfaces we have to use special equations discussed later in Section 1.1.8.

It is worth noting that the methods of solution of electromagnetic fields (both analytical—where possible and, particularly, numerical) are mostly based on algorithms starting from this form of Maxwell's equations. Their principal advantage consists in their ability to cope with nonlinearities, anisotropy, and other nontrivial aspects of the field computations.

1.1.3   Constitutive relations and equation of continuity

Besides Maxwell's equations the field vectors $\boldsymbol{E}$, $\boldsymbol{D}$, $\boldsymbol{H}$, and $\boldsymbol{B}$ are coupled by material (constitutive) relations. These may be presented in form

$$\boldsymbol{D} = \varepsilon \boldsymbol{E}, \tag{1.9}$$

$$\boldsymbol{B} = \mu \boldsymbol{H}, \tag{1.10}$$

$$\boldsymbol{J} = \gamma(\boldsymbol{E} + \boldsymbol{E}_{\mathrm{v}}), \tag{1.11}$$

where the symbols ε, μ, and γ stand for the permittivity, magnetic permeability, and electrical conductivity, respectively. These are generally tensorial, but very often are common scalar quantities that may be either constants or functions of the position, direction, local value of the field, or frequency. Quantity $\boldsymbol{E}_{\mathrm{v}}$ is an intensity of the impressed forces of, for instance, electrochemical, photovoltaic, thermoelectric, or diffusion origin.

Applying divergence to (1.5) and using (1.7) leads to the continuity equation for the conductive current,

$$\text{div } \boldsymbol{J} + \frac{\partial \varrho}{\partial t} = 0. \tag{1.12}$$

This equation (similarly as Maxwell's equations in the differential form) holds at all points of the domain where $\boldsymbol{J}$ is a continuously differentiable function of the coordinates and ϱ a continuously differentiable function of the coordinates and time.

1.1.4 Media and their characteristics

From the viewpoint of their electromagnetic properties, media can be divided into three basic classes: conductors, dielectrics, and magnetic materials. But first we will classify them with respect to more general attributes (uniformity, linearity, and isotropy). Only then will attention be paid to discussion of the mentioned classes, whose properties are, however, rather idealized.

- A medium is called homogeneous when its parameters (permittivity, permeability, electrical conductivity, and others) are not functions of the position. In an opposite case the medium is inhomogeneous. An example of a homogeneous medium is a copper conductor, while imperfectly mixed electrolyte represents an inhomogeneous medium whose physical properties may change from place to place. A medium can also be homogeneous by parts (it consists of several homogeneous subdomains whose parameters differ from each other).

- A medium is called linear when its parameters are independent of applied field. This property is typical for air, various gases, a lot of liquids, and nonmagnetic metals such as aluminum or copper. In nonlinear media, on the other hand, some parameters are field-dependent functions (such as magnetic permeability of iron).

- A medium is called isotropic when its physical properties do not depend on the direction of the applied field. In such a case these parameters are scalar quantities. In an opposite case the physical properties are tensorial quantities (and can be expressed in terms of matrices): for example, cold rolled oriented steel sheets for magnetic cores, piezoelectrics, and other materials.

- A medium is called disperse when its physical parameters are dependent on frequency of the applied field. Media without this property are called nondisperse.

1.1.5 Conductors

Ideal conductors are supposed to contain an unlimited amount of free charges. An external electric field produces motion of these charges to an equilibrium position characterized by zero internal field in the material (the field due to free charges in the conductor is exactly opposite to the original external field). The time necessary for such a redistribution of charges in good conductors (silver, copper, aluminum, etc.) is under normal conditions on the order of 10^{-18} s. That is why we can consider this redistribution practically instantaneous except for modeling extremely high-frequency effects.

1.1.6 Dielectrics

An external electric field described by vector $E(r, t)$ acting in materials without free charges creates from its atoms or molecules (containing bound charges) elementary electric dipoles generating an additional electric field of the opposite direction. This effect is called dielectric polarization and may be quantified by a vector of polarization $P(r, t)$ that at an arbitrary point gives the volume density of moments of elementary dipoles. This vector is expressed in terms of the applied field as

$$P = \varepsilon_0 \chi_e E, \qquad (1.13)$$

where $\varepsilon_0 \doteq 10^{-9}/36\pi$ [F/m] is the permittivity of vacuum and χ_e denotes the susceptibility of the material that may exhibit scalar or tensorial character. The total electric flux density $D(r, t)$ in the material now consists of the applied flux density and the polarization vector, which can be expressed (provided that χ_e is a scalar) as

$$D = \varepsilon_0 E + \varepsilon_0 \chi_e E = \varepsilon_0 (1 + \chi_e) E = \varepsilon E. \qquad (1.14)$$

The sum $1 + \chi_e$ is usually denoted ε_r and is referred to as the relative permittivity of the material. In fact, even this quantity is generally a tensor.

According to relations between vectors E, P, and D, we distinguish dielectrically linear and nonlinear media, dielectrically soft and hard media and finally dielectrically isotropic and anisotropic media. In dielectrically linear materials the dependence between the vectors is given by linear relations while in dielectrically nonlinear materials it is given by nonlinear vector functions. In dielectrically soft materials there is neither polarization P nor electric flux density D without applied electric field E, but in hard materials we find nonzero polarization P and electric flux density D even without the presence of any external field E. While in dielectrically isotropic materials all three vectors E, P, and D are collinear, in anisotropic materials they are not.

Most dielectric materials may be considered linear and perfectly soft. Some of them, called pyroelectrics, exhibit (within specific temperature ranges), however, spontaneous polarization even without any applied field. This polarization can also be affected by mechanical strains and stresses or various state variables.

As for electrically conductive materials, these may be in various applications modeled by a sufficiently high value of ε_r (the higher the polarization, the lower the electric field inside them).

1.1.7 Magnetic materials

Similarly, an external magnetic field described by vector $H(r, t)$ acting in various materials may influence motion of electrons in their atoms and, consequently, their magnetic moments. By their value, we distinguish diamagnetic, paramagnetic, and ferromagnetic materials.

Diamagnetic materials exhibit no magnetic moment in the absence of external fields. When such a field is applied, however, it affects the motion of electrons and a new magnetic field is induced acting against the original field. Thus, the field H is reduced there.

Particles (atoms, ions, molecules) in paramagnetic materials are characterized by a nonzero magnetic moment even without any external field. After applying such a field, particular moments orientate in its direction, thus producing its moderate increase.

Besides nonzero magnetic moments (similarly as paramagnetic materials) without external magnetic field, ferromagnetic materials contain Weiss domains in which particular moments exhibit the same direction. These directions generally differ from one domain to another, so that their effects are mutually compensated. An external magnetic field, however, orients the moments in individual domains to its direction, which causes its strong increase.

The described effects may be expressed by a vector quantity $M(r, t)$, referred to as magnetization. The basic relation between vectors H, M, and magnetic flux density B is given by formula

$$B = \mu_0(H + M), \qquad (1.15)$$

$\mu_0 \doteq 4\pi 10^{-7}$ H/m being the magnetic permeability of vacuum. Magnetization M is also a function of applied external field, which can be expressed as

$$M = \chi_m H, \qquad (1.16)$$

χ_m denoting the magnetic susceptibility that is of scalar or tensor character. Substitution of (1.16) into (1.15) yields

$$B = \mu_0(1 + \chi_m)H = \mu_0\mu_r H, \qquad (1.17)$$

where μ_r is the relative magnetic permeability.

Analogous to dielectrics, even magnetic materials are linear or nonlinear, soft or hard, and isotropic or anisotropic. But let us concentrate our attention on ferromagnetics, materials frequently used in practice.

Ferromagnetics are nonlinear materials in which vectors M and B are functions of not only applied field H, but also of the past history of the material. Magnetization M first grows with H, but from some given H typical for the material used its value practically does not change. The ferromagnetic is said to be saturated (magnetic moments in all present Weiss domains are oriented in the direction of the external field). Such behavior, however, is limited by the temperature. After exceeding Curie's point the originally ferromagnetic material becomes paramagnetic.

The steady-state dependence of B on H is given by the hysteresis curve. This curve is narrow in the case of soft ferromagnetics and wide for hard ferromagnetics. For the sake of simplicity, however, we often approximate at least narrow hysteresis curves (because modeling of hysteresis curves is a relatively complicated business) by magnetization curves that are obtained for the first magnetization of the material.

1.1.8   Conditions on interfaces

Both electric and magnetic fields have to satisfy certain interface conditions, in other words relations between the field vectors along both sides of the interface.

Consider an interface Γ (see Fig. 1.1) between two media of relative permittivities ε_{r1} and ε_{r2} and a point $P \in \Gamma$. The interface contains an electric charge of surface density σ. Let τ be the tangential plane to interface Γ at point P. Lines t and n represent a tangent and a normal, respectively, $\mathbf{t}_0$ and $\mathbf{n}_0$ being the corresponding unit vectors.

The interface conditions for the electric field then follow from integral equations (1.2) and (1.3) and read

$$E_{1t} = E_{2t}, \quad D_{2n} - D_{1n} = \sigma. \qquad (1.18)$$

Consider an analogous arrangement (Fig. 1.2) with relative magnetic permeabilities of individual media denoted as μ_{r1} and μ_{r2}. The interface carries electric current of surface density K_t.

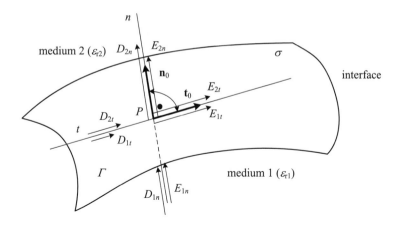

Figure 1.1.   Interface between two media in electric field.

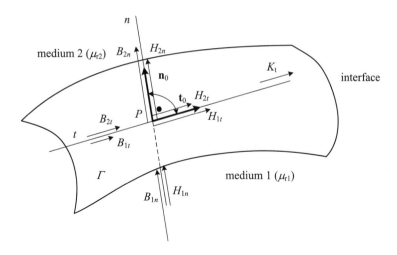

Figure 1.2.   Interface between two media in magnetic field.

Now the interface conditions for the magnetic field follow from integral equations (1.01) and (1.04) and read

$$B_{1n} = B_{2n}, \quad H_{2t} - H_{1t} = K_t. \tag{1.19}$$

The final boundary condition expresses a relation between current densities when a current passes from one medium of electrical conductivity γ_1 to another medium of conductivity γ_2 (Fig. 1.3). This interface condition follows from the continuity equation (1.12) and reads

$$J_{1n} = J_{2n}. \tag{1.20}$$

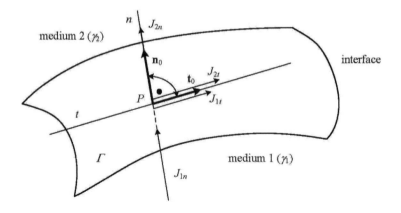

Figure 1.3. Interface between two media in current field.

1.2 POTENTIALS

Computation of electric or magnetic fields by means of the field vectors generally requires determination of all three components and, as was explained in the previous section, these vectors can exhibit discontinuities on various interfaces in the investigated domain. That is why other possibilities of field computations have been explored based on continuous scalar or vector functions, whose distribution would immediately provide the field vectors. These functions are called potentials and in the course of years several functions of this kind were suggested and successfully accepted as efficient tools for modeling of electromagnetic fields. In the low-frequency domain we practically use three of them that will be introduced and analyzed next.

1.2.1 Scalar electric potential

Consider equation (1.6) for steady-state electric field. In such a case the time derivative on the right-hand side vanishes, so that

$$\text{curl } \boldsymbol{E} = 0. \tag{1.21}$$

Now we can put

$$\boldsymbol{E} = -\text{grad } \varphi, \tag{1.22}$$

where continuous function φ is referred to as the scalar electric potential. The minus sign in (1.22) represents a convention that expresses the necessity to do work when a charge has to be moved toward a field produced by a charge (or their system) of the same sign. The electric potential may be interpreted as work necessary for transfer of a unit charge from one point of the electric field to another point. By definition the scalar electric potential is an ambiguous function (its value may change by a constant). However, we can norm this value by putting, for example, $\varphi(\infty) = 0$.

From (1.22) we can easily derive (using a Cartesian coordinate system, but the same holds in an arbitrary coordinate system) that for any two points A and B

$$\int_A^B \boldsymbol{E} \cdot \mathrm{d}\boldsymbol{l} = -\int_A^B \operatorname{grad} \varphi \cdot \mathrm{d}\boldsymbol{l} = -\int_A^B \left(\frac{\partial \varphi}{\partial x} \, \mathrm{d}x + \frac{\partial \varphi}{\partial y} \, \mathrm{d}y + \frac{\partial \varphi}{\partial z} \, \mathrm{d}z \right)$$

$$= -\int_A^B \mathrm{d}\varphi = \varphi_A - \varphi_B \,. \tag{1.23}$$

The integral is obviously independent of the integration path, only on the start and end positions. The difference of the electric potential at points A and B is called the voltage u_{AB}. Hence, for an arbitrary closed loop we obtain

$$\oint \boldsymbol{E} \cdot \mathrm{d}\boldsymbol{l} = 0 \tag{1.24}$$

(fields with this property are called conservative). This implies that no work is done when moving a charge around a closed path.

Sets of points of the field with the same potential (curves, surfaces) are called equipotentials. Their definition reads

$$\varphi = \text{const} \Leftrightarrow \mathrm{d}\varphi = 0 \Leftrightarrow \operatorname{grad} \varphi \cdot \mathrm{d}\boldsymbol{l} = 0 \Leftrightarrow \boldsymbol{E} \cdot \mathrm{d}\boldsymbol{l} = 0 \,, \tag{1.25}$$

where $\mathrm{d}\boldsymbol{l}$ is an element of path lying on the equipotential.

Lines orthogonal to equipotentials are called force lines and their definition reads

$$\operatorname{grad} \varphi \times \mathrm{d}\boldsymbol{l} = 0 \Leftrightarrow \boldsymbol{E} \times \mathrm{d}\boldsymbol{l} = \boldsymbol{0} \,, \tag{1.26}$$

where $\mathrm{d}\boldsymbol{l}$ is an element of this trajectory. These lines begin and end at the charges of opposite signs and, therefore, cannot be closed.

1.2.2 Magnetic vector potential

As the magnetic field is divergence-free (see (1.8)), we can define a vector function $\boldsymbol{A}$ by relation

$$\boldsymbol{B} = \operatorname{curl} \boldsymbol{A} \,. \tag{1.27}$$

This function, called magnetic vector potential, is again continuous and its distribution unambiguously gives distribution of the magnetic flux density. An opposite statement is, however, incorrect. The magnetic vector potential is ambiguous and may differ by the gradient of any scalar function. Several measures can be taken to constrain this function and one of them used for low-frequency modeling is Coulomb's condition,

$$\operatorname{div} \boldsymbol{A} = 0 \,. \tag{1.28}$$

In this way we obtain an unambiguous function except for a constant. Now let us have a look at the integral (similar to that in (1.24))

$$\oint \boldsymbol{A} \cdot \mathrm{d}\boldsymbol{l} \tag{1.29}$$

along a closed path. Using Stokes' theorem we can write

$$\oint \boldsymbol{A} \cdot \mathrm{d}\boldsymbol{l} = \int \mathrm{curl}\, \boldsymbol{A} \cdot \mathrm{d}\boldsymbol{S} = \int \boldsymbol{B} \cdot \mathrm{d}\boldsymbol{S} = \varPsi, \qquad (1.30)$$

where S denotes the area of the loop and $\varPsi$ the magnetic flux passing through it.

Sets of points at which $\boldsymbol{A}$ =const are called equipotential surfaces and lines given by equation $\boldsymbol{A} \times \mathrm{d}\boldsymbol{l} = \boldsymbol{0}$ are called the force lines. These always form closed loops.

Working with the magnetic vector potential is especially advantageous in 2D magnetic fields in which it has only one nonzero component and may, therefore, be handled as a scalar quantity.

1.2.3   Magnetic scalar potential

Consider a magnetic field produced by current carrying conductors or permanent magnets with sufficiently slow time variations. Outside the sources the field may be described by simplified equation (1.5)

$$\mathrm{curl}\, \boldsymbol{H} = \boldsymbol{0}, \qquad (1.31)$$

and hence we can introduce

$$\boldsymbol{H} = -\mathrm{grad}\, \varphi_{\mathrm{m}}. \qquad (1.32)$$

Function φ_{m} is called the magnetic scalar potential, which is similar to the scalar electric potential φ, continuous and differentiable and may change by a constant. This constant can be determined by putting $\varphi_{\mathrm{m}} = 0$ at a selected point.

Although work with the magnetic scalar potential may seem more friendly than with the magnetic vector potential, problems usually occur on the interfaces characterized by a step change of φ_{m}. On such surfaces the magnetic scalar potential is not defined. But on an interface without currents we can define its value so that it is continuous there.

As for the equipotentials and force lines, they are defined in the same way as in the case of the electric scalar potential φ.

1.3   MATHEMATICAL MODELS OF ELECTROMAGNETIC FIELDS

Mathematical models of electromagnetic fields are prevailingly given by partial differential equations (PDEs) derived from Maxwell's equations in the differential form for various field quantities, but from time to time even other models (integral, integrodifferential, or stochastic) may prove to be more advantageous. As for the field quantities themselves, these are either field vectors or potentials. As the potential description is more advantageous (as was explained in the previous section), it is just this conception that will be preferred here.

1.3.1   Static electric field

A static electric field is characterized by the absence of any time variations so that the partial derivatives of the corresponding quantities with respect to time vanish. Substitution of (1.9) into (1.7) provides

$$\mathrm{div}(\varepsilon \boldsymbol{E}) = \varrho. \qquad (1.33)$$

Further substitution from (1.22) for $\boldsymbol{E}$ gives

$$\mathrm{div}(\varepsilon\, \mathrm{grad}\, \varphi) = -\varrho, \qquad (1.34)$$

describing the distribution of electric potential φ in the investigated area. As was explained in the previous sections, permittivity ε may generally be a tensor. Provided it is a scalar and its value is constant, (1.34) may be simplified as follows:

$$\text{div grad } \varphi = -\frac{\varrho}{\varepsilon} . \tag{1.35}$$

This is the well-known Poisson equation of elliptic type for distribution of electric potential in a uniform linear medium. If the domain contains no free volume charges ($\varrho = 0$), we get classical Laplace's equation in the form

$$\text{div grad } \varphi = 0 . \tag{1.36}$$

Unambiguous solution of equations (1.34), (1.35) and (1.36) is determined by using correct boundary conditions (these will be discussed later on in more details).

Poisson's equation (1.34) in linear and homogeneous medium has a particular solution in the form

$$\varphi(\mathbf{r}') = \frac{1}{4\pi\varepsilon} \int_V \frac{\varrho(\mathbf{r})\mathrm{d}V}{|\mathbf{r}' - \mathbf{r}|} + \varphi_0 , \tag{1.37}$$

where $\mathbf{r}'$ denotes a reference point, $\mathbf{r}$ a general integration point, and integration is carried out over the volume V containing the volume charge ϱ. Finally, φ_0 is a constant. The significance of all symbols also follows from Fig. 1.4.

In the case of metal bodies (that may be considered perfectly conductive) the charge is distributed on their surfaces. Now formula (1.37) has to be modified as follows:

$$\varphi(\mathbf{r}') = \frac{1}{4\pi\varepsilon} \int_S \frac{\sigma(\mathbf{r})\mathrm{d}S}{|\mathbf{r}' - \mathbf{r}|} + \varphi_0 , \tag{1.38}$$

where the integration is performed over all charge carrying surfaces. The situation is depicted in Fig. 1.5.

Some references also provide an analogous formula for line charge τ:

$$\varphi(\mathbf{r}') = \frac{1}{4\pi\varepsilon} \int_l \frac{\tau(\mathbf{r})\mathrm{d}l}{|\mathbf{r}' - \mathbf{r}|} + \varphi_0 , \tag{1.39}$$

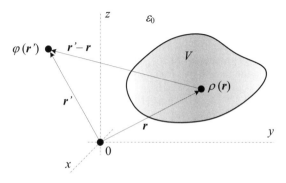

Figure 1.4.   Computation of electric potential from distribution of volume charge ϱ.

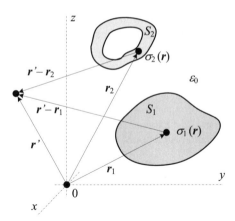

Figure 1.5.   Computation of potential from distribution of surface charge σ.

where the integration is carried out over the line of length l.

Practical calculations of such tasks are usually based on (1.38) (distribution of electric field in a system of metal electrodes). Their principal advantage consists in the fact that potential φ at any point of the electrode surface (where $|\mathbf{r}' - \mathbf{r}| = 0$) reaches the same and finite value, even when the integral itself is improper.

Possibilities of application of formula (1.37) are not so frequent (nevertheless, we could mention, for example, modeling of electric field produced by a thundercloud provided we are able to estimate the corresponding distribution of volume charge ρ). Formula (1.39) cannot be applied for determining potential on infinitely thin line conductors (the integral does not provide finite results for $|\mathbf{r}' - \mathbf{r}| = 0$)), but often it can be used for mapping electric fields in their vicinity.

Knowing the distribution of potential, electric field strength $\mathbf{E}$ may simply be calculated from the formula

$$\mathbf{E}(\mathbf{r}') = -\operatorname{grad}' \varphi(\mathbf{r}'), \tag{1.40}$$

where grad' is carried out with respect to the primed coordinates.

1.3.2   Static magnetic field

Consider a magnetic field produced by direct currents. Maxwell's equation in the differential form (1.5) then reads (the time derivative on its right-hand side is equal to zero)

$$\operatorname{curl} \mathbf{H} = \mathbf{J}. \tag{1.41}$$

Introducing $\mathbf{H}$ from (1.10) we obtain

$$\operatorname{curl}\left(\frac{1}{\mu}\mathbf{B}\right) = \mathbf{J} \tag{1.42}$$

(here it is necessary to remark that in the case of the tensorial character of permeability μ we should write μ^{-1} instead of $1/\mu$) and after substituting for $\mathbf{B}$ from (1.27) we finally have

$$\operatorname{curl}\left(\frac{1}{\mu}\operatorname{curl}\mathbf{A}\right) = \mathbf{J}. \tag{1.43}$$

This is a general equation describing static magnetic field in terms of vector potential $\mathbf{A}$. As far as magnetic permeability μ of the medium is constant (or, at least, constant by parts), it can be put outside the first curl and we can write

$$\operatorname{curl}\operatorname{curl}\mathbf{A} = \mu\mathbf{J}. \tag{1.44}$$

Further treatment of this equation depends on the coordinate system used (see Appendix A). In the Cartesian coordinates, for example, there holds

$$\operatorname{curl}\operatorname{curl}\mathbf{A} = \operatorname{grad}\operatorname{div}\mathbf{A} - \triangle\mathbf{A}$$

and with respect to Coulomb's condition (1.28) we obtain the vectorial Poisson equation

$$\triangle\mathbf{A} = -\mu\mathbf{J}, \tag{1.45}$$

Analogous to Section (1.3.2), for linear and homogeneous media there exists a particular solution to (1.45) in the form

$$\mathbf{A}(\mathbf{r}') = \frac{\mu}{4\pi}\int_V \frac{\mathbf{J}(\mathbf{r})\mathrm{d}V}{|\mathbf{r}'-\mathbf{r}|} + \mathbf{A}_0. \tag{1.46}$$

The significance of particular quantities follows from Fig. 1.6, $\mathbf{A}_0$ being a constant.

Some references also provide similar formulae for plane currents $\mathbf{K}$ (possibilities of its application, however, are rather rare):

$$\mathbf{A}(\mathbf{r}') = \frac{\mu}{4\pi}\int_S \frac{\mathbf{K}(\mathbf{r})\mathrm{d}S}{|\mathbf{r}'-\mathbf{r}|} + \mathbf{A}_0, \tag{1.47}$$

and for line currents I

$$\mathbf{A}(\mathbf{r}') = \frac{\mu I}{4\pi}\int_S \frac{\mathrm{d}\mathbf{l}}{|\mathbf{r}'-\mathbf{r}|} + \mathbf{A}_0. \tag{1.48}$$

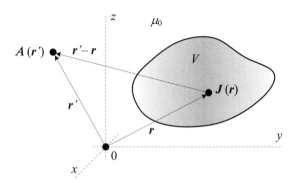

Figure 1.6. Computation of vector potential from distribution of current density $\mathbf{J}$.

The last formula is frequently used for mapping the magnetic field in the vicinity of thin conductors (but not on the line itself).

The comparison of the results obtained for static electric and magnetic fields shows that they are described by similar partial differential equations of the elliptic type or similar integral expressions. Nevertheless, there exists one important difference. Solution of the static electric field mostly starts from the knowledge of potential on electrically conductive surfaces (electrodes) while distribution of field sources – electric charge – is unknown in advance. On the other hand, computation of static magnetic fields usually starts from known field currents. That is why the methodology of solution of these fields may substantially differ depending on particular examples to be solved.

1.3.3   Quasistationary electromagnetic field

In this section we will formulate a mathematical model of an electromagnetic field with slow and medium time variations, where, generally, the time derivatives can no longer be neglected. Nevertheless, we can disregard the effect of displacement currents in equation (1.5). Indeed, let us modify this equation using (1.9) and (1.11). This gives

$$\text{curl } \boldsymbol{H} = \gamma \boldsymbol{E} + \frac{\partial \varepsilon \boldsymbol{E}}{\partial t} . \tag{1.49}$$

Consider now purely harmonic field quantities in linear media, so that we can replace all vectors by their phasors. In this way we obtain

$$\text{curl } \underline{\boldsymbol{H}} = \gamma \underline{\boldsymbol{E}} + \text{j} \cdot \omega \varepsilon \underline{\boldsymbol{E}} \tag{1.50}$$

and compare the absolute values of both coefficients on the right-hand side, that is, γ and $\omega \varepsilon$. In metals representing the principal object of our interest, electrical conductivity γ is on the order of $10^6 - 10^7$ S/m while the second term (considering frequency $f = 10^6$ Hz) for $\varepsilon = \varepsilon_0$ reaches values on the order of only 10^{-4} S/m.

Thus, the model of quasistationary electromagnetic field starts from the equations

$$\text{curl } \boldsymbol{H} = \boldsymbol{J}, \ \text{curl } \boldsymbol{E} = -\frac{\partial \boldsymbol{B}}{\partial t} . \tag{1.51}$$

While the first equation may directly be (in accordance with Section (1.3.2)) transferred to (1.43), it remains to process the second one. After substitution for $\boldsymbol{B}$ from (1.27) one obtains

$$\text{curl } \boldsymbol{E} = -\frac{\partial \text{ curl } \boldsymbol{A}}{\partial t}$$

and the interchange of the time and space operators leads to

$$\text{curl } \boldsymbol{E} = -\text{ curl } \frac{\partial \boldsymbol{A}}{\partial t} .$$

Removal of operator curl generally provides solution:

$$\boldsymbol{E} = -\frac{\partial \boldsymbol{A}}{\partial t} - \text{grad } \varphi - \boldsymbol{F}(t) \tag{1.52}$$

(application of curl on the second and third terms on the right-hand side gives zero). Now let us multiply (1.52) by electrical conductivity γ,

$$\gamma E = J = -\gamma \frac{\partial A}{\partial t} - \gamma \mathrm{grad}\varphi - \gamma F(t), \tag{1.53}$$

and have a look at all three terms from the viewpoint of their physical significance.

Obviously, the left-hand side represents the total current density at a given point that occurs on the right-hand side of (1.43). And the terms on the right-hand side of (1.53) represent its components. The first of them, given by the time variation of magnetic field, expresses the eddy current density so that we can put

$$-\gamma \frac{\partial A}{\partial t} = J_{\mathrm{eddy}}. \tag{1.54}$$

The second term represents the potential component of current density (without any curl) and may be interpreted as density delivered to the system from external sources that is known in advance. Thus, we will denote

$$-\gamma \, \mathrm{grad} \, \varphi = J_{\mathrm{ext}}. \tag{1.55}$$

Finally, the third term (a vector function dependent only on time) may represent an impressed current density of thermoelectric, photovoltaic, or another origin that is denoted as

$$-\gamma F(t) = J_{\mathrm{v}}. \tag{1.56}$$

In most applications the impressed current density J_{v} is equal to zero and we shall deal with it no longer. Substituting into (1.43) for J, one finally obtains the fundamental partial differential equation of parabolic type:

$$\mathrm{curl} \left(\frac{1}{\mu} \mathrm{curl} \, A \right) + \gamma \frac{\partial A}{\partial t} = -\gamma \, \mathrm{grad} \, \varphi = J_{\mathrm{ext}}. \tag{1.57}$$

Distribution of eddy current densities J_{eddy} in the system can be found only after solution of (1.57) using (1.54).

When all source and field quantities in (1.57) are harmonic (which requires permeability constant at least by parts), one can replace the vectors by their phasors and obtain

$$\mathrm{curl} \, \mathrm{curl} \, \underline{A} + \mathrm{j} \cdot \mu \omega \gamma \underline{A} = \mu \underline{J}_{\mathrm{ext}} \tag{1.58}$$

and, in Cartesian coordinate system, the well-known Helmholtz equation,

$$\triangle \underline{A} - \mathrm{j} \cdot \mu \omega \gamma \underline{A} = -\mu \underline{J}_{\mathrm{ext}}. \tag{1.59}$$

1.3.4 General electromagnetic field

General electromagnetic fields with fast time variations must be modeled by the complete system of Maxwell's equations. In this section we will present the model based on potentials φ and A.

The first Maxwell equation (1.5), together with (1.9) and (1.11) gives

$$\text{curl } \boldsymbol{H} = \gamma \boldsymbol{E} + \frac{\partial \varepsilon \boldsymbol{E}}{\partial t}, \tag{1.60}$$

while the second one (see (1.52) without respecting the impressed component) gives

$$\boldsymbol{E} = -\frac{\partial \boldsymbol{A}}{\partial t} - \text{grad } \varphi. \tag{1.61}$$

For the sake of simplicity, material parameters μ, ε, and γ are supposed to be independent of time. Substituting in (1.60) for $\boldsymbol{E}$ and for $\boldsymbol{H}$, we obtain

$$\text{curl} \left(\frac{1}{\mu} \text{curl } \boldsymbol{A} \right) = -\gamma \frac{\partial \boldsymbol{A}}{\partial t} - \gamma \text{ grad } \varphi - \varepsilon \gamma \frac{\partial^2 \boldsymbol{A}}{\partial t^2} - \varepsilon \gamma \text{ grad} \frac{\partial \varphi}{\partial t}, \tag{1.62}$$

while the second equation following from (1.8) reads

$$\text{div} \boldsymbol{D} = -\text{div} \left(\varepsilon \frac{\partial \boldsymbol{A}}{\partial t} + \varepsilon \text{ grad } \varphi \right) = \varrho. \tag{1.63}$$

In this case we usually do not use the supplementary calibration condition for vector potential $\boldsymbol{A}$ in form (1.28), but in another (Lorentz') form

$$\text{div} \boldsymbol{A} = -\mu \varepsilon \frac{\partial \varphi}{\partial t}. \tag{1.64}$$

Introducing (1.64) into (1.62) and (1.63) leads to their further simplifications. But these equations are beyond the scope of this book.

1.4   ENERGY AND FORCES IN ELECTROMAGNETIC FIELDS

As known, an electromagnetic field exhibits thermal and force effects, knowledge of which is often much more important than knowledge of the distribution of field quantities and potentials themselves. We can mention, for example, electric machines, apparatus, and a lot of other devices. Field energy is closely associated with the work that has to be exerted for its generation and represents the source of the mentioned force effects. These effects act on individual elements in the field in such a way that its total energy reaches its minimum (Thompson's principle).

This section is aimed at the possibilities of determining both energy and force effects in electromagnetic fields. Although formulas for their quantification seem to be relatively simple, their evaluation in complex systems containing nonlinear or anizotropic materials (or permanent magnets) requires a lot of effort. That is why we will not deal with these problems quite generally; the situation will be analyzed only in the fields of specific properties.

As for energy, we will independently explore the energy of the electric field and the magnetic field. And in the same manner we will explore the force (or torque) effects.

1.4.1 Energy of electric field

Let us start with determining the energy in an electric field of known distribution of vectors $\boldsymbol{E}$ and $\boldsymbol{D}$. The volume energy is given by formula

$$w_{\mathrm{e}} = \int_0^{\boldsymbol{D}} \boldsymbol{E}\,\mathrm{d}\boldsymbol{D}\,. \tag{1.65}$$

In the case of linear isotropic media we can make use of (1.9), so that

$$w_{\mathrm{e}} = \int_0^{\boldsymbol{D}} \frac{\boldsymbol{D}}{\varepsilon}\,\mathrm{d}\boldsymbol{D} = \frac{1}{2\varepsilon}|\boldsymbol{D}|^2 = \frac{\varepsilon}{2}|\boldsymbol{E}|^2\,, \tag{1.66}$$

where $|\boldsymbol{E}|$ is the module of electric field strength at the given point. The total energy in the domain of volume V is then

$$W_{\mathrm{e}} = \int_V w_{\mathrm{e}}\,\mathrm{d}V \tag{1.67}$$

and when its properties are linear

$$W_{\mathrm{e}} = \tfrac{1}{2} \int_V \varepsilon|\boldsymbol{E}|^2\,\mathrm{d}V \tag{1.68}$$

(permittivity ε was left in the integrand because it may change from one subdomain to another).

Numerical computation of the total energy W_{e} from the previous formula is, however, inconvenient. Normally, electric field is mostly modeled in terms of scalar potential φ. Determination of its distribution is burdened by an error. Another error is produced during numerical calculation of its gradient providing electric field strength $\boldsymbol{E}$, and one more error is caused by numerical integration of volume energy w_{e} over large area V.

That is why another approach to evaluation of the total field energy has been derived. If we confine ourselves to linear fields, it can be shown that formula (1.68) can be modified into form

$$W_{\mathrm{e}} = \tfrac{1}{2} \int_{V'} \varrho\varphi\,\mathrm{d}V \tag{1.69}$$

that is based on knowledge of the distribution of volume charge ϱ and potential φ in the domain. Moreover, integration is performed only over those subdomains V' of total volume V where $\varrho \neq 0$. As far as we work with surface charge σ,

$$W_{\mathrm{e}} = \tfrac{1}{2} \int_{S'} \sigma\varphi\,\mathrm{d}S\,. \tag{1.70}$$

Formulas (1.69) and (1.70) exhibit (in comparison with formula (1.68)) two advantages. First, they work directly with the field sources and potential, so that it is not necessary to determine the field vectors. Second, integration is carried out over much smaller subdomains, which leads to a substantial reduction of both the total error and computing time.

On the other hand, problems may occur with ambiguousness of potential φ that may change by a constant. The question is how to norm its value in order to obtain the correct value of energy. Let us consider $\varphi' = \varphi + C$, where C is a constant, and put it into (1.69).

Immediately we obtain

$$W'_e = \tfrac{1}{2}\int_{V'} \varrho(\varphi + C)\,dV = \tfrac{1}{2}\int_{V'}\varrho\varphi\,dV + \frac{C}{2}\int_{V'}\varrho\,dV = W_e + \frac{C}{2}\int_{V'}\varrho\,dV. \quad (1.71)$$

It is clear that when the charge in volume V' is balanced (so that $\int_{V'}\varrho\,dV = 0$), the result is for any C the same. In an opposite case (physically not quite correct) potential φ must appropriately be normalized or, in order to avoid problems with normalization, we can use less convenient relation (1.68).

1.4.2 Energy of magnetic field

Similar to the previous case, the volume energy w_m expressed in terms of field vectors H and B is given by

$$w_m = \int_0^{B} H\,dB. \quad (1.72)$$

In the case of linear isotropic media we can make use of (1.10), so that

$$w_m = \int_0^{B} H\,d(\mu H) = \frac{\mu}{2}|H|^2, \quad (1.73)$$

where $|H|$ is the module of magnetic field strength at the given point. The total energy in the domain of volume V is then

$$W_m = \int_V w_m\,dV \quad (1.74)$$

and when its properties are linear

$$W_m = \tfrac{1}{2}\int_V \mu|H|^2\,dV \quad (1.75)$$

(permeability μ was left in the integrand because it may change from one subdomain to another).

On the same grounds as in the previous case, formula (1.75) can be rewritten in the form

$$W_m = \tfrac{1}{2}\int_{V'} J\cdot A\,dV \quad (1.76)$$

that is based on the knowledge of distribution of current density J and magnetic vector potential A in the domain. Moreover, integration is performed only over those subdomains V' of total volume V where $J\neq 0$.

Even magnetic vector potential A may change by any constant vector k. Let us now find the value of

$$W'_m = \tfrac{1}{2}\int_{V'} J\cdot A'\,dV = \tfrac{1}{2}\int_{V'} J\cdot(A'+k)\,dV = W_m + \frac{k}{2}\int_{V'} J\,dV. \quad (1.77)$$

As far as $\int_{V'} J\,dV = 0$, both values are the same. If not, A has to be normalized appropriately or one can use formula (1.75).

1.4.3 Forces in electric field

Forces in electric fields can be divided into forces acting on free charges of volume or surface character and forces acting on dielectric materials without any free charge.

We shall start with a formula providing the force effect on a free charge Q of density ϱ in volume V that is placed in electric field $\boldsymbol{E}$. The corresponding volume force $\boldsymbol{f}$ is given as

$$\boldsymbol{f} = \varrho \boldsymbol{E} \tag{1.78}$$

and the total force is

$$\boldsymbol{F} = \int_V \boldsymbol{f} \, \mathrm{d}V = \int_V \varrho \boldsymbol{E} \, \mathrm{d}V . \tag{1.79}$$

Evaluation of force effects in a system of charged electrically conductive bodies starts from Coulomb's law. In a system of n point charges $Q_i, i = 1, \ldots, n$ placed in vacuum the force acting on the kth charge Q_k reads

$$\boldsymbol{F}_k = \frac{1}{4\pi\varepsilon_0} \sum_{i=1, i \neq k}^{n} \frac{Q_i Q_k}{r_{ik}^3} \boldsymbol{r}_{ik} . \tag{1.80}$$

But real systems are far from consisting of point charges. These are usually divided on surfaces of bodies of various geometries (see Fig. 1.7). In such a case

$$\boldsymbol{F}_k = \frac{1}{4\pi\varepsilon_0} \sum_{i=1, i \neq k}^{n} \int_{S_i} \int_{S_k} \frac{\sigma_i \sigma_k}{r_{ik}^3} \boldsymbol{r}_{ik} \, \mathrm{d}S_k \, \mathrm{d}S_i , \tag{1.81}$$

where r_{ik} is the module of vector $\boldsymbol{r}_{ik}$.

Another approach (that is sometimes used for quantification of forces acting on dielectric bodies) starts from the total energy of the system. The volume force $\boldsymbol{f}$ may also be

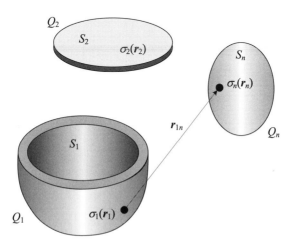

Figure 1.7. Computation of forces in a system of charged bodies.

determined from volume energy as

$$\boldsymbol{f} = -\operatorname{grad} w_{\mathrm{e}}$$

and the total force acting on an element of volume V is

$$\boldsymbol{F} = \int_{V} \boldsymbol{f} \, \mathrm{d}V = -\operatorname{grad} W_{\mathrm{e}} \,. \tag{1.82}$$

This approach requires, however, computation of field energy for two near positions of the investigated body. This is illustrated in Fig. 1.8 that depicts the process of attraction for a piece of dielectric between two electrodes of a capacitor after its connection to a voltage source. In order to find the force $\boldsymbol{F}$ acting on it at a given position, we have to find the total field energy $W_{\mathrm{e}1}$ and $W_{\mathrm{e}2}$ for two indicated positions 1 and 2 of dielectric and approximate (1.82) by

$$\boldsymbol{F} \doteq \mathbf{j} \, \frac{W_{\mathrm{e}1} - W_{\mathrm{e}2}}{\triangle y} \,, \tag{1.83}$$

where $\mathbf{j}$ is the unit vector in direction y.

Such a way of computation may lead, however, to significant errors because both numerator and denominator of the fraction are very small numbers.

The most versatile method (but not necessarily the best one) of determining forces in electric (and also magnetic) fields is Maxwell's approach based on evaluation of the forces acting in the actual position of the body on its surface.

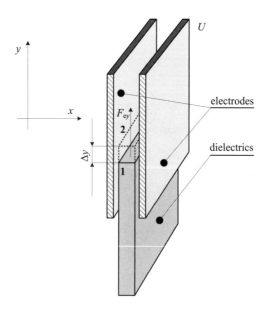

Figure 1.8.   Attraction of dielectric between two plates of a capacitor.

Let us start from the second Maxwell equation (1.6) modified for static field in vacuum in a Cartesian coordinate system. This equation reads

$$\operatorname{curl} \boldsymbol{E} = \boldsymbol{0}$$

and may be expanded in the following way

$$\varepsilon_0 (\operatorname{curl} \boldsymbol{E}) \times \boldsymbol{E} = \boldsymbol{0}. \tag{1.84}$$

Its component in the x direction may be written in the form

$$\varepsilon_0 [(\operatorname{curl} \boldsymbol{E}) \times \boldsymbol{E}]_x$$

$$= \varepsilon_0 \left[\frac{\partial}{\partial x} (E_x^2 - \tfrac{1}{2} E^2) + \frac{\partial}{\partial y} (E_x E_y) + \frac{\partial}{\partial z} (E_x E_z) - E_x \operatorname{div} \boldsymbol{E} \right] = 0; \tag{1.85}$$

an analogous relation would be obtained even for the remaining components. Finally, we can write

$$\varepsilon_0 \begin{pmatrix} \frac{\partial}{\partial x} (E_x^2 - \tfrac{1}{2} E^2) & + \frac{\partial}{\partial y} (E_x E_y) & + \frac{\partial}{\partial z} (E_x E_z) \\ \frac{\partial}{\partial x} (E_x E_y) & + \frac{\partial}{\partial y} (E_y^2 - \tfrac{1}{2} E^2) & + \frac{\partial}{\partial z} (E_y E_z) \\ \frac{\partial}{\partial x} (E_x E_z) & + \frac{\partial}{\partial y} (E_y E_z) & + \frac{\partial}{\partial z} (E_z^2 - \tfrac{1}{2} E^2) \end{pmatrix} = \varepsilon_0 \boldsymbol{E} (\operatorname{div} \boldsymbol{E}) = \rho \boldsymbol{E}. \tag{1.86}$$

Putting

$$\boldsymbol{S}^{\mathrm{e}} = \varepsilon_0 \begin{pmatrix} E_x^2 - \tfrac{1}{2} E^2 & E_x E_y & E_x E_z \\ E_y E_x & E_y^2 - \tfrac{1}{2} E^2 & E_y E_z \\ E_z E_x & E_z E_y & E_z^2 - \tfrac{1}{2} E^2 \end{pmatrix}, \tag{1.87}$$

we can write

$$\operatorname{div}^2 \boldsymbol{S}^{\mathrm{e}} = \rho \boldsymbol{E} = \boldsymbol{f}, \tag{1.88}$$

where $\operatorname{div}^2 \boldsymbol{S}^{\mathrm{e}}$ denotes the divergence of matrix $\boldsymbol{S}^{\mathrm{e}}$ by rows. The symbol $\boldsymbol{S}^{\mathrm{e}}$ itself represents Maxwell's tensor of stress in vacuum and its components S_{ij}^{e} may be interpreted as normal and tangential components of mechanical strains and stresses acting on individual surfaces of a volume body (see Fig. 1.9). The resultant force $\boldsymbol{F}$ acting on a given volume V can be (using Gauss' theorem that is valid even for the divergence of a tensor) calculated as

$$\boldsymbol{F} = \int_V \rho \boldsymbol{E} \, \mathrm{d}V = \int_V \operatorname{div}^2 \boldsymbol{S}^{\mathrm{e}} \, \mathrm{d}V = \oint_S \boldsymbol{S}^{\mathrm{e}} \, \mathrm{d}\boldsymbol{S}, \tag{1.89}$$

where the integration is carried out over the closed surface S bounding the volume V.

It is clear that the total force acting on a dielectric body may be calculated from the knowledge of distribution of the field vectors on its surface. Even when the methodology lacks physical sense (the space would have to be elastic), mathematically it provides correct results.

A simple two-dimensional illustration follows from Fig. 1.10. We want to find elementary force $\mathrm{d}\boldsymbol{F}$ acting on surface element $\mathrm{d}S = \mathrm{d}S_x$, $\mathrm{d}S_y = 0$. Modifying appropriately (1.86), we get

$$\boldsymbol{S}^{\mathrm{e}} = \varepsilon_0 \begin{pmatrix} E_x^2 - \tfrac{1}{2} E^2 & E_x E_y \\ E_y E_x & E_y^2 - \tfrac{1}{2} E^2 \end{pmatrix} = \varepsilon_0 \begin{pmatrix} \tfrac{1}{2} E_x^2 - \tfrac{1}{2} E_y^2 & E_x E_y \\ E_y E_x & \tfrac{1}{2} E_y^2 - \tfrac{1}{2} E_x^2 \end{pmatrix},$$

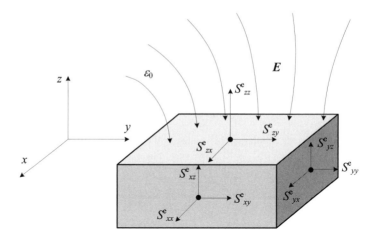

Figure 1.9.   Derivation of Maxwell's tensor.

and (1.89) provides

$$dF_x = \varepsilon_0 \left(\tfrac{1}{2} E_x^2 - \tfrac{1}{2} E_y^2 \right) dS_x , \quad dF_y = \varepsilon_0 E_y E_x dS_x ,$$

$$dF = \sqrt{(dF_x)^2 + (dF_y)^2} = \tfrac{1}{2} \varepsilon_0 (E_x^2 + E_y^2) dS_x = \tfrac{1}{2} \varepsilon_0 E^2 dS_x .$$

Figure 1.10 shows three examples. The first one (part **a**) is the case when $E_x > 0$, $E_y = 0$ and, subsequently, $dF_x = \tfrac{1}{2} \varepsilon_0 E_x^2 dS_x$, $dF_y = 0$. The resultant force $d\boldsymbol{F}$ has direction along the x axis. In the second example (part **b**) $E_x = E_y$. Now $dF_x = 0$, $dF_y = \varepsilon_0 E_x^2 dS_x$. The resultant force $d\boldsymbol{F}$ has direction along the y axis. Finally, in the third example (part **c**) we suppose that $E_x = 0$, $E_y > 0$. In this case $dF_x = -\tfrac{1}{2} \varepsilon_0 E_y^2$, $dF_y = 0$. The resultant

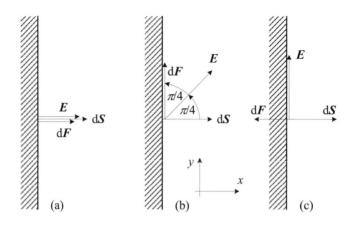

Figure 1.10.   Computation of 2D force effects using Maxwell's approach.

force $\mathrm{d}\boldsymbol{F}$ has direction along the $-x$ axis. It can generally be shown that vector $\boldsymbol{E}$ bisects the angle between $\mathrm{d}\boldsymbol{F}$ and $\mathrm{d}\boldsymbol{S}$.

1.4.4 Forces in magnetic field

Force $\boldsymbol{F}$ acting on charge Q that moves at a velocity $\boldsymbol{v}$ in a magnetic field of magnetic flux density $\boldsymbol{B}$ is given by the formula

$$\boldsymbol{F} = Q \cdot (\boldsymbol{v} \times \boldsymbol{B}). \tag{1.90}$$

The corresponding volume force is

$$\boldsymbol{f} = \frac{\mathrm{d}\boldsymbol{F}}{\mathrm{d}V} = \rho \cdot (\boldsymbol{v} \times \boldsymbol{B}). \tag{1.91}$$

As in conductors $\rho \cdot \boldsymbol{v} = \boldsymbol{J}$, we can write

$$\boldsymbol{f} = \boldsymbol{J} \times \boldsymbol{B}. \tag{1.92}$$

Force $\boldsymbol{F}$ acting on a conductor carrying current of density $\boldsymbol{J}$ whose volume is V in magnetic field $\boldsymbol{B}$ is then

$$\boldsymbol{F} = \int_V (\boldsymbol{J} \times \boldsymbol{B})\,\mathrm{d}V. \tag{1.93}$$

If the conductor is very thin

$$\boldsymbol{F} = I \int_l \mathrm{d}\boldsymbol{l} \times \boldsymbol{B}. \tag{1.94}$$

Analogous to the electric field, the volume density $\boldsymbol{f}$ of magnetic forces acting on a body can be derived from the volume magnetic field energy w_{m} using the formula

$$\boldsymbol{f} = -\operatorname{grad} w_{\mathrm{m}} = -\tfrac{1}{2}\operatorname{grad}(\boldsymbol{H} \cdot \boldsymbol{B}); \tag{1.95}$$

further processing of this equation depends on whether the body is linear or not. The total force acting on an element of volume V is

$$\boldsymbol{F} = \int_V \boldsymbol{f}\mathrm{d}V = -\operatorname{grad} W_{\mathrm{m}}. \tag{1.96}$$

The problems of this approach are the same as for the electric field.

Let us also present the approach based on Maxwell's tensor, at least for a magnetostatic field in a linear medium of permeability μ_0. We start from the first Maxwell equation (1.5) without the time derivative on the right-hand side in the form curl $\boldsymbol{H} = \boldsymbol{J}$, or, after a slight modification, curl $\boldsymbol{B} = \mu_0\boldsymbol{J}$. Now

$$\frac{1}{\mu_0}\operatorname{curl}\boldsymbol{B} \times \boldsymbol{B} = \boldsymbol{J} \times \boldsymbol{B}, \tag{1.97}$$

which, after some rearrangements in a Cartesian coordinate system, gives

$$\frac{1}{\mu_0}\begin{pmatrix} \frac{\partial}{\partial x}\left(B_x^2 - \frac{1}{2}B^2\right) & +\frac{\partial}{\partial y}(B_x B_y) & +\frac{\partial}{\partial z}(B_x B_z) \\ \frac{\partial}{\partial x}(B_x B_y) & +\frac{\partial}{\partial y}\left(B_y^2 - \frac{1}{2}B^2\right) & +\frac{\partial}{\partial z}(B_y B_z) \\ \frac{\partial}{\partial x}(B_x B_z) & +\frac{\partial}{\partial y}(B_y B_z) & +\frac{\partial}{\partial z}\left(B_z^2 - \frac{1}{2}B^2\right) \end{pmatrix} = \boldsymbol{J} \times \boldsymbol{B} = \boldsymbol{f}. \tag{1.98}$$

Putting

$$S^{\mathrm{m}} = \frac{1}{\mu_0} \begin{pmatrix} B_x^2 - \frac{1}{2}B^2 & B_x B_y & B_x B_z \\ B_y B_x & B_y^2 - \frac{1}{2}B^2 & B_y B_z \\ B_z B_x & B_z B_y & B_z^2 - \frac{1}{2}B^2 \end{pmatrix}, \qquad (1.99)$$

we can write

$$\mathrm{div}^2 S^{\mathrm{m}} = J \times B = f. \qquad (1.100)$$

Further work with the tensor is the same as for the electric field. For a static electromagnetic field we can combine both previous solutions, obtaining the formula

$$\mathrm{div}^2 S^{\mathrm{e}} + \mathrm{div}^2 S^{\mathrm{m}} = \varrho E + J \times B. \qquad (1.101)$$

In more general fields the resultant formula contains some more terms.

1.5   POWER BALANCE IN ELECTROMAGNETIC FIELDS

1.5.1   Energy in electromagnetic field and its transformation

As mentioned previously, the energy of an electromagnetic field is closely associated with the work necessary for its generation. But every real system is characterized by loss of this energy due to its transformation to other forms such as thermal and mechanical energies. And as far as the system should work on the same "electromagnetic" conditions, the loss must be compensated from external sources.

In the case that the system contains no moving parts, dissipation of electromagnetic energy is caused by its transformation into heat, which is a direct consequence of losses in the present media. These losses follow from the physical processes in them affected by the electromagnetic field such as the oscillation of molecules or rebuilding of the crystalline structure. Practically, of principal significance are Joule's losses and magnetization losses.

In the next section we will carry out, as an example, the balance of power in the electromagnetic field generated in a linear unmoving system, including any time dependence of its quantities.

1.5.2   Balance of power in linear electromagnetic field

Let us start from Maxwell's equations (1.5) and (1.6). After multiplying (in the scalar sense) the first of them by electric field strength E and the second one by magnetic field strength H, we obtain

$$E \cdot \mathrm{curl}\, H = E \cdot J + E \cdot \frac{\partial D}{\partial t}, \qquad (1.102)$$

$$H \cdot \mathrm{curl}\, E = -H \cdot \frac{\partial B}{\partial t}. \qquad (1.103)$$

Subtracting (1.103) from (1.102) provides

$$E \cdot \mathrm{curl}\, H - H \cdot \mathrm{curl}\, E = -\mathrm{div}(E \times H) = E \cdot J + E \cdot \frac{\partial D}{\partial t} + H \cdot \frac{\partial B}{\partial t}. \qquad (1.104)$$

Considering (1.65) and (1.72) for elementary volume energies of electric and magnetic fields, we can write

$$- \operatorname{div}(\boldsymbol{E} \times \boldsymbol{H}) = \boldsymbol{E} \cdot \boldsymbol{J} + \frac{\partial w_e}{\partial t} + \frac{\partial w_m}{\partial t} = \boldsymbol{E} \cdot \boldsymbol{J} + \frac{\partial w}{\partial t}, \tag{1.105}$$

where the symbol w stands for the total volume energy. Denoting

$$\boldsymbol{N} = \boldsymbol{E} \times \boldsymbol{H}, \tag{1.106}$$

known as Poynting's vector (expressing the flow of energy per time unit through a unit surface whose outward normal is perpendicular to both vectors $\boldsymbol{E}$ and $\boldsymbol{H}$), and using (1.11), we obtain

$$- \operatorname{div} \boldsymbol{N} = \boldsymbol{J} \cdot \left(\frac{\boldsymbol{J}}{\gamma} - \boldsymbol{E}_v \right) + \frac{\partial w}{\partial t}$$

or, after some rearrangement,

$$\boldsymbol{J} \cdot \boldsymbol{E}_v = \frac{|\boldsymbol{J}|^2}{\gamma} + \frac{\partial w}{\partial t} + \operatorname{div} \boldsymbol{N}, \tag{1.107}$$

whose terms may be interpreted in the following way:

- $\boldsymbol{J} \cdot \boldsymbol{E}_v$ is the volume power due to the impressed forces generated at a point,

- $|\boldsymbol{J}|^2/\gamma$ are specific Joule's losses in this volume,

- $\partial w / \partial t$ is the power necessary for changing the electromagnetic field in the volume, and

- $\operatorname{div} \boldsymbol{N}$ is the volume power that gets out of this elementary volume through its boundary.

Except for Joule's losses that are always of the positive sign, the remaining terms may be both positive and negative. Performing the volume integration of (1.107) finally provides

$$\int_V \boldsymbol{J} \cdot \boldsymbol{E}_v \, dV = \int_V \frac{|\boldsymbol{J}|^2}{\gamma} \, dV + \int_V \frac{\partial w}{\partial t} \, dV + \int_V \operatorname{div} \boldsymbol{N} \, dV, \tag{1.108}$$

and, using Gauss' theorem for the first term, we get

$$\int_V \boldsymbol{J} \cdot \boldsymbol{E}_v \, dV = \int_V \frac{|\boldsymbol{J}|^2}{\gamma} \, dV + \int_V \frac{\partial w}{\partial t} \, dV + \oint_S \boldsymbol{N} \cdot d\boldsymbol{S}. \tag{1.109}$$

This corresponds to (1.107) for a given volume V with boundary S.

CHAPTER 2

OVERVIEW OF SOLUTION METHODS

This chapter briefly classifies the methods for computation of electromagnetic fields and summarizes their advantages and drawbacks. It starts from a review of the most important continuous models in electromagnetics and techniques used for their analytical and particularly numerical solutions. Mentioned are their fundamental properties and mathematical aspects (convergence, stability, accuracy, etc.). Some of them are illustrated on typical examples.

2.1 CONTINUOUS MODELS IN ELECTROMAGNETISM

The basic continuous mathematical models in electromagnetism are mostly given in the form of partial differential equations (PDEs) of the second order. Alternatives to these models are models in the form of integral equations. From time to time, however, it is necessary to use other models (given by PDEs of higher orders or integrodifferential equations).

Every continuous problem may be well or ill posed. The problem is called well posed when it has a solution, and this solution is unique and continuously depends on the initial and boundary conditions. If any of these requirements is not satisfied, we speak about an ill posed problem. And in the same manner it is possible to define the posedness of the numerical problems.

There are usually no difficulties with the decision about the existence of the solution. If there exists a solution (no matter whether analytical or numerical), it is possible to say that the first condition is satisfied. Some problems may occur when the solution has to be

Integral Methods in Low-Frequency Electromagnetics. By I. Doležel, P. Karban, and P. Šolín.
Copyright © 2009 John Wiley & Sons, Inc.

calculated iteratively and none of the iterative processes converges. Such a result usually leads to the conclusion that the solution does not exist.

Many more problems are connected with the uniqueness, particularly in nonlinear systems. Ambiguousness was reported many times in association with solution of problems concerning, for instance, bifurcations or phase transitions. The corresponding mathematical models must be solved very carefully and sometimes the ambiguousness of the solution may be removed by imposing some suitable supplementary conditions.

The continuous dependence of the solution on continuously varying initial or boundary conditions is usually closely related to its uniqueness. However, problems may appear when small variations in these conditions lead to large changes in the solution (e.g. in systems with chaotic behavior).

More information related to the topic can be found in references devoted to the theory of differential [13–21] and integral [22–27] equations.

2.1.1   Differential models

The differential models in electromagnetism are given by various PDEs. The main groups of these equations are

- elliptic PDEs,

- parabolic PDEs,

- hyperbolic PDEs, and

- other PDEs.

Even when the formal appearance of these equations may sometimes seem similar, they have strongly different properties and their solution must usually be carried out by quite different methods. In the following we will (without exact mathematical background, which can be found in a lot of references) illustrate the mentioned groups on several typical examples.

2.1.1.1   Elliptic PDEs   The principal representatives of the elliptic PDEs in electromagnetism are Laplace's equation, Poisson's equation, and Helmholtz's equation. These PDEs contain the second (and sometimes also first) derivatives of the field describing the quantity with respect to the geometrical coordinates. This quantity (of scalar or vector character) is either independent of time or perfectly harmonic.

For example,

$$\frac{\partial^2 A_z}{\partial x^2} + \frac{\partial^2 A_z}{\partial y^2} = -\mu J_z$$

is Poisson's PDE describing the distribution of magnetic vector potential $\boldsymbol{A}$ (with only one nonzero component A_z) in a 2D Cartesian region of linear properties with current density $\boldsymbol{J}$ (also with only one nonzero component J_z) and permeability μ;

$$\frac{1}{r}\frac{\partial}{\partial r}\left(r\frac{\partial \varphi}{\partial r}\right) + \frac{\partial^2 \varphi}{\partial z^2} = \frac{\partial^2 \varphi}{\partial r^2} + \frac{1}{r}\frac{\partial \varphi}{\partial r} + \frac{\partial^2 \varphi}{\partial z^2} = 0$$

is Laplace's PDE describing the distribution of electric scalar potential φ in a 2D axisymmetric arrangement in linear media; and finally,

$$\frac{\partial^2 \boldsymbol{A}}{\partial x^2} + \frac{\partial^2 \boldsymbol{A}}{\partial y^2} + \frac{\partial^2 \boldsymbol{A}}{\partial z^2} + j \cdot \mu\omega\gamma\underline{\boldsymbol{A}} = 0$$

is Helmholtz's PDE for the phasor $\underline{\boldsymbol{A}}$ of magnetic vector potential $\boldsymbol{A}$ in a 3D linear medium without external field currents. The field is harmonic of angular frequency ω, with the permeability and electrical conductivity of the medium being μ and γ, respectively.

2.1.1.2 Parabolic PDEs The principal representative is the diffusion equation including not only the second (and sometimes also first) derivatives of the corresponding field quantity with respect to coordinates, but also its first derivative with respect to time. This equation can be used for the field description with not only magnetic vector potential, but also field vectors, for example,

$$\frac{\partial^2 H_z}{\partial r^2} + \frac{1}{r}\frac{\partial H_z}{\partial r} = \mu\gamma\frac{\partial H_z}{\partial t}$$

that describes the time variation of the axial component of magnetic field strength $H_z(r)$ in an axisymmetric infinitely long arrangement. The medium in the definition area has a constant permeability μ and electrical conductivity γ.

2.1.1.3 Hyperbolic PDEs Their principal representatives are the wave PDEs and PDEs describing the transmission of voltage, currents, and other quantities along a line with the distributed parameters. They are characterized by the presence of the second (and in some cases also first) derivative of the corresponding field quantity with respect to time. For example, the transmission equation for voltage on a single line reads

$$\frac{\partial^2 u}{\partial x^2} = R'G'u + (R'C' + L'G')\frac{\partial u}{\partial t} + L'C'\frac{\partial^2 u}{\partial t^2},$$

where R', L', C', and G' are the resistance, inductance, capacitance, and conductance per unit length, respectively, while the wave equation describing the time evolution of electric field strength $\boldsymbol{E}$ in a linear electrically conductive medium can be written in the form

$$\text{curl curl } \boldsymbol{E} = -\mu\gamma\frac{\partial \boldsymbol{E}}{\partial t} - \mu\varepsilon\frac{\partial^2 \boldsymbol{E}}{\partial t^2},$$

ε, μ, and γ being the permittivity, permeability, and electrical conductivity of the medium, respectively. Operator curl curl provides the second (and in some coordinate systems also first) derivatives with respect to the space variables.

2.1.1.4 Other PDEs Besides the above groups, from time to time one has to face problems described by other kinds of PDEs. For an illustration, we show one typical example concerning the time-dependent distribution of voltage in a single-layered coil during a fast transient (which represents a classical problem solved in the domain of electrical machines). The basic arrangement to be investigated is in Fig. 2.1.

The corresponding equivalent circuit with distributed parameters is depicted in Fig. 2.2. It is similar to that of a long line, but contains also the interturn (longitudinal) capacitances of value K' per unit length. Omitted are only the conductances because their influence is practically negligible here.

Now three basic circuit equations — first, Kirchhoff's law for node **2**,

$$i_{\text{L}} + i_{\text{K}} = C'\text{d}x\,\frac{\partial u}{\partial t} + i_{\text{L}} + \frac{\partial i_{\text{L}}}{\partial x}\,\text{d}x + i_{\text{K}} + \frac{\partial i_{\text{K}}}{\partial x}\,\text{d}x,$$

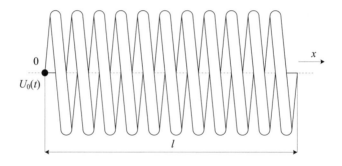

Figure 2.1. A single-layered coil.

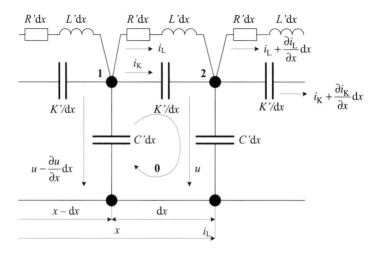

Figure 2.2. Equivalent circuit of a single-layered coil.

second, Kirchhoff's law for the voltage difference between nodes **1** and **2**,

$$i_K = \frac{K'}{dx} \cdot \frac{\partial}{\partial t} \left(u - \frac{\partial u}{\partial x} \, dx - u \right),$$

and third, Kirchhoff's law for the voltage in loop **0**,

$$u - \frac{\partial u}{\partial x} \, dx - R' dx - L' \frac{\partial i_L}{\partial t} \, dx = u \,,$$

provide after several manipulations the final PDE for the distribution of voltage in the form

$$K' \frac{\partial^4 u}{\partial x^2 \partial t^2} + \frac{R' K'}{L'} \frac{\partial^3 u}{\partial x^2 \partial t} + \frac{1}{L'} \frac{\partial^2 u}{\partial x^2} - C' \frac{\partial^2 u}{\partial t^2} - \frac{R' C'}{L'} \frac{\partial u}{\partial t} = 0 \,.$$

As far as the transversal conductance G' would be respected, we would obtain a similar PDE, but with more terms.

2.1.1.5 Boundary and initial conditions for PDEs A very important factor of all mentioned types of PDEs is the uniqueness of their solution. This has to be secured by imposing appropriate boundary (and in the case of time-dependent quantities also initial) conditions.

In electromagnetism we usually work with three types of boundary conditions. If a function f is defined on a domain Ω with boundary Γ (whose outward normal is n), we can specify the following:

- Dirichlet's condition (the knowledge of f along the boundary Γ),

- Neumann's condition (the knowledge of $\partial f / \partial n$ along the boundary Γ), and

- mixed condition (the knowledge of $a \cdot f + b \cdot \partial f / \partial n$ along the boundary Γ, a, b being constants).

The most frequent in electromagnetism is Neumann's condition. From time to time (e.g. when solving electromagnetic fields in rotating machines) one can meet specific boundary conditions of periodicity or antiperiodicity. But they represent nothing more than a modification of Dirichlet's and Neumann's conditions.

The initial conditions (where necessary) usually follow from knowledge of the starting state of the system that is to be investigated. In most cases the quantities under inspection start from zero.

2.1.2 Integral and integrodifferential models

Integral and integrodifferential models may represent an alternative to the differential models; however, their applicability is substantially lower and usually restricted to linear problems. Mostly we meet with three groups of these models:

- models described by Fredholm's equation of the first kind,

- models described by Fredholm's equation of the second kind, and

- models described by more general integrodifferential equations.

While the first two models can be used for solution of static or quasistatic (harmonic) problems, the last one is intended for solving nonstationary tasks or tasks with motion. The integrand then usually contains the derivative of the investigated function with respect to the time.

Similar to the case of differential models, methods of solution of these groups of equations also differ from one another.

2.1.2.1 Fredholm's integral equations of the first kind These equations are often used for finding the distribution of the surface charge in systems of electrodes in linear and uniform media. A typical equation of this kind reads

$$\varphi(r') = \frac{1}{4\pi\varepsilon} \int_S \frac{\sigma(r)\, \mathrm{d}S}{|r' - r|} + \varphi_0 \,,$$

where $\varphi(r')$ is a known potential of the electrode with surface S, ε the permittivity of the surrounding medium, $\sigma(r)$ the unknown surface charge density, and r the integration point. Finally, φ_0 is a constant of integration that must be determined from the total charge on the electrode (as far as its value is known).

Integral operators of the above kind are generally ill posed, so that the solutions of the corresponding equations often require special techniques (e.g. preconditioning).

2.1.2.2 Fredholm's integral equations of the second kind
Linear problems with harmonic eddy currents can often be modeled in terms of Fredholm's integral equation of the second kind. Consider an infinitely long massive nonmagnetic conductor of cross section S carrying harmonic current. The conductor is parallel with the z axis. The distribution of the phasor of the current density $\underline{J}_z$ then obeys the equation

$$- \underline{J}_z(x',y') + \mathrm{j} \cdot \frac{\mu_0 \omega \gamma}{4\pi} \int_S \underline{J}_z(x,y) \ln[(x-x')^2 + (y-y')^2]\, \mathrm{d}S + \underline{J}_{0z}\,,$$

where x', y' are the coordinates of the reference point, γ is the electrical conductivity of the conductor, ω is the angular frequency, and $\underline{J}_{0z}$ is a constant that has to be determined from the value of the phasor of the total current $\underline{I}$ (this case will be discussed in Chapter 4)

$$\int_S \underline{J}_z(x,y)\mathrm{d}S = \underline{I}\,.$$

2.1.2.3 Integrodifferential equations
Integrodifferential equations may be used for the description of linear problems with eddy currents of general time evolution. Consider again an infinitely long massive nonmagnetic conductor of cross section S parallel with the z axis that carries a general time-dependent current $i(t)$. The time evolution of current density over its cross section is now described by the equation

$$- J_z(x',y',t) + \frac{\mu_0 \gamma}{4\pi} \frac{\mathrm{d}}{\mathrm{d}t}\left(\int_S J_z(x,y,t) \ln[(x-x')^2 + (y-y')^2]\, \mathrm{d}S \right) + J_{0z}(t)\,,$$

where x', y' are the coordinates of the reference point, γ is the electrical conductivity of the conductor, and $J_{0z}(t)$ is an unknown function of time that has to be found from the total current using the equation

$$\int_S J_z(x,y,t)\, \mathrm{d}S = i(t)\,.$$

Even this model will be analyzed in Chapter 4.

2.1.2.4 Boundary and initial conditions
No boundary conditions must be imposed in case of the integral equations. In fact, they are part of the function in the integral called the kernel. On the other hand, sometimes one more condition (e.g. condition of the total charge or current, provided it is known) has to be added to secure the full unambiguousness of the solution.

The initial conditions have to be prescribed only for the integrodifferential equations, analogous to the case of the differential time-dependent models.

2.2 METHODS OF SOLUTION OF THE CONTINUOUS MODELS

The methods of solution of continuous models in electromagnetism may principally be split into four basic groups:

- analytical methods,
- numerical methods,

- methods based on stochastic approach, and

- specific methods based on neural networks, genetic algorithms, and so on.

Let us shortly mention the main attributes of these groups. More information about the analytical and numerical methods in electromagnetism (their classification and properties) will be given in Sections 2.3 and 2.4.

2.2.1 Analytical methods

The analytical methods represent the oldest (but accurate and reliable) techniques developed and used for mapping of field and various related quantities. Although they allow solving only linear and geometrically very simple arrangements (mostly 1D or 2D, very rarely even 3D), their principal advantage consists in the fact that the results are usually given in closed, physically clear forms. On the other hand, almost everything that could be solved by these methods was done in the past and since the 1970s their further development has practically ended.

Nevertheless, it would not be reasonable to ignore or even forget these seemingly "obsolete" methods. From time to time we have to cope with practical tasks that can be, after necessary simplifications, transformed onto arrangements solvable analytically. And the analytical solution shows us very well how the real results should look, so that we obtain at least correct qualitative ideas about the data that are to be calculated numerically. We can say that the analytical methods (as far as they are applicable) are useful especially from the prognostic viewpoint.

2.2.2 Numerical methods

Although the numerical methods are relatively young (their "serious" development started only in the second half of the twentieth century), soon they became the most efficient and versatile tool for mapping electromagnetic (and, of course, other physical) fields. Unlike the analytical solution that is continuous and known at any point of the definition area of the task, the numerical solution provides the field quantities at discrete points (nodes or other significant points of the discretization mesh) of this area while elsewhere it has to be found by means of interpolation or other possible techniques.

While the analytical solution is exact, the accuracy of the numerical solution depends on a number of various factors (selection of the numerical algorithm, numerical schemes, parameters of the mesh) and the process of solution has to be checked with respect to the stability, convergence of the results, and so on. (these concepts are explained later on). On the other hand, application of the numerical methods is often just routine work (at least to some extent) and the validity of the used techniques (represented by various procedures and computer codes) is fairly universal. This means that a lot of them may be used, either unchanged or after small modifications, for solution of similar tasks, such as for stationary electric or temperature fields.

2.2.3 Methods based on the stochastic approach

Like the Monte Carlo method, stochastic techniques first became popular in the 1950s and 1960s and were then widely used, for example, for mapping 2D static electric and magnetic fields. As the 2D algorithm was very simple and fast and the number of nodes did not exceed several thousand, the computations took a relatively short time. But later, with the development of sophisticated and reliable numerical methods, these techniques were almost abandoned. Nowadays, nevertheless, stochastic methods again appear in some areas of electromagnetism (signal propagation, hysteresis, geomagnetic field, optimization processes, etc.).

2.2.4 Specific methods

These methods (based on neural networks, genetic algorithms, etc.) are suitable particularly for solving low-dimensional systems and we will not deal with them in this book.

2.3   CLASSIFICATION OF THE ANALYTICAL METHODS

It is not the intention of the authors to give a comprehensive and exhaustive review of the analytical methods in electromagnetics. We just classify them with respect to the basic principles they are built on and show how they can be used for solution of several typical examples. Particulars are only referred to (the number of books and other references in this domain abounds).

2.3.1   Methods built on the basic laws of electromagnetics

These methods are mostly based on Maxwell's equations in the integral form or Gauss' and Stokes' theorems. A must is preliminary knowledge of the distribution of the field sources (charges, currents). A lot of simple examples can be found in the references such as

- electric field of a point charge or charged sphere,

- electric field of an infinitely long thin charged conductor or cylinder,

- electric field of an infinite charged plane, and

- magnetic field of a long, direct current carrying cylindrical conductor.

The results are very simple, the field vectors have usually only one nonzero component that is, moreover, a function of only one variable. Potentials of these fields may also be calculated, mostly in the same or similar manner.

As an illustration, we present the computation of distribution of the electric field produced by an infinitely long electrically conductive cylinder of radius R, whose axis is identical with the z axis and that is charged by charge Q' per meter (see Fig. 2.3). The surrounding medium has constant permittivity ε.

The solution follows from (1.3). The dielectric flux density $\boldsymbol{D}$ has only one nonzero component $D_r(r)$ in the radial direction and there holds

$$\int_C D_r(r)\mathrm{d}S' = Q'\,,$$

where the integration is carried out over the shell C of the cylinder of radius $r > R$, whose length is 1 m. Hence,

$$2\pi r D_r(r) = Q' \quad \Rightarrow \quad D_r(r) = \frac{Q'}{2\pi r}$$

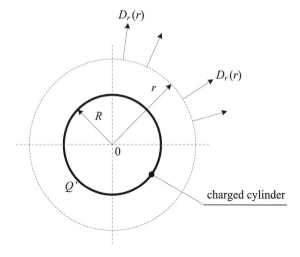

Figure 2.3.   An infinitely long charged cylinder.

and

$$E_r(r) = \frac{Q'}{2\pi\varepsilon r}\,,\quad \varphi(r) = -\frac{Q'}{2\pi\varepsilon}\ln r + \varphi_0\,,$$

where φ_0 is an integration constant.

2.3.2   Methods based on various transforms

Another group of analytical methods is based on techniques allowing transformation of the solved arrangement onto another, simpler arrangement solvable by the basic laws of electromagnetics mentioned in the previous section. The second step is the back transform of the result obtained.

The most famous methods belonging to this class are

- conformal mapping,

- Schwarz-Christoffel transform,

- method of the complex potential, and

- method of images.

All these methods are suitable for solution of both electric and magnetic fields in specific 2D arrangements.

2.3.2.1   Conformal mapping   Conformal mapping is an efficient tool for modeling planar linear static electric and magnetic fields in domains with or without field sources (charges or currents), and with a sufficiently smooth boundary. Its basic principle consists in finding an analytical function of complex variable that would transform the investigated domain into a simpler arrangement whose solution is either easier or even known. The most important property of this mapping is that both its real and imaginary parts satisfy

Laplace's equation and, at a given intersection, it preserves the angles of two arbitrary curves. In this manner we are usually able to transform practically any system of force lines and equipotentials into an equivalent Cartesian or polar system. Another property of this mapping is preservation of the distribution of energy and its total value in the original and transformed domains (which results in the invariance of inductances and capacitances). If the sum of currents in the domain is not equal to zero, we have to take into account a back conductor that is in the original arrangement located at infinity, but in the transformed area we must also consider its effects.

Let us illustrate the method on a typical example. It is necessary to map the electric field between two very long charged cylindrical electrodes whose arrangement is depicted in Fig. 2.4. The relative permittivity ε_r of the surrounding medium (air) is 1.

It is first necessary to find a function that is able to transform the investigated arrangement into a rectangular area in Cartesian coordinates. Generally, it is not a simple task, but there exist extensive lists of analytical functions of different properties. One of them that is suitable for solution of the above problem is

$$w = \ln \frac{z - d}{z + d}, \tag{2.1}$$

where

$$z = x + jy, \quad w = u + jv,$$

and d is a constant. Separating the real and imaginary parts of (2.1), we obtain equations of two systems of circles in the form

$$(x + d \coth u)^2 + y^2 = \frac{d^2}{\sinh^2 u} \tag{2.2}$$

and

$$x^2 + (y - d \cot v)^2 = \frac{d^2}{\sin^2 v}. \tag{2.3}$$

The second step is finding such values of u_1, u_2, and d that, after the back transform, provide the arrangement in Fig. 2.4. So it must hold (see (2.2) and (2.3)) that

$$R_1 = -\frac{d}{\sinh u_1}, \quad R_2 = \frac{d}{\sinh u_2}, \quad d \coth u_2 - d \coth u_1 = a$$

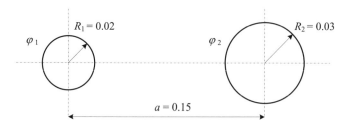

Figure 2.4. Two infinitely long cylindrical electrodes.

and hence, after a cumbersome computation,

$$u_1 = -\cosh^{-1}\frac{a^2 + R_2^2 - R_1^2}{2aR_1} = -1.97329\,,\quad u_2 = \cosh^{-1}\frac{a^2 + R_1^2 - R_2^2}{2aR_2} = 1.59073\,,$$

$$d = \frac{1}{2a}\sqrt{a^4 + R_1^4 + R_2^4 - 2a^2R_1^2 - 2a^2R_2^2 - 2R_1^2R_2^2} = 0.0705534\,.$$

When changing u in interval $\langle u_1, u_2 \rangle$ and v in interval $\langle 0, 2\pi \rangle$ (in the exterior of this interval function v repeats), we may interpret the lines $u = \text{const}$ and $v = \text{const}$ as the equipotentials and force lines in the rectangular area depicted in Fig. 2.5.

Now, for the values of $u = \text{const}$ corresponding to equipotentials in Fig. 2.5 we can, using (2.2), construct the equipotentials in plane x, y; see Fig. 2.6.

In the same way we could, using (2.3), construct the force lines in plane x, y. Finally, the capacity C' per unit length between two considered cylinders, that is equal in both planes

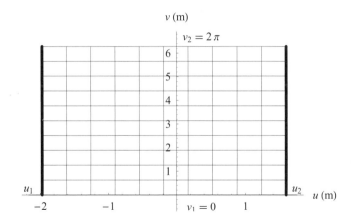

Figure 2.5. A rectangular grid in the transformed area.

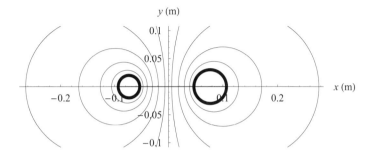

Figure 2.6. Equipotential lines in the system of two long cylindrical electrodes.

u, v and x, y, follows from the formula for a plate capacitor:

$$C' = \varepsilon_0 \cdot \frac{v_2 - v_1}{u_2 - u_1} = \frac{10^{-9}}{36\pi} \frac{2\pi}{u_2 - u_1} = 15.55879 \text{ pF/m}.$$

A more detailed description of the method with complete mathematical background and many examples can be found in numerous references. Monographs about the complex analysis exist [28, 29]. Reference 30 is devoted to classical methods of conformal mapping while Ref. 31 deals with its computational aspects. Simple examples in the domain of electrical engineering are solved in a great deal of classical books [32–33] but even more sophisticated tasks are solved in recent papers [34–35].

2.3.2.2 *Schwarz–Christoffel transform*

As far as the boundary of the domain forms a polygon (that can be open or closed), we can successfully apply the Schwarz–Christoffel transform. Its principle consists in the generation of such analytical functions that are capable of the conformal mapping of a field inside or outside such a polygon. While the generation process itself is relatively simple, the resultant analytical function is usually given by a complicated integral. That is why the mapping of fields bounded by polygons with more than four vertices is quite a difficult business. Otherwise, the basic features of this mapping (that is realized by similar functions as the conformal mapping) are practically the same. More information about this technique can be found, for instance, in a comprehensive monograph [36] and classical books on electromagnetism 32, 33, but from time to time we can find its applications even in more recent papers [37–41].

2.3.2.3 *Complex potential*

The method of the complex potential is an efficient tool for mapping of static linear 2D magnetic fields described by the scalar magnetic potential ψ or 1D magnetic vector potential A (which means that this potential has only one nonzero component). The complex potential may be represented by any analytical function. Similarly, its real and imaginary parts can again be interpreted as equations of the force lines and equipotentials. The investigated arrangements are homogeneous or may also contain infinitely large magnetic walls.

Let us calculate, for example, the magnetic field produced by a long bundle conductor consisting of n parallel thin wires arranged in a regular polygon (see Fig. 2.7). The radius of the circumscribed circle is R and the total current transmitted by the bundle is I (so that every thin conductor carries current I/n). Magnetic permeability of the surrounding medium is μ_0.

The complex potential P at reference point $z = x + \mathrm{j}\,y$ produced by a thin conductor carrying current I/n located at point $z_i = x_i + \mathrm{j}\,y_i$ is

$$P(z) = \mathrm{j}\,\frac{I/n}{2\pi} \ln(z - z_i).$$

The complex potential produced by n conductors arranged in a regular polygon is given by the superposition of all partial potentials, that is

$$P(z) = \mathrm{j}\,\frac{I/n}{2\pi} \ln[(z - z_1) \cdot (z - z_2) \cdot \cdots \cdot (z - z_n)],$$

which gives

$$P(z) = \mathrm{j}\,\frac{I/n}{2\pi} \ln[z^n - R^n],$$

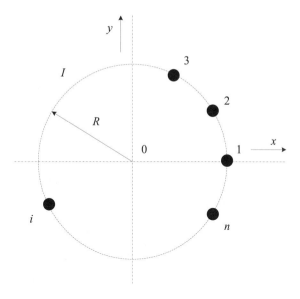

Figure 2.7. Arrangement of the bundle conductor.

because the points $z_1, z_2, \ldots, z_n$ are distributed regularly on the circle of radius R.
Magnetic flux density $\boldsymbol{B}$ is then

$$\boldsymbol{B} = -\mu_0 \left| \frac{\mathrm{d}P}{\mathrm{d}z} \right|^* = \mathrm{j}\, \frac{\mu_0 I}{2\pi} \left| \frac{z^{n-1}}{z^n - R^n} \right|^*$$

(the asterisk denoting the complex conjugate) while the force lines are given by the imaginary part of $P(z)$,

$$\mathrm{Im}[P(z)] = \mathrm{Im}\left[\mathrm{j}\, \frac{I/n}{2\pi} \ln(z^n - R^n) \right] = \frac{I}{2\pi n}\, \mathrm{Im}[\mathrm{j} \cdot \ln(z^n - R^n)] = \mathrm{const}.$$

Figures 2.8–2.10 show the results for $n = 5$, $R = 0.2\,\mathrm{m}$, and $I = 1\,\mathrm{A}$. Figure 2.8 depicts the field distribution (distribution of the force lines) in the system while Fig. 2.9 shows the distribution of the module of magnetic flux density.

Finally Fig. 2.10 shows the distribution of the module of magnetic flux density along the x axis. The same distribution is (due to symmetry) along every straight line starting at point 0 and passing through any wire in the polygon.

More information on the topic may be found in classical monographs concerning the theory of electrical engineering [1, 32, 33] but the methodology can also be found in more recent papers [44].

2.3.2.4 *Method of images*
From time to time it is necessary to map an electric field in the charge arrangement (point charge, line charge, surface charge) – a perfectly electrically conductive surface (plane, cylindrical surface, etc.). Because such a surface always represents an equipotential, in simpler geometries it is often possible to substitute its effects

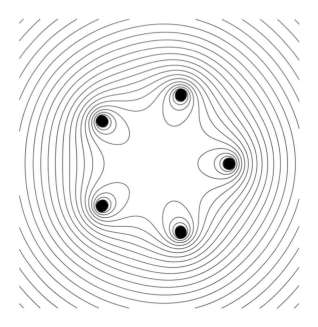

Figure 2.8. Magnetic field distribution in the system.

by a fictitious charge of the opposite sign that is placed behind it. The same holds for simple magnetostatic fields.

A typical example is determination of the capacitance per unit length of a thin conductor placed eccentrically in a metal sheath of circular cross section; see Fig. 2.11. The shell is considered perfectly electrically conductive. The relative permittivity of the medium inside the sheath is ε_r.

The solution starts from determining electric potential at an arbitrary point P in a system of two long parallel thin conductors **1** and **2** of radius r (see Fig. 2.12) in a medium of relative permittivity ε_r.

The potential at point P is now given by the expression

$$\varphi(P) = \frac{\tau}{2\pi\varepsilon_0\varepsilon_r} \ln \frac{d_{2P}}{d_{1P}}. \tag{2.4}$$

where τ denotes the line charge on the conductor per unit length. Usually we do not know the value of τ, but we do know the potential of this conductor with respect to earth (for example). In order to find τ, we put the reference point P on the surface of conductor **1**, at its intersection with line **12**. Then we obtain

$$\varphi_c = \frac{\tau}{2\pi\varepsilon_0\varepsilon_r} \ln \frac{a-r}{r},$$

and since usually $r \ll a$, we may finally write

$$\varphi_c = \frac{\tau}{2\pi\varepsilon_0\varepsilon_r} \ln \frac{a}{r}. \tag{2.5}$$

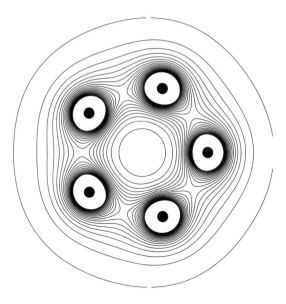

Figure 2.9. Distribution of the module of magnetic flux density in the system.

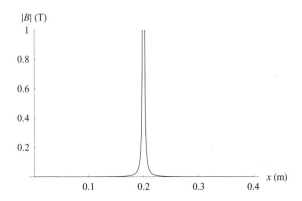

Figure 2.10. Distribution of the module of magnetic flux density along the x axis.

Hence,

$$\tau = \frac{2\pi\varepsilon_0\varepsilon_\mathrm{r}\varphi_c}{\ln(a/r)},$$

and now we can substitute for τ in (2.4).

Let us return to the original example itself. First, we try to replace the sheath by another (fictitious) conductor **2** placed in its exterior, whose still unknown distance with respect to the center of the sheath is b. In this way we obtain the arrangement in Fig. 2.12 again. Second, we find the potential at two reference points X and Y (Fig. 2.11) whose values (as

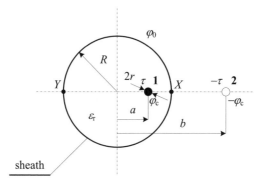

Figure 2.11. A thin conductor **1** of radius r placed eccentrically in a metal sheath.

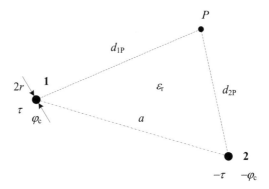

Figure 2.12. Potential in a system of two charged parallel thin conductors.

the sheath is perfectly electrically conductive) must be the same. Now we have

$$\varphi(X) = \varphi_0 = \frac{\tau}{2\pi\varepsilon_0\varepsilon_r} \ln \frac{b - R}{R - a} = \varphi(Y) = \frac{\tau}{2\pi\varepsilon_0\varepsilon_r} \ln \frac{b + R}{R + a}, \tag{2.6}$$

so that

$$b = \frac{R^2}{a}.$$

After substitution into (2.6) we get

$$\varphi_0 = \frac{\tau}{2\pi\varepsilon_0\varepsilon_r} \ln \frac{R}{a}.$$

Potential of conductor **1** itself may be expressed (in accordance with (2.5)) as

$$\varphi_c = \frac{\tau}{2\pi\varepsilon_0\varepsilon_r} \ln \frac{b - a}{r} = \frac{\tau}{2\pi\varepsilon_0\varepsilon_r} \ln \frac{R^2 - a^2}{ar}$$

and the difference between the potentials of the conductor and sheath is

$$\varphi_c - \varphi_0 = \frac{\tau}{2\pi\varepsilon_0\varepsilon_r} \ln \frac{R^2 - a^2}{Rr} .$$

The capacitance per unit length of the system is then

$$C' = \frac{\tau}{\varphi_c - \varphi_0} = \frac{2\pi\varepsilon_0\varepsilon_r}{\ln\left(\dfrac{R^2 - a^2}{Rr}\right)} .$$

More details about the method in common with numerous relevant examples can particularly be found in classical monographs [1, 32, 33], but various authors employ the methodology even in relatively recent papers containing more sophisticated examples [42, 43].

2.3.3 Direct solution of the field equations

In a few practical tasks, the field equations can be solved directly in the analytical manner. But there is usually a number of limitations. The field must be produced by simple sources in simple geometries, and its distribution has to depend on only one coordinate. In more complicated (2D and 3D) problems we can sometimes use the method of separation of variables. But even this technique is practically restricted to fields depending on two variables defined in rectangular, circular, or other areas of simple forms.

The function to be determined is now supposed in the form of the product of two functions, each of them being dependent on only one variable. These functions are given in the forms of infinite series whose type depends on the coordinate system (trigonometric and hyperbolic functions in Cartesian coordinates x, y, hyperbolic and Bessel functions in cylindrical coordinates r, z, and trigonometric and power functions in polar coordinates r, α) and their coefficients must be determined from the boundary conditions.

The fundamental ideas of the variable separation method will be shown on an example in Fig. 2.13 that was studied by several authors [32, 45]. We consider two electrically conductive cylinders (separated from each other by distance $2a$) of the same internal radius R, whose length is infinite. The cylinder on the left carries potential φ_1 while the cylinder on the right potential φ_2. The task is to find the distribution of potential φ in the system.

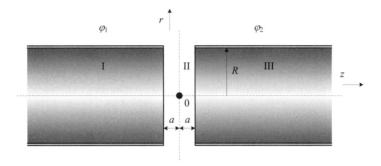

Figure 2.13.   Two infinitely long conductive cylinders separated by an air gap.

The task will be solved in cylindrical coordinates. The potential in the investigated system is a function of coordinates r and z and its distribution is described by Laplace's equation in the form

$$\frac{1}{r}\frac{\partial}{\partial r}\left(r\frac{\partial\varphi}{\partial r}\right) + \frac{\partial^2\varphi}{\partial z^2} = 0. \tag{2.7}$$

Consider now $\varphi(r, z) = \kappa(r) \cdot \lambda(z)$. Substituting this product into (2.7) provides

$$\frac{1}{\kappa^2}\frac{1}{r}\frac{\partial}{\partial r}\left(r\frac{\partial\kappa}{\partial r}\right) + \frac{1}{\lambda^2}\frac{\partial^2\lambda}{\partial z^2} = 0. \tag{2.8}$$

At this moment we can split (2.8) in the following manner:

$$\frac{1}{\lambda^2}\frac{\partial^2\lambda}{\partial z^2} = m^2, \quad \frac{1}{\kappa^2}\frac{1}{r}\frac{\partial}{\partial r}\left(r\frac{\partial\kappa}{\partial r}\right) = -m^2, \tag{2.9}$$

where m is an arbitrary constant; without any loss of generality we can assume that m is an arbitrary integer or a term of a series equivalent to the set of integers. The solution of both equations in (2.9) is

$$\lambda(z) = A_m e^{mz} + B_m e^{-mz} \tag{2.10}$$

and

$$\kappa(r) = C_m J_0(mr) + D_m Y_0(mr), \tag{2.11}$$

where J_0 and Y_0 are Bessel functions of the first and second kinds and of zero order. As $\lim_{r\to 0} Y_0(mr) = \infty$ and potential along the z axis must be finite, the constant D_m must be equal to zero. Now we have to consider three different regions (I, II, and III, see Fig. 2.13) and in each of them the constant m can reach any value. Nevertheless, we will suppose that constants m form a set equivalent to the set of integers, as mentioned before. In this way we obtain the solutions in particular regions in the form

$$\varphi_{\mathrm{I}} = \varphi_1 + \sum_{k=1}^{\infty}\left(A_k^{\mathrm{I}}e^{m_k z} + B_k^{\mathrm{I}}e^{-m_k z}\right)\cdot C_k^{\mathrm{I}}J_0(m_k r), \tag{2.12}$$

$$\varphi_{\mathrm{II}} = \frac{\varphi_1 + \varphi_2}{2} + \frac{(\varphi_2 - \varphi_1)z}{2a} + \sum_{k=1}^{\infty}\left(A_k^{\mathrm{II}}e^{m_k z} + B_k^{\mathrm{II}}e^{-m_k z}\right)\cdot C_k^{\mathrm{II}}J_0(m_k r), \tag{2.13}$$

$$\varphi_{\mathrm{III}} = \varphi_2 + \sum_{k=1}^{\infty}\left(A_k^{\mathrm{III}}e^{m_k z} + B_k^{\mathrm{III}}e^{-m_k z}\right)\cdot C_k^{\mathrm{III}}J_0(m_k r). \tag{2.14}$$

The first terms on the left-hand side of the above equations represent the average values of potential with respect to the z axis.

In (2.12) constants B_k^{I} must be equal to zero, otherwise with $z \to \infty$ the potential would also grow to ∞, which is physically impossible. The same holds for A_k^{III} in (2.14). In this way we obtain

$$\varphi_{\mathrm{I}} = \varphi_1 + \sum_{k=1}^{\infty} E_k^{\mathrm{I}}e^{m_k z} \cdot J_0(m_k r), \tag{2.15}$$

$$\varphi_{\mathrm{II}} = \frac{\varphi_1 + \varphi_2}{2} + \frac{(\varphi_2 - \varphi_1)z}{2a} + \sum_{k=1}^{\infty}\left(E_k^{\mathrm{II}}e^{m_k z} + F_k^{\mathrm{II}}e^{-m_k z}\right)\cdot J_0(m_k r), \tag{2.16}$$

$$\varphi_{\text{III}} = \varphi_2 + \sum_{k=1}^{\infty} F_k^{\text{III}} \mathrm{e}^{-m_k z} \cdot J_0(m_k r) \,, \tag{2.17}$$

where $E_k^{\text{I}} = A_k^{\text{I}} C_k^{\text{I}}$, $E_k^{\text{II}} = A_k^{\text{II}} C_k^{\text{II}}$, $F_k^{\text{II}} = B_k^{\text{II}} C_k^{\text{II}}$, and $F_k^{\text{III}} = B_k^{\text{III}} C_k^{\text{III}}$. Now it remains to find the above constants. We may proceed in the following manner:

- In region I the potential for $r = R$ equals φ_1, so that (see(2.15)) we have

$$\sum_{k=1}^{\infty} E_k^{\text{I}} \mathrm{e}^{m_k z} \cdot J_0(m_k R) = 0 \,.$$

  We see that values $m_k R$ must be roots of function J_0. So first we find these roots and dividing them by R we obtain the values of m_k, $k = 1, \dots, \infty$.

- The same holds for region III.

- Potential must be continuous along the interfaces I–II and II–III. Hence (compare (2.15) with (2.16) for $z = -a$ and (2.16) with (2.17) for $z = a$), we obtain

$$\sum_{k=1}^{\infty} E_k^{\text{I}} \mathrm{e}^{-m_k a} \cdot J_0(m_k r) = \sum_{k=1}^{\infty} \left(E_k^{\text{II}} \mathrm{e}^{-m_k a} + F_k^{\text{II}} \mathrm{e}^{m_k a} \right) \cdot J_0(m_k r)$$

  and

$$\sum_{k=1}^{\infty} \left(E_k^{\text{II}} \mathrm{e}^{m_k a} + F_k^{\text{II}} \mathrm{e}^{-m_k a} \right) \cdot J_0(m_k r) = \sum_{k=1}^{\infty} F_k^{\text{III}} \mathrm{e}^{-m_k a} \cdot J_0(m_k r) \,.$$

  The comparison provides the following results:

$$E_k^{\text{I}} \mathrm{e}^{-m_k a} = E_k^{\text{II}} \mathrm{e}^{-m_k a} + F_k^{\text{II}} \mathrm{e}^{m_k a}, \quad k = 1, \dots, \infty \,,$$

$$E_k^{\text{II}} \mathrm{e}^{m_k a} + F_k^{\text{II}} \mathrm{e}^{-m_k a} = F_k^{\text{III}} \mathrm{e}^{-m_k a}, \quad k = 1, \dots, \infty \,. \tag{2.18}$$

- Finally, for $z = 0$ (region II) the potential, due to symmetry, must reach value $0.5(\varphi_1 + \varphi_2)$. From (2.16) we immediately obtain

$$\sum_{k=1}^{\infty} \left(E_k^{\text{II}} + F_k^{\text{II}} \right) \cdot J_0(m_k r) = 0 \,,$$

so that

$$E_k^{\text{II}} + F_k^{\text{II}} = 0, \quad k = 1, \dots, \infty \,. \tag{2.19}$$

Using (2.18) and (2.19), one can express the potential in particular regions I, II, and III as follows:

$$\varphi_{\text{I}}(r, z) = \varphi_1 + \sum_{k=1}^{\infty} E_k^{\text{II}} \left(1 - \mathrm{e}^{2m_k a} \right) \mathrm{e}^{m_k z} \cdot J_0(m_k r) \,, \tag{2.20}$$

$$\varphi_{\text{II}}(r, z) = \frac{\varphi_1 + \varphi_2}{2} + \frac{(\varphi_2 - \varphi_1) z}{2a} + \sum_{k=1}^{\infty} E_k^{\text{II}} \left(\mathrm{e}^{m_k z} - \mathrm{e}^{-m_k z} \right) \cdot J_0(m_k r) \,, \tag{2.21}$$

$$\varphi_{III}(r,z) = \varphi_2 + \sum_{k=1}^{\infty} E_k^{II} \left(e^{2m_k a} - 1\right) e^{-m_k z} \cdot J_0(m_k r).$$ (2.22)

The last step is to find the coefficients E_k^{II}, $k = 1, \dots, \infty$, which is, principally, not so easy. Several attempts described by various authors in older references lead to acceptable results, but these results were either not quite accurate, or handling them was rather awkward (one of these possibilities consisted in the comparison of the gradients of potential along the boundaries I–II and II–III). The best way of finding them, however, is to minimize the electric field energy in the domain. The algorithm consists of the following steps:

- Determination of both components of electric field strength and its module in all three domains I, II, and III using the formulas

$$E_r = -\frac{\partial \varphi}{\partial r}, \quad E_z = -\frac{\partial \varphi}{\partial z}, \quad E = \sqrt{E_r^2 + E_z^2}.$$

- Computation of the electric field energy given by the formula

$$W = \frac{\varepsilon_0}{2} \int_{V_I + V_{II} + V_{III}} E^2 dV.$$

- Minimization of this energy with respect to coefficients E_k^{II}, $k = 1, \dots, \infty$. This process provides their values in the form

$$E_k^{II} = (\varphi_1 - \varphi_2) \frac{e^{-m_k a}}{2a \cdot R \cdot m_k^2 \cdot J_1(m_k R)},$$

where J_1 is a Bessel function of the first kind and first order.

The algorithm is tested on an example of two cylinders in the arrangement depicted in Fig. 2.13. The shell of each cylinder is supposed to be infinitely thin. The geometrical dimensions are $a = 0.02$ m, $R = 0.05$ m, $\varphi_1 = 50$ V, and $\varphi_2 = 100$ V. For the number of terms of the expansion of the Bessel functions $n = 20$ is the distribution of potential near the air gap depicted in Fig. 2.14.

More sophisticated techniques of this kind can also be used together with the method of images and various transforms.

A comprehensive survey of the methodology can be found in several monographs [20] and numerous practical examples in the domain of electrical engineering are solved in older books [1, 32, 33] and numerous papers. Often the method is used in combination with numerical methods and is employed for mapping fields in air. Worth mentioning are Refs. 46–49.

2.4 NUMERICAL METHODS AND THEIR CLASSIFICATION

Partial differential equations describing most problems in electromagnetism can be solved by the analytical methods only rarely. Moreover, the spectrum of problems solvable analytically has practically been exhausted and this is the main reason why their further development has ended.

During the last fifty years it was the numerical methods that became the basic tool for processing complicated tasks in electromagnetism. Unlike the analytical methods, they do

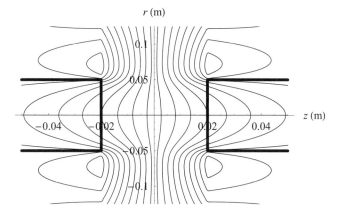

Figure 2.14. Distribution of the scalar potential near the air gap.

not provide the exact distribution of the wanted quantity in the whole definition area, but only its approximate values at selected discrete points, called nodes. The values at other points are then found from the above values, using various interpolation and extrapolation techniques.

The basic aim associated with the development of the numerical methods is to achieve the highest possible agreement between the calculated approximate values and exact solution for the shortest computing time. However, this is not an easy business, as the exact solution is usually unknown. Of course, the quality of any approximate method can be tested on analytically solvable arrangements. But even if its results in such a case are outstanding, this experience cannot, unfortunately, be generalized, particularly when the problem to be solved is nonlinear and/or nonstationary. Every method of this kind, even when functioning reliably for most common problems, may sometimes fail. But the reason is not rooted in the method itself, but in various circumstances accompanying its practical realization. We can mention the ill-posedness of the solved task, round-off errors, and truncation errors.

Even so, it is of high importance for every numerical method to have an error estimator, which is a mathematical formula that allows the method to quantify the error. Formulas of this kind depend on the equation used, on the method, and also on simplifying assumptions. On the other hand, yet not every problem has such an estimator and the available ones often have serious limitations.

Despite a very broad spectrum, since the very beginning of their discovery the numerical methods have been split into two fundamental groups:

- differential methods and

- integral or integrodifferential methods.

Each of these groups contains several subgroups that differ by the particular approach to the problem and algorithm used for its solution. There exist, moreover, methods that combine some features of both these groups.

Thanks to very fast progress in the area, each of these subgroups contains a great number of versions differing from one another, each of them being suitable for solving a specific class of tasks.

In the following sections we will summarize the most important characteristics of these numerical methods and show particular steps of their application.

2.5 DIFFERENTIAL METHODS

Differential methods are based on the numerical solution of the field equations in the differential form and their principal idea mostly consists in approximation of their solution in smaller domains (e.g. finite elements). The group of these methods is relatively wide and may be split into three main subgroups:

- difference methods,

- methods of weighted residuals, and

- variational methods.

2.5.1 Difference methods

Difference methods are based on the difference approximation of the partial differential equations. It means that the partial derivative of any order of a function at a given point is approximated by an expression containing values of this function at several neighbor points and their mutual distances. The fundamentals of this method were developed more than two centuries ago, perhaps by Gauss and his contemporaries. The first algorithms appeared, nevertheless, only in the second half of the nineteenth century, but due to (from the then viewpoint) considerable complexity they were applied only for the solution of a few very simple problems.

Very fast development of the difference methods in the 1950s and 1960s appeared hand in hand with the development of more and more powerful computers. Quite a high popularity was won the simplest five-point (in 2D) or seven-point (in 3D) version of the method, where the unknown value of the function at a point is given as a linear combination of the values of the same function at four (in 2D) or six (in 3D) nearest points.

2.5.1.1 The simplest version   Its basic scheme for a 3D Cartesian grid is depicted in Fig. 2.15. Suppose that the figure represents a part of the domain where the distribution of the scalar electric potential φ is to be found.

Potential φ at points 1 and 2 can be approximated by expressions

$$\varphi_1 \approx \varphi_0 + \left(\frac{\partial \varphi}{\partial x}\right)_0 \cdot a + \left(\frac{\partial^2 \varphi}{\partial x^2}\right)_0 \cdot \frac{a^2}{2}$$

representing the first three terms of Taylor's expansion (the terms of higher orders are neglected). Analogously,

$$\varphi_2 \approx \varphi_0 - \left(\frac{\partial \varphi}{\partial x}\right)_0 \cdot b + \left(\frac{\partial^2 \varphi}{\partial x^2}\right)_0 \cdot \frac{b^2}{2} . \tag{2.23}$$

After dividing the first equation by parameter a and the second by parameter b and summing up the results, we obtain

$$\left(\frac{\partial^2 \varphi}{\partial x^2}\right)_0 = 2\left(\frac{\varphi_1 a + \varphi_2 b}{ab(a+b)} - \frac{\varphi_0}{ab}\right) . \tag{2.24}$$

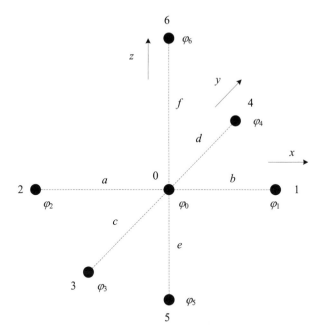

Figure 2.15. The seven-point scheme.

In the same way one could derive in the directions of the y axis and z axis

$$\left(\frac{\partial^2 \varphi}{\partial y^2}\right)_0 = 2\left(\frac{\varphi_3 c + \varphi_4 d}{cd(c+d)} - \frac{\varphi_0}{cd}\right) \tag{2.25}$$

and

$$\left(\frac{\partial^2 \varphi}{\partial z^2}\right)_0 = 2\left(\frac{\varphi_5 e + \varphi_6 f}{ef(e+f)} - \frac{\varphi_0}{ef}\right). \tag{2.26}$$

Processing of the Laplace equation describing stationary electric field in a Cartesian domain leads (at the node with index 0) to equation

$$A_0\varphi_1 + B_0\varphi_2 + C_0\varphi_3 + D_0\varphi_4 + E_0\varphi_5 + F_0\varphi_6 = G_0\varphi_0, \tag{2.27}$$

where

$$A_0 = \frac{2}{a(a+b)}, \ B_0 = \frac{2}{b(a+b)}, \ C_0 = \frac{2}{c(c+d)}, \ D_0 = \frac{2}{d(c+d)},$$

$$E_0 = \frac{2}{e(e+f)}, \ F_0 = \frac{2}{f(e+f)}, \ G_0 = A_0 + B_0 + C_0 + D_0 + E_0 + F_0.$$

The described algorithm leads to a system of common algebraic equations whose solution provides the values of function φ at all internal nodes of the grid. As for the boundary, it is assumed to be characterized by Dirichlet's or Neumann's condition. The system matrix is a band matrix and the width of the band in this case is relatively small. Its construction is very easy.

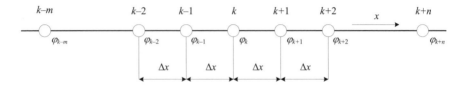

Figure 2.16. A higher-order 1D scheme.

2.5.1.2 *Higher-order finite difference methods*   In the course of years, more sophisticated versions of the method based on the algorithms of higher orders of accuracy began to appear. While the mentioned seven-point method (for 3D arrangements) starts from just three terms of Taylor's expansion, the higher-order methods work with more terms and also with more points. Higher accuracy is reached at the expense of more complicated structure of the system matrix whose band is now wider.

First, we shall illustrate the method on a 1D simple example (see Fig. 2.16). For the sake of simplicity suppose that the nodes along the x axis are distributed equidistantly.

Let us approximate the jth derivative ($j = 1, 2, 3, \ldots$) of function φ with respect to x at point k as a linear combination of values $\varphi_{k-m}, \ldots, \varphi_{k+n}$, that is,

$$\left(\frac{\partial^j \varphi}{\partial x^j}\right)_k = \frac{\sum_{i=k-m}^{i=k+n} \alpha_i \varphi_i}{(\Delta x)^j} . \tag{2.28}$$

The aim is to determine the unknown coefficients α_i, $i = k - m, \ldots, k + n$. We start from Taylor's expansion of function φ at point k, taking into account the first $n + m + 1$ terms. Generally,

$$\varphi_{k+i} \doteq \varphi_k + \sum_{j=-m}^{j=n} \left(\frac{\partial^{j+m+1} \varphi}{\partial x^{j+m+1}}\right)_k \frac{(i\Delta x)^{j+m+1}}{(j+m+1)!} , \quad i = -m, \ldots, n .$$

For example, when $m = 2$, $n = 2$, and $i = -1$, we have

$$\varphi_{k-1} \doteq \varphi_k - \left(\frac{\partial \varphi}{\partial x}\right)_k \Delta x + \left(\frac{\partial^2 \varphi}{\partial x^2}\right)_k \frac{(\Delta x)^2}{2} - \left(\frac{\partial^3 \varphi}{\partial x^3}\right)_k \frac{(\Delta x)^3}{6} + \left(\frac{\partial^4 \varphi}{\partial x^4}\right)_k \frac{(\Delta x)^4}{24} ,$$

and for $m = 2$, $n = 2$, and $i = 2$,

$$\varphi_{k+2} \doteq \varphi_k + \left(\frac{\partial \varphi}{\partial x}\right)_k 2\Delta x + \left(\frac{\partial^2 \varphi}{\partial x^2}\right)_k \frac{(2\Delta x)^2}{2} + \left(\frac{\partial^3 \varphi}{\partial x^3}\right)_k \frac{(2\Delta x)^3}{6} + \left(\frac{\partial^4 \varphi}{\partial x^4}\right)_k \frac{(2\Delta x)^4}{24} .$$

Substituting the above results into (2.28) and comparing the terms corresponding to the particular derivatives with respect to x, we easily obtain a system of algebraic equations in the following form:

$$\sum_{i=1}^{i=m+n+1} \alpha_i = 0$$

for the zeroth derivatives;

$$\sum_{i=1}^{i=m+n+1} \frac{(i-1-m)^1}{1!} \alpha_i = 0\,,$$

$$\vdots$$

for the jth derivatives;

$$\sum_{i=1}^{i=m+n+1} \frac{(i-1-m)^j}{j!} \alpha_i = 1$$

$$\vdots$$

and

$$\sum_{i=1}^{i=m+n+1} \frac{(i-1-m)^{n+m}}{(n+m)!} \alpha_i = 0$$

for the $(m+n)$th derivatives. The right-side vector contains zeros except for the $(j+1)$st element that is equal to 1.

For example, the typical system matrix for $m=2$ and $n=2$ reads

$$\boldsymbol{A} = \begin{pmatrix} 1 & 1 & 1 & 1 & 1 \\ -2 & -1 & 0 & 1 & 2 \\ 2 & \frac{1}{2} & 0 & \frac{1}{2} & 2 \\ -\frac{4}{3} & -\frac{1}{6} & 0 & \frac{1}{6} & \frac{4}{3} \\ \frac{2}{3} & \frac{1}{24} & 0 & \frac{1}{24} & \frac{2}{3} \end{pmatrix}\,,$$

its element with indices i and j being given by the formula

$$a_{ij} = \frac{(j-1-m)^{i-1}}{i!}\,, \quad i,j = 1,\ldots,m+n+1\,.$$

Its inverse is

$$\boldsymbol{A}^{-1} = \begin{pmatrix} 0 & \frac{1}{12} & -\frac{1}{12} & -\frac{1}{2} & 1 \\ 0 & -\frac{2}{3} & \frac{4}{3} & 1 & -4 \\ 1 & 0 & -\frac{5}{2} & 0 & 6 \\ 0 & \frac{2}{3} & \frac{4}{3} & -1 & -4 \\ 0 & -\frac{1}{12} & -\frac{1}{12} & \frac{1}{2} & 1 \end{pmatrix}\,.$$

Now for the first derivative $(j=1)$ at point k in (2.28) we obtain

$$\alpha_1 = \frac{1}{12}\,, \quad \alpha_2 = -\frac{2}{3}\,, \quad \alpha_3 = 0\,, \quad \alpha_4 = \frac{2}{3}\,, \quad \alpha_5 = -\frac{1}{12}$$

(the coefficients being given by the elements in the second column of matrix $\boldsymbol{A}^{-1}$), so that

$$\left(\frac{\partial \varphi}{\partial x}\right)_k \doteq \frac{\varphi_{k-2} - 8\varphi_{k-1} + 8\varphi_{k+1} - \varphi_{k+2}}{12\Delta x}\,.$$

Analogously, the second derivative ($j = 2$) of function φ at the central point k may be approximated by the formula

$$\left(\frac{\partial^2 \varphi}{\partial x^2}\right)_k \doteq \frac{-\varphi_{k-2} + 16\varphi_{k-1} - 30\varphi_k + 16\varphi_{k+1} - \varphi_{k+2}}{12(\Delta x)^2},$$

where the coefficients are the elements of the third column of matrix $\boldsymbol{A}^{-1}$.

Another example is calculated for $m = 0$ and $n = 3$. The system matrix is now

$$\boldsymbol{A} = \begin{pmatrix} 1 & 1 & 1 & 1 \\ 0 & 1 & 2 & 3 \\ 0 & \frac{1}{2} & 2 & \frac{9}{2} \\ 0 & \frac{1}{6} & \frac{4}{3} & \frac{9}{2} \end{pmatrix}$$

and the corresponding inverse matrix is

$$\boldsymbol{A}^{-1} = \begin{pmatrix} 1 & -\frac{11}{6} & 2 & -1 \\ 0 & 3 & -5 & 3 \\ 0 & -\frac{3}{2} & 4 & -3 \\ 0 & \frac{1}{3} & -1 & 1 \end{pmatrix}.$$

So, for example,

$$\left(\frac{\partial \varphi}{\partial x}\right)_k \doteq \frac{-11\varphi_k + 18\varphi_{k+1} - 9\varphi_{k+2} + 2\varphi_{k+3}}{6\Delta x}$$

(the coefficients being the elements of the second column of matrix $\boldsymbol{A}^{-1}$),

$$\left(\frac{\partial^2 \varphi}{\partial x^2}\right)_k \doteq \frac{2\varphi_k - 5\varphi_{k+1} + 4\varphi_{k+2} - \varphi_{k+3}}{(\Delta x)^2}$$

(the coefficients being the elements of the third column of matrix $\boldsymbol{A}^{-1}$), and

$$\left(\frac{\partial^3 \varphi}{\partial x^3}\right)_k \doteq \frac{-\varphi_k + 3\varphi_{k+1} - 3\varphi_{k+2} + \varphi_{k+3}}{(\Delta x)^3}$$

(the coefficients are the elements of the fourth column of matrix $\boldsymbol{A}^{-1}$).

In the same manner we can construct analogous approximations of the partial derivatives of function φ in the remaining directions y and z.

If the points in a particular direction are not distributed equidistantly, the corresponding expressions are no longer so simple and include complete information about the position of particular points taking part in the approximation. That is why regular grids are preferred for higher-order difference schemes.

The accuracy of the higher-order difference methods based on $m + n + 1$ points is of the $(m + n)$th order.

2.5.1.3 *Advantages and disadvantages of the difference methods* Despite their simplicity, the difference methods did not become too popular. The principal reason consisted in the necessity of covering the investigated area by a topologically orthogonal discretization grid. In the case of domains with curvilinear boundaries or interfaces, it is very difficult to realize. A number of authors tried to develop special difference algorithms

even for nonorthogonal meshes, but they were highly nontrivial and awkward and the technical community did not adopt them. Another reason was the problems on interfaces. As is known, Maxwell's equations in the differential form do not hold along them and, consequently, neither do their difference approximations. The interfaces had to be described by approximations of the interface conditions, which also leads to some complications associated with the building of the corresponding algorithms for assembling the system matrices. The third reason at that time (1970s) was the rapid growth of popularity of the variational methods, particularly the finite element method.

At present, the finite difference methods are used (due to their simplicity) for education of students who employ them for the solution of simple, mostly planar tasks. But their implementation into professional codes has practically been abandoned.

Very comprehensive information about the difference method can be found in a lot of relevant monographs [51–54].

2.5.2 Weighted residual methods

This group of methods is perhaps the most general and versatile tool for solving partial differential equations and may often be used even for solution of such problems where other methods (difference or variational) fail. These methods are based on the minimization of the weighted error in the investigated domain.

Consider a partial differential equation defined on domain Ω in the form

$$L\varphi = 0\,, \tag{2.29}$$

where L is a differential operator and φ an unknown solution. This solution can depend on both spatial coordinates and time and we suppose that it is approximated by the series

$$\varphi' = \sum_{i=1}^{n} \alpha_i(t) f_i(u)\,. \tag{2.30}$$

where functions $f_i(u)$, $i = 1, \ldots, n$ are called testing functions (symbol u denoting a set of coordinates, e.g. x, y, and z) and $\alpha_i(t)$, $i = 1, \ldots, n$ represent unknown coefficients that can generally be functions of time. The testing functions must satisfy the boundary conditions and their set has to be linearly independent and complete. Typical examples are functions of polynomial character.

But for such an approximated solution, the right-side hand of (2.29) does provides not zero, but a nonzero quantity R called the residuum . So we obtain

$$L\varphi' = R\,. \tag{2.31}$$

Now the goal is to find the coefficients $\alpha_i(t)$, $i = 1, \ldots, n$ that would minimize the value of R. This may be achieved by imposing the condition

$$\int_{\Omega} R \cdot W_j(u) \mathrm{d}\Omega = 0\,, \tag{2.32}$$

where $W_j(u)$, $j = 1, \ldots, m$, are appropriate weight functions. The way of selecting the weight functions is the principal factor for classifying the version of the weighted residual method. We will mention the following five variants:

- method of subdomains,

- collocation method,

- least-square method,

- method of moments, and

- Galerkin's method.

2.5.2.1 Method of subdomains The definition area Ω is first divided into m subdomains Ω_j, $j = 1, \ldots, m$. The weight functions $W_j(u)$, $j = 1, \ldots, m$ are now defined as

$$W_j(u) = 1 \text{ in the subdomain } \Omega_j, \quad W_j(u) = 0 \text{ elsewhere.}$$

The selection of the subdomains is quite arbitrary. In many cases the uniform subdivision appears to be the most advantageous. But in some cases the accuracy of the results may grow with the level of nonuniformity of the division.

2.5.2.2 Collocation method In this case the weight function at point u_j is represented by Dirac's function in the form

$$W_j(u) = \delta(u - u_j), \; j = 1, \ldots, m.$$

Every point like u_j then exhibits no error.

2.5.2.3 Least-square method In this case the weight functions are defined as the derivatives of the residuum with respect to the coefficients of the approximative solution, that is,

$$W_j(u) = \frac{\partial R}{\partial \alpha_j}, \; j = 1, \ldots, m.$$

In fact, the process represents the minimization of the integral $\int_\Omega R^2 d\Omega$ because by definition

$$\frac{\partial}{\partial \alpha_j} \int_\Omega R^2 d\Omega = 0, \; j = 1, \ldots, m.$$

2.5.2.4 Method of moments If the weight functions are considered in the form $W_j(u) = \sum_{i=0}^{j-1} a_{i,j} u^i$, we speak about the method of moments.

2.5.2.5 Galerkin's method Now the weight functions are identical with the testing functions, so that $m = n$ and $W_j(u) = f_j(u)$, $j = 1, \ldots, m$. This selection is very advantageous, particularly in the case where the testing functions are mutually orthogonal.

For an illustration we will present a simple 1D example that is solved using this method. Consider an infinite thin metal cylinder of radius R (see Fig. 2.17) whose interior of permittivity ε_r contains nonuniformly distributed volume charge of density $\varrho = \varrho_0(R^2 - r^2)$ (ϱ_0 being a constant). The cylinder itself is grounded, that is, its potential $\varphi(R) = 0$. The task is to find the distribution of potential φ along its radius, that is, $\varphi(r), r \in \langle 0, R \rangle$.

We will first solve the problem exactly. It is clearly described by Poisson's equation in the form

$$\frac{1}{r} \frac{d}{dr} \left(r \frac{d\varphi}{dr} \right) = -\frac{\varrho}{\varepsilon_0 \varepsilon_r} = -\frac{\varrho_0(R^2 - r^2)}{\varepsilon_0 \varepsilon_r} \tag{2.33}$$

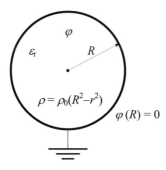

Figure 2.17.   The investigated cylinder.

with boundary condition $\varphi(R) = 0$. From (2.33) we first obtain

$$\frac{\mathrm{d}}{\mathrm{d}r}\left(r\frac{\mathrm{d}\varphi}{\mathrm{d}r}\right) = -\frac{\varrho_0(R^2 - r^2)r}{\varepsilon_0\varepsilon_{\mathrm{r}}}$$

and, after integration with respect to r,

$$r\frac{\mathrm{d}\varphi}{\mathrm{d}r} = -\frac{\varrho_0(2R^2 - r^2)r^2}{4\varepsilon_0\varepsilon_{\mathrm{r}}} + C,$$

where C is an integration constant. Hence,

$$\frac{\mathrm{d}\varphi}{\mathrm{d}r} = -\frac{\varrho_0(2R^2 - r^2)r}{4\varepsilon_0\varepsilon_{\mathrm{r}}} + \frac{C}{r},$$

so that, after next integration with respect to r,

$$\varphi = -\frac{\varrho_0(4R^2 - r^2)r^2}{16\varepsilon_0\varepsilon_{\mathrm{r}}} + C\ln r + D,$$

where D is another constant. Evidently, the constant C has to be equal to zero, because for $r \to 0$ the value of potential φ would grow to infinity. And the value of constant D follows from the boundary condition $\varphi(R) = 0$. Immediately we obtain

$$D = \frac{3\varrho_0 R^4}{16\varepsilon_0\varepsilon_{\mathrm{r}}},$$

so that the exact solution reads

$$\varphi = \frac{\varrho_0(R^2 - r^2)(3R^2 - r^2)}{16\varepsilon_0\varepsilon_{\mathrm{r}}}. \tag{2.34}$$

Now we shall deal with the approximate solution φ'. It is necessary first to select the testing functions. Let us choose

$$f_i(r) = (R^2 - r^2)^i, \quad i = 1, \dots, k, \tag{2.35}$$

where $k \geq 2$ is an integer. All the testing functions evidently satisfy the boundary condition. The approximate solution is now given in the form

$$\varphi' = \sum_{i=1}^{k} \alpha_i f_i(r), \qquad (2.36)$$

where α_i, $i = 1, \ldots, k$ are the unknown coefficients.

Substituting (2.36) into (2.33) we obtain

$$\begin{aligned}
\text{Res} &= \frac{1}{r}\frac{d}{dr}\left(r\frac{d\varphi'}{dr}\right) + \frac{\varrho_0(R^2 - r^2)}{\varepsilon_0 \varepsilon_r} \\
&= \frac{1}{r}\frac{d}{dr}\left(r \cdot \frac{d\sum_{i=1}^{k}\alpha_i(R^2 - r^2)^i}{dr}\right) + \frac{\varrho_0(R^2 - r^2)}{\varepsilon_0 \varepsilon_r},
\end{aligned}$$

and after carrying out the derivatives we have

$$\text{Res} = 4\sum_{i=1}^{k} i \cdot \alpha_i \cdot (R^2 - r^2)^{i-2}(ir^2 - R^2) + \frac{\varrho_0(R^2 - r^2)}{\varepsilon_0 \varepsilon_r}.$$

This expression is, in fact, the residual (see (2.31)) that is, at least in this example, denoted as Res in order to avoid confusing with symbol R that is used for the radius of the cylinder.

For Galerkin's technique, the weight functions $W_j(r)$ are identical with the testing functions, i.e.

$$W_j(r) = (R^2 - r^2)^j, \quad j = 1, \ldots, k, \qquad (2.37)$$

and these functions will be applied to the integration of (2.32). In this manner we obtain a system of equalities in the form

$$\int_0^R \text{Res} \cdot W_j(r)dr = 0, \quad j = 1, \ldots, k$$

or, after substituting for the residual Res and $W_j(r)$,

$$\int_0^R \left[4\sum_{i=1}^{k} i \cdot \alpha_i \cdot (R^2 - r^2)^{i-2}(ir^2 - R^2) + \frac{\varrho_0(R^2 - r^2)}{\varepsilon_0 \varepsilon_r}\right] \cdot (R^2 - r^2)^j dr = 0,$$

$$j = 1, \ldots, k.$$

The integration for particular values of i and j provides the following results:

$$\int_0^R 4i \cdot \alpha_i \cdot (R^2 - r^2)^{i+j-2}(ir^2 - R^2)dr = -i \cdot \alpha_i \frac{(i + 2j + 1)\sqrt{\pi}\, R^{2i+2j-1}\Gamma(i + j - 1)}{\Gamma(i + j + \frac{1}{2})},$$

$$\int_0^R \frac{\varrho_0}{\varepsilon_0 \varepsilon_r}(R^2 - r^2)^{j+1}dr = \frac{\varrho_0}{\varepsilon_0 \varepsilon_r}\frac{\sqrt{\pi}\, R^{3+2j}\Gamma(2 + j)}{2\Gamma(j + \frac{5}{2})},$$

so that we obtain a system of equations in the form

$$\sum_{i=1}^{k} -\frac{i \cdot (i+2j+1)\sqrt{\pi}\, R^{2i+2j-1}\Gamma(i+j-1)}{\Gamma(i+j+\frac{1}{2})} \cdot \alpha_i + \frac{\varrho_0}{\varepsilon_0 \varepsilon_r}\frac{\sqrt{\pi}\, R^{3+2j}\Gamma(2+j)}{2\Gamma(j+\frac{5}{2})} = 0\,,$$

$$j = 1, \ldots, k\,,$$

whose solution provides the values of α_i, $i = 1, \ldots, k$.

Let us first consider $k = 1$. In this case we obtain just one equation for α_1 in the form

$$\frac{8\alpha_1}{3} = \frac{8\varrho_0 R^2}{15\varepsilon_0 \varepsilon_r}\,.$$

Hence,

$$\alpha_1 = \frac{\varrho_0 R^2}{5\varepsilon_0 \varepsilon_r}\,,$$

and from (2.36) we have

$$\varphi' = \frac{\varrho_0 R^2}{5\varepsilon_0 \varepsilon_r}(R^2 - r^2)\,. \tag{2.38}$$

For $k = 2$ we obtain two equations in the form

$$\frac{8\alpha_1}{3} + \frac{16\alpha_2 R^2}{5} = \frac{8\varrho_0 R^2}{15\varepsilon_0 \varepsilon_r}\,,$$

$$\frac{32\alpha_1}{15} + \frac{64\alpha_2 R^2}{21} = \frac{16\varrho_0 R^2}{35\varepsilon_0 \varepsilon_r}\,.$$

Hence,

$$\alpha_1 = \frac{\varrho_0}{\varepsilon_0 \varepsilon_r}\frac{R^2}{8}\,, \quad \alpha_2 = \frac{\varrho_0}{\varepsilon_0 \varepsilon_r}\frac{1}{16}\,,$$

and, after substitution to (2.36), we have

$$\varphi' = \frac{\varrho_0 (R^2 - r^2)(3R^2 - r^2)}{16\varepsilon_0 \varepsilon_r}\,, \tag{2.39}$$

which is already equal to the exact solution (2.34). Finally, for $k = 3$ we obtain three equations,

$$\frac{8\alpha_1}{3} + \frac{16\alpha_2 R^2}{5} + \frac{128\alpha_3 R^4}{35} = \frac{8\varrho_0 R^2}{15\varepsilon_0 \varepsilon_r}\,,$$

$$\frac{32\alpha_1}{15} + \frac{64\alpha_2 R^2}{21} + \frac{128\alpha_3 R^4}{35} = \frac{16\varrho_0 R^2}{35\varepsilon_0 \varepsilon_r}\,,$$

$$\frac{64\alpha_1}{35} + \frac{128\alpha_2 R^2}{45} + \frac{4096\alpha_3 R^4}{1155} = \frac{128\varrho_0 R^2}{315\varepsilon_0 \varepsilon_r}\,,$$

with solution

$$\alpha_1 = \frac{\varrho_0}{\varepsilon_0 \varepsilon_r}\frac{R^2}{8}\,, \quad \alpha_2 = \frac{\varrho_0}{\varepsilon_0 \varepsilon_r}\frac{1}{16}\,, \quad \alpha_3 = 0\,.$$

It is clear that this solution is identical with the solution for $k = 2$, and it can easily be shown that the same holds even for every $k \geq 3$.

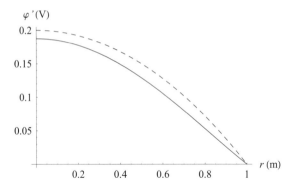

Figure 2.18. An approximate solution for $k = 1$ (dashed line) and the exact solution for $k = 2$ (full line).

For an illustration, consider that $\varrho_0/\varepsilon_0\varepsilon_r = 1$ and $R = 1$. Now for $k = 1$ (see (2.38)) we obtain

$$\varphi' = \tfrac{1}{5}(1 - r^2)$$

and for $k = 2$ (exact solution (2.39))

$$\varphi' = \frac{(1 - r^2)(3 - r^2)}{16}.$$

The corresponding graphs are shown in Fig. 2.18.

More detailed information on the above methods can be found in every mathematical book aimed at numerical solution of partial differential equations and even in various technical monographs [18, 55–59].

2.5.3 Variational and other related methods

The variational methods are based on the variational representation of the partial differential equations. The problem of solving a physical field is transformed into a problem of determining a functional (which is usually a quantity related to the field energy) and finding conditions on which the solution of the original partial differential equation also extremizes this functional (this condition is the Euler–Lagrange equation that, applied to the functional, provides the original PDE). The most famous variational techniques are the Ritz method and the finite element method that is perhaps not so general, but, without any doubt, the most effective and with the widest spectrum of applications.

The variational methods may be used successfully for solving fields in any kind of media (nonlinear, anisotropic, etc.). As the functional (related to the energy of the system) is a scalar additive quantity, we obtain its total value by summing of its values in particular cells of the discretization mesh. The conditions along the internal interfaces of the investigated domain are satisfied naturally.

In the next sections we will explain in more detail the significance of the concept of the "functional," methods of finding its value, and a way of extremizing it using the so-called Euler–Lagrange equation.

2.5.3.1 *Functional and its determination*   The functional is generally an instruction assigning to a function (from a given class of functions of prescribed properties and defined in some domain) a certain number. As an example, we can mention its definite integral over the domain and its maximum value in this domain.

Now we will try to transform the above definition into mathematical language. Let a function f of independent variables x, y, z be defined in a 3D domain Ω with boundary Γ. In region Ω the function is continuous and continuously differentiable and its value on boundary Γ is known. Then, the value defined as

$$L = \int_\Omega f(x, y, z)\,\mathrm{d}\Omega \tag{2.40}$$

may represent a functional.

The potential energy of physical fields may often be expressed as a stationary value of a functional

$$L = \int_\Omega f\left(x, y, z, u, \frac{\partial u}{\partial x}, \frac{\partial u}{\partial y}, \frac{\partial u}{\partial z}\right)\mathrm{d}\Omega, \tag{2.41}$$

where $u = u(x, y, z)$. The corresponding Euler–Lagrange equation for this functional reads [69]

$$\frac{\partial}{\partial x}\left(\frac{\partial f}{\partial u'_x}\right) + \frac{\partial}{\partial y}\left(\frac{\partial f}{\partial u'_y}\right) + \frac{\partial}{\partial z}\left(\frac{\partial f}{\partial u'_z}\right) - \frac{\partial f}{\partial u} = 0. \tag{2.42}$$

This equation should be identical to the corresponding partial differential equation that was used for the description of the field.

Now the question is how to find the function $f(x, y, z, u, \partial u/\partial x, \partial u/\partial y, \partial u/\partial z)$ (or directly the functional L) for a given partial differential equation. First, there does not exist a universal method (moreover, not every PDE has such a functional). But in the case where the functional exists, we can determine it using two principal methods:

- method of residual excitation and

- Poynting's vector method.

For illustration we will explain the first of them.

Consider Poisson's equation in the form

$$\Delta\varphi = \beta \tag{2.43}$$

defined in domain Ω. We know that the corresponding functional L of required properties exists and we are going to find it using the method of residual excitation. In (2.43) φ denotes the exact solution of this equation and β the excitation function.

If φ' is an approximate solution, so that $\Delta\varphi' = \beta'$, let us call the residuum R the expression $(\beta - \beta')$ and let us construct a functional

$$L = \int_\Omega \varphi R\,\mathrm{d}\Omega. \tag{2.44}$$

After substituting for R we immediately obtain

$$L = \int_\Omega \varphi(\Delta\varphi - \beta')\mathrm{d}\Omega. \tag{2.45}$$

The integral on the right-hand side expresses the residual energy. Now we can show that the minimization of functional L provides the original Poisson equation. Let us first carry out the following transform:

$$L = \int_\Omega \nabla(\varphi \cdot \nabla\varphi) d\Omega - \int_\Omega (\nabla\varphi)^2) d\Omega - \int_\Omega \varphi\beta' d\Omega. \tag{2.46}$$

Applying Gauss' theorem on the first integral on the right-hand side provides

$$L = \int_\Gamma (\varphi \cdot \nabla\varphi) d\Gamma - \int_\Omega (\nabla\varphi)^2) d\Omega - \int_\Omega \varphi\beta' d\Omega, \tag{2.47}$$

where Γ is the boundary of domain Ω.

The Euler–Lagrange equation related to this functional provides

$$2\triangle\varphi = \beta'$$

and hence

$$\beta' = 2\beta.$$

After substituting for β' into the integral identity (2.47), we obtain

$$L = \oint_\Gamma \varphi \cdot \nabla\varphi \, d\Gamma - \int_\Omega ((\nabla\varphi)^2 + 2\varphi\beta) d\Omega. \tag{2.48}$$

If the boundary conditions to the problem (either Dirichlet or Neumann) are equal to zero, the integral along the boundary Γ in (2.48) vanishes.

2.5.3.2 Ritz method
This method assumes the solution in the form of a combination of testing functions with unknown coefficients. The coefficients are then determined from the condition that the partial derivatives of the corresponding functional with respect to these coefficients are equal to zero. This leads to a solution of a system of linear or nonlinear algebraic equations. In this way we obtain the best solution on the selected set of testing functions, whose accuracy, however, may grow with the selection of another set of these functions. The testing functions have to satisfy the boundary conditions of the problem.

Consider a PDE in the form

$$A\varphi = \psi, \tag{2.49}$$

where A is a differential operator, φ the solution, and ψ the right-hand side. This equation is defined in domain Ω with boundary Γ and along this boundary the value of unknown function φ is supposed to be known. Let the corresponding functional L (it must exist, otherwise the Ritz method cannot be applied) be a function of φ.

Assume the solution φ in the form

$$\varphi = \sum_{i=1}^n a_i f_i, \tag{2.50}$$

where f_i, $i = 1, \ldots, n$, are the testing functions and a_i, $i = 1, \ldots, n$ the unknown coefficients. These are determined from the condition

$$\frac{\partial L(\varphi)}{\partial a_i} = 0, \quad i = 1, \ldots, n. \tag{2.51}$$

Again we will show the application of the Ritz method on the charged cylinder solved at the end of section 2.5.2. The distribution of potential φ is governed here by equation (2.33), whose exact solution is given by formula (2.34).

Consider first the approximate solution as

$$\varphi' = \alpha_1(R^2 - r^2).$$

Now the corresponding functional (2.47) may be expressed as

$$L = -\int_S \left((\nabla\varphi')^2 - 2\varphi'\frac{\varrho_0(R^2 - r^2)}{\varepsilon_0\varepsilon_r}\right)dS,$$

where S is the cross section of the cylinder. Since

$$\nabla\varphi' = -2r\alpha_1,$$

the value of the functional L is

$$L = -\frac{2\pi R^4}{3}\alpha_1(3\alpha_1 - KR^2),$$

and its minimization with respect to α_1 provides

$$\alpha_1 = \frac{\varrho_0 R^2}{6\varepsilon_0\varepsilon_r}. \qquad (2.52)$$

Finally, we obtain

$$\varphi' = \frac{\varrho_0 R^2}{6\varepsilon_0\varepsilon_r}(R^2 - r^2). \qquad (2.53)$$

For $k = 2$ we have

$$\varphi' = \alpha_1(R^2 - r^2) + \alpha_2(R^2 - r^2)^2.$$

In the same way as in the previous case, we obtain two linear algebraic equations for α_1 and α_2 in the form

$$6\alpha_1 + 4\alpha_2 R^2 = R^2\frac{\varrho_0}{\varepsilon_0\varepsilon_r}$$

and

$$16\alpha_1 + 16\alpha_2 R^2 = 3R^2\frac{\varrho_0}{\varepsilon_0\varepsilon_r}.$$

Hence,

$$\alpha_1 = \frac{\varrho_0 R^2}{8\varepsilon_0\varepsilon_r}, \quad \alpha_2 = \frac{\varrho_0}{16\varepsilon_0\varepsilon_r},$$

so that

$$\varphi' = \frac{\varrho_0}{16\varepsilon_0\varepsilon_r}(R^2 - r^2)(3R^2 - r^2),$$

which is again the exact solution.

For $k \geq 2$ we would obtain the same values of α_1 and α_2, while α_3, α_4, and so on are equal to zero. The graphs for $k = 1$ and $k = 2$ are shown in Fig. 2.19.

Comprehensive information about variational principles may be found in a great number of references [60–62].

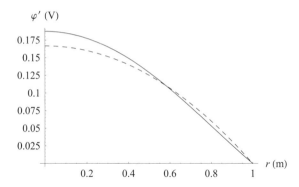

Figure 2.19. An approximate solution for $k = 1$ (dashed line) and the exact solution for $k = 2$ (full line).

2.5.3.3 *Finite element method* The first references about the finite element method come from a German mathematician, Richard Courant, who studied its fundamentals in 1943. Nevertheless, it was first practically tested in the 1960s, in the domain of structural analysis. Its first applications in electromagnetics date to the years 1967–1968 and since then it has been utilized in a number of branches, from the proposal of large electrical devices to the proposal of microstructures.

The method itself may be considered as a specific case of the Ritz technique. Instead of solving the PDE describing the field distribution in the prescribed domain, an energy-related functional is sought whose value is then extremized in order to find the nodal values of the function describing the field. But unlike the Ritz technique, there is not a strong demand on the trial functions to satisfy the boundary conditions of the task. The only demand is usually the continuity of the trial functions along the interfaces between every pair of elements, because this property significantly contributes to the simplification of the assembly of the system matrix. It is not necessary to pay any attention to the interfaces of various media because the corresponding conditions are satisfied there automatically.

As the finite element method nowadays represents the principal technique for solving electromagnetic fields, we will describe its main attributes in the following section 2.6.

2.6 FINITE ELEMENT METHOD

As in the case of other numerical methods, this technique intended for approximate solutions of partial differential and also integral equations. It allows solving both steady state and evolutionary problems.

The finite element method is versatile, robust, and very flexible for modeling complicated geometries. It functions for various media (nonlinear, anisotropic, etc.) and provides results that are in accordance with physical reality. That is why we shall deal with its selected aspects in more detail than the other mentioned methods. But even these details are rather rough. Exhaustive information on the finite element method can be found in the monographs [63–93], and its application in thousands of papers in hundreds of scientific journals.

The method consists of several steps:

- definition of the boundary value problem (partial differential equation, specification of geometry, material and media properties, spatial and temporal distribution of field quantities, etc.);

- determination of the boundary conditions (that generally may be time dependent);

- finding of the energy-related functional;

- discretization of the investigated domain using the finite elements;

- selection of the functions approximating the real distribution of the field quantity in every element; these functions are expressed in terms of trial functions based on the nodal values of the field quantity (other significant points of the element such as centers of the edges or faces may be used as well);

- extremization of the functional with respect to all nodal values of the sought field quantity (this procedure leads to the solution of a system of linear or nonlinear algebraic equations in steady problems, but in evolutionary problems we have to solve a system of linear or nonlinear ordinary differential equations where the variable is time);

- evaluation of the results, mapping of the field; and obtaining field and other related quantities.

As the first two points in the above list (concerning the input data of the task solved) are common for practically all methods and the problems associated with finding functionals were briefly discussed before, we will start with the discretization of the definition area and selection of the trial functions in particular elements.

2.6.1   Discretization of the definition area and selection of the approximate functions

The discretization itself strongly depends on the dimensionality of the investigated region. In 1D arrangements the elements are abscissas, in 2D mostly triangles (less quadrilaterals), and in 3D tetrahedra and hexahedra (nevertheless, a number of more complicated elements were also studied in the past). The functions approximating the real distribution of the sought quantity in the elements are selected not only with respect to the dimensionality but also with respect to the coordinate system, type of problem, and other features (e.g., boundary conditions, or whether the task is solved in the time or frequency domain). The most typical functions are polynomials, but widely used are also trigonometric functions, real or complex Bessel functions, and various orthogonal systems such as Legendre or Hermite polynomials. Generally, hundreds of variants of the finite element method (FEM) were described in the last forty years, differing from one another by some of the mentioned aspects. But we will focus our attention only on some of them, where the approximating functions are formed by low-order polynomials.

We shall illustrate the introduction of the approximate functions on a simple 1D example. Consider a simple differential equation in the form

$$\frac{\mathrm{d}^2 y}{\mathrm{d}x^2} = x\,\mathrm{e}^x, \quad x \in \langle 0, 2 \rangle$$

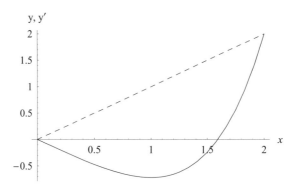

Figure 2.20.   An approximate abscissa (dashed line) and the exact solution (full line).

with boundary conditions

$$y(0) = 0, \; y(2) = 2,$$

whose exact solution is obviously

$$y = e^x(x - 2) + 2.$$ (2.54)

We will try first to replace the above exact solution by an abscissa whose beginning and end points are given by the boundary conditions. Its equation evidently reads

$$y_a = x.$$

Both exact solution and approximate abscissa are depicted in Fig. 2.20.

It can be seen that the accuracy of this approximation is very low. The maximum value of the error follows from the equation

$$\frac{d(y - y_a)}{dx} = 1 - e^x(x - 1) = 0 \; \Rightarrow \; x = 1.27846, \; (y - y_a)_{\max} = 1.86959.$$

Now we shall approximate the function (2.54) by a second-order polynomial in the form

$$y_a = a + bx + cx^2$$

with the condition of collocating both end points of the definition interval, that is,

$$y_a(0) = 0 \; \Rightarrow \; a = 0,$$

$$y_a(2) = 2 \; \Rightarrow \; b + 2c = 1.$$

The equation for the third parameter can be obtained using three different ways: *point collocation*, *weighted residual technique*, and *least-square method*.

The *point collocation* consists in a mostly random choice of an internal point from the considered interval (in our case interval $\langle 0, 2\rangle$) with the corresponding (exact) value of y. Putting, for example, $x = 1$, we obtain from (2.54) $y = -0.718282$. So the third equation reads

$$b + c = 2 - e$$

and, hence, $b = -2.436564$, $c = 1.718282$. In this case the approximation polynomial is

$$y_a = -2.436564x + 1.718282x^2.$$

The *weighted residual technique* is based on finding the functional related to the considered differential equation. As was shown before, in (2.47), the functional reads

$$L = \int_0^2 \left[\left(\frac{dy}{dx} \right)^2 + 2yxe^x \right] dx,$$

where (as a consequence of the collocation at both end points of the interval)

$$y_a = (1 - 2c)x + cx^2.$$

After substitution for y into the expression for the functional L we have

$$L = -2 + \frac{8c^2}{3} + 4e^2 - 4c(e^2 - 5),$$

and putting its derivative with respect to c equal to zero we obtain

$$c = \frac{3(e^2 - 5)}{4}.$$

Now the polynomial approximating the solution is

$$y_a = \frac{3(e^2 - 5)}{4}x^2 - \left(\frac{3e^2}{2} - \frac{13}{2} \right) x.$$

Finally, the *least-square method* is based on the minimization of the quadratic difference between the exact and approximate curve. This quantity Q is calculated as

$$Q = \int_0^2 \left[e^x(x - 2) + 2 - (1 - 2c)x - cx^2 \right]^2 dx.$$

After the calculation we have

$$Q = \frac{233}{12} + \frac{16c^2}{15} - \frac{15e^2}{4} + \frac{4c}{3}(3e^2 - 25),$$

so that

$$\frac{dQ}{dc} = \frac{4}{15}(8c - 125 + 15e^2) = 0 \;\Rightarrow\; c = \frac{1}{8}(125 - 15e^2).$$

Now

$$y_a = \frac{125 - 15e^2}{8}x^2 + \left(\frac{15e^2}{4} - \frac{121}{4} \right) x.$$

The results are depicted in Fig. 2.21.

It can be seen that even now the accuracy of the approximate functions is low. Possible ways of its increasing consist in

- dividing the interval into more subintervals in which the function is also approximated by linear or quadratic functions, or

- using polynomials of higher degrees.

Now we will introduce the concept of the *shape functions* . Let us start from Fig. 2.22 containing $n - 1$ linear elements defined by n points $(x_i, y_i), i = 1, \ldots, n$. Suppose that in every element the function y is approximated by an abscissa connecting its end points.

In the first interval $\langle x_1, x_2 \rangle$ the linear approximation of function $y = y(x)$ is given by the formula

$$y = y_1 + \frac{y_2 - y_1}{x_2 - x_1}(x - x_1),$$

which can be rewritten in the following way:

$$y = y_1 \frac{x_2 - x}{x_2 - x_1} + y_2 \frac{x - x_1}{x_2 - x_1}.$$

The functions

$$\xi_1(x) = \frac{x_2 - x}{x_2 - x_1}, \quad \xi_2(x) = \frac{x - x_1}{x_2 - x_1} \tag{2.55}$$

are called the shape functions (see Fig. 2.23). Their characteristic properties follow from these relations:

- $\xi_i(x_j) = \delta_{ij}, \ i, j = 1, 2 \ (\delta_{ij}$ denoting Kronecker's delta),

- $\sum_{i=1}^{2} \xi_i(x) = 1$ for any $x \in \langle x_1, x_2 \rangle$.

Now the function y may be written in the form

$$y = y_1 \xi_1(x) + y_2 \xi_2(x). \tag{2.56}$$

Analogously, we can find the shape functions in the remaining intervals.

Consider again the arrangement depicted in Fig. 2.22. Now we will suppose that function $y(x)$ is a polynomial passing through all points $(x_i, y_i), i = 1, \ldots, n$. The degree of such a polynomial is $n - 1$ and may be written in the form

$$y = a_0 + a_1 x + a_2 x^2 + \ldots + a_{n-1} x^{n-1}.$$

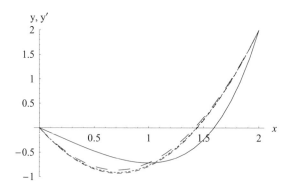

Figure 2.21.   Exact solution (full line), point collocation (long dashing), weighted residual method (short dashing), and least-square method (dotted line).

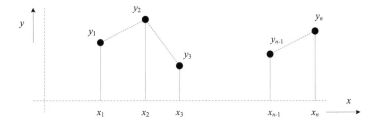

Figure 2.22.   Linear elements in 1D.

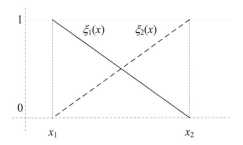

Figure 2.23.   The shape function for an element.

Its coefficients can easily be calculated by solving the system

$$y_1 = a_0 + a_1 x_1 + a_2 x_1^2 + \ldots + a_{n-1} x_1^{n-1} \,,$$

$$y_2 = a_0 + a_1 x_2 + a_2 x_2^2 + \ldots + a_{n-1} x_2^{n-1} \,,$$

$$\vdots$$

$$y_{n-1} = a_0 + a_1 x_{n-1} + a_2 x_{n-1}^2 + \ldots + a_{n-1} x_{n-1}^{n-1} \,.$$

The solution, however, generally does not look too friendly. But it may be transformed into Lagrange's form (similar to (2.56)),

$$y = \sum_{i=1}^{n} y_i \xi_i(x) \,,$$

where

$$\xi_i(x) = \frac{\prod_{j=1, j \neq i}^{n} (x - x_j)}{\prod_{j=1, j \neq i}^{n} (x_i - x_j)} \,. \tag{2.57}$$

Again we have

- $\xi_i(x_j) = \delta_{ij}, \quad i, j = 1, n \,;$

- $\sum_{i=1}^{n} \xi_i(x) = 1$ for any $x \in \langle x_1, x_n \rangle \,.$

For an illustration, consider four points $(x_i, y_i), i = 1, \ldots, 4$ whose coordinates are given in Fig. 2.24. The corresponding shape functions $\xi_i(x), i = 1, \ldots, 4$ are depicted in Fig. 2.25.

Finally, the shape of Lagrange's polynomial is shown in Fig. 2.26. The polynomial is given by the equation

$$y = \frac{x}{6}(x - 5)^2 .$$

In the next paragraphs the ideas for processing of 1D elements will be extended to 2D and 3D cases. Consider first a 2D triangular element with vertices **1**, **2**, and **3** depicted in Fig. 2.27. Let a function $z = z(x, y)$ be approximated by a bilinear form

$$z = a_0 + a_1\,x + a_2\,y . \tag{2.58}$$

The unknown values a_0, a_1, and a_2 represent the solution of a system of equations:

$$z_1 = a_0 + a_1\,x_1 + a_2\,y_1 ,$$

$$z_2 = a_0 + a_1\,x_2 + a_2\,y_2 ,$$

$$z_3 = a_0 + a_1\,x_3 + a_2\,y_3 .$$

Substituting into (2.58) we immediately obtain

$$z = \begin{pmatrix} 1 & x & y \end{pmatrix} \cdot \begin{pmatrix} 1 & x_1 & y_1 \\ 1 & x_2 & y_2 \\ 1 & x_3 & y_3 \end{pmatrix}^{-1} \cdot \begin{pmatrix} z_1 \\ z_2 \\ z_3 \end{pmatrix} . \tag{2.59}$$

The inverse of the central matrix is

$$\begin{pmatrix} 1 & x_1 & y_1 \\ 1 & x_2 & y_2 \\ 1 & x_3 & y_3 \end{pmatrix}^{-1} = \frac{1}{2S} \cdot \begin{pmatrix} u_1 & u_2 & u_3 \\ v_2 & v_2 & v_3 \\ w_1 & w_2 & w_3 \end{pmatrix} ,$$

where

$$S = \tfrac{1}{2}(x_2 y_3 - x_3 y_2 + x_3 y_1 - x_1 y_3 + x_1 y_2 - x_2 y_1)$$

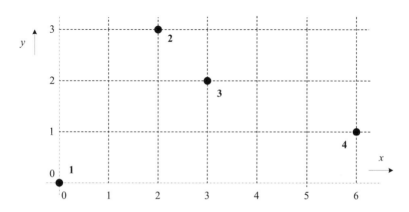

Figure 2.24. The arrangement with four points.

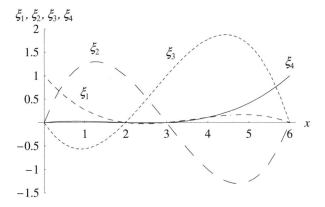

Figure 2.25. Particular shape functions for the solved example.

is the area of the triangle and

$$u_1 = x_2 y_3 - x_3 y_2 , \quad u_2 = x_3 y_1 - x_1 y_3 , \quad u_3 = x_1 y_2 - x_2 y_1 ,$$
$$v_1 = y_2 - y_3 , \quad v_2 = y_3 - y_1 , \quad v_3 = y_1 - y_2 ,$$
$$w_1 = x_3 - x_2 , \quad w_2 = x_1 - x_3 , \quad w_3 = x_2 - x_1 .$$

Finally, we can write

$$z = \frac{u_1 + v_1 x + w_1 y}{2S} z_1 + \frac{u_2 + v_2 x + w_2 y}{2S} z_2 + \frac{u_3 + v_3 x + w_3 y}{2S} z_3 ,$$

where

$$\xi_j(x,y) = \frac{u_j + v_j x + w_j y}{2S} , \quad j = 1, \ldots, 3 ,$$

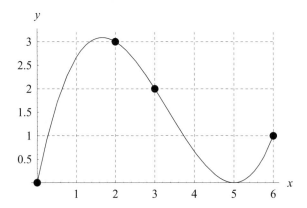

Figure 2.26. Lagrange's polynomial for the solved example.

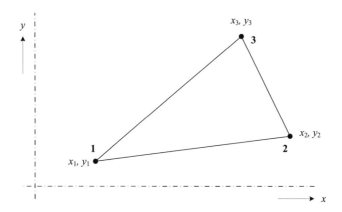

Figure 2.27.   A general linear triangle.

are the shape functions corresponding to particular vertices **1, 2,** and **3**. Evidently there holds again

$$\xi_i(x_j, y_j) = \delta_{ij} \ \text{ for } \ i, j = 1, \dots, 3$$

and

$$\sum_{i=1}^{3} \xi_i(x, y) = 1 \ \text{ for any } \ (x, y) \in S \,.$$

It is not so easy to construct higher-order elements of 2D triangular shape as in the 1D case. For example, approximate function z in quadratic elements is defined as the following polynomial in variables x and y:

$$z = a_0 + a_1\, x + a_2\, y + a_3\, x^2 + a_4\, xy + a_5\, y^2;$$

and we need six points with the given values of function z; see Fig. 2.28. Here three more points are located at the midpoints of all three sides of the triangle.

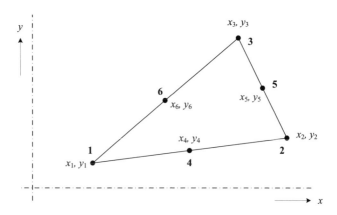

Figure 2.28.   A general quadratic triangle.

Now the unknown coefficients $a_i, i = 0, \ldots, 5$, follow from the system of six algebraic equations for the values of function z at points **1–6**, so that, in accordance with Fig. 2.28, we obtain

$$
z = \begin{pmatrix} 1 & x & y & x^2 & xy & y^2 \end{pmatrix} \cdot \begin{pmatrix} 1 & x_1 & y_1 & x_1^2 & x_1 y_1 & y_1^2 \\ 1 & x_2 & y_2 & x_2^2 & x_2 y_2 & y_2^2 \\ 1 & x_3 & y_3 & x_3^2 & x_3 y_3 & y_3^2 \\ 1 & x_4 & y_4 & x_4^2 & x_4 y_4 & y_4^2 \\ 1 & x_5 & y_5 & x_5^2 & x_5 y_5 & y_5^2 \\ 1 & x_6 & y_6 & x_6^2 & x_6 y_6 & y_6^2 \end{pmatrix}^{-1} \cdot \begin{pmatrix} z_1 \\ z_2 \\ z_3 \\ z_4 \\ z_5 \\ z_6 \end{pmatrix} . \tag{2.60}
$$

In this case the shape functions have much more complicated forms. Nevertheless, they again satisfy relations (2.57).

Finally, we will analyze a general 3D tetrahedral element (see Fig. 2.29.) with vertices V_1, V_2, V_3, V_4.

Here the linear function approximating the real physical quality has the form

$$
w = a_0 + a_1 x + a_2 y + a_3 z ,
$$

whose coefficients $a_0, \ldots, a_3$ follow from the system of equations

$$
\begin{aligned}
w_1 &= a_0 + a_1 x_1 + a_2 y_1 + a_3 z_1 , \\
w_2 &= a_0 + a_1 x_2 + a_2 y_2 + a_3 z_2 , \\
w_3 &= a_0 + a_1 x_3 + a_2 y_3 + a_3 z_3 , \\
w_4 &= a_0 + a_1 x_4 + a_2 y_4 + a_3 z_4 .
\end{aligned} \tag{2.61}
$$

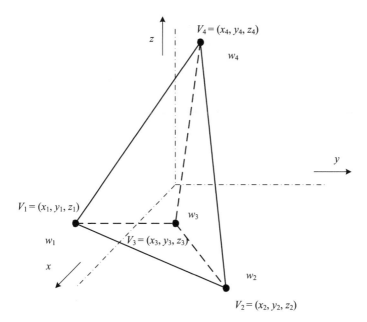

Figure 2.29.   A general linear tetrahedral element.

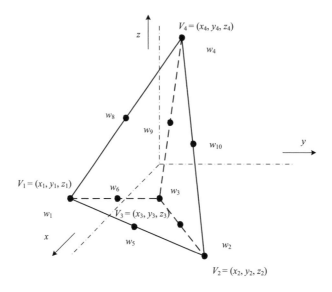

Figure 2.30. A general quadratic tetrahedral element.

Hence, in the same way as in the previous case, we obtain

$$w = \begin{pmatrix} 1 & x & y & z \end{pmatrix} \cdot \begin{pmatrix} 1 & x_1 & y_1 & z_1 \\ 1 & x_2 & y_2 & z_2 \\ 1 & x_3 & y_3 & z_3 \\ 1 & x_4 & y_4 & z_4 \end{pmatrix}^{-1} \cdot \begin{pmatrix} w_1 \\ w_2 \\ w_3 \\ w_4 \end{pmatrix}. \tag{2.62}$$

Provided we use a quadratic tetrahedral element, we have to add six more significant points, for example, the centers of its sides (see Fig. 2.30).

In this case the approximation function has the form of

$$w = a_0 + a_1 x + a_2 y + a_3 z + a_4 x^2 + a_5 y^2 + a_6 z^2 + a_7 xy + a_8 xz + a_9 yz,$$

where coefficients $a_0, \ldots, a_9$ follow from the system of equations

$$w_1 = a_0 + a_1 x_1 + a_2 y_1 + a_3 z_1 + a_4 x_1^2 + a_5 y_1^2 + a_6 z_1^2 + a_7 x_1 y_1 + a_8 x_1 z_1 + a_9 y_1 z_1,$$

$$w_2 = a_0 + a_1 x_2 + a_2 y_2 + a_3 z_2 + a_4 x_2^2 + a_5 y_2^2 + a_6 z_2^2 + a_7 x_2 y_2 + a_8 x_2 z_2 + a_9 y_2 z_2,$$

$$w_3 = a_0 + a_1 x_3 + a_2 y_3 + a_3 z_3 + a_4 x_3^2 + a_5 y_3^2 + a_6 z_3^2 + a_7 x_3 y_3 + a_8 x_3 z_3 + a_9 y_3 z_3,$$

$$\vdots$$

$$w_{10} = a_0 + a_1 x_{10} + a_2 y_{10} + a_3 z_{10} + a_4 x_{10}^2$$
$$+ a_5 y_{10}^2 + a_6 z_{10}^2 + a_7 x_{10} y_{10} + a_8 x_{10} z_{10} + a_9 y_{10} z_{10}.$$

Hence,

$$w = \begin{pmatrix} 1 & x & \cdots & xz & yz \end{pmatrix}$$

$$\cdot \begin{pmatrix} 1 & x_1 & y_1 & z_1 & x_1^2 & y_1^2 & z_1^2 & x_1y_1 & x_1z_1 & y_1z_1 \\ 1 & x_2 & y_2 & z_2 & x_2^2 & y_2^2 & z_2^2 & x_2y_2 & x_2z_2 & y_2z_2 \\ \vdots & \vdots & \vdots & \vdots & \vdots & \vdots & \vdots & \vdots & \vdots & \vdots \\ 1 & x_{10} & y_{10} & z_{10} & x_{10}^2 & y_{10}^2 & z_{10}^2 & x_{10}y_{10} & x_{10}z_{10} & y_{10}z_{10} \end{pmatrix}^{-1} \cdot \begin{pmatrix} w_1 \\ w_2 \\ \vdots \\ w_{10} \end{pmatrix}. \qquad (2.63)$$

2.6.2 Computation of the functional and its extremization

As energy-related functionals are additive quantities (like energy), the easiest way is to find the contribution to the functional in particular elements of the discretization mesh and sum them up. The resultant functional is then an expression whose value depends on all nodal values of the physical quantity that is to be found.

We shall illustrate it for two cases. The first one is a 3D electrostatic field; the second one is a 2D harmonic magnetic field. For the sake of simplicity, both fields are supposed to be linear.

2.6.2.1 3D electrostatic field   The functional for this problem is expressed by (2.47), where $\beta = -\varrho/\varepsilon$, ϱ being the volume charge and $\varepsilon = \varepsilon_0\varepsilon_r$ being the permittivity (distribution of both these quantities is supposed to be known in advance). Moreover, we will suppose that the boundary conditions of the Dirichlet or Neumann type are homogeneous, that is,

$$\varphi = 0, \quad \frac{d\varphi}{dn} = 0,$$

where n denotes the normal. Now the functional acquires the form

$$L = -\int_\Omega \left[(\nabla\varphi)^2)d\Omega - \varphi\frac{2\varrho}{\varepsilon} \right] d\Omega. \qquad (2.64)$$

Suppose that the discretization mesh consists of linear tetrahedra. In every tetrahedron the potential (quantity whose distribution is to be found) is approximated by a trilinear function

$$\varphi_j = a_{j0} + a_{j1}x + a_{j2}y + a_{j3}z,$$

where j is the index of the element. Now

$$\nabla\varphi = \mathbf{i}a_{j1} + \mathbf{j}a_{j2} + \mathbf{k}a_{j3},$$

where $\mathbf{i}$, $\mathbf{j}$, and $\mathbf{k}$ are the unit vectors in the corresponding directions. Coefficients a_{j0}, a_{j1}, a_{j2}, and a_{j3} must be calculated from (2.61).

Now the contribution to the functional L from the jth element is

$$L_j = -\int_{\Omega_j} \left[a_{j1}^2 + a_{j2}^2 + a_{j3}^2 - \frac{2\varrho_j}{\varepsilon_j}(a_{j0} + a_{j1}x + a_{j2}y + a_{j3}z) \right] d\Omega,$$

which gives

$$L_j = -(a_{j1}^2 + a_{j2}^2 + a_{j3}^2)V_j + \frac{2\varrho_j}{\varepsilon_j}\int_{\Omega_j}(a_{j0} + a_{j1}x + a_{j2}y + a_{j3}z)d\Omega, \qquad (2.65)$$

where V_j is the volume of the jth tetrahedron. Computation of the integral in (2.65) is a relatively complicated business, but the result still has a reasonable appearance.

2.6.2.2 2D harmonic magnetic field

We will describe the problem in terms of phasor $\underline{A}$ of the magnetic vector potential A. If the problem is characterized by homogeneous boundary conditions

$$\underline{A} = 0 \quad \text{or} \quad \frac{\mathrm{d}\underline{A}}{\mathrm{d}n} = 0 \,,$$

the corresponding functional may be written in the form

$$L = \int_{\Omega} \left[\frac{\boldsymbol{B} \cdot \boldsymbol{B}}{\mu} - 2\underline{\boldsymbol{J}} \cdot \underline{\boldsymbol{A}} + j\omega\gamma\underline{\boldsymbol{A}} \cdot \underline{\boldsymbol{A}} \right] \mathrm{d}\Omega \,, \tag{2.66}$$

where $\mu = \mu_0\mu_\mathrm{r}$ denotes the permeability, γ the electrical conductivity, ω the angular frequency, and $\boldsymbol{J}$ the external current density. In a 2D arrangement in Cartesian coordinates x, y, both the phasors of external current density and magnetic vector potential have only one nonzero component in the z direction, so that we can write

$$L = \int_{\Omega} \left[\frac{\boldsymbol{B} \cdot \boldsymbol{B}}{\mu} - 2\underline{J}_z \cdot \underline{A}_z + j\omega\gamma\underline{A}_z \cdot \underline{A}_z \right] \mathrm{d}\Omega \,. \tag{2.67}$$

As for the phasor of magnetic flux density $\underline{\boldsymbol{B}}$, it has two components in the plane x, y:

$$\underline{\boldsymbol{B}} = \mathbf{i}\underline{B}_x + \mathbf{j}\underline{B}_y \,,$$

where $\mathbf{i}$ and $\mathbf{j}$ are the corresponding unit vectors. If the distribution of magnetic vector potential in the jth element Ω_j of surface S_j (see Fig. 2.31) is described by a bilinear form

$$A_{zj} = a_{0j} + a_{1j}x + a_{2j}y \,, \tag{2.68}$$

we obtain (using relation $\boldsymbol{B} = \operatorname{curl} A$)

$$B_{xj} = \frac{\mathrm{d}A_{zj}}{\mathrm{d}y} = a_{2j} \,, \quad B_{yj} = -\frac{\mathrm{d}A_{zj}}{\mathrm{d}a} = a_{1j}$$

and

$$|\boldsymbol{B}|^2 = a_{1j}^2 + a_{2j}^2 \,.$$

It is obvious that magnetic flux density in the whole jth element is independent of coordinates x and y. Thus, it is a constant, so that constant must also be the corresponding permeability, no matter whether the element contains ferromagnetics or not.

Now we have to calculate the coefficients a_{0j}, a_{1j}, and a_{2j} using (2.59). We easily obtain

$$a_{0j} = \frac{A_{z3j}(x_{2j}y_{1j} - x_{1j}y_{2j}) + A_{z2j}(x_{1j}y_{3j} - x_{3j}y_{1j}) + A_{z1j}(x_{3j}y_{2j} - x_{2j}y_{2j})}{2S_j} \,,$$

$$a_{1j} = \frac{A_{z3j}(y_{2j} - y_{1j}) + A_{z2j}(y_{1j} - y_{3j}) + A_{z1j}(y_{3j} - y_{2j})}{2S_j} \,,$$

$$a_{2j} = \frac{A_{z3j}(x_{2j} - x_{1j}) + A_{z2j}(x_{1j} - x_{3j}) + A_{z1j}(x_{3j} - x_{2j})}{2S_j} \,,$$

where

$$2S_j = x_{1j}(y_{2j} - y_{3j}) + x_{2j}(y_{3j} - y_{1j}) + x_{3j}(y_{1j} - y_{2j}) \qquad (2.69)$$

is the double surface of the triangle.

Using the above results, the contribution to the functional L from the jth element may be written as follows:

$$L_j = \frac{a_{1j}^2 + a_{2j}^2}{\mu_j} \cdot S_j - \int_{\Omega_j} \left[2J_{zj} \cdot A_{zj} - j\omega\gamma_j A_{zj}^2\right] d\Omega. \qquad (2.70)$$

After substituting for A_{zj} from (2.68) and (2.69) we obtain

$$L_j = \frac{a_{1j}^2 + a_{2j}^2}{\mu_j} \cdot S_j - 2J_{zj} \int_{\Omega_j} (a_{0j} + a_{1j}x + a_{2j}y) \, d\Omega$$

$$+ j\omega\gamma_j \int_{\Omega_j} (a_{0j} + a_{1j}x + a_{2j}y)^2 \, d\Omega.$$

Denoting

$$x_{0j} = \tfrac{1}{3}(x_{1j} + x_{2j} + x_{3j}), \quad y_{0j} = \tfrac{1}{3}(y_{1j} + y_{2j} + y_{3j})$$

as the barycentric coordinates of the triangle, we can write

$$L_j = \frac{a_{1j}^2 + a_{2j}^2}{\mu_j} \cdot S_j - J_{zj}(a_{0j} + a_{1j}x_{0j} + a_{2j}y_{0j}) + \frac{j}{12}\omega\gamma_j \cdot [6a_{0j}^2 + a_{1j}^2(9x_{0j}^2 - P_j)$$

$$+ a_{2j}^2(9y_{0j}^2 - Q_j) + 12a_{0j}(a_{1j}x_{0j} + a_{2j}y_{0j}) + a_{1j}a_{2j}(9x_{0j}y_{0j} + R_j)], \qquad (2.71)$$

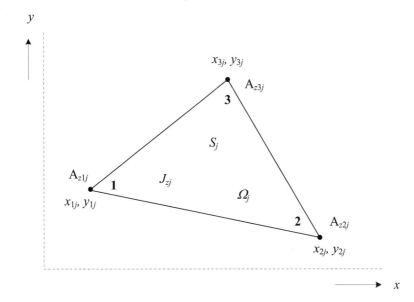

Figure 2.31.   Computation of relevant quantities on a triangular element.

where

$$P_j = x_{1j}x_{2j} + x_{2j}x_{3j} + x_{3j}x_{1j}\,,$$
$$Q_j = y_{1j}y_{2j} + y_{2j}y_{3j} + y_{3j}y_{1j}\,,$$
$$R_j = x_{1j}y_{1j} + x_{2j}y_{2j} + x_{3j}y_{3j}\,.$$

2.6.3 Further prospectives

Although it might seem that the development of this method is at its end and nothing novel can be contributed in the domain, such an opinion would be far from reality. Nowadays, intensive research is being conducted particularly in the area of finite element methods of higher orders of accuracy, with automatic or semiautomatic mesh adaptivity. In the case of coupled problems, quite new technologies are being developed that make it possible to avoid splitting the operators and that work with different meshes for mapping different physical fields. Extensive research is being conducted in the area of "hanging nodes" that strongly extend the possibilities of adaptivity. More information about the actual situation in the domain can be found in recent monographs and papers [94–98].

2.7 INTEGRAL AND INTEGRODIFFERENTIAL METHODS

Under the integral and integrodifferential methods we usually understand methods used for the solution of various integral or integrodifferential equations. Nevertheless, in this group we can also include technologies for evaluation of a great number of definite and indefinite integrals that occur in the expressions for the field quantities in linear and homogeneous fields or algorithms combining both solution of the integral equations and evaluation of integral expressions (e.g., boundary element method).

These methods represent an alternative to differential methods, particularly when the differential formulation of the task is ill-posed (e.g., some eddy current problems, problems where it is not easy to implement the boundary conditions, or problems with motion).

These methods will be analyzed in detail in Chapters 3, 4, and 5.

2.8 IMPORTANT MATHEMATICAL ASPECTS OF NUMERICAL METHODS

Every method for numerical processing of the field describing PDEs leads to a system of linear or nonlinear algebraic equations. If the field is, moreover, nonstationary, we have to solve such a system at every time step. It is clear that the results must be affected by various errors arising during the numerical process. So it is necessary to have tools that would allow a decision on whether the resultant errors are still acceptable or not.

In this section we will only revise the most important concepts concerning the quality of the numerical solution of partial differential equations. Detailed information can be found in a great deal of references [99].

The quality of the results generally depends on five properties of the developed numerical schemes:

- consistency,

- stability,

- convergence,

- accuracy, and

- efficiency.

Consistency means a fair agreement between the solved partial differential equation and proposed numerical scheme. It is necessary that the system of algebraic equations is a sufficiently good representation of the original PDE.

Stability of the numerical scheme means that it is not too sensitive to small perturbations such as round-off or other numerical errors. Not every scheme is numerically stable, or is stable only for some conditions.

Convergence means that the approximate solution converges to the exact solution of the PDE when the spacing of the mesh (and time step) approaches zero.

Accuracy of the numerical scheme means how much the results obtained by the corresponding approximate solution differ from the exact solution.

And finally, the efficiency is also an important concept that is not yet well defined. But the method (or numerical scheme) is efficient when the results are sufficiently accurate and obtained in a short time.

Some of these concepts will be explained in more detail in the following sections.

2.8.1   Stability

Numerical stability is a concept associated particularly (but not only) with nonstationary physical fields representing the parabolic and hyperbolic initial and boundary value problems. In the course of their numerical solution, the results determined at one time level are used for computation of the results at the following time level. And it is necessary to find the conditions on which the accompanying errors do not grow and, consequently, do not lead to unacceptable results at higher time levels. As for the mentioned errors, we can split them into three groups:

- round-off errors due to computation with a finite number of numerals,

- truncation errors, and

- errors caused by discretization (nonaccurate setting of the right-hand sides and initial or boundary conditions).

Practical computations must always be based on stable numerical processes.

As for the stability itself, it is an internal property of the selected difference formula and does not depend directly on the approximated partial differential equation. Every equation of this kind may be approximated by a numerical scheme that is

- stable under all conditions,

- conditionally stable (stable under specified conditions), or

- always unstable.

The evaluation of numerical schemes with respect to their stability is generally a difficult task. Nevertheless, in many cases it may be validated in several ways. The most frequent techniques are the matrix method and von Neumann's method.

2.8.2 Convergence

Consider an operator equation

$$L\varphi = 0 \,, \tag{2.72}$$

where L is an operator and φ an unknown function of the spatial and time variables defined in domain Ω. Let a point $p \in \Omega$. A numerical scheme used for solution of (2.72) is convergent if

$$\lim \varphi_{\text{approx}}(p) = \varphi_{\text{exact}}(p) \text{ for } \Delta x \to 0 \text{ and } \Delta t \to 0 \,, \tag{2.73}$$

where Δx denotes the spatial discretization while Δt represents the temporal discretization.

It is very difficult to prove that a general numerical scheme is convergent. Nevertheless, in linear cases there holds an equivalence theorem saying that for properly posed linear problems solved by finite differences satisfying the condition of consistency it is stability that is the principal condition of convergence. In such a case this theorem holds for any discretization, which is typical for a number of boundary value or initial and boundary value problems.

Convergence of the numerical schemes can be investigated in cases where we know the analytical solution. When the exact solution is not known, the convergence is usually investigated using appropriate numerical experiments.

2.8.3 Accuracy

Accuracy of the results is influenced by several factors. The first one is given by the discretization of the problem. Generally, accuracy grows with finer mesh; on the other hand, generating finer meshes has its limits in computer resources (memory). Important also are round-off errors and their accumulation in the process of computation.

Of course, accuracy can be improved to some extent. We can carry out, for example, better discretization of the definition area of the problem, or use a more appropriate numerical scheme.

2.9 NUMERICAL SCHEMES FOR PARABOLIC EQUATIONS

In low-frequency electromagnetism we often work with PDEs of the parabolic type, particularly in association with the investigation of the time evolution of eddy currents. Their numerical solution is somewhat specific (in comparison with the elliptic PDEs describing the static fields) because, as is usual for the initial and boundary value problems, it must proceed from one time level to the next one. Two fundamental numerical schemes—explicit and implicit—have been proposed for this purpose, each of them with somewhat different mathematical properties. Of course, during the last fifty years a lot of various modifications of these two basic schemes have been developed and successfully applied [55, 56].

Analogous schemes can be applied even for the solution of integrodifferential equations describing the same or similar physical processes that will be discussed later on. And that is why it might be useful to derive both these schemes, at least for one of the simplest possible arrangements, and explain their differences.

Consider a diffusion differential equation for the magnetic vector potential $\boldsymbol{A}$ in cylindrical coordinates, in a medium of electrical conductivity γ and relative magnetic permeability μ_{r}. Both these quantities are considered constant. Moreover, the magnetic vector potential is supposed to have only one nonzero component A_z that depends only on radius r. Now this equation reads

$$\frac{\partial^2 A_z}{\partial r^2} + \frac{1}{r}\frac{\partial A_z}{\partial r} = \mu_0 \mu_r \gamma \cdot \frac{\partial A_z}{\partial t} . \tag{2.74}$$

The solution is to be carried out in a domain $\Omega(r,t)$, $r \in \langle R_1, R_2 \rangle$, $t \in \langle 0, T \rangle$. The initial and boundary conditions are known.

At first, we cover the domain $\Omega(r,t)$ with a rectangular grid; see Fig. 2.32. For the sake of simplicity, let all spatial steps and also temporal steps be equal, having values Δr and Δt, respectively.

The partial derivatives in (2.74) will be replaced by the corresponding difference approximations. Of great importance is how the difference approximations are chosen and handled.

2.9.1 Explicit scheme

The derivatives with respect to the geometrical variables are approximated on the jth level and to the $(j + 1)$st level we get using the forward derivative with respect to time t on the jth level. In this way we obtain

$$\left[\frac{\partial^2 A_z}{\partial r^2}\right]_{(i,j)} \doteq \frac{A_{z(i+1,j)} - 2A_{z(i,j)} + A_{z(i-1,j)}}{(\Delta r)^2} ,$$

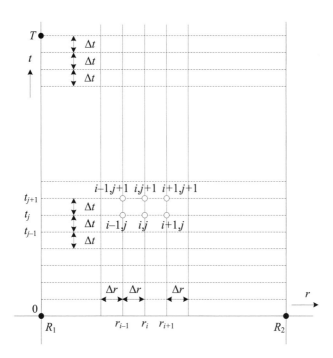

Figure 2.32. The grid for solving (2.74).

using the central derivative

$$\left[\frac{\partial A_z}{\partial r}\right]_{(i,j)} \doteq \frac{A_{z(i+1,j)} - A_{z(i-1,j)}}{2\Delta r}$$

and finally

$$\left[\frac{\partial A_z}{\partial t}\right]_{(i,j)} \doteq \frac{A_{z(i,j+1)} - A_{z(i,j)}}{\Delta t}. \tag{2.75}$$

After substituting these relations into (2.74), we find

$$A_{z(i,j+1)} = a_{i,j} A_{z(i,j)} + b_{i,j} A_{z(i+1,j)} + c_{i,j} A_{z(i-1,j)},$$

where

$$a_{i,j} = 1 - \frac{2\Delta t}{\mu_0 \mu_r \gamma (\Delta r)^2}, \quad b_{i,j} = \frac{\Delta t}{\mu_0 \mu_r \gamma}\left[\frac{1}{(\Delta r)^2} + \frac{1}{2 r_i \Delta r}\right],$$

$$c_{i,j} = \frac{\Delta t}{\mu_0 \mu_r \gamma}\left[\frac{1}{(\Delta r)^2} - \frac{1}{2 r_i \Delta r}\right]. \tag{2.76}$$

It is clear that the explicit scheme allows one to directly determine the values of function A_z on the $(j+1)$st level.

The explicit schemes are often stable only conditionally. Before using them we have to know the corresponding condition of stability that requires some limitation on the value of Δt. On the other hand, its application is very easy from the viewpoint of the numerical solution; on every time level only relatively simple algebraic expressions have to be evaluated.

2.9.2   Implicit scheme

The derivatives with respect to the geometrical variables are approximated on the $(j+1)$st level while for the time derivative we will use the backward scheme. Using the same notation as in previous case, we get

$$\frac{A_{z(i+1,j+1)} - 2A_{z(i,j+1)} + A_{z(i-1,j+1)}}{(\Delta r)^2} + \frac{1}{r_i}\frac{A_{z(i+1,j+1)} - A_{z(i-1,j+1)}}{2\Delta r}$$

$$= \mu_0 \mu_r \gamma \frac{A_{z(i,j+1)} - A_{z(i,j)}}{\Delta t}, \tag{2.77}$$

and after some modifications

$$d_{i,j} A_{z(i,j+1)} + e_{i,j} A_{z(i+1,j+1)} + f_{i,j} A_{z(i-1,j+1)} = A_{z(i,j)},$$

where

$$d_{i,j} = 1 + \frac{2\Delta t}{\mu_0 \mu_r \gamma (\Delta r)^2}, \quad e_{i,j} = -\frac{\Delta t}{\mu_0 \mu_r \gamma}\left[\frac{1}{(\Delta r)^2} + \frac{1}{2 r_i \Delta r}\right],$$

$$f_{i,j} = -\frac{\Delta t}{\mu_0 \mu_r \gamma}\left[\frac{1}{(\Delta r)^2} - \frac{1}{2 r_i \Delta r}\right]. \tag{2.78}$$

The implicit difference approximation represents one row of a system of linear algebraic equations. After assembling the corresponding matrix and solving the system, we obtain the distribution of function A_z on the $(j + 1)$st time level.

The implicit formulas are usually stable and allow computations with any value of Δt.

CHAPTER 3

SOLUTION OF ELECTROMAGNETIC FIELDS BY INTEGRAL EXPRESSIONS

3.1 INTRODUCTION

Solution of electric and magnetic fields by means of integral expressions represents a well-known and reliable calculation technique. Its application, however, is restricted to several classes of linear problems in homogeneous media with sufficiently simple geometries.

Possibilities of mapping electric fields by this technique are rather rare. The reason is that most of the relevant problems are characterized by the knowledge of electric potential along electrically conductive surfaces. In order to find electric field distribution in such a system, we must first determine distribution of the charge on these surfaces, which generally leads to the solution of a system of the first-kind Fredholm integral equations, and only then to use integral expressions for calculation of the field quantities. Therefore, the technique can practically be applied only for a few tasks that are either artificial (at least to some extent) or exhibit full symmetry (distribution of the charge is known in advance). Nevertheless, this chapter contains several common tasks that may conveniently be solved in this way.

Solution of magnetic fields in this manner is possible in much wider extent, for example, fields generated by various systems of direct current carrying nonmagnetic conductors in linear media. Here the technique represents a powerful tool, particularly in those cases where the integrals can be calculated analytically or semianalytically. Moreover, the results may immediately be used for computation of subsequent integral quantities such as the total field energy, self-inductances and mutual inductances, and force and torque effects in the system. The chapter presents several useful examples of thin and massive conductors and also cylindrical coils, even with nonnegligible lead.

Integral Methods in Low-Frequency Electromagnetics. By I. Doležel, P. Karban, and P. Šolín.

83

3.2 1D INTEGRATION AREA

3.2.1 Review of typical problems

These tasks almost always represent more or less idealized arrangements. In this way we can determine, for example, electric fields of long single uniformly charged conductors of simple geometries (circular cross section) and also their magnetic fields provided that they carry direct currents. Another case is a charged or current carrying circular loop formed by a filamentary conductor of negligible cross section. Of course, now the field quantities exhibit singularities. Nevertheless, when we are interested in far fields, we can use this approximation because it provides sufficiently accurate results at very low computational costs.

3.2.2 Electric field generated by a solitary filamentary conductor of infinite length

From the physical viewpoint, such a task is practically unreal due to two reasons: the first one is the unreal geometry of the conductor (its cross section is negligibly small and its length is infinite); the second one is the unbalance of the electric charges in the investigated system. On the other hand, however, its results may immediately be used for description of far fields of physically real (but, of course, somewhat idealized) arrangements.

Consider an infinitely long filamentary conductor whose longitudinal axis is identical with the z axis (see Fig. 3.1). Let the conductor be uniformly charged by charge Q' per meter. The task is to find the distribution of the potential and the electric field in its neighborhood. The calculation does not respect any influence of earth or other electrically conductive bodies. Permittivity of the surrounding medium is ε_0.

The dielectric flux Ψ' per unit length at any radius $r > 0$ is equal to charge Q' per unit length, so that

$$\Psi' = Q' = \boldsymbol{D} \cdot \boldsymbol{S}', \tag{3.1}$$

where $\boldsymbol{S}'$ is the area of the cylinder of radius r per unit length. As both vectors $\boldsymbol{D}$ and $\boldsymbol{S}'$ are of the same direction (they have only one nonzero component in the radial direction),

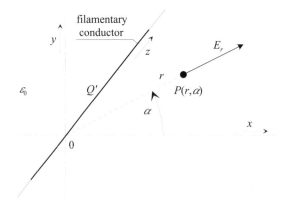

Figure 3.1.   Charged filamentary conductor of infinite length.

at any point $P(r, \alpha)$ we can write

$$Q' = \varepsilon_0 E_r \cdot S' = \varepsilon_0 E_r \cdot 2\pi r, \quad r > 0,$$

and, hence,

$$E_r = E_r(r) = \frac{Q'}{2\pi r \varepsilon_0}, \quad r > 0. \tag{3.2}$$

Electric potential produced by the conductor is a function of r and may be expressed as

$$\varphi(r) = -\int E_r dr = -\frac{Q'}{2\pi\varepsilon_0} \ln r + \varphi_0, \quad r > 0. \tag{3.3}$$

Unfortunately, potential φ cannot be normalized in the standard way, that is, we are not able to find such a value of φ_0 that would provide $\lim_{r\to\infty} \varphi(r) = 0$.

For a line conductor charged by $Q' = 10^{-9}$ C/m, Fig. 3.2 shows the function $E_r(r)$ and Fig. 3.3 the function $\varphi(r)$ for $\varphi_0 = 0$.

3.2.3 Electric field of charged thin circular ring

One of the elements often used in various practical applications is a charged metal circular ring of finite dimensions (mostly of circular or rectangular cross section).

When we want to know the field distribution in an area sufficiently distant from the ring, we can replace it by an infinitely thin circular filament of radius R (see Fig. 3.4, whose center lies at the origin of a cylindrical coordinate system). The calculation does not take into account any influence of earth or other electrically conductive bodies. Due to the symmetry, the total electric charge Q is distributed along the filament uniformly, with line charge density

$$\tau = \frac{Q}{2\pi R}. \tag{3.4}$$

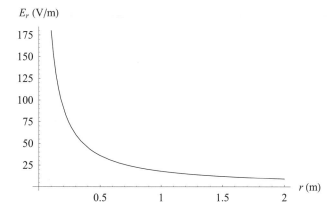

Figure 3.2. The graph of function $E_r(r)$ for $Q' = 10^{-9}$ C/m.

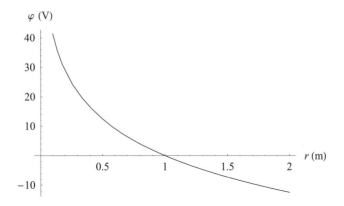

Figure 3.3.   The graph of function $\varphi(r)$ for $Q' = 10^{-9}$ C/m and $\varphi_0 = 0$.

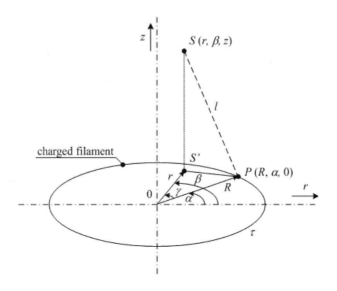

Figure 3.4.   Arrangement of the charged circular filament.

Contribution to the potential φ at the reference point $S(r, \beta, z)$ from an elementary charge at the integration point $P(R, \alpha, 0)$ is

$$d\varphi(r, \beta, z) = \frac{\tau}{4\pi\varepsilon_0} \cdot \frac{R\,d\gamma}{l}, \tag{3.5}$$

where

$$l = \sqrt{R^2 + r^2 - 2Rr\cos(\alpha - \beta) + z^2}. \tag{3.6}$$

Since $\alpha - \beta = \gamma$, we simply obtain

$$\varphi(r, \beta, z) = \frac{\tau}{4\pi\varepsilon_0} \cdot \int_{\gamma=0}^{2\pi} \frac{R \, d\gamma}{\sqrt{R^2 + r^2 - 2Rr \cos\gamma + z^2}} + \varphi_0 . \tag{3.7}$$

The potential is obviously independent of angle β (symmetry). Putting $\varphi_0 = 0$, after some rearrangements in the above integral we finally have

$$\varphi(r, z) = \frac{R\tau}{\pi\varepsilon_0 \sqrt{(R+r)^2 + z^2}} \cdot \int_{\delta=0}^{\pi/2} \frac{d\delta}{\sqrt{1 - k^2 \sin^2\delta}} = \frac{R\tau \cdot F(k^2)}{\pi\varepsilon_0 \sqrt{(R+r)^2 + z^2}} , \tag{3.8}$$

where

$$0 \le k^2 = \frac{4rR}{(R+r)^2 + z^2} < 1 \tag{3.9}$$

and $F(k^2)$ is a complete elliptic integral of the first kind of argument k^2. Its values are tabulated in a lot of various references or may easily be calculated by standard very fast and accurate procedures (for details see Appendix B).

As the potential φ is a function of variables r and z, the vector of electric field strength $\mathbf{E}$ has only two components, E_r and E_z (the component E_β being identically equal to zero). Using (3.7) we can express their values at point $U(r, \beta, z)$ in the form

$$E_r(r, z) = -\frac{\partial\varphi}{\partial r} = \frac{\tau}{4\pi\varepsilon_0} \cdot \int_{\gamma=0}^{2\pi} \frac{R(r - R\cos\gamma) \, d\gamma}{\sqrt{[R^2 + r^2 - 2Rr\cos\gamma + z^2]^3}} , \tag{3.10}$$

$$E_z(r, z) = -\frac{\partial\varphi}{\partial z} = \frac{\tau}{4\pi\varepsilon_0} \cdot \int_{\gamma=0}^{2\pi} \frac{Rz \, d\gamma}{\sqrt{[R^2 + r^2 - 2Rr\cos\gamma + z^2]^3}} . \tag{3.11}$$

Denoting

$$m^2 = \frac{r^2 + R^2 + z^2}{2rR} \tag{3.12}$$

and rearranging (3.10) and (3.11), we obtain

$$E_r(r, z) = \frac{\tau}{4\pi\varepsilon_0} \cdot \frac{2}{\sqrt{(2rR)^3}}$$

$$\cdot \left[rR \int_{\gamma=0}^{\pi} \frac{d\gamma}{\sqrt{(m^2 - \cos\gamma)^3}} - R^2 \int_{\gamma=0}^{\pi} \frac{\cos\gamma \, d\gamma}{\sqrt{(m^2 - \cos\gamma)^3}} \right] , \tag{3.13}$$

$$E_z(r, z) = \frac{\tau}{4\pi\varepsilon_0} \cdot \frac{2Rz}{\sqrt{(2rR)^3}} \int_{\gamma=0}^{\pi} \frac{d\gamma}{\sqrt{(m^2 - \cos\gamma)^3}} . \tag{3.14}$$

Application of formulas summarized in Appendix B finally provides

$$E_r(r, z) = \frac{\tau}{4\pi\varepsilon_0} \cdot \frac{2R}{r\sqrt{(r+R)^2 + z^2}} \left[\frac{r^2 - R^2 - z^2}{(r-R)^2 + z^2} \cdot E(k^2) + F(k^2) \right] , \tag{3.15}$$

$$E_z(r, z) = \frac{\tau}{4\pi\varepsilon_0} \cdot \frac{4Rz}{((r-R)^2 + z^2)\sqrt{(r+R)^2 + z^2}} \cdot E(k^2) , \tag{3.16}$$

where k^2 is given by (3.9).

As mentioned before, the filament itself represents a set of singular points at which the field quantities cannot be evaluated because their limits reach infinity there. On the other hand, along the z axis their distribution is given by quite simple expressions:

$$\varphi(0, z) = \frac{R\tau}{2\varepsilon_0 \sqrt{R^2 + z^2}}, \quad E_r(0, z) = 0, \quad E_z(0, z) = \frac{Rz\tau}{2\varepsilon_0 \sqrt{(R^2 + z^2)^3}}. \quad (3.17)$$

For illustration, the next three figures show several results obtained for a thin loop of radius $R = 0.2$ m and total charge $Q = 10^{-9}$ C. Figure 3.5 shows the distribution of the equipotential lines in the axial cut of the arrangement and Fig. 3.6 the distribution of the module $|\boldsymbol{E}| = \sqrt{E_r^2 + E_z^2}$ of corresponding electric field strength.

Finally, Fig. 3.7 shows the distribution of the module of electric field strength $|\boldsymbol{E}|$ along the z axis for $z > 0$.

3.2.4   Magnetic field generated by a solitary filamentary conductor of infinite length

The task is practically unreal due to the same reasons that were mentioned in Section 3.2.2 for the electric field of such a conductor. But the results may conveniently be used, for example, for description of external fields produced by long massive cylindrical conductors whose radii $R > 0$.

Consider an infinitely long filamentary conductor whose longitudinal axis is identical with the z axis (see Fig. 3.8). The conductor placed in a medium of permeability μ_0 carries current $i(t)$.

Magnetic field strength $\boldsymbol{H}$ at the distance r from the conductor has only one nonzero component in the circumferential direction α, whose value is (see (1.5)) given by the relation

$$H_\alpha(r, t) = \frac{i(t)}{2\pi r}$$

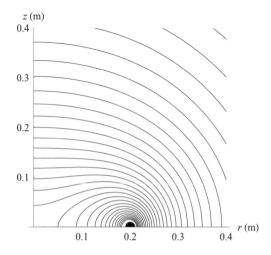

Figure 3.5.   Distribution of the equipotentials in the vicinity of the loop.

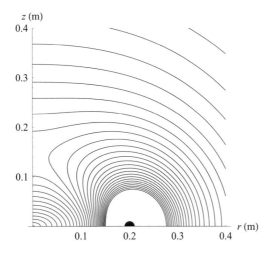

Figure 3.6.   Distribution of the module of electric field strength in the vicinity of the loop.

and, analogously,

$$B_\alpha(r, t) = \frac{\mu_0 i(t)}{2\pi r} .$$ (3.18)

Distribution of the magnetic vector potential $\mathbf{A}$ (that has only one nonzero component $A_z(r, t)$ in the z direction) follows from the relation

$$A_z(r, t) = -\int B_\alpha(r, t)\mathrm{d}r = -\frac{\mu_0 i(t)}{2\pi} \ln r + A_{z0}(t) ,$$ (3.19)

where $A_{z0}(t)$ is an arbitrary function of time. For $r \to 0$ the function $A_z(r, t)$ exhibits a singularity. Figures 3.9 and 3.10 depict the components $B_\alpha(r)$ and $A_z(r)$ for a constant current $I = 10$ A and $A_{z0}(t) = 0$.

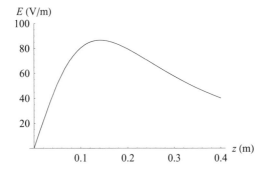

Figure 3.7.   Distribution of the module of electric field strength along the z axis.

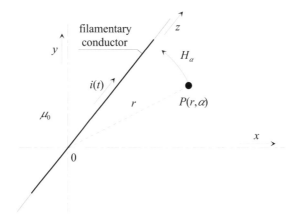

Figure 3.8. Filamentary conductor of infinite length carrying current $i(t)$.

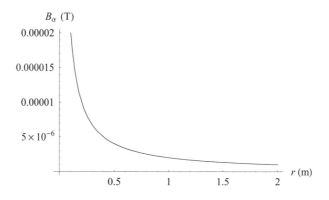

Figure 3.9. The graph of function $B_\alpha(r)$ for $I = 10$ A.

3.2.5 Magnetic field of thin circular current carrying loop

Unlike thin charged rings that represent real physical objects, a thin current carrying circular turn is only an idealized element.

Nevertheless, mapping of its field provides a good idea of the distribution of the magnetic field in similar real arrangements (e.g., coils of small height). Consider a solitary filamentary turn of radius R (see Fig. 3.11) carrying direct current I, whose center lies at the origin of a cylindrical coordinate system.

At an arbitrary regular point $U(r, \beta, z)$ the current I produces magnetic vector potential $\mathbf{A}$ with only one nonzero component A_β in the tangential direction. It is expressed by the formula

$$A_\beta(r, \beta, z) = \frac{\mu_0 I}{4\pi} \oint_c \frac{\cos \gamma \, dc}{l} + A_{\beta 0}, \qquad (3.20)$$

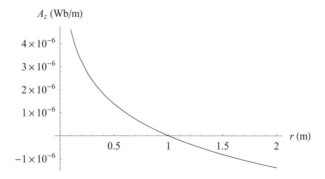

Figure 3.10. The graph of function $A_z(r)$ for $I = 10$ A and $A_{z0}(t) = 0$.

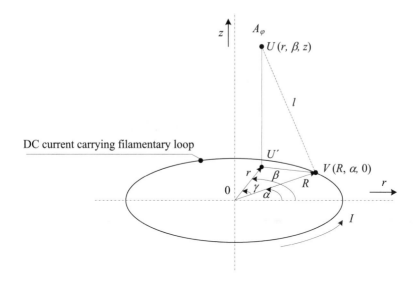

Figure 3.11. A thin direct current carrying circular turn.

where $l = \sqrt{r^2 + R^2 - 2rR\cos\gamma + z^2}$ and integration is performed all over the turn. Since A_β is independent of angle γ, after a simple rearrangement (considering $A_{\beta 0} = 0$) we obtain

$$A_\beta(r, z) = \frac{\mu_0 I}{4\pi} \int_{\gamma=0}^{2\pi} \frac{R\cos\gamma \, d\gamma}{\sqrt{R^2 + r^2 - 2Rr\cos\gamma + z^2}}. \qquad (3.21)$$

Using again the parameter k^2 introduced in (3.9), the above integral may be rewritten as

$$A_\beta(r, z) = \frac{\mu_0 I}{4\pi} \cdot \frac{R}{\sqrt{(r + R)^2 + z^2}}$$

$$\cdot \left[\left(\frac{2}{k^2} - 1 \right) \int_{\gamma=0}^{2\pi} \frac{d\gamma}{\sqrt{1 - k^2 \cos^2 \frac{\gamma}{2}}} - \frac{2}{k^2} \int_{\gamma=0}^{2\pi} \sqrt{1 - k^2 \cos^2 \frac{\gamma}{2}} \, d\gamma \right]$$

$$= \frac{\mu_0 I}{\pi} \cdot \frac{R}{\sqrt{(r + R)^2 + z^2}} \cdot \left[\left(\frac{2}{k^2} - 1 \right) F(k^2) - \frac{2}{k^2} E(k^2) \right], \qquad (3.22)$$

where $E(k)$ is a complete elliptic integral of the second kind and $F(k)$ of the first kind.

The vector of magnetic flux density $\boldsymbol{B}$ has again two nonzero components $B_r(r, z)$ and $B_z(r, z)$ that may be determined from the relation $\boldsymbol{B} = \text{curl } \boldsymbol{A}$ in a cylindrical coordinate system. Starting from (3.22) we have

$$B_r(r, z) = -\frac{\partial A_\beta(r, z)}{\partial z} = \frac{\mu_0 I R z}{4\pi} \cdot \int_{\gamma=0}^{2\pi} \frac{\cos \gamma \, d\gamma}{l^3}, \qquad (3.23)$$

$$B_z(r, z) = \frac{1}{r} \frac{\partial [r A_\beta(r, z)]}{\partial r} = \frac{\mu_0 I R}{4\pi} \cdot \int_{\gamma=0}^{2\pi} \left[\frac{\cos \gamma}{lr} - \frac{\cos \gamma (r - R \cos \gamma)}{l^3} \right] d\gamma. \quad (3.24)$$

Now it is necessary to remove the singularity for $r = 0$ occurring in the first term of integral (3.24). Its integration "by parts" with respect to γ using $u' = \cos \gamma$ and $v = l$ provides

$$B_z(r, z) = \frac{\mu_0 I R}{4\pi} \cdot \int_{\gamma=0}^{2\pi} \frac{R - r \cos \gamma}{l^3} \, d\gamma. \qquad (3.25)$$

Introducing m^2 from (3.12), the integral expressions (3.23) and (3.25) may be rearranged as follows

$$B_r(r, z) = \frac{\mu_0 I}{4\pi} \frac{2Rz}{\sqrt{(2rR)^3}} \cdot \int_{\gamma=0}^{\pi} \frac{\cos \gamma \, d\gamma}{\sqrt{(m^2 - \cos \gamma)^3}}, \qquad (3.26)$$

$$B_z(r, z) = \frac{\mu_0 I}{4\pi} \cdot \frac{2}{\sqrt{(2rR)^3}}$$

$$\cdot \left[R^2 \int_{\gamma=0}^{\pi} \frac{d\gamma}{\sqrt{(m^2 - \cos \gamma)^3}} - rR \int_{\gamma=0}^{\pi} \frac{\cos \gamma \, d\gamma}{\sqrt{(m^2 - \cos \gamma)^3}} \right]. \quad (3.27)$$

Both of the above integrals can be calculated again using formulas in Appendix B. After their evaluation we obtain

$$B_r(r, z) = \frac{\mu_0 I}{4\pi} \cdot \frac{2z}{r\sqrt{(r + R)^2 + z^2}} \left[\frac{r^2 + R^2 + z^2}{(r - R)^2 + z^2} \cdot E(k^2) + F(k^2) \right], \qquad (3.28)$$

$$B_z(r, z) = \frac{\mu_0 I}{4\pi} \cdot \frac{2}{\sqrt{(r + R)^2 + z^2}} \left[\frac{R^2 - r^2 - z^2}{(r - R)^2 + z^2} \cdot E(k^2) + F(k^2) \right], \qquad (3.29)$$

k^2 being given by (3.9).

For the special case $r = 0$ we get

$$A_\beta(0, z) = 0 \,,$$

$$B_r(0, z) = 0 \,,$$

$$B_z(0, z) = \frac{\mu_0 I R^2}{2\sqrt{[R^2 + z^2]^3}} \,. \tag{3.30}$$

The following example solves the magnetic field distribution of a thin loop for radius $R = 0.2$ m and $I = 100$ A. Figure 3.12 shows the distribution of force lines in its meridian cut (their equation being given by the relation $r \cdot A_\beta(r, z) = \text{const}$) while Fig. 3.13 depicts the distribution of the module of magnetic flux density $|B| = \sqrt{B_r^2 + B_z^2}$. Finally, Fig. 3.14 shows the distribution of $|B|$ along the z axis.

It should be mentioned that the current passing through the filament may exhibit time dependence. A magnetic field produced by such a current varies correspondingly.

3.2.6   Electric field generated by a system of uniformly charged parallel thin filaments of infinite length

Sometimes we have to determine the distribution of electric field quantities produced by a system of long parallel conductors of small cross sections (a typical example is the electric field near a three-phase overhead line). When evaluating their values at a sufficient distance from the conductors, we can substitute thin filaments for them.

Consider an arrangement consisting of n infinitely long thin filaments as shown in Fig. 3.15. All filaments are parallel with axis z, charged by line charges $\tau_1, \ldots, \tau_n$, and

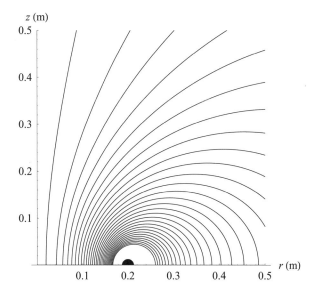

Figure 3.12.   Distribution of force lines in the vicinity of the thin ring ($R = 0.2$ m, $I = 100$ A).

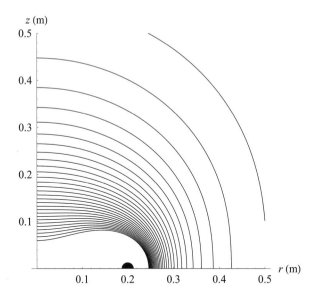

Figure 3.13.   Distribution of the module $|\boldsymbol{B}|$ of magnetic flux density in the vicinity of the thin ring ($R = 0.2$ m, $I = 100$ A).

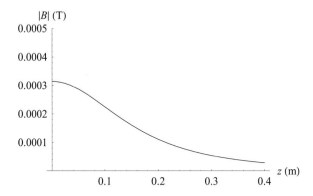

Figure 3.14.   Distribution of the module $|\boldsymbol{B}|$ of magnetic flux density along the z axis ($R = 0.2$ m, $I = 100$ A).

their intersections with plane $z = 0$ are at points $x_i, y_i, i = 1, \ldots, n$. Suppose the balance of charge is expressed by the relation

$$\sum_{i=1}^{n} \tau_i = 0 \,. \tag{3.31}$$

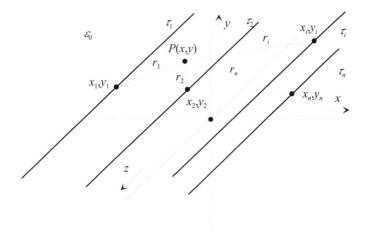

Figure 3.15. A system of thin charged parallel conductors of infinite length.

The task is to find the value of potential and electric field strength at an arbitrary point $P(x, y)$ (that is not identical with any of the conductors) provided that the permittivity of the surrounding medium is ε_0. The field quantities are obviously independent of the z coordinate. The influence of the earth is neglected. Using (3.3), potential $\varphi(P)$ is given by

$$\varphi(P(x, y)) = -\frac{1}{2\pi\varepsilon_0} \sum_{i=1}^{n} \tau_i \ln r_i + \varphi_0, \tag{3.32}$$

where $r_i = \sqrt{(x - x_i)^2 + (y - y_i)^2} > 0$. Substituting for τ_n from (3.31) we obtain

$$\varphi(P(x, y)) = -\frac{1}{2\pi\varepsilon_0} \sum_{i=1}^{n-1} \tau_i \ln \frac{r_i}{r_n} + \varphi_0. \tag{3.33}$$

It is obvious that the potential $\varphi(P(x, y))$ is always finite.

Electric field strength $\mathbf{E}$, which is also independent of the z coordinate, has two components given by the fractions

$$E_x(P) = -\frac{\partial \varphi(P)}{\partial x} = \frac{1}{2\pi\varepsilon_0} \sum_{i=1}^{n} \tau_i \cdot \frac{x - x_i}{(x_i - x)^2 + (y_i - y)^2}, \tag{3.34}$$

$$E_y(P) = -\frac{\partial \varphi(P)}{\partial y} = \frac{1}{2\pi\varepsilon_0} \sum_{i=1}^{n} \tau_i \cdot \frac{y - y_i}{(x_i - x)^2 + (y_i - y)^2}. \tag{3.35}$$

Finally, the module of $\mathbf{E}$ is

$$|\mathbf{E}(P)| = \sqrt{E_x^2(P) + E_y^2(P)}. \tag{3.36}$$

Another important case of this type is the distribution of the electric field in the same arrangement, but with the influence of the earth (of rake angle β) whose surface is considered to be perfectly electrically conductive. Particulars are depicted in Fig. 3.16. The earth is substituted by conductors placed at a depth that is equal to the distance of the real conductors from its surface. Thus, the only task is to find their coordinates $x'_i, y'_i, i = 1, \ldots, n$, and then to use the results (3.33)–(3.35). After several simple calculations we get

$$x'_i = x_i + 2l_i \sin \beta, \quad y'_i = y_i - 2l_i \cos \beta, \quad i = 1, \ldots, n. \tag{3.37}$$

Of course, charges of a particular conductor may change with time. Such cases are typical, for example, for overhead power lines. The computation of electric field in the vicinity of a three-phase overhead power line will be shown later on.

3.2.7 Magnetic field generated by a system of currents carrying parallel filamentary conductors of infinite length

Formulas for the distribution of the magnetic vector potential and relevant components of the magnetic flux density are derived on the assumption that the system is not influenced by the presence of the earth or other electrically conductive bodies. Such a system with n conductors carrying generally time-variable currents $i_j(t), j = 1, \ldots, n$, is depicted in Fig. 3.17. The magnetic permeability of the system is supposed to be μ_0.

The z-component of the magnetic vector potential $\boldsymbol{A}$ at any point $P(x, y)$ that is not identical with any of the conductors (see (3.17)) is given as

$$A_z(x, y, t) = -\frac{\mu_0}{2\pi} \sum_{j=1}^{n} i_j(t) \ln r_j + A_{z0}(t), \tag{3.38}$$

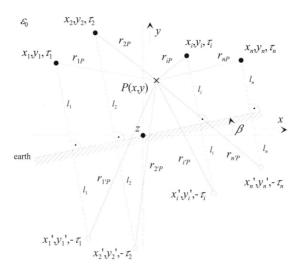

Figure 3.16. A system of thin charged parallel conductors of infinite length taking into account the influence of the earth.

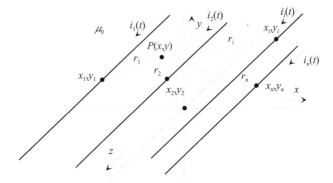

Figure 3.17.   A system of filamentary parallel current carrying conductors of infinite length.

where $r_j = \sqrt{(x - x_j)^2 + (y - y_j)^2} > 0$. Both components of the magnetic flux density $B_x(x, y, t)$ and $B_y(x, y, t)$ are then given as

$$B_x(x, y, t) = \frac{\partial A_z}{\partial y} = -\frac{\mu_0}{2\pi} \sum_{j=1}^{n} i_j(t) \frac{y - y_j}{(x - x_j)^2 + (y - y_j)^2} \qquad (3.39)$$

and

$$B_y(x, y, t) = -\frac{\partial A_z}{\partial x} = \frac{\mu_0}{2\pi} \sum_{j=1}^{n} i_j(t) \frac{x - x_j}{(x - x_j)^2 + (y - y_j)^2}. \qquad (3.40)$$

3.3   2D INTEGRATION AREA

3.3.1   Review of typical problems

Typical problems in this domain are linear magnetic fields produced by one or more long massive nonmagnetic conductors carrying direct currents. such as direct conductors of various cross sections, their systems, cylindrical coils, and other similar arrangements. Distribution of the magnetic field (magnetic vector potential and magnetic flux density) both inside and outside the conductors is always given by a sum of double integrals carried out over the relevant cross sections.

From the domain of electrostatics we will calculate an example aimed at the determination of the distribution of voltage and electric field strength in the domain of a thundercloud.

3.3.2   Magnetic field of an infinitely long massive conductor carrying DC current

This is an idealized problem whose results, nevertheless, may be used for description of magnetic fields in systems of sufficiently long parallel massive conductors. Consider first a conductor of a general cross section S that is parallel to the z axis (see Fig. 3.18). The conductor carries direct current (DC) I of density $J = I/S$.

Magnetic flux density **B** at point $P(x', y', z')$ has only two components in directions x and y. Contributions to these components from the indicated filament f of cross section

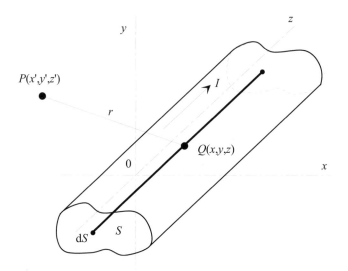

Figure 3.18.   A massive conductor of a general cross section.

$\mathrm{d}S$ are given by the well-known formulas

$$\mathrm{d}B_x(x',y') = -\frac{\mu_0 J\,\mathrm{d}S}{2\pi} \cdot \frac{y-y'}{(x-x')^2 + (y-y')^2} \,,$$

$$\mathrm{d}B_y(x',y') = \frac{\mu_0 J\,\mathrm{d}S}{2\pi} \cdot \frac{x-x'}{(x-x')^2 + (y-y')^2} \,. \tag{3.41}$$

Starting from the definition $\boldsymbol{B} = \mathrm{curl}\,\boldsymbol{A}$ in Cartesian coordinates, we easily obtain

$$\mathrm{d}B_x(x',y') = \frac{\partial \mathrm{d}A_z(x',y')}{\partial y'}, \quad \mathrm{d}B_y(x',y') = -\frac{\partial \mathrm{d}A_z(x',y')}{\partial x'} \tag{3.42}$$

so that

$$\mathrm{d}A_z(x',y') = -\frac{\mu_0 I}{4\pi S} \ln[(x-x')^2 + (y-y')^2]\mathrm{d}S\,. \tag{3.43}$$

After the integration we have

$$A_z(x',y') = -\frac{\mu_0 I}{4\pi S} \int_S \ln[(x-x')^2 + (y-y')^2]\mathrm{d}S + A_{0z}\,, \tag{3.44}$$

where A_{0z} is an arbitrary constant. This integral can be calculated analytically or numerically, depending on the geometry of the cross section. Neither magnetic flux density nor magnetic vector potential depends on the z' coordinate of the reference point.

Consider a long straight conductor of rectangular cross section depicted in Fig. 3.19. Provided that $A_{0z} = 0$ we immediately obtain

$$A_z(x',y') = -\frac{\mu_0 I}{4\pi ab} \int_{b_1}^{b_2} \int_{a_1}^{a_2} \ln[(x-x')^2 + (y-y')^2]\mathrm{d}x\,\mathrm{d}y\,.$$

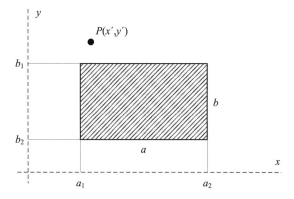

Figure 3.19. A massive conductor of rectangular cross section.

Putting

$$s = x' - a_1, \quad t = x' - a_2, \quad u = y' - b_1, \quad v = y' - b_2,$$

we have

$$A_z(x', y') = \frac{\mu_0 I}{4\pi ab} \cdot (p + q + r + s),$$

where

$$p = 3a_2 b_2 - 3a_2 b_1 - 3a_1 b_2 + 3a_1 b_1 = 3ab,$$

$$\begin{aligned}
q = &-t^2 \cdot \arctan \frac{v}{t} - v^2 \cdot \arctan \frac{t}{v} + t^2 \cdot \arctan \frac{u}{t} + u^2 \cdot \arctan \frac{t}{u} \\
&+ s^2 \cdot \arctan \frac{v}{s} + v^2 \cdot \arctan \frac{s}{v} - s^2 \cdot \arctan \frac{u}{s} - u^2 \cdot \arctan \frac{s}{u},
\end{aligned}$$

$$r = -tv \cdot \ln[t^2 + v^2] + tu \cdot \ln[t^2 + u^2] + sv \cdot \ln[t^2 + v^2] - su \cdot \ln[s^2 + u^2].$$

(3.45)

Components of the magnetic flux density at the same point are

$$B_x(x', y') = \frac{\mu_0 I}{4\pi ab} \cdot (e + f),$$

where

$$e = -2v \cdot \arctan \frac{v}{t} + 2u \cdot \arctan \frac{u}{t} + 2v \cdot \arctan \frac{v}{s} - 2u \cdot \arctan \frac{u}{s},$$

$$f = t \cdot \ln[t^2 + v^2] - t \cdot \ln[t^2 + u^2] - s \cdot \ln[s^2 + v^2] + s \cdot \ln[s^2 + u^2], \quad (3.46)$$

and

$$B_y(x', y') = \frac{\mu_0 I}{4\pi ab} \cdot (g + h),$$

where

$$g = -2t \cdot \arctan\frac{v}{t} + 2t \cdot \arctan\frac{u}{t} + 2s \cdot \arctan\frac{v}{s} - 2s \cdot \arctan\frac{u}{s},$$
$$h = -v \cdot \ln[t^2 + v^2] + u \cdot \ln[t^2 + u^2] + v \cdot \ln[s^2 + v^2] - u \cdot \ln[s^2 + u^2]. \quad (3.47)$$

Finally, the module of magnetic flux density at point $P(x', y')$ is

$$|\boldsymbol{B}(x', y')| = \sqrt{B_x^2(x', y') + B_y^2(x', y')}.$$

Special attention has to be paid to several limiting cases ($s \rightarrow 0$, $t \rightarrow 0$, $u \rightarrow 0$, or $v \rightarrow 0$). But computation of the corresponding limits in expressions (3.45), (3.46), and (3.47) for both vector potential and magnetic flux density encounters no difficulties.

The magnetic field of additional conductors with rectangular cross section is given by superposition of their particular fields.

For an illustration, we calculate the distribution of the magnetic field of a direct current carrying long hollow rectangular conductor, whose arrangement and dimensions follow from Fig. 3.20. The current density is 8×10^6 A/m². The results are calculated in two steps, making use of the superposition: first we find the magnetic field of the massive conductor without the hole and then we subtract the magnetic field produced by the current of the same density in a fictitious conductor in the hole.

Since the problem is linear, the shapes of the magnetic force lines and the lines of constant magnetic flux density do not depend on the current. Both fields are depicted in Figs. 3.21 and 3.22.

Finally, Figs. 3.23 and 3.24 show the distributions of the magnetic flux density along two dashed lines a and b depicted in Fig. 3.20. While the distribution in Fig. 3.24 is quite typical, the distribution in Fig. 3.23 is strongly distorted due to the hole inside the conductor.

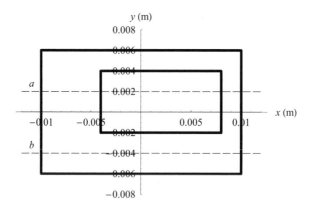

Figure 3.20. The arrangement of the investigated hollow conductor.

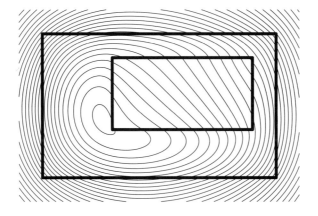

Figure 3.21.   Magnetic field of the hollow conductor.

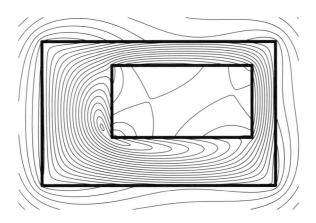

Figure 3.22.   Distribution of the module of the magnetic flux density in the region of the hollow conductor.

3.3.3 Magnetic field of a massive ring of rectangular cross section

A massive direct current carrying ring represents an unreal, idealized object. The knowledge of its magnetic field and other related quantities (self-inductance and radial forces acting in it) represents, however, the basis for determination of these quantities in cylindrical air-core coils that are widely used in many practical applications.

Consider first a massive circular ring of rectangular cross section carrying direct current I of density J_φ (Fig. 3.25).

The current density J_φ is not distributed uniformly over the cross section of the ring, but it is indirectly proportional to the corresponding radius. This follows from the condition $\operatorname{curl} \boldsymbol{J} = 0$ (where, moreover, only the tangential component $J_\varphi(r, z)$ is nonzero) in the

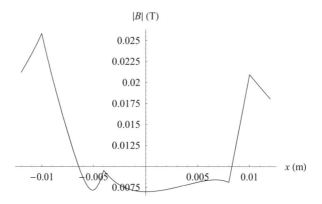

Figure 3.23. Distribution of magnetic flux density along line a (see Fig. 3.20).

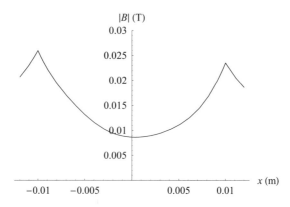

Figure 3.24. Distribution of magnetic flux density along line b (see Fig. 3.20).

cylindrical coordinate system. In such a case

$$\operatorname{curl} \mathbf{J} = -\mathbf{r}_0 \frac{\partial J_\varphi}{\partial z} + \mathbf{z}_0 \frac{1}{r} \cdot \frac{\partial(rJ_\varphi)}{\partial r} = 0 \Rightarrow rJ_\varphi = K, \qquad (3.48)$$

where $\mathbf{r}_0$ and $\mathbf{z}_0$ are the unit vectors in the corresponding directions. The unknown constant K follows from the condition

$$\int_{R_1}^{R_2} \int_{Z_1}^{Z_2} J_\varphi \, dz \, dr = \int_{R_1}^{R_2} \int_{Z_1}^{Z_2} \frac{K}{r} \, dz \, dr = I, \qquad (3.49)$$

and, hence,

$$K = \frac{I}{(Z_2 - Z_1) \ln(R_2/R_1)} \Rightarrow J_\varphi(r) = \frac{I}{r(Z_2 - Z_1) \ln(R_2/R_1)}$$

$$= \frac{I}{r \cdot h \ln(R_2/R_1)}. \qquad (3.50)$$

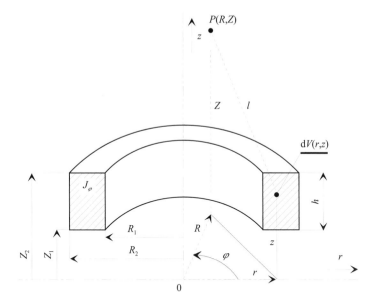

Figure 3.25. A circular ring of the rectangular cross section.

The basic quantity of interest is the magnetic vector potential $\mathbf{A}(R, Z)$ that has only the component $A_\varphi(R, Z)$. This is given by

$$A_\varphi(R, Z) = \frac{\mu_0}{4\pi} \int_V \frac{J_\varphi \cos \varphi}{l} \, dV \, , \tag{3.51}$$

where (see Fig. 3.25) $l = \sqrt{r^2 + R^2 - 2rR \cos \varphi + (Z - z)^2}$ and $dV = r \, dr \, d\varphi \, dz$, V denoting the volume of the ring. Two more important quantities are the components of the magnetic flux density $B_r(R, Z)$ and $B_z(R, Z)$. These follow from the relations

$$B_r(R, Z) = -\frac{\partial A_\varphi(R, Z)}{\partial Z} = \frac{\mu_0}{4\pi} \int_V \frac{J_\varphi(Z - z) \cos \varphi}{l^3} \, dV \, , \tag{3.52}$$

$$B_z(R, Z) = \frac{1}{R} \frac{\partial[R \, A_\varphi(R, Z)]}{\partial R}$$

$$= \frac{\mu_0}{4\pi R} \int_V \frac{J_\varphi[r(r - R \cos \varphi) + (Z - z)^2] \cos \varphi}{l^3} \, dV \, . \tag{3.53}$$

After substituting for J_φ from (3.50), for l and for dV, and putting $h = Z_2 - Z_1$ (the height of the ring), we obtain

$$A_\varphi(R, Z) = C \int_{\varphi=0}^{2\pi} \int_{r=R_1}^{R_2} \int_{z=Z_1}^{Z_2} \frac{\cos \varphi}{\sqrt{r^2 + R^2 - 2rR \cos \varphi + (Z - z)^2}} \, dz \, dr \, d\varphi \, , \tag{3.54}$$

$$B_r(R, Z) = C \int_{\varphi=0}^{2\pi} \int_{r=R_1}^{R_2} \int_{z=Z_1}^{Z_2} \frac{(Z-z)\cos\varphi}{\sqrt{[r^2 + R^2 - 2rR\cos\varphi + (Z-z)^2]^3}} \, dz \, dr \, d\varphi,$$

(3.55)

$$B_z(R, Z) = \frac{C}{R} \int_{\varphi=0}^{2\pi} \int_{r=R_1}^{R_2} \int_{z=Z_1}^{Z_2} \frac{[r(r - R\cos\varphi) + (Z-z)^2]\cos\varphi}{\sqrt{[r^2 + R^2 - 2rR\cos\varphi + (Z-z)^2]^3}} \, dz \, dr \, d\varphi,$$

(3.56)

where

$$C = \frac{\mu_0 I}{4\pi(Z_2 - Z_1)\ln(R_2/R_1)}.$$

(3.57)

Now we compute these integrals with respect to r and z. For (3.54) we first get the internal integral in the form

$$\int_r \int_z \frac{1}{\sqrt{r^2 + R^2 - 2rR\cos\varphi + (Z-z)^2}} \, dz \, dr$$

$$= (r - R \cdot \cos\varphi)\ln[z - Z + l] + (z - Z) \cdot \ln[r - R\cos\varphi + l]$$

$$- R \cdot \sin\varphi \arctan \frac{(z-Z)(r - R\cos\varphi)}{R \cdot l \sin\varphi},$$

(3.58)

with the significance of symbol l being explained before. Similarly, for the internal integral in (3.55) we obtain

$$\int_r \int_z \frac{Z - z}{\sqrt{[r^2 + R^2 - 2rR\cos\varphi + (Z-z)^2]^3}} \, dz \, dr = \ln[r - R \cdot \cos\varphi + l].$$

(3.59)

A little more complicated is computation of the internal integral in (3.56), because we have to remove its singularity for $R = 0$. In order to do so, we first rearrange the integrand,

$$\frac{1}{R} \cdot \frac{[r(r - R\cos\varphi) + (Z-z)^2]\cos\varphi}{\sqrt{[r^2 + R^2 - 2rR\cos\varphi + (Z-z)^2]^3}} = \frac{\cos\varphi}{Rl} + \frac{(r\cos\varphi - R)\cos\varphi}{l^3}.$$

For the first term on the right-hand side we now apply the "by parts" technique with respect to φ, introducing $u' = \cos\varphi$ and $v = 1/Rl$. After some manipulation we have

$$\frac{1}{R} \cdot \int_{\varphi=0}^{2\pi} \frac{[r(r - R\cos\varphi) + (Z-z)^2]\cos\varphi}{\sqrt{[r^2 + R^2 - 2rR\cos\varphi + (Z-z)^2]^3}} \, d\varphi = \int_{\varphi=0}^{2\pi} \frac{r - R\cos\varphi}{l^3} \, d\varphi,$$

and now we can easily find that

$$\int_r \int_z \frac{r - R\cos\varphi}{\sqrt{[r^2 + R^2 - 2rR\cos\varphi + (Z-z)^2]^3}} \, dz \, dr = -\ln[z - Z + l].$$

(3.60)

The results may be written in the following forms:

$$A_\varphi(R, Z) = C \cdot [f(R_2, R, Z_2 - Z) - f(R_2, R, Z_1 - Z)$$

$$-f(R_1, R, Z_2 - Z) + f(R_1, R, Z_1 - Z)],$$

(3.61)

$$B_r(R, Z) = C \cdot [g(R_2, R, Z_2 - Z) - g(R_2, R, Z_1 - Z)$$

$$-g(R_1, R, Z_2 - Z) + g(R_1, R, Z_1 - Z)],$$

(3.62)

$$B_z(R, Z) = C \cdot [h(R_2, R, Z_2 - Z) - h(R_2, R, Z_1 - Z)$$
$$-h(R_1, R, Z_2 - Z) + h(R_1, R, Z_1 - Z)], \tag{3.63}$$

where, for example,

$$f(R_2, R, Z_2 - Z) = \int_{\varphi=0}^{2\pi} [(R_2 - R \cdot \cos \varphi) \cdot \ln[Z_2 - Z + l_{22}]$$
$$+ (Z_2 - Z) \cdot \ln[R_2 - R \cos \varphi + l_{22}]$$
$$- R \cdot \sin \varphi \arctan \frac{(Z_2 - Z)(R_2 - R \cos \varphi)}{R \cdot l_{22} \sin \varphi}] \cos \varphi \, d\varphi, \tag{3.64}$$

$$g(R_2, R, Z_2 - Z) = \int_{\varphi=0}^{2\pi} \ln[R_2 - R \cdot \cos \varphi + l_{22}] \cos \varphi \, d\varphi, \tag{3.65}$$

$$h(R_2, R, Z_2 - Z) = -\int_{\varphi=0}^{2\pi} \ln[Z_2 - Z + l_{22}] \, d\varphi, \tag{3.66}$$

and

$$l_{22} = \sqrt{R_2^2 + R^2 - 2R_2 R \cos \varphi + (Z - Z_2)^2}. \tag{3.67}$$

The other functions are obtained by standard interchanging of the indices.

For an illustration, the next few figures contain selected results obtained for the arrangement in Fig. 3.26. The dimensions of the ring are $R_1 = 0.01 \, \text{m}$, $R_2 = 0.02 \, \text{m}$, $Z_1 = -0.01 \, \text{m}$, and $Z_2 = 0.01 \, \text{m}$ and the total current $I = 1600 \, \text{A}$.

Figure 3.27 contains the distribution of the force lines (that are given by the formula $R A_\varphi(R, Z) = \text{const}$) inside the ring and near it.

Figure 3.28 shows the distribution of lines of the constant module of magnetic flux density, and, finally, Figs. 3.29 and 3.30 show the distribution of this quantity along the z axis and radius r for $z = 0$.

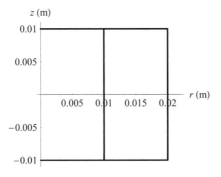

Figure 3.26. Arrangement of the investigated ring.

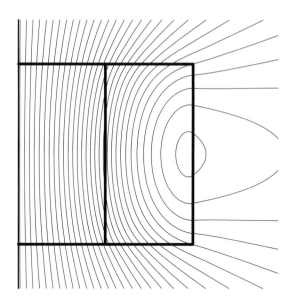

Figure 3.27.   Magnetic field in the domain of the investigated ring.

Detailed solution of the above problem (including various limiting cases) can be found in Ref. 106.

3.4   FORCES ACTING IN THE SYSTEM OF LONG MASSIVE CONDUCTORS

Let us start from Fig. 3.31, showing the basic geometry of two conductors parallel with to the z axis. The conductors of cross sections S_1 and S_2 carry direct currents of densities J_1 and J_2, respectively.

The force per unit length, $\boldsymbol{F}'_2$, acting on the conductor **2** is given by

$$\boldsymbol{F}'_2 = \int_{S_2} (\boldsymbol{J}_2 \times \boldsymbol{B})\, \mathrm{d}S\,, \tag{3.68}$$

where $\boldsymbol{B}$ is the magnetic field produced by conductor **1**. Its particular components are

$$F'_{x,2} = -\int_{S_2} B_y J_2\, \mathrm{d}S\,, \quad F'_{y,2} = \int_{S_2} B_x J_2\, \mathrm{d}S\,. \tag{3.69}$$

After substituting for B_x and B_y from (3.41) we obtain

$$F'_{x,2} = -\frac{\mu_0 J_1 J_2}{2\pi} \int_{S_2} \left[\int_{S_1} \frac{x - x'}{(x - x')^2 + (y - y')^2}\, \mathrm{d}S_1 \right] \mathrm{d}S_2\,,$$

$$F'_{y,2} = -\frac{\mu_0 J_1 J_2}{2\pi} \int_{S_2} \left[\int_{S_1} \frac{y - y'}{(x - x')^2 + (y - y')^2}\, \mathrm{d}S_1 \right] \mathrm{d}S_2\,, \tag{3.70}$$

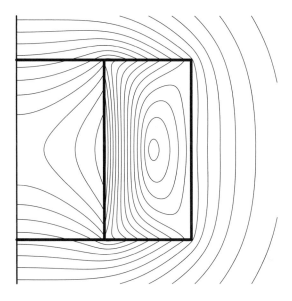

Figure 3.28.   Lines of the constant module of magnetic flux density.

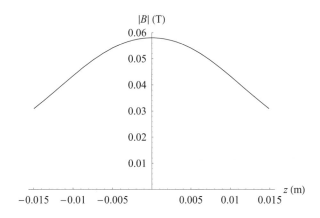

Figure 3.29.   Module of the magnetic flux density along the z axis.

where $\mathrm{d}S_1 = \mathrm{d}y\,\mathrm{d}x$ and $\mathrm{d}S_2 = \mathrm{d}y'\,\mathrm{d}x'$. In a system of more conductors we easily make use of the principle of superposition.

Unfortunately, integral (3.70) can be calculated analytically only for polygonal or circular cross sections. In more complicated cases some integrations must be performed numerically.

For an illustration we present two examples aimed at finding forces between two parallel long conductors. The first one determines forces (3.70) acting between two conductors of rectangular cross sections in a general position, as depicted in Fig. 3.32.

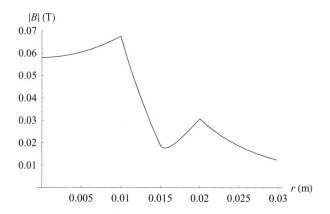

Figure 3.30.   Module of the magnetic flux density along the radius r for $z = 0$.

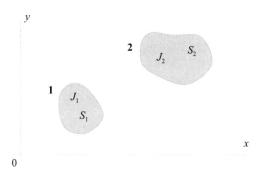

Figure 3.31.   Arrangement of the conductors.

According to (3.70) we have

$$F'_{x,2} = -\frac{\mu_0 J_1 J_2}{2\pi} \int_{y'=d_1}^{d_2} \int_{x'=c_1}^{c_2} \left[\int_{y=b_1}^{b_2} \int_{x=a_1}^{a_2} \frac{x - x'}{(x - x')^2 + (y - y')^2} \, dx \, dy \right] dx' \, dy' \,,$$

$$F'_{y,2} = -\frac{\mu_0 J_1 J_2}{2\pi} \int_{y'=d_1}^{d_2} \int_{x'=c_1}^{c_2} \left[\int_{y=b_1}^{b_2} \int_{x=a_1}^{a_2} \frac{y - y'}{(x - x')^2 + (y - y')^2} \, dx \, dy \right] dx' \, dy' \,.$$

Let us first denote

$$P(x, y, x', y') = \frac{1}{6} \cdot (y' - y) \left[(y' - y)^2 - 3(x' - x)^2 \right] \arctan \frac{x' - x}{y' - y}$$

$$- \frac{1}{12} \cdot (x' - x) \left[(x' - x)^2 - 3(y' - y)^2 \right] \ln \left((x' - x)^2 + (y' - y)^2 \right) \,,$$

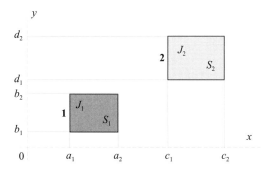

Figure 3.32.   Two long conductors of rectangular cross sections in a general position.

$$Q(x, y, x', y') = \frac{1}{6} \cdot (x' - x) \left[(x' - x)^2 - 3(y' - y)^2 \right] \arctan \frac{y' - y}{x' - x}$$
$$- \frac{1}{12} \cdot (y' - y) \left[(y' - y)^2 - 3(x' - x)^2 \right] \ln \left((x' - x)^2 + (y' - y)^2 \right)$$

and now the results read

$$F_x^l = \frac{\mu_0 J_1 J_2}{2\pi}$$
$$\cdot \left[P(a_2, b_2, c_2, d_2) + P(a_2, b_2, c_1, d_1) + P(a_2, b_1, c_2, d_1) + P(a_2, b_1, c_1, d_2) \right.$$
$$+ P(a_1, b_2, c_2, d_1) + P(a_1, b_2, c_1, d_2) + P(a_1, b_1, c_2, d_2) + P(a_1, b_1, c_1, d_1)$$
$$- P(a_2, b_2, c_2, d_1) - P(a_2, b_2, c_1, d_2) + P(a_2, b_1, c_2, d_2) + P(a_2, b_1, c_1, d_1)$$
$$\left. - P(a_1, b_2, c_2, d_2) - P(a_1, b_2, c_1, d_1) + P(a_1, b_1, c_2, d_1) + P(a_1, b_1, c_1, d_2) \right],$$

$$F_y^l = \frac{\mu_0 J_1 J_2}{2\pi}$$
$$\cdot \left[Q(a_2, b_2, c_2, d_2) + Q(a_2, b_2, c_1, d_1) + Q(a_2, b_1, c_2, d_1) + Q(a_2, b_1, c_1, d_2) \right.$$
$$+ Q(a_1, b_2, c_2, d_1) + Q(a_1, b_2, c_1, d_2) + Q(a_1, b_1, c_2, d_2) + Q(a_1, b_1, c_1, d_1)$$
$$- Q(a_2, b_2, c_2, d_1) - Q(a_2, b_2, c_1, d_2) + Q(a_2, b_1, c_2, d_2) + Q(a_2, b_1, c_1, d_1)$$
$$\left. - Q(a_1, b_2, c_2, d_2) - Q(a_1, b_2, c_1, d_1) + Q(a_1, b_1, c_2, d_1) + Q(a_1, b_1, c_1, d_2) \right].$$

We end with an analogous example when one of the conductors is circular (Fig.33). As known, the module of magnetic flux density generated by a conductor of circular cross section of radius R in a nonmagnetic medium at a distance $r \geq R$ is given by $|\mathbf{B}| = \mu_0 I / 2\pi r$. Its components at the reference point $P(x', y')$ are

$$B_x(x', y') = -\frac{\mu_0 I_1}{2\pi} \cdot \frac{b - y'}{(a - x')^2 + (b - y')^2},$$

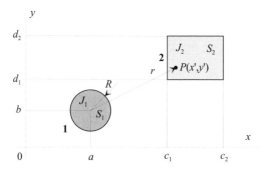

Figure 3.33.   Arrangement with one circular conductor.

$$B_y(x', y') = \frac{\mu_0 I_1}{2\pi} \cdot \frac{a - x'}{(a - x')^2 + (b - y')^2} , \tag{3.71}$$

where $I_1 = J_1 S_1$. The components of the force per unit length acting on conductor **2** are now

$$F'_{x,2} = -\frac{\mu_0 I_1 J_2}{2\pi} \int_{y'=d_1}^{d_2} \int_{x'=c_1}^{c_2} \frac{a - x'}{(a - x')^2 + (b - y')^2} \, dx' \, dy',$$

$$F'_{y,2} = -\frac{\mu_0 I_1 J_2}{2\pi} \int_{y'=d_1}^{d_2} \int_{x'=c_1}^{c_2} \frac{b - y'}{(a - x')^2 + (b - y')^2} \, dx' \, dy'$$

and hence

$$F'_{x,2} = -\frac{\mu_0 I_1 J_2}{2\pi}$$
$$\cdot \left[\left[(a - x') \arctan \frac{b - y'}{a - x'} + \frac{1}{2} \cdot (b - y') \ln[(a - x')^2 + (b - y')^2] \right]_{x'=c_1}^{c_2} \right]_{y'=d_1}^{d_2} ,$$

$$F'_{y,2} = -\frac{\mu_0 I_1 J_2}{2\pi}$$
$$\cdot \left[\left[(b - y') \arctan \frac{a - x'}{b - y'} + \frac{1}{2} \cdot (a - x') \ln[(a - x')^2 + (b - y')^2] \right]_{x'=c_1}^{c_2} \right]_{y'=d_1}^{d_2} .$$

3.4.1   Self-inductance of a massive ring of rectangular cross section

The computation starts from the energy of its magnetic field given by

$$W = \frac{1}{2} \int_V \boldsymbol{J} \cdot \boldsymbol{A} \, dV , \tag{3.72}$$

where the integral is performed over the whole volume of the turn. Since both current density $\boldsymbol{J}$ (we consider again the direct current) and magnetic vector potential $\boldsymbol{A}$ have only one nonzero component in the circumferential direction φ, we can write

$$W = \frac{1}{2} \int_V J_\varphi \cdot A_\varphi \, dV , \tag{3.73}$$

where, moreover,

$$J_\varphi = J_\varphi(R), \quad A_\varphi = A_\varphi(R, Z). \tag{3.74}$$

With respect to Fig. 3.34 we obtain

$$W = \frac{1}{2} \int_{\psi=0}^{2\pi} \int_{Z=Z_1}^{Z_2} \int_{R=R_1}^{R_2} J_\varphi(R) \cdot A_\varphi(R, Z) \cdot R \, dR \, dZ \, d\psi . \tag{3.75}$$

Substitution of (3.50) for $J_\varphi(R)$ provides

$$J_\varphi(R) = \frac{K}{R}, \quad K = \frac{I}{(Z_2 - Z_1) \ln[R_2/R_1]} \tag{3.76}$$

and integrating (3.75) with respect to ψ (neither J_φ nor A_φ depend on this parameter) we get

$$W = \pi K \int_{Z=Z_1}^{Z_2} \int_{R=R_1}^{R_2} A_\varphi(R, Z) \, dR \, dZ . \tag{3.77}$$

Magnetic vector potential $A_\varphi(R, Z)$ is given by (see (3.54))

$$A_\varphi(R, Z) = \frac{\mu_0}{4\pi} \int_{\varphi=0}^{2\pi} \int_{z=Z_1}^{Z_2} \int_{r=R_1}^{R_2} \frac{J_\varphi(r) \cdot \cos\varphi \cdot r \, dr \, dz \, d\varphi}{\sqrt{r^2 + R^2 - 2rR\cos\varphi + (z - Z)^2}} . \tag{3.78}$$

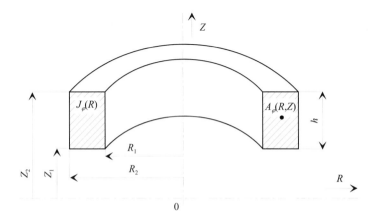

Figure 3.34.   Computation of the self-inductance of a massive ring.

After back substitution of (3.78) into (3.77) and using (3.50) again we finally obtain

$$
W = \frac{\mu_0 K^2}{4}
$$
$$
\cdot \int_{\varphi=0}^{2\pi} \cos\varphi \int_{z=Z_1}^{Z_2} \int_{Z=Z_1}^{Z_2} \int_{r=R_1}^{R_2} \int_{R=R_1}^{R_2} \frac{dr\,dR\,dz\,dZ\,d\varphi}{\sqrt{r^2 + R^2 - 2rR\cos\varphi + (z - Z)^2}}\,.
$$
$$(3.79)$$

Comparison of this expression with

$$
W = \tfrac{1}{2}LI^2
$$

immediately provides the self-inductance in the form

$$
L = \frac{\mu_0}{(Z_2 - Z_1)^2 \cdot [\ln(R_2/R_1)]^2}
$$
$$
\cdot \int_{\varphi=0}^{\pi} \cos\varphi \int_{z=Z_1}^{Z_2} \int_{Z=Z_1}^{Z_2} \int_{r=R_1}^{R_2} \int_{R=R_1}^{R_2} \frac{dr\,dR\,dz\,dZ\,d\varphi}{\sqrt{r^2 + R^2 - 2rR\cos\varphi + (z - Z)^2}}\,.
$$
$$(3.80)$$

While the first four integrations may be carried out analytically, the last one, with respect to angle φ, has to be performed numerically. The result (putting $Z_2 - Z_1 = h$) reads

$$
L = \frac{\mu_0}{h^2 \cdot [\ln(R_2/R_1)]^2} \cdot [F(R_2, R_2, h) + F(R_1, R_1, h) - 2F(R_1, R_2, h)]\,, \quad (3.81)
$$

where generally

$$
F(r, R, h) = \int_{\varphi=0}^{\pi} f(r, R, h, \varphi)d\varphi \qquad (3.82)
$$

and

$$
\begin{aligned}
f(r, R, h, \varphi) =&\; \frac{h^3 \cos \varphi}{3 \sin \varphi} \arctan \frac{h \sin \varphi \sqrt{r^2 + R^2 - 2rR\cos \varphi + h^2}}{h^2 \cos \varphi + rR \sin^2 \varphi} \\
&- hr^2 \sin^2 \varphi \cos \varphi \arctan \frac{h(R - r \cos \varphi)}{r \sin \varphi \sqrt{r^2 + R^2 - 2rR\cos \varphi + h^2}} \\
&- hR^2 \sin^2 \varphi \cos \varphi \arctan \frac{h(r - R \cos \varphi)}{R \sin \varphi \sqrt{r^2 + R^2 - 2rR\cos \varphi + h^2}} \\
&- r \cos \varphi \left(\frac{r^2 \sin^2 \varphi}{3} - h^2 \right) \ln[R - r \cos \varphi + \sqrt{r^2 + R^2 - 2rR\cos \varphi + h^2}] \\
&- R \cos \varphi \left(\frac{R^2 \sin^2 \varphi}{3} - h^2 \right) \ln[r - R \cos \varphi + \sqrt{r^2 + R^2 - 2rR\cos \varphi + h^2}] \\
&+ \frac{r^3 \sin^2 \varphi \cos \varphi}{3} \ln[R - r \cos \varphi + \sqrt{r^2 + R^2 - 2rR\cos \varphi}] \\
&+ \frac{R^3 \sin^2 \varphi \cos \varphi}{3} \ln[r - R \cos \varphi + \sqrt{r^2 + R^2 - 2rR\cos \varphi}] \\
&+ \frac{r(R - r \cos \varphi) + R(r - R \cos \varphi)}{2} \cdot h \cdot \cos \varphi \ln \frac{\sqrt{r^2 + R^2 - 2rR\cos \varphi + h^2} + h}{\sqrt{r^2 + R^2 - 2rR\cos \varphi + h^2} - h} \\
&+ \frac{r(R - r \cos \varphi) + R(r - R \cos \varphi)}{3} \cos \varphi \\
&\cdot \left(\sqrt{r^2 + R^2 - 2rR\cos \varphi} - \sqrt{r^2 + R^2 - 2rR\cos \varphi + h^2} \right).
\end{aligned}
\tag{3.83}
$$

Before numerical integration of (3.82) it is necessary to determine the limits of function $f(r, R, h, \varphi)$ at points $\varphi = 0$ and $\varphi = \pi$. There holds

$$
\begin{aligned}
\lim_{\varphi \to 0} &\, f(r, R, h, \varphi) \\
=&\; -\frac{1}{2} h(r - R)^2 \ln \frac{\sqrt{(r - R)^2 + h^2} + h}{\sqrt{(r - R)^2 + h^2} - h} \\
&+ h^2 R \ln[r - R + \sqrt{(r - R)^2 + h^2}] \\
&+ h^2 r \ln[R - r + \sqrt{(r - R)^2 + h^2}] \\
&+ \frac{1}{3} \sqrt{[(r - R)^2 + h^2]^3} - \frac{1}{3}(r - R)^2 |r - R|
\end{aligned}
\tag{3.84}
$$

and

$$
\begin{aligned}
\lim_{\varphi \to \pi} f(r, R, h, \varphi) =&\; -\frac{1}{2} h(r + R)^2 \ln \frac{\sqrt{(r + R)^2 + h^2} + h}{\sqrt{(r + R)^2 + h^2} - h} \\
&- h^2 (R + r) \ln[r + R + \sqrt{(r + R)^2 + h^2}] \\
&+ \frac{1}{3} \sqrt{[(r + R)^2 + h^2]^3} - \frac{1}{3}(r + R)^3.
\end{aligned}
\tag{3.85}
$$

Both these limits are finite, so the numerical integration of function $f(r, R, h, \varphi)$ causes no difficulties.

Two limiting cases of the ring are sometimes used. The first one is a ring of negligible thickness ($R_1 \rightarrow R_2$) and the second one is a ring of negligible height ($h \rightarrow 0$). Their self-inductances can be obtained using, for example, the l'Hôpital rule applied to (3.81). But this way is very complicated and time consuming. A more effective manner is to calculate them directly from the modified formula (3.80). There holds

$$L_{R_2 \rightarrow R_1} = \lim_{R_2 \rightarrow R_1} \frac{\mu_0}{h^2 \cdot [\ln(R_2/R_1)]^2}$$

$$\cdot \int_{\varphi=0}^{\pi} \cos\varphi \int_{z=Z_1}^{Z_2} \int_{Z=Z_1}^{Z_2} \int_{r=R_1}^{R_2} \int_{R=R_1}^{R_2} \frac{dr\,dR\,dz\,dZ\,d\varphi}{\sqrt{r^2 + R^2 - 2rR\cos\varphi + (z-Z)^2}}$$

$$= \lim_{R_2 \rightarrow R_1} \frac{\mu_0}{h^2 \cdot [\ln(R_2/R_1)]^2}$$

$$\cdot \int_{\varphi=0}^{\pi} \cos\varphi \int_{z=Z_1}^{Z_2} \int_{Z=Z_1}^{Z_2} \int_{r=R_1}^{R_2} \int_{R=R_1}^{R_2} \frac{dr\,dR\,dz\,dZ\,d\varphi}{\sqrt{2R_1^2(1-\cos\varphi) + (z-Z)^2}}$$

$$\lim_{R_2 \rightarrow R_1} \frac{\mu_0(R_2 - R_1)^2}{h^2 \cdot [\ln(R_2/R_1)]^2}$$

$$\cdot \int_{\varphi=0}^{\pi} \cos\varphi \int_{z=Z_1}^{Z_2} \int_{Z=Z_1}^{Z_2} \frac{dz\,dZ\,d\varphi}{\sqrt{2R_1^2(1-\cos\varphi) + (z-Z)^2}}$$

$$= \frac{\mu_0 R_1^2}{h^2} \cdot \int_{\varphi=0}^{\pi} \cos\varphi \int_{z=Z_1}^{Z_2} \int_{Z=Z_1}^{Z_2} \frac{dz\,dZ\,d\varphi}{\sqrt{2R_1^2(1-\cos\varphi) + (z-Z)^2}}$$

$$= \frac{\mu_0}{3} \left(\left[\left(\frac{4R_1^2}{h^2} - 1 \right) \mathrm{E}(k^2) + \mathrm{F}(k^2) \right] \sqrt{4R_1^2 + h^2} - \frac{8R_1^3}{h^2} \right), \tag{3.86}$$

where F and E denote the complete elliptic integrals of the first and second kinds with

$$k^2 = \frac{4R_1^2}{4R_1^2 + h^2}.$$

The second limit provides

$$L_{h \rightarrow 0} = \lim_{h \rightarrow 0} \frac{\mu_0}{h^2 \cdot [\ln(R_2/R_1)]^2}$$

$$\cdot \int_{\varphi=0}^{\pi} \cos\varphi \int_{z=Z_1}^{Z_2} \int_{Z=Z_1}^{Z_2} \int_{r=R_1}^{R_2} \int_{R=R_1}^{R_2} \frac{dr\,dR\,dz\,dZ\,d\varphi}{\sqrt{r^2 + R^2 - 2rR\cos\varphi + (z-Z)^2}}$$

$$= \lim_{h \rightarrow 0} \frac{\mu_0}{h^2 \cdot [\ln(R_2/R_1)]^2} \cdot \int_{\varphi=0}^{\pi} \cos\varphi \int_{z=Z_1}^{Z_2} \int_{Z=Z_1}^{Z_2} \int_{r=R_1}^{R_2} \int_{R=R_1}^{R_2} \frac{dr\,dR\,dz\,dZ\,d\varphi}{\sqrt{r^2 + R^2 - 2rR\cos\varphi}}$$

$$= \frac{\mu_0}{\left[\ln\frac{R_2}{R_1}\right]^2} \cdot \int_{\varphi=0}^{\pi} \cos\varphi \int_{r=R_1}^{R_2} \int_{R=R_1}^{R_2} \frac{dr\,dR\,d\varphi}{\sqrt{r^2 + R^2 - 2rR\cos\varphi}}$$

$$= \frac{4\mu_0(R_2 - R_1)}{[\ln(R_2/R_1)]^2} \cdot (\mathrm{E}(k^2) - 1), \tag{3.87}$$

where E denotes the complete elliptic integral of the second kind with

$$k^2 = \frac{4R_1 R_2}{(R_1 + R_2)^2} .$$

More comprehensive information about the computation of self-inductances and mutual inductances in the systems of circular rings and solenoidal coils can be found in Refs. 107 and 108.

3.4.2   Radial force on a massive ring of rectangular cross section

The total radial force acting on the ring follows from the relation for volume force $\boldsymbol{f} = \boldsymbol{J} \times \boldsymbol{B}$ in the cylindrical coordinates. Its value is

$$F_r = \int_V J_\varphi B_z \mathrm{d}V , \qquad (3.88)$$

where V is the volume of the ring. The force acts out of the ring and tends to increase its radius. Using the previously derived formulas for J_φ (3.50) and B_z (3.56), we obtain

$$F_r = K \int_{\psi=0}^{2\pi} \int_{R=R_1}^{R_2} \int_{Z=Z_1}^{Z_2} B_z \, \mathrm{d}R \, \mathrm{d}Z \, \mathrm{d}\psi$$

$$= 2\pi K \int_{R=R_1}^{R_2} \int_{Z=Z_1}^{Z_2} B_z(R, Z) \, \mathrm{d}R \, \mathrm{d}Z , \qquad (3.89)$$

where

$$B_z(R, Z) = \frac{\mu_0 K}{4\pi} \int_{\varphi=0}^{2\pi} \int_{r=R_1}^{R_2} \int_{z=Z_1}^{Z_2} \frac{(r - R \cos \varphi) \, \mathrm{d}r \, \mathrm{d}z \, \mathrm{d}\varphi}{\sqrt{[r^2 + R^2 - 2rR \cos \varphi + (z - Z)^2]^3}}$$

and

$$K = \frac{I}{h \ln(R_2/R_1)} .$$

The first four integrations with respect to r, R, z, and Z may be carried out analytically. Finally, we get

$$\begin{aligned} F_r = \mu_0 \cdot K^2 \\ \cdot [M(R_2, R_2, Z_2, Z_2) + M(R_2, R_1, Z_2, Z_1) + M(R_2, R_1, Z_1, Z_2) \\ + M(R_1, R_2, Z_1, Z_2) + M(R_1, R_2, Z_2, Z_1) + M(R_2, R_2, Z_1, Z_1) \\ + M(R_1, R_1, Z_2, Z_2) + M(R_1, R_1, Z_2, Z_2) - M(R_2, R_1, Z_1, Z_1) \\ - M(R_1, R_2, Z_1, Z_1) - M(R_1, R_1, Z_2, Z_1) - M(R_1, R_1, Z_1, Z_2) \\ - M(R_2, R_2, Z_2, Z_1) - M(R_2, R_2, Z_1, Z_2) - M(R_2, R_1, Z_2, Z_2) \\ - M(R_1, R_2, Z_2, Z_2)] , \end{aligned} \qquad (3.90)$$

where

$$M(r, R, z, Z) = \int_{\varphi=0}^{\pi} m(r, R, z, Z, \varphi) \mathrm{d}\varphi \qquad (3.91)$$

and

$$m(r, R, z, Z, \varphi) = (z - Z)(R - r\cos\varphi)\ln[z - Z + \sqrt{r^2 + R^2 - 2rR\cos\varphi + (z - Z)^2}]$$
$$+ \frac{(z - Z)^2 - r^2\sin^2\varphi}{2} \cdot \ln[R - r\cos\varphi + \sqrt{r^2 + R^2 - 2rR\cos\varphi + (z - Z)^2}]$$
$$- (z - Z)r\sin\varphi\arctan\frac{(R - r\cos\varphi)(z - Z)}{r\sin\varphi \cdot \sqrt{r^2 + R^2 - 2rR\cos\varphi + (z - Z)^2}}$$
$$- \frac{R - r\cos\varphi}{2}\sqrt{r^2 + R^2 - 2rR\cos\varphi + (z - Z)^2}. \tag{3.92}$$

Before numerical integration of (3.91) it is again necessary to determine the limits of $m(r, R, z, Z, \varphi)$ at points $\varphi = 0$ and $\varphi = \pi$. Their values are

$$\lim_{\varphi \to 0} m(r, R, z, Z, \varphi) = -\tfrac{1}{2}(r - R)\sqrt{(r - R)^2 + (z - Z)^2}$$
$$+ \tfrac{1}{2}(z - Z)^2\ln[R - r + \sqrt{(r - R)^2 + (z - Z)^2}]$$
$$+ (R - r)(z - Z)\ln[z - Z + \sqrt{(r - R)^2 + (z - Z)^2}] \tag{3.93}$$

and

$$\lim_{\varphi \to \pi} m(r, R, z, Z, \varphi) = -\frac{1}{2}(r + R)\sqrt{(r + R)^2 + (z - Z)^2}$$
$$+ \frac{1}{2}(z - Z)^2\ln[R + r + \sqrt{(r + R)^2 + (z - Z)^2}]$$
$$+ (R + r)(z - Z)\ln[z - Z + \sqrt{(r + R)^2 + (z - Z)^2}]. \tag{3.94}$$

Even here the limits are finite, so that the numerical integration of function $m(r, R, z, Z, \varphi)$ causes no difficulties.

Consider again the two limiting cases of the ring (a ring of negligible thickness ($R_1 \to R_2$) and another ring of negligible height ($h \to 0$). The corresponding radial forces acting on them are given by

$$F_{r,R_2 \to R_1} = \lim_{R_2 \to R_1} \frac{\mu_0 I^2}{h^2 \cdot [\ln(R_2/R_1)]^2}$$

$$\cdot \int_{\varphi=0}^{\pi} \int_{z=Z_1}^{Z_2} \int_{Z=Z_1}^{Z_2} \int_{r=R_1}^{R_2} \int_{R=R_1}^{R_2} \frac{(r - R\cos\varphi)dr\,dR\,dz\,dZ\,d\varphi}{\sqrt{(r^2 + R^2 - 2rR\cos\varphi + (z - Z)^2)^3}}$$

$$= \lim_{R_2 \to R_1} \frac{\mu_0 I^2}{h^2 \cdot [\ln(R_2/R_1)]^2}$$

$$\cdot \int_{\varphi=0}^{\pi} \int_{z=Z_1}^{Z_2} \int_{Z=Z_1}^{Z_2} \int_{r=R_1}^{R_2} \int_{R=R_1}^{R_2} \frac{R_1(1 - \cos\varphi)dr\,dR\,dz\,dZ\,d\varphi}{\sqrt{(2R_1^2(1 - \cos\varphi) + (z - Z)^2)^3}}$$

$$= \lim_{R_2 \to R_1} \frac{\mu_0 I^2 (R_2 - R_1)^2}{h^2 \cdot [\ln(R_2/R_1)]^2} \cdot \int_{\varphi=0}^{\pi} \int_{z=Z_1}^{Z_2} \int_{Z=Z_1}^{Z_2} \frac{R_1(1 - \cos\varphi)dz\,dZ\,d\varphi}{\sqrt{(2R_1^2(1 - \cos\varphi) + (z - Z)^2)^3}}$$

$$= \frac{\mu_0 I^2 R_1^2}{h^2} \cdot \int_{\varphi=0}^{\pi} \int_{z=Z_1}^{Z_2} \int_{Z=Z_1}^{Z_2} \frac{R_1(1 - \cos\varphi)dz\,dZ\,d\varphi}{\sqrt{(2R_1^2(1 - \cos\varphi) + (z - Z)^2)^3}}$$

$$= \frac{4\mu_0 I^2 R_1^2}{h^2} \left(\sqrt{1 + \frac{h^2}{4R_1^2}} \cdot E(k^2) - 1 \right), \tag{3.95}$$

where E denotes the complete elliptic integral of the second kind with

$$k^2 = \frac{4R_1^2}{4R_1^2 + h^2}.$$

Analogously

$$F_{r,h \to 0} = \lim_{h \to 0} \frac{\mu_0 I^2}{h^2 \cdot [\ln(R_2/R_1)]^2}$$

$$\cdot \int_{\varphi=0}^{\pi} \int_{z=Z_1}^{Z_2} \int_{Z=Z_1}^{Z_2} \int_{r=R_1}^{R_2} \int_{R=R_1}^{R_2} \frac{(r - R\cos\varphi)dr\,dR\,dz\,dZ\,d\varphi}{\sqrt{(r^2 + R^2 - 2rR\cos\varphi + (z - Z)^2)^3}}$$

$$= \lim_{h \to 0} \frac{\mu_0 I^2}{h^2 \cdot [\ln(R_2/R_1)]^2}$$

$$\cdot \int_{\varphi=0}^{\pi} \int_{z=Z_1}^{Z_2} \int_{Z=Z_1}^{Z_2} \int_{r=R_1}^{R_2} \int_{R=R_1}^{R_2} \frac{(r - R\cos\varphi)dr\,dR\,dz\,dZ\,d\varphi}{\sqrt{(r^2 + R^2 - 2rR\cos\varphi)^3}}$$

$$= \frac{\mu_0 I^2}{[\ln(R_2/R_1)]^2} \cdot \int_{\varphi=0}^{\pi} \int_{r=R_1}^{R_2} \int_{R=R_1}^{R_2} \frac{(r - R\cos\varphi)dr\,dR\,d\varphi}{\sqrt{(r^2 + R^2 - 2rR\cos\varphi)^3}}$$

$$= \frac{\mu_0 I^2}{[\ln(R_2/R_1)]^2} \cdot \int_{\varphi=0}^{\pi} [\ln(R_1 - R_2\cos\varphi + \sqrt{R_1^2 + R_2^2 - 2R_1 R_2\cos\varphi})$$

$$+ \ln(R_2 - R_1\cos\varphi + \sqrt{R_1^2 + R_2^2 - 2R_1 R_2\cos\varphi}) - \ln R_1 - \ln R_2$$

$$- 2\ln(1 - \cos\varphi - \sqrt{2 - 2\cos\varphi})]d\varphi. \tag{3.96}$$

The last integral has to be evaluated numerically.

3.4.3   Cylindrical air-core coils and their parameters

Consider an air-core coil wound by a massive conductor of rectangular cross section. When the lead of its helicoid is small and may be neglected, we can (very accurately) obtain the distribution of its magnetic field by the superposition of magnetic fields of its individual turns (see (3.54), (3.55), and (3.56)). This way is relatively simple and respects the arrangement of the coil, interturn insulation, and other particulars. Since the coil consists of several sufficiently densely wound layers (the thickness of interturn insulation is small), each layer can be treated as one massive turn.

More complicated is determination of the total inductance of such a coil, particularly when its structure is complicated and consists of several mutually separated layers or sub-coils. The semianalytical methodology of computation based on the integral expressions starts from Fig. 3.35, showing two separated ideal massive concentric turns.

Turn 1 carries current I_1 of nonuniform density $J_{\varphi 1}$. The magnetic field generated by this current at A (that has only the circumferential component A_φ) is

$$A_\varphi(R, Z) = \frac{\mu_0}{4\pi} \int_{V_1} \frac{J_{\varphi 1} \cos \varphi}{l} \mathrm{d}V . \tag{3.97}$$

Here symbol l denotes the distance between the reference point P and the general integration point, and integration is carried out over the volume of ring 1. In accordance with (3.49)

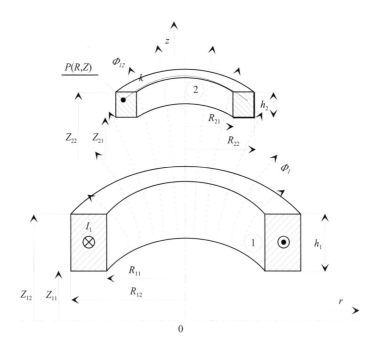

Figure 3.35.   Two ideal massive concentric turns.

and (3.54) we have

$$A_\varphi(R, Z) = \frac{\mu_0 K_1}{4\pi} \int_{\varphi=0}^{2\pi} \int_{r=R_{11}}^{R_{12}} \int_{z=Z_{11}}^{Z_{12}} \frac{\cos\varphi \, dz \, dr \, d\varphi}{\sqrt{r^2 + R^2 - 2rR\cos\varphi + (z - Z)^2}}, \quad (3.98)$$

where

$$K_1 = \frac{I_1}{(Z_{12} - Z_{11}) \ln(R_{21}/R_{11})}.$$

The mutual inductance M_{12} of a pair of turns can be defined in two ways, either by means of the linkage energy or in terms of the linkage flux. The first way starts from the assumption that even turn 2 carries current I_1. On this assumption we can define

$$M_{12} = \frac{2W_{12}}{I_1^2}. \quad (3.99)$$

The symbol W_{12} stands for energy of the mutual linkage that is given by

$$W_{12} = \frac{1}{2} \int_{V_2} A_\varphi(R, Z) J_{\varphi 2}(R) dV, \quad (3.100)$$

where $J_{\varphi 2}$ denotes the circumferential component of the current density in turn 2. In an analogous way we can write

$$W_{12} = \frac{K_2}{2} \int_{\varphi=0}^{2\pi} \int_{R=R_{21}}^{R_{22}} \int_{Z=Z_{21}}^{Z_{22}} A_\varphi(R, Z) \, dZ \, dR \, d\psi, \quad (3.101)$$

where

$$K_2 = \frac{I_1}{(Z_{22} - Z_{21}) \ln(R_{22}/R_{21})}.$$

Due to the symmetry the magnetic vector potential $A_\varphi(R, Z)$ is independent of ψ, so the corresponding integration can be carried out immediately. After substitution for $A_\varphi(R, Z)$ from (3.98) we finally obtain

$$M_{12} = \frac{\mu_0}{(Z_{22} - Z_{21})(Z_{12} - Z_{11}) \ln(R_{22}/R_{21}) \ln(R_{21}/R_{11})}$$
$$\cdot \int_{\varphi=0}^{2\pi} \int_{r=R_{11}}^{R_{12}} \int_{R=R_{21}}^{R_{22}} \int_{z=Z_{11}}^{Z_{12}} \int_{Z=Z_{21}}^{Z_{22}} \frac{\cos\varphi \, dr \, dR \, dz \, dZ \, d\varphi}{\sqrt{r^2 + R^2 - 2rR\cos\varphi + (z - Z)^2}}.$$
$$(3.102)$$

It is obvious that the formula is symmetric to all subscripts; the consequence of this fact is

$$M_{12} = M_{21}.$$

Moreover, if turns 1 and 2 are identical (i.e., $R_{11} = R_{21}$, $R_{12} = R_{22}$, $Z_{11} = Z_{21}$, $Z_{12} = Z_{22}$), we obtain the formula for the self-inductance (3.80) derived earlier.

The second way of determining M_{12} starts from the static definition of the inductance

$$M_{12} = \frac{\Phi_{12}}{I_1}, \quad (3.103)$$

where Φ_{12} denotes the magnetic flux due to the field current in turn 1 linked with turn 2. Let k be a circle of radius R going through the reference point $P(R, Z) \in V_2$ (see Fig. 3.35). The total magnetic flux Φ_R passing through it is given by

$$\Phi_R = \int_{S_k} B_z(R, Z)\mathrm{d}S, \tag{3.104}$$

where S_k is the area of the circle. Moreover,

$$B_z(R, Z) = \frac{1}{R}\frac{\partial}{\partial R}[R \cdot A_\varphi(R, Z)]$$

so that

$$\Phi_R = \int_{\psi=0}^{2\pi}\int_{R=0}^{R}\frac{1}{R}\frac{\partial}{\partial R}[R \cdot A_\varphi(R, Z)]R\,\mathrm{d}R\,\mathrm{d}\psi = 2\pi R A_\varphi(R, Z). \tag{3.105}$$

Calculating the mean value of Φ_R within the whole turn 2 (under consideration of the inverse proportionality of magnetic quantities with respect to radius R), we have

$$\Phi_{12} = \frac{\int_{S_2}(\Phi_R/R)\mathrm{d}S}{\int_{S_2}(1/R)\mathrm{d}S},$$

where S_2 is the cross section of turn 2. The above formula gives

$$\Phi_{12} = 2\pi\frac{\int_{R=R_{21}}^{R_{22}}\int_{Z=Z_{21}}^{Z_{22}}A_\varphi(R, Z)\mathrm{d}Z\,\mathrm{d}R}{\int_{R=R_{21}}^{R_{22}}\int_{Z=Z_{21}}^{Z_{22}}(1/R)\mathrm{d}Z\mathrm{d}R}. \tag{3.106}$$

Substituting for $A_\varphi(R, Z)$ from (3.98) we obtain (3.102) again.

After quadruple analytical integration of (3.102) with respect to r, R, z, and Z, we get

$$
\begin{aligned}
M_{12} = &\frac{\mu_0}{(Z_{22} - Z_{21})(Z_{12} - Z_{11})\ln(R_{22}/R_{21})\ln(R_{21}/R_{11})}\\
&\cdot [W(R_{12}, R_{22}, Z_{12}, Z_{22}) + W(R_{12}, R_{22}, Z_{11}, Z_{21}) + W(R_{12}, R_{21}, Z_{12}, Z_{21})\\
&+ W(R_{12}, R_{21}, Z_{11}, Z_{22}) + W(R_{11}, R_{21}, Z_{11}, Z_{21}) + W(R_{11}, R_{21}, Z_{12}, Z_{22})\\
&+ W(R_{11}, R_{22}, Z_{12}, Z_{21}) + W(R_{11}, R_{22}, Z_{11}, Z_{22}) - W(R_{12}, R_{22}, Z_{12}, Z_{21})\\
&- W(R_{12}, R_{22}, Z_{11}, Z_{22}) - W(R_{12}, R_{21}, Z_{12}, Z_{22}) - W(R_{12}, R_{21}, Z_{11}, Z_{21})\\
&- W(R_{11}, R_{21}, Z_{11}, Z_{22}) - W(R_{11}, R_{21}, Z_{12}, Z_{21}) - W(R_{11}, R_{22}, Z_{11}, Z_{21})\\
&- W(R_{11}, R_{22}, Z_{12}, Z_{22})].
\end{aligned} \tag{3.107}
$$

Here

$$W(r, R, z, Z) = \int_{\varphi=0}^{\pi} w(r, R, z, Z, \varphi)\mathrm{d}\varphi$$

and

$$w(r, R, z, Z, \varphi) = \cos\varphi \cdot \frac{r(R - r\cos\varphi) + R(r - R\cos\varphi)}{6}$$

$$\cdot \sqrt{r^2 + R^2 - 2rR\cos\varphi + (z - Z)^2}$$

$$- \cos\varphi \cdot \frac{r(R - r\cos\varphi) + R(r - R\cos\varphi)}{2}(z - Z)$$

$$\cdot \ln[z - Z + \sqrt{r^2 + R^2 - 2rR\cos\varphi + (z - Z)^2}]$$

$$+ \frac{(z - Z)R^2}{2} \sin\varphi \cdot \cos\varphi \cdot \arctan \frac{(z - Z)(r - R\cos\varphi)}{R\sin\varphi \cdot \sqrt{r^2 + R^2 - 2rR\cos\varphi + (z - Z)^2}}$$

$$+ \frac{(z - Z)r^2}{2} \sin\varphi \cdot \cos\varphi \cdot \arctan \frac{(z - Z)(R - r\cos\varphi)}{r\sin\varphi \cdot \sqrt{r^2 + R^2 - 2rR\cos\varphi + (z - Z)^2}}$$

$$+ \left[\frac{r^2 \sin^2\varphi}{6} - \frac{(z - Z)^2}{2}\right] r\cos\varphi \cdot \ln[R - r\cos\varphi + \sqrt{r^2 + R^2 - 2rR\cos\varphi + (z - Z)^2}]$$

$$+ \left[\frac{R^2 \sin^2\varphi}{6} - \frac{(z - Z)^2}{2}\right] R\cos\varphi \cdot \ln[r - R\cos\varphi + \sqrt{r^2 + R^2 - 2rR\cos\varphi + (z - Z)^2}]$$

$$- \frac{(z - Z)^3 \cos\varphi}{6 \sin\varphi} \arctan \frac{(z - Z)\sin\varphi \sqrt{r^2 + R^2 - 2rR\cos\varphi + (z - Z)^2}}{(z - Z)^2 \cos\varphi + rR \cdot \sin^2\varphi}. \qquad (3.108)$$

Only a few terms in function w (3.108) can be integrated analytically. That is why this calculation has to be done numerically. For this purpose we first have to find its limits for $\varphi \to 0$ and $\varphi \to \pi$.

We easily find

$$\lim_{\varphi \to 0} w(r, R, z, Z, \varphi) =$$

$$-\frac{1}{6}\sqrt{[(r - R)^2 + (z - Z)^2]^3}$$

$$+ \frac{(z - Z)(r - R)^2}{2} \ln[z - Z + \sqrt{(r - R)^2 + (z - Z)^2}]$$

$$- \frac{(z - Z)^2}{2} \cdot (r\ln[R - r + \sqrt{(r - R)^2 + (z - Z)^2}]$$

$$+ R\ln[r - R + \sqrt{(r - R)^2 + (z - Z)^2}]), \qquad (3.109)$$

$$\lim_{\varphi \to \pi} w(r, R, z, Z, \varphi) =$$

$$-\frac{1}{6}\sqrt{[(r + R)^2 + (z - Z)^2]^3}$$

$$+ \frac{(z - Z)^2(r + R)}{2} \ln[R + r + \sqrt{(r + R)^2 + (z - Z)^2}]$$

$$+ \frac{(z - Z)(r + R)^2}{2} \ln[z - Z + \sqrt{(r + R)^2 + (z - Z)^2}]. \qquad (3.110)$$

Both limits are finite, so the numerical integration causes no problems.

Consider now the coil depicted in Fig. 3.36. The coil consists of two segments. Let the first segment contain four layers (each of them having N_1 turns) and the second segment three layers with N_2 turns. Each layer in the arrangement carries current in the same direction.

Let us first determine the self-inductance of layer 1 in segment 1. If the layer is wound sufficiently densely (so that it may be considered a massive turn), the value of its self-inductance L_{11} is given by formula (3.81) for the massive turn multiplied by N_1^2. Similarly, the mutual inductance between, for example, the first and third layer M_{13} is then given by (3.107) that is also multiplied by N_1^2. Of course, the mutual inductance between any two layers in different segments is obtained analogously, but formula (3.107) must be multiplied by product $N_1 N_2$.

Now, the self-inductance of segment 1 is given by

$$L_1 = L_{11} + L_{22} + L_{33} + L_{44} + 2M_{12} + 2M_{13} + 2M_{14} + 2M_{23} + 2M_{24} + 2M_{34} ,$$

while the self-inductance of the segment 2 is

$$L_2 = L_{55} + L_{66} + L_{77} + 2M_{56} + 2M_{57} + 2M_{67} .$$

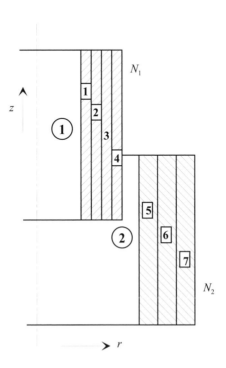

Figure 3.36.   A coil consisting of two segments.

The total inductance L of the system is

$$L = L_1 + L_2 + 2M_{15} + 2M_{16} + 2M_{17} + 2M_{25} + 2M_{26} + 2M_{27}$$

$$+2M_{35} + 2M_{36} + 2M_{37} + 2M_{45} + 2M_{46} + 2M_{47}.$$

In general, if segment 1 is wound by m layers and segment 2 by n layers, the number of partial self- and mutual inductances to be calculated is

$$\tfrac{1}{2}(m+n)(m+n+1). \tag{3.111}$$

It is obvious that exact calculation of the self-inductance of multilayered coils would be awkward and time consuming. For this reason a relatively wide range of research has been conducted, to determine for which conditions it is permissible to consider the current density in every layer uniform (and not indirectly proportional to the corresponding radius). In such a case the whole segment can be handled as one massive turn whose fictitious self-inductance is given by (3.81) and the real inductance is then obtained as this value multiplied by the second power of the total number of turns in the segment.

After a thorough analysis we came to the following results. If the ratio between the external and internal radii of any layer (whose number is n) in the segment satisfies the nonequality

$$\kappa = \max_i \frac{R_{2i}}{R_{1i}} \leq 1.1, \quad i = 1, \ldots, n,$$

and

$$n \geq 3,$$

we can use an approximation that the distribution of the current density across the segment is uniform, with an error not exceeding 0.2%. On the other hand, errors of the same magnitude may appear due to neglecting, for example, the influence of the interturn and interlayer insulation or the lead of the helicoid of the winding.

In order to complete our considerations, it is necessary to determine the mutual inductance between two general concentric massive turns (see Fig. 3.35) when the current density over its cross sections is assumed uniform. In this case we have

$$M_{12} = \frac{\mu_0}{(Z_{22}-Z_{21})(Z_{12}-Z_{11})(R_{22}-R_{21})((R_{12}-R_{11}))}$$

$$\cdot \int_{\varphi=0}^{2\pi}\int_{r=R_{11}}^{R_{12}}\int_{R=R_{21}}^{R_{22}}\int_{z=Z_{11}}^{Z_{12}}\int_{Z=Z_{21}}^{Z_{22}} \frac{\cos\varphi\, r\, R\, dr\, dR\, dz\, dZ\, d\varphi}{\sqrt{r^2 + R^2 - 2rR\cos\varphi + (z-Z)^2}}.$$

$$\tag{3.112}$$

After four analytical integrations with respect to r, R, z, and Z, we obtain

$$
\begin{aligned}
M_{12} =\ & \frac{\mu_0}{(Z_{22} - Z_{21})(Z_{12} - Z_{11})(R_{22} - R_{21})((R_{12} - R_{11}))} \\
& \cdot [V(R_{12}, R_{22}, Z_{12}, Z_{22}) + V(R_{12}, R_{22}, Z_{11}, Z_{21})V(R_{12}, R_{21}, Z_{12}, Z_{21}) \\
& + V(R_{12}, R_{21}, Z_{11}, Z_{22}) + V(R_{11}, R_{21}, Z_{11}, Z_{21}) + V(R_{11}, R_{21}, Z_{12}, Z_{22}) \\
& + V(R_{11}, R_{22}, Z_{12}, Z_{21}) + V(R_{11}, R_{22}, Z_{11}, Z_{22}) - V(R_{12}, R_{22}, Z_{12}, Z_{21}) \\
& - V(R_{12}, R_{22}, Z_{11}, Z_{22}) - V(R_{12}, R_{21}, Z_{12}, Z_{22}) - V(R_{12}, R_{21}, Z_{11}, Z_{21}) \\
& - V(R_{11}, R_{21}, Z_{11}, Z_{22}) - V(R_{11}, R_{21}, Z_{12}, Z_{21}) - V(R_{11}, R_{22}, Z_{11}, Z_{21}) \\
& - V(R_{11}, R_{22}, Z_{12}, Z_{22})].
\end{aligned}
\tag{3.113}
$$

Here

$$
V(r, R, z, Z) = \int_{\varphi=0}^{\pi} v(r, R, z, Z, \varphi)\mathrm{d}\varphi
$$

and

$$
\begin{aligned}
v(r, R, z, Z, \varphi) =\ & -\cos\varphi \cdot \frac{3\cos^2\varphi(r^4 + R^4) + rR\cos\varphi(r^2 + R^2) - 2(r^2 + R^2)^2}{30} \\
& \cdot \sqrt{r^2 + R^2 - 2rR\cos\varphi + (z - Z)^2} \\
& -\cos\varphi \cdot \left[\frac{3(z - Z)^2(r^2 + R^2)}{40} + \frac{(z - Z)^4}{60\sin^2\varphi}\right] \sqrt{r^2 + R^2 - 2rR\cos\varphi + (z - Z)^2} \\
& +\cos\varphi \cdot \frac{2(r^4 + R^4)\cos^2\varphi - (r^2 + R^2)^2}{8}(z - Z) \\
& \cdot \ln[z - Z + \sqrt{r^2 + R^2 - 2rR\cos\varphi + (z - Z)^2}] \\
& + \frac{(z - Z)R^4}{4}\sin\varphi \cdot \cos^2\varphi \cdot \arctan\frac{(z - Z)(r - R\cos\varphi)}{R\sin\varphi \cdot \sqrt{r^2 + R^2 - 2rR\cos\varphi + (z - Z)^2}} \\
& + \frac{(z - Z)r^4}{4}\sin^2\varphi \cdot \cos\varphi \cdot \arctan\frac{(z - Z)(R - r\cos\varphi)}{r\sin\varphi \cdot \sqrt{r^2 + R^2 - 2rR\cos\varphi + (z - Z)^2}} \\
& + \left[\frac{r^2\sin^2\varphi}{5} - \frac{(z - Z)^2}{3}\right]\frac{r^3}{2}\cos^2\varphi \\
& \cdot \ln[R - r\cos\varphi + \sqrt{r^2 + R^2 - 2rR\cos\varphi + (z - Z)^2}] \\
& + \left[\frac{R^2\sin^2\varphi}{5} - \frac{(z - Z)^2}{3}\right]\frac{R^3}{2}\cos^2\varphi \\
& \cdot \ln[r - R\cos\varphi + \sqrt{r^2 + R^2 - 2rR\cos\varphi + (z - Z)^2}] \\
& + \frac{(z - Z)^5\cos^2\varphi}{60\sin^3\varphi}\arctan\frac{(z - Z)\sin\varphi\sqrt{r^2 + R^2 - 2rR\cos\varphi + (z - Z)^2}}{(z - Z)^2\cos\varphi + rR \cdot \sin^2\varphi}.
\end{aligned}
\tag{3.114}
$$

The limits of function v at points $\varphi = 0$ and $\varphi = \pi$ are

$$\lim_{\varphi \to 0} v(r, R, z, Z, \varphi) = \frac{(z - Z)(r^2 - R^2)^2}{8} \ln[z - Z + \sqrt{(r - R)^2 + (z - Z)^2}]$$

$$- \frac{(z - Z)^2}{6}(r^3 \ln[r - R + \sqrt{(r - R)^2 + (z - Z)^2}])$$

$$+ \frac{(z - Z)^2}{6}R^3 \ln[R - r + \sqrt{(r - R)^2 + (z - Z)^2}])$$

$$- \frac{1}{30}(r - R)^2(r^2 + 3rR + R^2)\sqrt{(r - R)^2 + (z - Z)^2}$$

$$- \frac{(z - Z)^2}{20}\left[\frac{(r - R)^2 + (z - Z)^2}{9} + \frac{rR}{3} + \frac{3(r^2 + R^2)}{2}\right]\sqrt{(r - R)^2 + (z - Z)^2}$$

$$(3.115)$$

and

$$\lim_{\varphi \to \pi} v(r, R, z, Z, \varphi) = -\frac{(z - Z)(r^2 - R^2)^2}{8} \ln[z - Z + \sqrt{(r + R)^2 + (z - Z)^2}]$$

$$- \frac{(z - Z)^2}{6}(r^3 + R^3) \ln[R + r + \sqrt{(r + R)^2 + (z - Z)^2}]$$

$$+ \frac{1}{30}(r + R)^2(r^2 - 3rR + R^2)\sqrt{(r + R)^2 + (z - Z)^2}$$

$$+ \frac{(z - Z)^2}{20}\left[\frac{(r + R)^2 + (z - Z)^2}{9} - \frac{rR}{3} + \frac{3(r^2 + R^2)}{2}\right]\sqrt{(r + R)^2 + (z - Z)^2}.$$

$$(3.116)$$

Even these limits are finite, so that the function v can be integrated numerically without any difficulties. Similar to the case of the massive circular turn, more detailed information about the topic can be found in Refs. 107 and 108.

The last parameters to be determined are the radial and axial forces acting in particular turns of cylindrical coils. Let us start again from Fig. 3.35 showing two turns in a general position, and find the total radial and axial forces acting on the turn with index 2. The turns carry currents I_1 and I_2, respectively.

From the general vector formula $f = J \times B$ for the volume force, we obtain

$$F_{r,2} = \int_{V_2} J_{\varphi,2} B_z \, dV \tag{3.117}$$

and

$$F_{z,2} = -\int_{V_2} J_{\varphi,2} B_r \, dV, \tag{3.118}$$

where $J_{\varphi,2}(R) = K/R$, K is given by (3.4.3), and $B_r(R, Z)$ and $B_z(R, Z)$ are the radial and axial components, respectively of the magnetic flux density in turn 2.

While the radial force in turn 2 is produced by currents I_1 and I_2 in both turns, the axial force is produced only by current I_1. As neither $J_{\varphi,2}(R)$ nor $B_z(R, Z)$ depends on the azimuth ψ, immediately we can write

$$F_{r,2} = 2\pi K \int_{R=R_{21}}^{R_{22}} \int_{Z=Z_{21}}^{Z_{22}} B_z(R,Z)\,\mathrm{d}R\,\mathrm{d}Z\,,$$

$$F_{z,2} = -2\pi K \int_{R=R_{21}}^{R_{22}} \int_{Z=Z_{21}}^{Z_{22}} B_r(R,Z)\,\mathrm{d}R\,\mathrm{d}Z\,, \qquad (3.119)$$

where

$$B_r(R,Z) = \frac{\mu_0 K_1}{4\pi} \int_{\varphi=0}^{2\pi} \int_{r=R_{11}}^{R_{12}} \int_{z=Z_{11}}^{Z_{12}} \frac{\cos\varphi(Z-z)\,\mathrm{d}r\,\mathrm{d}z\,\mathrm{d}\varphi}{\sqrt{(r^2+R^2-2rR\cos\varphi+(z-Z)^2)^3}}$$

and

$$B_z(R,Z) = \frac{\mu_0 K_1}{4\pi} \int_{\varphi=0}^{2\pi} \int_{r=R_{11}}^{R_{12}} \int_{z=Z_{11}}^{Z_{12}} \frac{(r-R\cos\varphi)\,\mathrm{d}r\,\mathrm{d}z\,\mathrm{d}\varphi}{\sqrt{(r^2+R^2-2rR\cos\varphi+(z-Z)^2)^3}}$$

$$+\frac{\mu_0 K_2}{4\pi} \int_{\varphi=0}^{2\pi} \int_{r=R_{21}}^{R_{22}} \int_{z=Z_{211}}^{Z_{22}} \frac{(r-R\cos\varphi)\,\mathrm{d}r\,\mathrm{d}z\,\mathrm{d}\varphi}{\sqrt{(r^2+R^2-2rR\cos\varphi+(z-Z)^2)^3}}\,. \qquad (3.120)$$

Substitution of (3.120) into (3.119) and consequent quadruple analytical integration with respect to r, R, z, and Z provides

$$\begin{aligned}
F_{r,2} = \mu_0 K_1 K_2 \\
\cdot\, [&M(R_{12},R_{22},Z_{12},Z_{22}) + M(R_{12},R_{22},Z_{11},Z_{21}) + M(R_{12},R_{21},Z_{12},Z_{21}) \\
+ &M(R_{12},R_{21},Z_{11},Z_{22}) + M(R_{11},R_{21},Z_{11},Z_{21}) + M(R_{11},R_{21},Z_{12},Z_{22}) \\
+ &M(R_{11},R_{22},Z_{12},Z_{21}) + M(R_{11},R_{22},Z_{11},Z_{22}) - M(R_{12},R_{22},Z_{12},Z_{21}) \\
- &M(R_{12},R_{22},Z_{11},Z_{22}) - M(R_{12},R_{21},Z_{12},Z_{22}) - M(R_{12},R_{21},Z_{11},Z_{21}) \\
- &M(R_{11},R_{21},Z_{11},Z_{22}) - M(R_{11},R_{21},Z_{12},Z_{21}) - M(R_{11},R_{22},Z_{11},Z_{21}) \\
- &M(R_{11},R_{22},Z_{12},Z_{22})] \\
+ \mu_0 K_2^2 \\
\cdot\, [&M(R_{22},R_{22},Z_{22},Z_{22}) + M(R_{22},R_{22},Z_{21},Z_{21}) + M(R_{22},R_{21},Z_{22},Z_{21}) \\
+ &M(R_{22},R_{21},Z_{21},Z_{22}) + M(R_{21},R_{21},Z_{21},Z_{21}) + M(R_{21},R_{21},Z_{12},Z_{22}) \\
+ &M(R_{21},R_{22},Z_{22},Z_{21}) + M(R_{21},R_{22},Z_{21},Z_{22}) - M(R_{22},R_{22},Z_{22},Z_{21}) \\
- &M(R_{22},R_{22},Z_{11},Z_{22}) - M(R_{22},R_{21},Z_{22},Z_{22}) - M(R_{22},R_{21},Z_{21},Z_{21}) \\
- &M(R_{21},R_{21},Z_{21},Z_{22}) - M(R_{21},R_{21},Z_{22},Z_{21}) - M(R_{21},R_{22},Z_{21},Z_{21}) \\
- &M(R_{21},R_{22},Z_{22},Z_{22})]\,, \qquad (3.121)
\end{aligned}$$

where

$$M(r,R,z,Z) = \int_{\varphi=0}^{\pi} m(r,R,z,Z,\varphi)\mathrm{d}\varphi$$

and $m(r,R,z,Z,\varphi)$ is given by (3.92). Its limits for $\varphi=0$ and $\varphi=\pi$ are identical with (3.93) and (3.94).

The axial force is analogously

$$F_{z,2} = \mu_0 K_1 K_2$$
$$\cdot[N(R_{12}, R_{22}, Z_{12}, Z_{22}) + N(R_{12}, R_{22}, Z_{11}, Z_{21}) + N(R_{12}, R_{21}, Z_{12}, Z_{21})$$
$$+N(R_{12}, R_{21}, Z_{11}, Z_{22}) + N(R_{11}, R_{21}, Z_{11}, Z_{21}) + N(R_{11}, R_{21}, Z_{12}, Z_{22})$$
$$+N(R_{11}, R_{22}, Z_{12}, Z_{21}) + N(R_{11}, R_{22}, Z_{11}, Z_{22}) - N(R_{12}, R_{22}, Z_{12}, Z_{21})$$
$$-N(R_{12}, R_{22}, Z_{11}, Z_{22}) - N(R_{12}, R_{21}, Z_{12}, Z_{22}) - N(R_{12}, R_{21}, Z_{11}, Z_{21})$$
$$-N(R_{11}, R_{21}, Z_{11}, Z_{22}) - N(R_{11}, R_{21}, Z_{12}, Z_{21}) - N(R_{11}, R_{22}, Z_{11}, Z_{21})$$
$$-N(R_{11}, R_{22}, Z_{12}, Z_{22})],   \tag{3.122}$$

where

$$N(r, R, z, Z) = \int_{\varphi=0}^{\pi} n(r, R, z, Z, \varphi) \mathrm{d}\varphi$$

and

$$n(r, R, z, Z, \varphi) = R(z - Z)\ln[r - R\cos\varphi + \sqrt{r^2 + R^2 - 2rR\cos\varphi + (z - Z)^2}]$$
$$+ r(z - Z)\ln[R - r\cos\varphi + \sqrt{r^2 + R^2 - 2rR\cos\varphi + (z - Z)^2}]$$
$$+ \frac{R(r - R\cos\varphi) + r(R - r\cos\varphi)}{2}$$
$$\cdot \ln[z - Z + \sqrt{r^2 + R^2 - 2rR\cos\varphi + (z - Z)^2}]$$
$$- \frac{R^2}{2}\sin\varphi\cos\varphi\arctan\frac{(r - R\cos\varphi)(z - Z)}{R\sin\varphi \cdot \sqrt{r^2 + R^2 - 2rR\cos\varphi + (z - Z)^2}}$$
$$- \frac{r^2}{2}\sin\varphi\cos\varphi\arctan\frac{(R - r\cos\varphi)(z - Z)}{R\sin\varphi \cdot \sqrt{r^2 + R^2 - 2rR\cos\varphi + (z - Z)^2}}$$
$$+ \frac{(z - Z)^2}{2}\frac{\cos\varphi}{\sin\varphi}\arctan\frac{(z - Z)\sin\varphi\sqrt{r^2 + R^2 - 2rR\cos\varphi + (z - Z)^2}}{rR\sin^2\varphi + (z - Z)^2\cos\varphi}.$$
$$\tag{3.123}$$

As always, for the sake of the numerical integration, we have to find the limits of the function $n(r, R, z, Z, \varphi)$ at singular points $\varphi = 0$ and $\varphi = \pi$. There holds

$$\lim_{\varphi \to 0} n(r, R, z, Z, \varphi) = \frac{z - Z}{2}\sqrt{(r - R)^2 + (z - Z)^2}$$
$$- \frac{(r - R)^2}{2}\ln[z - Z + \sqrt{(r - R)^2 + (z - Z)^2}]$$
$$+ R(z - Z)\ln[r - R + \sqrt{(r - R)^2 + (z - Z)^2}]$$
$$+ r(z - Z)\ln[R - r + \sqrt{(r - R)^2 + (z - Z)^2}],$$
$$\tag{3.124}$$

$$\lim_{\varphi \to \pi} n(r, R, z, Z, \varphi) = \frac{z - Z}{2}\sqrt{(r + R)^2 + (z - Z)^2}$$
$$+ \frac{(r + R)^2}{2} \ln[z - Z + \sqrt{(r + R)^2 + (z - Z)^2}]$$
$$- (r + R)(z - Z)\ln[r + R + \sqrt{(r + R)^2 + (z - Z)^2}].$$

$$(3.125)$$

Even these limits are finite.

Analogously, as in the case of the inductance, the forces acting in multilayered coils of complicated structures can be found by superposition of forces acting between particular turns. If any layer is wound sufficiently densely, with a negligible error we can consider it a massive turn. The results must be multiplied by the number of turns corresponding to the relevant layers.

More details on the computation of forces in cylindrical air-core coils can be found in Refs. 109 and 110.

3.4.4 Electric field of an idealized thundercloud

In this example we will map the distribution of voltage and electric field strength in the domain of an idealized thundercloud provided that we know the distribution of its electric charge.

A common thundercloud and distribution of its charge are depicted in Fig. 3.37. While the lower part of the thundercloud is a seat of negative charge, its upper part carries positive charge, but a smaller amount. The total charge of the thundercloud is negative. The maximum density of electric charge ϱ in the thundercloud (that can be found mostly in its center) is on the order of 10^{-9} C/m^3. The potential of earth is supposed to be $\varphi = 0$.

Now it is necessary to calculate the distribution of potential in the domain of the idealized thundercloud provided that we know the distribution of specific electric charge $\varrho(r, z)$. If we suppose that the relative permittivity ε_r of the thundercloud and its large vicinity is uniform and constant (this is a strong simplification because the thundercloud contains a mixture of water and ice) we can, using the method of images, write (see Fig. 3.38)

$$\varphi(T) = \varphi(R, \Phi, Z) = \frac{1}{4\pi\varepsilon_0\varepsilon_r}$$
$$\cdot \left[\int_{\varphi=0}^{2\pi} \int_{r=0}^{R_1} \int_{z=Z_1}^{Z_2} \frac{\varrho r\,dr\,dz\,d\varphi}{d_1} - \int_{\varphi=0}^{2\pi} \int_{r=0}^{R_1} \int_{z=Z_1}^{Z_2} \frac{\varrho r\,dr\,dz\,d\varphi}{d_2} \right], \qquad (3.126)$$

where T is a reference point and d_1 and d_2 are the distances between this point and the general integration point P_1 and its image P_2, respectively. We easily obtain

$$d_1 = \sqrt{r^2 + R^2 - 2rR\cos\varphi + (z - Z)^2},$$

$$d_2 = \sqrt{r^2 + R^2 - 2rR\cos\varphi + (z + Z)^2}.$$

Now it is necessary to approximate the real distribution of $\varrho(r, z)$. This problem has been dealt with by several authors. For example, Pasko et al. [104] and later Tong et al.

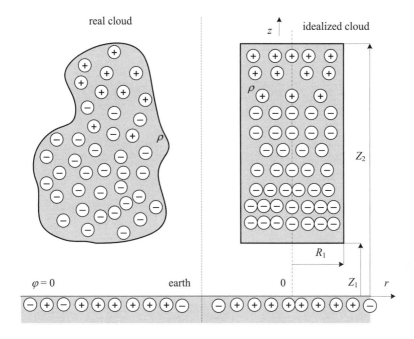

Figure 3.37. Real and idealized thunderclouds.

[105] use Gauss' probabilistic distribution with respect to both r and z, but in such a case the charge density is negative everywhere. Moreover, this distribution is also dependent on time. Somewhat easier is to approximate it (at any time level) by a product of two second-order polynomials,

$$\varrho(r, z) = (a_0 + a_1 r + a_2 r^2)(b_0 + b_1 z + b_2 z^2),$$

where the coefficients $a_0, \ldots, b_2$, are generally functions of time. But we focus our effort on a selected time instant, that is, we suppose that their values are given.

Now the computation of (3.126) is conditioned by evaluation of the integrals

$$\int_{\varphi=0}^{2\pi} \int_{r=0}^{R_1} \int_{z=Z_1}^{Z_2} \frac{r^i z^j \, dr \, dz \, d\varphi}{\sqrt{r^2 + R^2 - 2rR \cos \varphi + (z - Z)^2}} \tag{3.127}$$

and

$$\int_{\varphi=0}^{2\pi} \int_{r=0}^{R_1} \int_{z=Z_1}^{Z_2} \frac{r^i z^j \, dr \, dz \, d\varphi}{\sqrt{r^2 + R^2 - 2rR \cos \varphi + (z + Z)^2}}, \tag{3.128}$$

where $i = 1, 2, 3$ and $j = 0, 1, 2$.

Integration of every integral with respect to r and z may be performed analytically. But we will present only three of them, considering $a_1 = a_2 = 0$ (this means that the specific

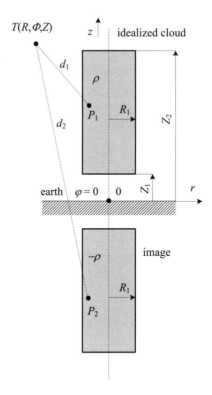

Figure 3.38.   Method of images for the idealized thundercloud.

charge does not depend on the radius r).

$$
\begin{aligned}
I_{00} &= \int_{\varphi=0}^{2\pi} \int_{r=0}^{R_1} \int_{z=Z_1}^{Z_2} \frac{r\,\mathrm{d}r\,\mathrm{d}z\,\mathrm{d}\varphi}{\sqrt{r^2 + R^2 - 2rR\cos\varphi + (z-Z)^2}} \\
&= \int_{\varphi=0}^{\pi} [i00(R_2, Z_2) - i00(R_1, Z_2) - i00(R_2, Z_1) + i00(R_1, Z_1)]\mathrm{d}\varphi\,,
\end{aligned}
$$

where

$$
\begin{aligned}
i00(r, z) &= (z - Z)\sqrt{r^2 + R^2 - 2rR\cos\varphi + (z-Z)^2} \\
&\quad + (r^2 - R^2\cos(2\varphi)) \\
&\qquad \cdot \ln[z - Z + \sqrt{r^2 + R^2 - 2rR\cos\varphi + (z-Z)^2}] \\
&\quad + 2R(z - Z)\cos\varphi \\
&\qquad \cdot \ln[r - R\cos\varphi + \sqrt{r^2 + R^2 - 2rR\cos\varphi + (z-Z)^2}] \\
&\quad - R^2\sin(2\varphi)\arctan\frac{(z-Z)(r - R\cos\varphi)}{} \\
&\qquad \cdot R\sin\varphi\sqrt{r^2 + R^2 - 2rR\cos\varphi + (z-Z)^2}\,,
\end{aligned}
\tag{3.129}
$$

$$
\begin{aligned}
I_{01} &= \int_{\varphi=0}^{2\pi} \int_{r=0}^{R_1} \int_{z=Z_1}^{Z_2} \frac{rz \, dr \, dz \, d\varphi}{\sqrt{r^2 + R^2 - 2rR\cos\varphi + (z - Z)^2}} \\
&= \int_{\varphi=0}^{\pi} [i01(R_2, Z_2) - i01(R_1, Z_2) - i01(R_2, Z_1) + i01(R_1, Z_1)] d\varphi \,,
\end{aligned}
$$

where

$$
\begin{aligned}
i01(r, z) &= \frac{4(z - Z)^2 + 4r^2 + R^2 - 6(z - Z)Z - 2rR\cos\varphi - 3R^2\cos(2\varphi)}{6} \\
&\quad \cdot \sqrt{r^2 + R^2 - 2rR\cos\varphi + (z - Z)^2} \\
&\quad + (-r^2 Z + R^2 Z\cos(2\varphi)) \ln[z - Z + \sqrt{r^2 + R^2 - 2rR\cos\varphi + (z - Z)^2}] \\
&\quad + (z - Z)R(z - 3Z)\cos\varphi \\
&\quad \cdot \ln[r - R\cos\varphi + \sqrt{r^2 + R^2 - 2rR\cos\varphi + (z - Z)^2}] \\
&\quad + R^2 Z\sin(2\varphi)\arctan\frac{(z - Z)(r - R\cos\varphi)}{R\sin\varphi\sqrt{r^2 + R^2 - 2rR\cos\varphi + (z - Z)^2}} \\
&\quad + R^3\cos\varphi\sin^2\varphi\coth^{-1}\frac{r - R\cos\varphi}{\sqrt{r^2 + R^2 - 2rR\cos\varphi + (z - Z)^2}} \,,
\end{aligned}
$$

$$(3.130)$$

and

$$
\begin{aligned}
I_{02} &= \int_{\varphi=0}^{2\pi} \int_{r=0}^{R_1} \int_{z=Z_1}^{Z_2} \frac{rz^2 \, dr \, dz \, d\varphi}{\sqrt{r^2 + R^2 - 2rR\cos\varphi + (z - Z)^2}} \\
&= \int_{\varphi=0}^{\pi} [i02(R_2, Z_2) - i02(R_1, Z_2) - i02(R_2, Z_1) + i02(R_1, Z_1)] d\varphi \,,
\end{aligned}
$$

where

$$
\begin{aligned}
i02(r, z) = {} & \frac{1}{12}(r^2(3z - 19Z) + R^2(z - 5Z) + 2(z - Z)(3z^2 - 14zZ + 17Z^2) \\
& - 2rR(z - 5Z)\cos\varphi - 2R^2(z - 7Z)\cos(2\varphi)) \\
& \cdot \sqrt{r^2 + R^2 - 2rR\cos\varphi + (z - Z)^2} \\
& + \frac{1}{12}(-3r^2(r^2 + 2R^2 - 4Z^2) + 8r^3R\cos\varphi + 2R^2(R^2 - 6Z^2)\cos(2\varphi) \\
& - R^4\cos(4\varphi)) \cdot \ln[z - Z + \sqrt{r^2 + R^2 - 2rR\cos\varphi + (z - Z)^2}] \\
& + \frac{2}{3}R(z - 2Z)^2\cos\varphi \\
& \cdot \ln[r - R\cos\varphi + \sqrt{r^2 + R^2 - 2rR\cos\varphi + (z - Z)^2}] \\
& + \frac{2}{3}R^2\cos\varphi\sin\varphi(-3Z^2 + R^2\sin^2\varphi) \\
& \cdot \arctan\frac{(z - Z)(r - R\cos\varphi)}{R\sin\varphi\sqrt{r^2 + R^2 - 2rR\cos\varphi + (z - Z)^2}} \\
& + \frac{2}{3}RZ\cos\varphi(Z^2 - 3R^2\sin^2\varphi) \\
& \cdot \coth^{-1}\frac{r - R\cos\varphi}{\sqrt{r^2 + R^2 - 2rR\cos\varphi + (z - Z)^2}}.
\end{aligned}
\tag{3.131}
$$

Now we shall investigate the distribution of electric potential in the thundercloud for the following parameters: $R_1 = 3000$ m, $Z_1 = 1000$ m, $Z_2 = 15000$ m, and the total charge $Q = -40$ C. The volume of the cloud $V = \pi R_1^2(Z_2 - Z_1) = 395.84 \times 10^9$ m^3 and the average specific charge $\varrho_0 = Q/V = -40/395.84/10^9 \doteq -10^{-10}$ C/m^3.

We will compare four cases of the distribution of the specific charge (the total charge remaining the same value, $Q = -40$ C):

1. The charge density is uniform and its value all over the cloud is $\varrho_0 = -10^{-10}$ C/m^3.

2. The charge density everywhere in the cloud is negative but grows linearly from its bottom to its top, where it vanishes.

3. The charge density changes linearly from its bottom to its top, but at the top it is positive and reaches 40% of its absolute value at the bottom.

4. The charge density grows parabolically from the bottom to the top with the condition $\varrho(1000) = -210^{-10}$ C/m^3 and $\varrho(15000) = 10^{-10}$ C/m^3.

The corresponding dependencies $\varrho = \varrho(z)$ are depicted in Fig. 3.39, together with their equations.

Figure 3.40 shows the distribution of potential in the cloud (bounded by the bold line) and its vicinity for the distribution of specific charge corresponding to line 1 in Fig. 3.39. The figure also contains the distribution of potential along the z axis in order to obtain the maximum potential in the cloud with respect to the earth, whose potential is considered zero.

Figures 3.41 and 3.42 show a situation that is closer to physical reality. Now the charge density changes linearly with the z coordinate. While in the former case its value is non-positive everywhere (line 2 in Fig. 3.39), in the latter one the top of the cloud is supposed

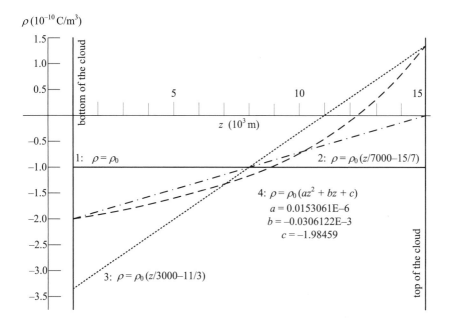

Figure 3.39. Considered dependencies of charge density ϱ.

to be charged positively (line 3 in Fig. 3.39). Both figures are supplemented with another graph showing the distribution of potential along the z axis.

3.5 3D INTEGRATION AREA

3.5.1 Review of typical problems

Surprisingly, the problems that can be solved by means of integral expressions are not so frequent because they are limited by the presence of exclusively linear and uniform media. Moreover, the field currents (that are supposed to be known in advance) must be permanent in time, otherwise the methodology would fail due to eddy currents generated in electrically conductive parts of the system. And these requirements are satisfied practically only in case of air-core coils with nonnegligible lead and their systems.

3.5.2 Magnetic field around a helicoidal air-core coil

Let a conductor of rectangular crosssection be wound in a helix (see Fig. 3.43). The figure also contains the necessary geometrical data. Symbols R_1 and R_2 denote the inner and outer radii of the helix, h the height of the conductor, and angle ψ the lead. Quantities Φ_1 and Φ_2 determine the starting and ending angles of the helix with respect to the chosen system of cylindrical coordinates r, φ, and z.

Derivation of the integral expressions for mapping the magnetic field of the coil starts from Fig. 3.44. Let $Q \equiv Q(R, \Phi, Z)$ be a reference point (at which we want to find the field quantities) and $P \equiv dV(r, \varphi, z)$ be a general integration point characterized by the presence

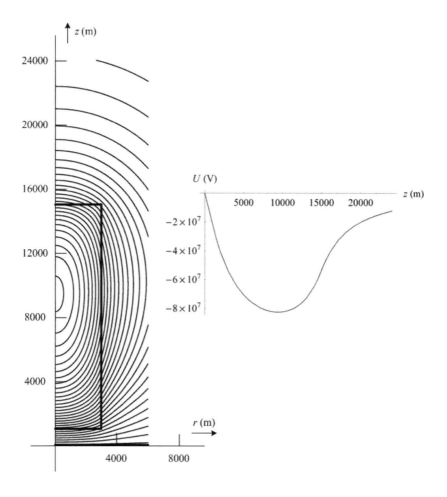

Figure 3.40. Distribution of potential in the cloud and its vicinity for charge density according to line 1 in Fig. 3.39.

of nonzero field current density whose vector is $\boldsymbol{J}$. The field current density obviously has two components, J_φ and J_z, in the tangential and axial directions, respectively,

$$J_\varphi = J \cos \psi, \quad J_z = J \sin \psi,$$

where $J = |\boldsymbol{J}|$ is the module of the current density given by

$$J = \frac{1}{r} \cdot \frac{I}{h \cos \psi \ln(R_2/R_1)},$$

I being the field current. Quantity J is not constant within the conductor; its value is inversely proportional to the corresponding radius, as was explained in Section 3.3.

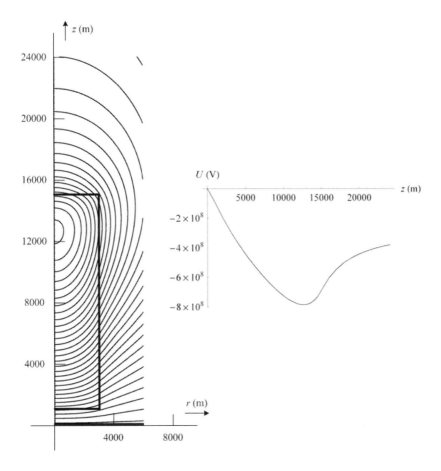

Figure 3.41.   Distribution of potential in the cloud and its vicinity for charge density according to line 2 in Fig. 3.39.

Starting from the basic vectorial relation for magnetic vector potential A at the reference point Q [111],

$$A(Q) = \frac{\mu_0}{4\pi} \int_V \frac{J\, \mathrm{d}V}{|l|} ,$$

where V stands for the volume of the helix, in the cylindrical coordinate system we obtain the following component equations:

$$A_r(R, \Phi, Z) = -\frac{\mu_0}{4\pi} \int_V \frac{J_\varphi \sin(\varphi - \Phi)\, \mathrm{d}V}{|l|}$$
$$= \frac{\mu_0}{4\pi} \int_{r=R_1}^{R_2} \int_{\varphi=\Phi_1}^{\Phi_2} \int_{z=\vartheta_1}^{\vartheta_2} \frac{J_\varphi \sin(\varphi - \Phi)r\, \mathrm{d}r\, \mathrm{d}\varphi \mathrm{d}z}{|l|} , \qquad (3.132)$$

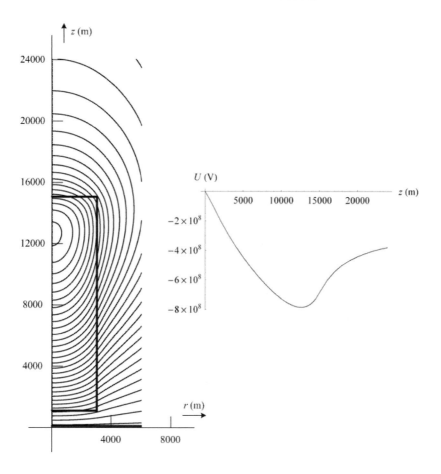

Figure 3.42.   Distribution of potential in the cloud and its vicinity for charge density according to line 3 in Fig. 3.39.

$$A_\varphi(R, \Phi, Z) = \frac{\mu_0}{4\pi} \int_V \frac{J_\varphi \cos(\varphi - \Phi)\, dV}{|\mathbf{l}|}$$

$$= \frac{\mu_0}{4\pi} \int_{r=R_1}^{R_2} \int_{\varphi=\Phi_1}^{\Phi_2} \int_{z=\vartheta_1}^{\vartheta_2} \frac{J_\varphi \cos(\varphi - \Phi) r\, dr\, d\varphi\, dz}{|\mathbf{l}|}, \qquad (3.133)$$

$$A_z(R, \Phi, Z) = \frac{\mu_0}{4\pi} \int_V \frac{J_z\, dV}{|\mathbf{l}|}$$

$$= \frac{\mu_0}{4\pi} \int_{r=R_1}^{R_2} \int_{\varphi=\Phi_1}^{\Phi_2} \int_{z=\vartheta_1}^{\vartheta_2} \frac{J_z r\, dr\, d\varphi dz}{|\mathbf{l}|}, \qquad (3.134)$$

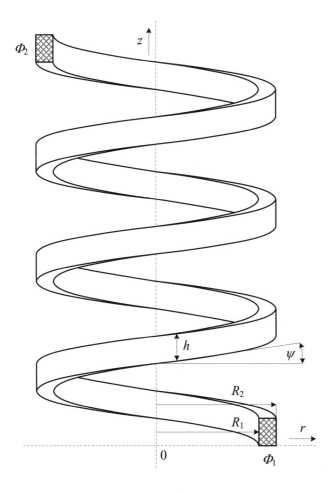

Figure 3.43. Geometry of the investigated helicoidal coil.

where

$$\vartheta_1 = R_a(\varphi - \Phi_1) \cdot \tan\psi,$$
$$\vartheta_2 = h + R_a(\varphi - \Phi_1) \cdot \tan\psi,$$
$$R_a = \frac{R_1 + R_2}{2}, \tag{3.135}$$

and $\boldsymbol{l}$ is a vector oriented from point P to point Q,

$$\boldsymbol{l} \equiv (R - r\cos(\Phi - \varphi), r\sin(\Phi - \varphi), Z - z),$$

with module

$$l = \sqrt{r^2 + R^2 - 2rR\cos(\Phi - \varphi) + (Z - z)^2}.$$

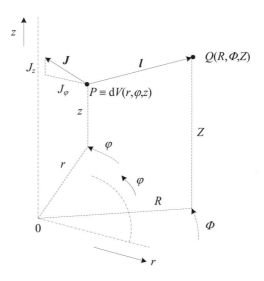

Figure 3.44.   Derivation of the field equations.

The components of magnetic flux density $\boldsymbol{B}$ follow from the definition $\boldsymbol{B} = \operatorname{curl} \boldsymbol{A}$ in cylindrical coordinates. Immediately we have

$$
\begin{aligned}
B_r(R, \Phi, Z) &= \frac{1}{R} \frac{\partial A_z}{\partial \Phi} - \frac{\partial A_\varphi}{\partial Z} \\
&= \frac{\mu_0}{4\pi} \cdot \int_{r=R_1}^{R_2} \int_{\varphi=\Phi_1}^{\Phi_2} \int_{z=\vartheta_1}^{\vartheta_2} \frac{J_\varphi \cos(\Phi - \varphi)(Z - z) - J_z r \sin(\Phi - \varphi)}{|\boldsymbol{l}|^3} r \, dr \, d\varphi \, dz \,,
\end{aligned}
$$

(3.136)

$$
\begin{aligned}
B_\varphi(R, \Phi, Z) &= \frac{\partial A_r}{\partial Z} - \frac{\partial A_z}{\partial R} \\
&= \frac{\mu_0}{4\pi} \cdot \int_{r=R_1}^{R_2} \int_{\varphi=\Phi_1}^{\Phi_2} \int_{z=\vartheta_1}^{\vartheta_2} \frac{J_z(R - r\cos(\Phi - \varphi)) - J_\varphi \sin(\Phi - \varphi)(Z - z)}{|\boldsymbol{l}|^3} r \, dr \, d\varphi \, dz \,,
\end{aligned}
$$

(3.137)

$$
\begin{aligned}
B_z(R, \Phi, Z) &= \frac{A_\varphi}{R} + \frac{\partial A_\varphi}{\partial R} - \frac{1}{R} \cdot \frac{\partial A_r}{\partial \Phi} \\
&= \frac{\mu_0}{4\pi} \cdot \int_{r=R_1}^{R_2} \int_{\varphi=\Phi_1}^{\Phi_2} \int_{z=\vartheta_1}^{\vartheta_2} \frac{J_\varphi(r - R\cos(\Phi - \varphi))}{|\boldsymbol{l}|^3} r \, dr \, d\varphi \, dz,
\end{aligned}
$$

(3.138)

Denoting

$$p = \tan\psi, \quad \gamma = \varphi - \Phi, \quad C = \frac{I}{h\ln(R_2/R_1)},$$

the above formulas can be modified as follows

$$
A_r(R,\Phi,Z)
= -\frac{\mu_0 C}{4\pi} \int_{\gamma=\Phi_1-\Phi}^{\Phi_2-\Phi} \int_{r=R_1}^{R_2} \int_{z=\vartheta_1}^{\vartheta_2} \frac{\sin\gamma \, dz \, dr \, d\gamma}{\sqrt{r^2 + R^2 - 2rR\cos\gamma + (Z-z)^2}},
$$
(3.139)

$$
A_\varphi(R,\Phi,Z)
= -\frac{\mu_0 C}{4\pi} \int_{\gamma=\Phi_1-\Phi}^{\Phi_2-\Phi} \int_{r=R_1}^{R_2} \int_{z=\vartheta_1}^{\vartheta_2} \frac{\cos\gamma \, dz \, dr \, d\gamma}{\sqrt{r^2 + R^2 - 2rR\cos\gamma + (Z-z)^2}},
$$
(3.140)

$$
A_z(R,\Phi,Z)
= -\frac{\mu_0 p C}{4\pi} \int_{\gamma=\Phi_1-\Phi}^{\Phi_2-\Phi} \int_{r=R_1}^{R_2} \int_{z=\vartheta_1}^{\vartheta_2} \frac{dz \, dr \, d\gamma}{\sqrt{r^2 + R^2 - 2rR\cos\gamma + (Z-z)^2}},
$$
(3.141)

$$
B_r(R,\Phi,Z)
= \frac{\mu_0 C}{4\pi} \cdot \int_{\gamma=\Phi_1-\Phi}^{\Phi_2-\Phi} \int_{r=R_1}^{R_2} \int_{z=\vartheta_1}^{\vartheta_2} \frac{(p\,r\sin\gamma - (z-Z)\cos\gamma)dz \, dr \, d\gamma}{[\sqrt{r^2 + R^2 - 2rR\cos\gamma + (Z-z)^2}]^3},
$$
(3.142)

$$
B_\varphi(R,\Phi,Z)
= \frac{\mu_0 C}{4\pi} \cdot \int_{\gamma=\Phi_1-\Phi}^{\Phi_2-\Phi} \int_{r=R_1}^{R_2} \int_{z=\vartheta_1}^{\vartheta_2} \frac{(p(R - r\cos\gamma) - (z-Z)\sin\gamma) \, dz \, dr \, d\gamma}{[\sqrt{r^2 + R^2 - 2rR\cos\gamma + (Z-z)^2}]^3},
$$
(3.143)

$$B_z(R, \Phi, Z)$$
$$= \frac{\mu_0 C}{4\pi} \cdot \int_{\gamma = \Phi_1 - \Phi}^{\Phi_2 - \Phi} \int_{r=R_1}^{R_2} \int_{z=\vartheta_1}^{\vartheta_2} \frac{(r - R\cos\gamma)\, dz\, dr\, d\gamma}{[\sqrt{r^2 + R^2 - 2rR\cos\gamma + (Z-z)^2}]^3} \,,$$

$$(3.144)$$

where

$$\vartheta_1 = pR_a(\gamma + \Phi - \Phi_1)\,,$$
$$\vartheta_2 = h + pR_a(\gamma + \Phi - \Phi_1)\,.$$

All these integrals can be calculated analytically with respect to variables r and z. Gradually we obtain

$$A_r(R, \Phi, Z) =$$
$$-\frac{\mu_0 C}{4\pi} \cdot [F_{\mathrm{ar}}(R_2, \vartheta_2) - F_{\mathrm{ar}}(R_1, \vartheta_2) - F_{\mathrm{ar}}(R_2, \vartheta_1) + F_{\mathrm{ar}}(R_1, \vartheta_1)]\,,$$

where

$$F_{\mathrm{ar}}(r, z) = \int_{\gamma = \Phi_1 - \Phi}^{\Phi_2 - \Phi} f_{\mathrm{ar}}(r, z) \sin\gamma \, d\gamma$$

and

$$f_{\mathrm{ar}}(r, z) = (r - R\cos\gamma)\ln(z - Z + \sqrt{r^2 + R^2 - 2rR\cos\gamma + (Z-z)^2}\,)$$
$$+ (z - Z)\ln(r - R\cos\gamma + \sqrt{r^2 + R^2 - 2rR\cos\gamma + (Z-z)^2}\,)$$
$$- R\sin\gamma \arctan \frac{(r - R\cos\gamma)(z - Z)}{R\sin\gamma\sqrt{r^2 + R^2 - 2rR\cos\gamma + (Z-z)^2}}\,,$$

$$(3.145)$$

$$A_\varphi(R, \Phi, Z)$$
$$= \frac{\mu_0 C}{4\pi} \cdot [F_{\mathrm{af}}(R_2, \vartheta_2) - F_{\mathrm{af}}(R_1, \vartheta_2) - F_{\mathrm{af}}(R_2, \vartheta_1) + F_{\mathrm{af}}(R_1, \vartheta_1)]\,,$$

where

$$F_{\mathrm{af}}(r, z) = \int_{\gamma = \Phi_1 - \Phi}^{\Phi_2 - \Phi} f_{\mathrm{af}}(r, z) \cos\gamma \, d\gamma$$

and

$$
\begin{aligned}
f_{\mathrm{af}}(r, z) =\ & (r - R\cos\gamma) \ln(z - Z + \sqrt{r^2 + R^2 - 2rR\cos\gamma + (Z - z)^2}\,) \\
& + (z - Z) \ln(r - R\cos\gamma + \sqrt{r^2 + R^2 - 2rR\cos\gamma + (Z - z)^2}\,) \\
& - R\sin\gamma \arctan \frac{(r - R\cos\gamma)(z - Z)}{R\sin\gamma\sqrt{r^2 + R^2 - 2rR\cos\gamma + (Z - z)^2}}\,,
\end{aligned}
$$

$$(3.146)$$

$$
\begin{aligned}
& A_z(R, \Phi, Z) \\
& = \frac{\mu_0 pC}{4\pi} \cdot [F_{\mathrm{az}}(R_2, \vartheta_2) - F_{\mathrm{az}}(R_1, \vartheta_2) - F_{\mathrm{az}}(R_2, \vartheta_1) + F_{\mathrm{az}}(R_1, \vartheta_1)]\,,
\end{aligned}
$$

where

$$
F_{\mathrm{az}}(r, z) = \int_{\gamma=\Phi_1-\Phi}^{\Phi_2-\Phi} f_{\mathrm{az}}(r, z)\,\mathrm{d}\gamma
$$

and

$$
\begin{aligned}
f_{\mathrm{az}}(r, z) =\ & (r - R\cos\gamma) \ln(z - Z + \sqrt{r^2 + R^2 - 2rR\cos\gamma + (Z - z)^2}\,) \\
& + (z - Z) \ln(r - R\cos\gamma + \sqrt{r^2 + R^2 - 2rR\cos\gamma + (Z - z)^2}\,) \\
& - R\sin\gamma \arctan \frac{(r - R\cos\gamma)(z - Z)}{R\sin\gamma\sqrt{r^2 + R^2 - 2rR\cos\gamma + (Z - z)^2}}\,,
\end{aligned}
$$

$$(3.147)$$

$$
\begin{aligned}
& B_r(R, \Phi, Z) \\
& = \frac{\mu_0 C}{4\pi} \cdot [F_{\mathrm{br}}(R_2, \vartheta_2) - F_{\mathrm{br}}(R_1, \vartheta_2) - F_{\mathrm{br}}(R_2, \vartheta_1) + F_{\mathrm{br}}(R_1, \vartheta_1)]\,,
\end{aligned}
$$

where

$$
F_{\mathrm{br}}(r, z) = \int_{\gamma=\Phi_1-\Phi}^{\Phi_2-\Phi} f_{\mathrm{br}}(r, z)\,\mathrm{d}\gamma
$$

and

$$
\begin{aligned}
f_{\mathrm{br}}(r, z) =\ & -p\sin\gamma \ln(z - Z + \sqrt{r^2 + R^2 - 2rR\cos\gamma + (Z - z)^2}\,) \\
& + \cos\gamma \ln(r - R\cos\gamma + \sqrt{r^2 + R^2 - 2rR\cos\gamma + (Z - z)^2}\,) \\
& + p\cos\gamma \arctan \frac{(r - R\cos\gamma)(z - Z)}{R\sin\gamma\sqrt{r^2 + R^2 - 2rR\cos\gamma + (Z - z)^2}}\,,
\end{aligned}
$$

$$(3.148)$$

$$B_\varphi(R, \Phi, Z)$$
$$= \frac{\mu_0 C}{4\pi} \cdot [F_{\mathrm{bf}}(R_2, \vartheta_2) - F_{\mathrm{bf}}(R_1, \vartheta_2) - F_{\mathrm{bf}}(R_2, \vartheta_1) + F_{\mathrm{bf}}(R_1, \vartheta_1)],$$

where

$$F_{\mathrm{bf}}(r, z) = \int_{\gamma = \Phi_1 - \Phi}^{\Phi_2 - \Phi} f_{\mathrm{bf}}(r, z)\, \mathrm{d}\gamma$$

and

$$\begin{aligned}
f_{\mathrm{bf}}(r, z) &= p \cos\gamma \ln(z - Z + \sqrt{r^2 + R^2 - 2rR\cos\gamma + (Z - z)^2}) \\
&+ \sin\gamma \ln(r - R\cos\gamma + \sqrt{r^2 + R^2 - 2rR\cos\gamma + (Z - z)^2}) \\
&+ p \sin\gamma \arctan \frac{(r - R\cos\gamma)(z - Z)}{R\sin\gamma\sqrt{r^2 + R^2 - 2rR\cos\gamma + (Z - z)^2}},
\end{aligned}$$

$$(3.149)$$

$$B_z(R, \Phi, Z)$$
$$= \frac{\mu_0 C}{4\pi} \cdot [F_{\mathrm{bz}}(R_2, \vartheta_2) - F_{\mathrm{bz}}(R_1, \vartheta_2) - F_{\mathrm{bz}}(R_2, \vartheta_1) + F_{\mathrm{bz}}(R_1, \vartheta_1)],$$

where

$$F_{\mathrm{bz}}(r, z) = \int_{\gamma = \Phi_1 - \Phi}^{\Phi_2 - \Phi} f_{\mathrm{bz}}(r, z)\, \mathrm{d}\gamma$$

and

$$f_{\mathrm{bz}}(r, z) = -\ln(z - Z + \sqrt{r^2 + R^2 - 2rR\cos\gamma + (Z - z)^2}). \qquad (3.150)$$

The last integrals in (3.145)–(3.150) with respect to γ cannot be calculated analytically. Nevertheless, all integrands are relatively simple and continuous functions of γ and their numerical integration (see Appendix C) causes no difficulties.

For an illustration we will present some results obtained for the following parameters (the influence of feeding conductors being neglected):

- arrangement (see Fig. 3.43) with 3.5 turns,

- $R_1 = 0.1$ m, $R_2 = 0.11$ m, $h = 0.02$ m, $\tan\psi = 0.1$, and

- $I = 1000$ A.

We calculated the distribution of function rA_φ (this function gives not an exact, but a relatively good idea about the magnetic field of the coil in planes $\Phi = $ const) for angles $\Phi = 0°$, $\Phi = 90°$, $\Phi = 180°$, and $\Phi = 270°$. The results are depicted in Figs. 3.45 and 3.46.

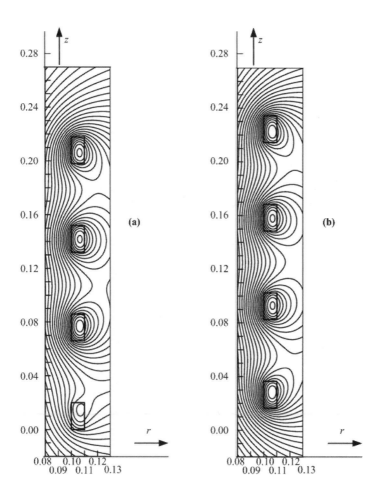

Figure 3.45.   Distribution of function $r A_\varphi$ in the vicinity of the turns of the coil: (**a**) $\Phi = 0°$, **b**) $\Phi = 90°$.

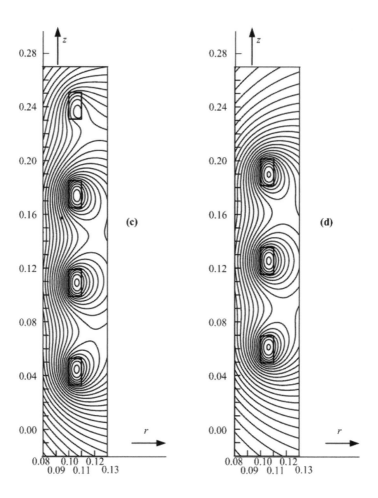

Figure 3.46.   Distribution of function rA_φ in the vicinity of the turns of the coil: (**c**) $\Phi = 180°$, (**d**) $\Phi = 270°$.

CHAPTER 4

INTEGRAL AND INTEGRODIFFERENTIAL METHODS

In this chapter we present and illustrate by examples several integral and integrodifferential methods suitable for the direct solution of static and low-frequency electromagnetic fields in linear and homogeneous (at least by parts) media.

4.1 INTEGRAL VERSUS DIFFERENTIAL MODELS

In principle, problems of the above type can always be tackled by means of differential methods. However, these methods are very sensitive to the quality of meshes, which, moreover, have to match very accurately the geometry of all subdomains as well as all material interfaces. Mesh generation is extremely time consuming when working with complicated 3D geometries (see, e.g., Fig. 4.1 that depicts an inductor for induction heating of large metal bodies).

If such 3D geometry, in addition, is time dependent (e.g., if some part of the computational arrangement is moving), the differential approach may simply get out of hand.

It is worth realizing that differential methods always need to truncate the infinite space to a finite computational domain, which in turn requires the employment of some artificial boundary conditions. A number of nontrivial techniques have been proposed to deal with the boundary truncation in finite difference and finite element methods (FEMs). One of them, based on the one-way wave equation, is called the Engquist–Majda absorbing boundary conditions (ABCs) [100]. Researchers have also combined FEM with the method of moments (MOM) to come up with a hybrid modeling scheme [101]. In these hybrid methods, the FEM is applied inside the volume of interest and the MOM is applied on the surface.

Integral Methods in Low-Frequency Electromagnetics. By I. Doležel, P. Karban, and P. Šolín.
Copyright © 2009 John Wiley & Sons, Inc.

Figure 4.1.   Meshing can become tedious with complicated 3D geometries.

Finite thickness absorbing layers have also been investigated. Recently, Berenger [102] introduced a novel and efficient method, called the perfectly matched layer (PML) method. This provides a reflectionless interface between the region of interest and the PMLs at all incident angles. The layers themselves are lossy, so that after a few layers the wave is significantly attenuated. Berenger formulated the PMLs for use in the finite difference time domain (FDTD) techniques. Sacks and other researchers adapted the PML concept to the FEM [103].

In contrast to differential methods, integral approaches do not require artificial boundaries and usually they require much less meshing. Typically, their primary objective is the distribution of the field sources such as electric charge density or density of electric currents in linear and homogeneous (at least by parts) systems. The distribution of the electromagnetic field is then found in a next step using standard relations such as integral expressions.

Historically, probably the first monograph on integral methods in electromagnetism [112] was written by Harrington in 1960 (its second and third extended editions appeared much later—in the 1980s and 1990s). The book contains the general formulations for integral equations describing the distribution of the source quantities (charges and currents). Nevertheless, its key parts are devoted to higher frequencies (particularly in connection with scattering) and only limited attention is paid to the problems of static or slowly time-varying electromagnetic fields.

The first practical computations of low-frequency eddy currents based on integral methods appeared only in the 1970s and 1980s. The reason was that the state-of-the-art of numerical methods for integral equations, together with the lack of efficient methods for processing linear algebraic systems with dense matrices, did not allow one to fully exploit their potential. Worth mentioning from that time are three pioneering papers–Refs. 113–115. The first one deals with the numerical solution of eddy currents in 2D electrically conductive structures. The 2D domain is here replaced by a network consisting of current carrying line elements. This representation leads to the substitution of Kirchhoff's laws for Maxwell's equations. For obtaining the time evolution of eddy currents the nodal and loop equations are solved repeatedly, at discrete time levels. The second paper solves harmonic currents in 2D Cartesian structures containing systems of thin conductors. The mathematical model is formulated on the basis of second-kind Fredholm's integral equations. This model is supplemented with the condition of the total current in every conductor. The last paper extends the methodology to 3D structures. Nevertheless, the authors work with conductors whose thicknesses are substantially smaller than the depth of penetration, so that the current is supposed to flow only along their surfaces. That is why the case is, in fact, also two-dimensional.

Typical is also a cluster of papers (from the 1980s and 1990s) of Greek origin [116–120] and several others. These papers deal with modeling of eddy currents in systems of long conductors (that are either filamentary or of circular cross section) with shielding elements in the form of concentric or nonconcentric, well electrically conductive pipes of various thicknesses. Partial problems were mostly solved by combinations of analytical and numerical methods, somewhere also with integral formulations for harmonic quantities.

The only integral technique that became relatively very popular in 1980s and 1990s was the boundary element method (BEM). This technique is based on Green's identity and works with a free-space Green's function that depends on the system of coordinates used. The BEM can be used for solution of specific 2D and 3D problems described mostly by Laplace's, Poisson's, or Helmholtz' equation. The technique consists of two steps. The first one solves Dirichlet's and Neumann's (or mixed) conditions along the boundary (this solution is described by a specific second-kind Fredholm integral equation) while the second step provides the distribution of the required quantity in the interior of the definition area that is determined by means of integral expressions.

In the course of years a lot of versions of this technique have appeared that were intended either for independent use or for applications in combination with other existing numerical methods such as the FEM. More information about the method (and relevant references) will be given in Chapter 5.

Nowadays, development of integral and integrodifferential methods in electromagnetism continues, but mainly in the field of higher frequencies and scattering. Available are several monographs, proceedings, and a number of papers [121–127]. In the area of static, quasistatic, or low-frequency electromagnetism the progress is somewhat slower, but research continues. Available is one monograph covering some topics [128] and a group of papers that may approximately be divided into three groups:

- Research in the area of nonstandard mathematical procedures and algorithms in integral methods and evaluation of their properties and capabilities. For example, Albanese et al. [129] compare the properties of differential and integral formulations for solution of transients with eddy currents. A special method suggested by the authors transfers the problem of eddy currents in nonlinear medium into another problem of analyzing an equivalent electric network (which means, that, in fact, no "classical" integral method is used for its solution). Tsukerman [130] focuses on the stability of the MOM in electromagnetism. The method is here understood in a narrower sense, just for the computation of the field sources—distribution of charge density or current density. The principal focus is on the distribution of charge on the surfaces of conductors, which is a problem characterized by ill posedness. The author investigates how the method is applicable for solving ill-posed problems, what limitations the method brings, and how these limitations can be reduced by using appropriate regularization techniques. The work contains several interesting conclusions and results validated by the FEM. Maouche and Féliachi [131] describe a discretized integral method for solution of eddy currents in an axisymmetric arrangement with motion that was tested on the problem of electromagnetic forming. Rubinacci et al. [132] deal with the possibility of effective solution of linear systems described by dense matrices by means of methods based on the multipole expansion and wavelet transform.

- Improvement and acceleration of semianalytical or numerical computations of very complicated (mostly multiple) definite integrals occurring in the algorithms for numerical solution of the integral equations. Even when this is a mathematical domain, relevant papers may be found even in engineering journals. For an illustration, Lean and Wexler [133] deal with the improvement of Gauss' integration that consists in shifting of Gauss' points by means of a nonlinear polynomial transform of odd order, allowing the integration of singular kernel $1/r$ on generally curved surfaces. The algorithm is demonstrated on an example of transient scattering of an electromagnetic wave.

- Application of selected integral algorithms for solution of particular technical problems. Lei et al. [134] focus on an integral analysis of magnetic field generated by a coil of an arbitrary shape in the vicinity of a conductor of rectangular cross section. The paper also contains a number of recommendations concerning treatment of singularities occurring in some definite integrals (they are determined as limits of certain functions at prescribed points). Kwon et al. [135] present another integral method consisting in the application of Coulomb's calibration condition on the integral expression for magnetic vector potential. The algorithm is applied to an electrically conductive parallelepiped of rectangular cross section in which the eddy currents are generated by an external harmonic magnetic field. Interesting also is the paper by Ciric and Curiac [136], which presents an integral equation for analysis of eddy currents induced in a massive conductor. The magnetic vector potential inside the conductor is expressed by means of unknown current density on its surface, while outside the conductor it can be found from the solution of Laplace's equation. Finally, Gagnoud [137] applies selected integral techniques to the numerical simulation of levitation melting of nonmagnetic metals.

Even when the papers mentioned in the previous paragraphs bring a lot of interesting knowledge, the theory of integral methods in electromagnetics cannot be considered finished. For example, development in the area of adaptive integral methods of higher orders of accuracy in the near future may become a powerful and reliable tool for investigation of some types of electromagnetic fields.

Integral models typically are based on the following assumptions:

- The solved arrangement consists of (piecewise) linear materials and (piecewise) homogeneous media.

- The total electric charge Q is only distributed on the surface of objects (not in the interior).

- The charge density σ produces the same electric potential φ at every point of the surface.

The solutions to integral equations typically are very smooth; complications only can occur at singular points (such as sharp reentrant corners or edges) where the charge density σ (as well as the electric field strength $|E|$) may grow to infinity. Besides the computation of electric fields produced by charged bodies, another major application of integral techniques is the computation of the distribution of eddy currents in linear homogeneous systems, particularly when their individual subregions are geometrically incommensurable and/or subject to motion. The application of integral techniques leads to Fredholm's integral equations of the second kind or to more complex integrodifferential equations.

4.2 THEORETICAL FOUNDATIONS

In this section we provide some theoretical background for integral techniques whose selected applications to practical problems will be presented in the next sections of this chapter.

4.2.1 Electrostatic fields produced by charged bodies

Consider a system of n electrically conductive bodies $\Omega_1, \Omega_2, \ldots, \Omega_n$ depicted in Fig. 4.2. The bodies carry charges $Q_1, Q_2, \ldots, Q_n$ and may be subject to motion. The task is to find the following at any given time instant:

- the distribution of charge on their surfaces,

- the distribution of electric field that they produce, and

- Coulomb's forces acting on every one of them.

To begin with, let us determine the electric potential φ at an arbitrary exterior or surface point X. The potential $\varphi(X)$ is given by

$$\varphi(X) = \frac{1}{4\pi\varepsilon_0} \sum_{i=1}^{n} \int_{S_i} \frac{\sigma_i}{r_{X,i}} \, dS_i + \varphi_0 \,, \tag{4.1}$$

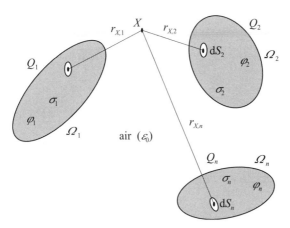

Figure 4.2.   The investigated system of charged bodies.

where the symbol S_i denotes the boundary of Ω_i with surface charge density $\sigma_i, i = 1, 2, \ldots, n$. Furthermore, $r_{X,i}$ stands for the distance between point X and an integration point of the ith surface and φ_0 is a constant.

In the next step we will find the charge distribution on the surfaces of all bodies $\Omega_1, \Omega_2, \ldots, \Omega_n$. Using the fact that the surface of any perfectly electrically conductive body is an equipotential area, for any point $X_j \in S_j$ we obtain a system of first-kind Fredholm's integral equations,

$$\varphi(X_j) = \varphi_j = \frac{1}{4\pi\varepsilon_0} \sum_{i=1}^{n} \int_{S_i} \frac{\sigma_i}{r_{X_j,i}} \, dS_i + \varphi_0 , \quad j = 1, 2, \ldots, n . \tag{4.2}$$

However, the potentials $\varphi(X_j)$ are not known in advance. Therefore, system (4.2) has to be supplemented with additional conditions for the total charges $Q_1, Q_2, \ldots, Q_n$ on the surfaces of the bodies $\Omega_1, \Omega_2, \ldots, \Omega_n$,

$$\int_{S_i} \sigma_i \, dS_i = Q_i , \quad i = 1, 2, \ldots, n . \tag{4.3}$$

After solving (4.2) and (4.3) we are able to compute $\varphi(X)$ via (4.1).

Finally, Coulomb's force $\mathbf{F}_j$ acting on the body Ω_j in the system can be calculated using the formula

$$\mathbf{F}_j = \frac{1}{4\pi\varepsilon_0} \sum_{i=1}^{n} \int_{S_j} \int_{S_i} \frac{\sigma_j \sigma_i}{r_{j,i}^3} \mathbf{r}_{j,i} \, dS_i \, dS_j , \quad j = 1, 2, \ldots, n . \tag{4.4}$$

4.2.2   Eddy currents in linear homogeneous systems

Let us consider a linear system consisting of n electrically conductive elements Ω_j, $j = 1, 2, \ldots, n$ of arbitrary shapes (see Fig. 4.3) carrying external field currents $i_j(t)$, $j = 1, 2, \ldots, n$ of general time dependence. Some of these currents may be zero. All elements in the system can move at arbitrary velocities $\mathbf{v}_j(t)$, $j = 1, 2, \ldots, n$.

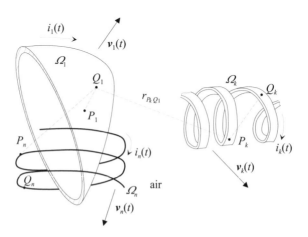

Figure 4.3.   General system of current carrying bodies with moving parts.

The nonstationary magnetic field produced by field currents $i_j(t)$ generates eddy currents in every electrically conductive part of the system. We are interested in the time evolution of the following quantities:

- current densities in Ω_j, $j = 1, 2, \ldots, n$,

- specific and total Joule losses in Ω_j, $j = 1, 2, \ldots, n$,

- specific and total dynamic forces acting on Ω_j, $j = 1, 2, \ldots, n$, and

- magnetic field in the system.

Knowledge of these quantities is essential for further thermal, mechanical, and other computations, for example continual induction heating of nonmagnetic metal bodies and behavior of massive conductors in multiphase systems during short circuits.

This problem can be solved via the magnetic vector potential $\boldsymbol{A}$. The value $\boldsymbol{A}(Q_j, t)$ is given by the superposition of components produced by instantaneous current densities in all involved elements Ω_j, $j = 1, 2, \ldots, n$ (see Fig. 4.3), and the component $\boldsymbol{A}_{j0}(t)$, which is an unknown function of time. Using the linearity of the system, we can write

$$\boldsymbol{A}(Q_j, t) = \frac{\mu_0}{4\pi} \sum_{i=1}^{n} \int_{\Omega_i} \frac{\boldsymbol{J}_i(P_i, t) \cdot dV_i}{r_{P_i Q_j}(t)} + \boldsymbol{A}_{j0}(t) . \tag{4.5}$$

Here, the symbol $\boldsymbol{J}_i(P_i, t)$ stands for the vector of total current density at the integration point $P_i \in \Omega_i$ and time t, and $r_{P_i Q_j}(t)$ is the distance between the reference point Q_j and the point of integration P_i (Fig. 4.3 depicts such a distance between the points Q_1 and P_k). The total current density $\boldsymbol{J}_i(P_i, t)$ in the ith element consists of the uniform current density $\boldsymbol{J}_{\text{ext},i}(P_i, t)$ delivered from the corresponding external current source and eddy current density $\boldsymbol{J}_{\text{eddy},i}(P_i, t)$. If there is no external source, then $\boldsymbol{J}_{\text{ext},i}(P_i, t) = \boldsymbol{0}$.

Maxwell's equation

$$\text{curl } \boldsymbol{E} = -\frac{d\boldsymbol{B}}{dt} = -\frac{d}{dt}(\text{curl } \boldsymbol{A})$$

yields

$$\boldsymbol{E} = -\frac{d\boldsymbol{A}}{dt} - \text{grad } \varphi + \boldsymbol{g}(t) , \tag{4.6}$$

where φ is any scalar function of spatial coordinates (usually interpreted as electrical potential) and $\boldsymbol{g}(t)$ is any vector-valued function of time. As no element is supposed to be connected to any supplementary source of electric field strength (e.g., of thermoelectric or electrochemical origin), we put $\boldsymbol{g}(t) = \boldsymbol{0}$. Electric field strength in all elements is then only given by the source value and time variation of the vector potential $\boldsymbol{A}$. The vector of eddy current density $\boldsymbol{J}_{\text{eddy},j}$, $j = 1, 2, \ldots, n$ can be obtained from

$$\boldsymbol{J}_{\text{eddy},j}(Q_j, t) = \boldsymbol{J}_j(Q_j, t) - \boldsymbol{J}_{\text{ext},j}(t) = -\gamma_j \boldsymbol{E}(Q_j, t) = -\gamma_j \cdot \frac{d\boldsymbol{A}(Q_j, t)}{dt} ,$$

$$j = 1, 2, \ldots, n, \quad (4.7)$$

where γ_j denotes the electrical conductivity of element Ω_j. The substitution for $\boldsymbol{A}(Q_j, t)$ from (4.5) leads to

$$\boldsymbol{J}_j(Q_j, t) + \frac{\mu_0 \gamma_j}{4\pi} \cdot \frac{\mathrm{d}}{\mathrm{d}t} \sum_{i=1}^{n} \int_{\Omega_i} \frac{\boldsymbol{J}_i(P_i, t) \cdot \mathrm{d}V_i}{r_{P_i Q_j}(t)} - \boldsymbol{J}_{\mathrm{ext}, j}(t) + \gamma_j \frac{\mathrm{d}\boldsymbol{A}_{j,0}(t)}{\mathrm{d}t} = \boldsymbol{0},$$

$$j = 1, 2, \ldots, n.$$

This formula can be further modified as follows:

$$\boldsymbol{J}_j(Q_j, t) + \frac{\mu_0 \gamma_j}{4\pi} \cdot \frac{\mathrm{d}}{\mathrm{d}t} \sum_{i=1}^{n} \int_{\Omega_i} \frac{\boldsymbol{J}_i(P_i, t) \cdot \mathrm{d}V_i}{r_{P_i Q_j}(t)} + \boldsymbol{J}_{j0}(t) = \boldsymbol{0}, \quad j = 1, 2, \ldots, n, \quad (4.8)$$

where

$$\boldsymbol{J}_{j0}(t) = -\boldsymbol{J}_{\mathrm{ext}, j}(t) + \gamma_j \frac{\mathrm{d}\boldsymbol{A}_{j,0}(t)}{\mathrm{d}t}$$

is an unknown function of time. This function can be determined from the following condition of the total current in the jth part Ω_j:

$$\int_{S_j} \boldsymbol{J}_j(Q_j, t) \, \mathrm{d}S_j = i_j(t), \quad j = 1, 2, \ldots, n, \quad (4.9)$$

the integration being carried out over a suitable cross section S_j of Ω_j. If the jth body carries no source current, the condition (4.9) is not prescribed and in such a case the last term in (4.8)—$\boldsymbol{J}_{j0}(t)$—vanishes.

Let us return to (4.8) once more. After performing the derivative in the second term on the left-hand side, we obtain

$$\boldsymbol{J}_j(Q_j, t) + \frac{\mu_0 \gamma_j}{4\pi} \cdot \sum_{i=1}^{n} \int_{\Omega_i} \frac{\mathrm{d}\boldsymbol{J}_i(P_i, t)}{\mathrm{d}t} \cdot \frac{\mathrm{d}V_i}{r_{P_i Q_j}(t)}$$

$$- \frac{\mu_0 \gamma_j}{4\pi} \cdot \sum_{i=1}^{n} \int_{\Omega_i} \frac{\left(\boldsymbol{v}_{ij}(t) \cdot \boldsymbol{r}_{P_i Q_j}(t)\right) \boldsymbol{J}_i(P_i, t) \mathrm{d}V_i}{r_{P_i Q_j}^3(t)} + \boldsymbol{J}_{j0}(t) = \boldsymbol{0}, \quad j = 1, 2, \ldots, n, \quad (4.10)$$

where $\boldsymbol{v}_{ij}(t) = \boldsymbol{v}_i(t) - \boldsymbol{v}_j(t)$ and $\boldsymbol{r}_{P_i Q_j}(t) = \boldsymbol{r}_{P_i}(t) - \boldsymbol{r}_{Q_j}(t)$. The second and third terms on the left-hand side denote the components of eddy currents due to transformation and motion, respectively.

System (4.10) supplemented with condition (4.9) provides the time dependence of current densities $\boldsymbol{J}_j$. The specific and total Joule losses w_J and $W_{\mathrm{J}j}(t)$ in the jth body and specific dynamic forces $\boldsymbol{f}_j(Q_j, t)$ acting on it can be determined as follows:

$$w_{\mathrm{J}j}(Q_j, t) = \frac{\boldsymbol{J}_j^2(Q_j, t)}{\gamma_j}, \quad W_{\mathrm{J}j}(t) = \int_{\Omega_j} w_{\mathrm{J}j}(Q_j, t) \mathrm{d}V_j, \quad (4.11)$$

$$\boldsymbol{f}_j(Q_j, t) = \boldsymbol{J}_j(Q_j, t) \times \boldsymbol{B}_j(Q_j, t) = \boldsymbol{J}_j(Q_j, t) \times \mathrm{curl}_j\left(\boldsymbol{A}(Q_j, t)\right). \quad (4.12)$$

After substituting for $\boldsymbol{A}(Q_j, t)$ from (4.5), the total force $\boldsymbol{F}_j(t)$ can be expressed as

$$
\begin{aligned}
\boldsymbol{F}_j(t) &= \int_{\Omega_j} \boldsymbol{f}_j(Q_j, t) \mathrm{d}V_j \\
&= \frac{\mu_0}{4\pi} \int_{\Omega_j} \boldsymbol{J}_j(Q_j, t) \times \left(\sum_{i=1}^{n} \int_{\Omega_i} \mathrm{curl}_j \left[\frac{\boldsymbol{J}_i(P_i, t)}{r_{P_i Q_j}(t)} \right] \mathrm{d}V_i \right) \mathrm{d}V_j .
\end{aligned} \tag{4.13}
$$

The symbol curl_j stands for curl carried out with respect to the coordinates of the reference point Q_j.

4.2.3 Planar and axisymmetric arrangements

In this section let us extend the previous results to planar arrangements in the x, y coordinate system and axisymmetric arrangements in the r, z coordinate system.

First, consider the planar system depicted in Fig. 4.4.

In order to solve the problem, first we need to find the distribution of the current density $\boldsymbol{J}$ over the cross section S of a long massive conductor carrying a time-variable current $i(t)$, as shown in Fig. 4.5. The electrical conductivity of the massive conductor is γ.

In this case, both the current density $\boldsymbol{J}$ and vector potential $\boldsymbol{A}$ have only one nonzero component in the z-direction (J_z and A_z, respectively). Consider a thin filament $\mathrm{d}S$ of the conductor that carries an elementary current $\mathrm{d}i = J_z \mathrm{d}S$. The elementary current $\mathrm{d}i$

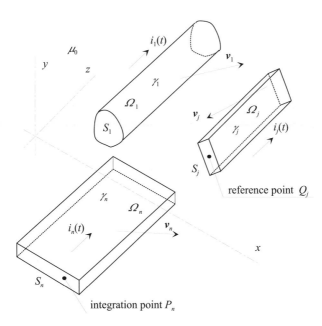

Figure 4.4. Current carrying bodies with moving parts in the x, y coordinate system.

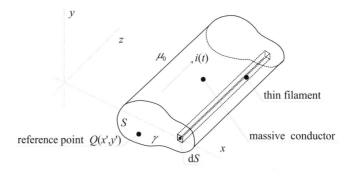

Figure 4.5.   Long single massive conductor carrying time-variable current.

produces at a reference point $Q(x', y')$ a magnetic field $\boldsymbol{B}$ with components

$$dB_x(x', y') = \frac{\mu_0 J_z(x, y)dS}{2\pi} \cdot \frac{y - y'}{(x - x')^2 + (y - y')^2} = \frac{\partial dA_z(x', y')}{\partial y'},$$

$$dB_y(x', y') = -\frac{\mu_0 J_z(x, y)dS}{2\pi} \cdot \frac{x - x'}{(x - x')^2 + (y - y')^2} = -\frac{\partial dA_z(x', y')}{\partial x'}, \quad (4.14)$$

and thus

$$A_z(x', y') = -\frac{\mu_0}{4\pi} \int_S J_z(x, y) \ln[(x - x')^2 + (y - y')^2]dS + A_{0z}. \quad (4.15)$$

This holds for any time t.

The same result can be obtained alternatively. The magnetic flux density $\boldsymbol{B}$ (which only has a nonzero tangential component B_α) near a current (I) carrying filament in nonmagnetic media (see Fig. 4.6) is expressed as

$$B_\alpha(r) = \frac{\mu_0 I}{2\pi r}. \quad (4.16)$$

As in an axisymmetric arrangement,

$$B_\alpha(r) = -\frac{\partial A_z}{\partial r}, \quad (4.17)$$

we immediately obtain

$$A_z(r) = -\int B_\alpha(r)\, dr = -\frac{\mu_0 I}{2\pi} \ln r + A_{0z}. \quad (4.18)$$

For massive conductors we have to substitute for $I = \int J_z\, dS$. After inserting $\ln r$ into this integral, we obtain (4.15) again.

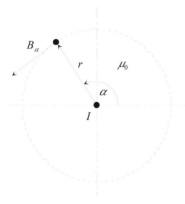

Figure 4.6. Magnetic flux density near a long thin current carrying conductor.

According to (4.7), for the component of eddy current density produced by time variation of magnetic field it holds that

$$J_{z,\text{eddy}} = J_z - J_{z,\text{ext}} = -\gamma \cdot \frac{\mathrm{d}A_z}{\mathrm{d}t} \,. \tag{4.19}$$

Therefore, after combining with (4.15), we obtain

$$J_z - J_{z,\text{ext}} - \gamma \cdot \frac{\mathrm{d}}{\mathrm{d}t}\left(\frac{\mu_0}{4\pi}\int_S J_z(x,y)\ln[(x-x')^2 + (y-y')^2]\mathrm{d}S + A_{0z}\right) = 0\,.$$

This can be further rewritten into

$$-J_z + \frac{\mu_0\gamma}{4\pi}\cdot\frac{\mathrm{d}}{\mathrm{d}t}\int_S J_z(x,y)\ln[(x-x')^2 + (y-y')^2]\mathrm{d}S + J_{0z} = 0\,, \tag{4.20}$$

which is similar to (4.8). Finally, after performing the time derivative in a system with n conductors (Fig. 4.4) which can move with respect to one another, one obtains a direct analogue to (4.10),

$$-J_{zj}(Q_j,t) + \frac{\mu_0\gamma_j}{2\pi}\cdot\left(\sum_{i=1}^n \int_{S_i} \frac{\mathrm{d}J_{zi}(P_i,t)}{\mathrm{d}t}\cdot\ln[r_{P_iQ_j}(t)]\,\mathrm{d}S\right)$$

$$+\frac{\mu_0\gamma_j}{2\pi}\cdot\left(\sum_{i=1}^n \int_{S_i} J_{zi}(P_i,t)\cdot\frac{\mathbf{v}_{ij}(t)\cdot\mathbf{r}_{P_iQ_j}(t)}{r_{P_iQ_j}^2(t)}\cdot\mathrm{d}S\right) + J_{zj0}(t) = 0\,,$$

$$j = 1, 2, \ldots, n\,. \tag{4.21}$$

Here, all symbols have the same meaning as in (4.10). The indirect condition used to determine the unknowns $J_{zj0}(t), j = 1, 2, \ldots, n$ is analogous to (4.9).

Next, let us look at the axisymmetric case depicted in Fig. 4.7. This time we can use formula (4.10) again, taking into account that both the current density $\mathbf{J}$ and the vector potential $\mathbf{A}$ only have a nonzero tangential component (J_φ and A_φ, respectively).

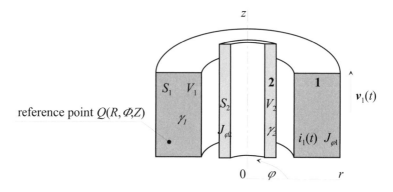

Figure 4.7.   Current carrying bodies with moving parts in the r, z coordinate system.

4.3   STATIC AND HARMONIC PROBLEMS IN ONE DIMENSION

In the previous section we derived continuous integral/integrodifferential models for the distribution of field sources (surface charge densities and eddy current densities) in linear homogeneous systems. Knowledge of these quantities is needed in order to determine the field distribution and other quantities that are necessary for subsequent mechanical and thermal calculations. Now we will employ these models to solve selected practical problems.

We begin with three typical one-dimensional examples: An electric field produced by a charged thin ring, distribution of the current density along the radius of a harmonic current carrying massive conductor of circular cross section and the distribution of the current density in a long circular system consisting of a harmonic current carrying massive hollow cylindrical conductor—a coaxial shielding pipe.

4.3.1   Electric field of a thin charged circular ring

Perfectly conductive rings of small thickness play an important role in various applications. Such a ring of internal radius R_1 and external radius R_2, carrying a charge Q, is depicted in Fig. 4.8. The task is to find the following:

- the distribution of the charge density on the ring and

- the electric field surrounding the ring.

Since the ring is a perfect conductor, the electric potential on this surface is constant. Thus, using (4.2), for any point $M(R, \alpha, 0)$, $R_1 \leq R \leq R_2, 0 \leq \alpha < 2\pi$ we can write

$$\varphi(M) = \frac{1}{4\pi\varepsilon_0} \int_S \frac{\sigma}{l} \, \mathrm{d}S + \varphi_0 \,, \tag{4.22}$$

where the charge density σ satisfies the additional condition

$$Q = \int_S \sigma \, \mathrm{d}S \,. \tag{4.23}$$

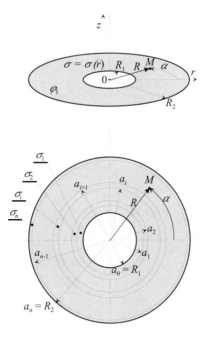

Figure 4.8.   Geometry of the thin circular ring.

Here, the symbol S stands for the surface of the ring, l is the distance between M and a general integration point, and φ_0 is an arbitrary constant (which can be set to zero without loss of generality). Due to the axial symmetry of the ring, the charge density σ is a function of the radius r only. Hence, (4.22) yields

$$\varphi(M) = \frac{1}{4\pi\varepsilon_0} \int_{\alpha=0}^{2\pi} \int_{r=R_1}^{R_2} \frac{r \cdot \sigma(r)}{\sqrt{r^2 + R^2 - 2rR\cos\alpha}} \, dr \, d\alpha + \varphi_0 \,. \tag{4.24}$$

The first-kind Fredholm integral equation (4.24) with the supplementary condition (4.23) is approximated numerically in the following way.

Let the ring be divided into n subrings with internal radii a_{j-1} and external radii a_j, $j = 1, 2, \ldots, n$ (see Fig. 4.8). We select reference points M_i, $i = 1, 2, \ldots, n$ corresponding to the radii $b_i = (a_{i-1} + a_i)/2$, $i = 1, 2, \ldots, n$. At each point M_i we have $\varphi(M_i) = \varphi$. Relations (4.24) and (4.23) can be approximated by the discrete system

$$(\varphi - \varphi_0)\frac{4\pi\varepsilon_0}{Q} = K = \sum_{j=1}^{n} \frac{\sigma_j}{Q} \int_{\alpha=0}^{2\pi} \int_{r=a_{j-1}}^{a_j} \frac{r}{\sqrt{r^2 + b_i^2 - 2rb_i\cos\alpha}} \, dr \, d\alpha \,,$$

$$i = 1, 2, \ldots, n, \tag{4.25}$$

$$\pi \sum_{j=1}^{n} (a_j^2 - a_{j-1}^2)\frac{\sigma_j}{Q} = 1 \,. \tag{4.26}$$

The unknowns are the constant K and the values of σ_j/Q, $j = 1, 2, \ldots, n$. System (4.25) and (4.26) can be written in matrix form:

$$\mathbf{S}\mathbf{L} = \mathbf{P}, \tag{4.27}$$

where $\mathbf{S}$ is a square matrix of rank $n + 1$ with entries

$$s_{ij} = \int_{\alpha=0}^{2\pi} \int_{r=a_{j-1}}^{a_j} \frac{r}{\sqrt{r^2 + b_i^2 - 2rb_i \cos \alpha}} \, dr \, d\alpha, \quad i, j = 1, 2, \ldots, n,$$

$$s_{i,n+1} = -1, \quad i = 1, 2, \ldots, n, \quad s_{n+1,j} = \pi(a_j^2 - a_{j-1}^2), \quad j = 1, 2, \ldots, n,$$

$$s_{n+1,n+1} = 0. \tag{4.28}$$

The vector $\mathbf{L}$ contains the unknowns

$$l_i = \frac{\sigma_i}{Q}, \quad i = 1, 2, \ldots, n, \quad l_{n+1} = K, \tag{4.29}$$

and the right-hand side vector $\mathbf{P}$ has the form

$$p_i = 0, \quad i = 1, 2, \ldots, n, \quad p_{n+1} = 1. \tag{4.30}$$

The values of s_{ij} are calculated as follows:

$$
\begin{aligned}
s_{ij} &= \int_{\alpha=0}^{2\pi} \int_{r=a_{j-1}}^{a_j} \frac{r}{\sqrt{r^2 + b_i^2 - 2rb_i \cos \alpha}} \, dr \, d\alpha \\
&= 2 \int_{\alpha=0}^{\pi} \left[\sqrt{r^2 + b_i^2 - 2rb_i \cos \alpha} \right. \\
&\qquad \left. + b_i \cos \alpha \ln \left(r - b_i \cos \alpha + \sqrt{r^2 + b_i^2 - 2rb_i \cos \alpha} \right) \right]_{r=a_{j-1}}^{a_j} d\alpha. \tag{4.31}
\end{aligned}
$$

Using integration by parts in the second term, we obtain

$$
\begin{aligned}
s_{ij} &= 2(a_j + b_i)\mathrm{E}(k_{ij}) + 2(a_j - b_i)\mathrm{F}(k_{ij}) \\
&\quad - 2(a_{j-1} + b_i)\mathrm{E}(k_{i,j-1}) - 2(a_{j-1} - b_i)\mathrm{F}(k_{i,j-1}), \tag{4.32}
\end{aligned}
$$

where

$$k_{ij} = \frac{4a_j b_i}{(a_j + b_i)^2}, \quad k_{i,j-1} = \frac{4a_{j-1} b_i}{(a_{j-1} + b_i)^2}.$$

Here, $\mathrm{E}(k_{ij})$ denotes the complete elliptic integral of the second kind of argument k_{ij}, and $\mathrm{F}(k_{ij})$ is the corresponding complete first-kind elliptic integral (see Appendix B).

With an approximation of the charge density σ in hand, we can calculate the potential φ at any spatial point $N(R, \alpha, Z)$ via a standard integral expression

$$\varphi(N) = \frac{1}{4\pi\varepsilon_0} \sum_{i=1}^{n} \sigma_i \int_{\alpha=0}^{2\pi} \int_{r=a_{i-1}}^{a_i} \frac{r}{\sqrt{r^2 + R^2 - 2rR \cos \alpha + Z^2}} \, dr \, d\alpha + \varphi_0, \tag{4.33}$$

where

$$
\int_{\alpha=0}^{2\pi} \int_{r=a_{i-1}}^{a_i} \frac{r}{\sqrt{r^2 + R^2 - 2rR\cos\alpha + Z^2}} \, dr \, d\alpha
$$
$$
= 2 \int_{\alpha=0}^{\pi} \left[\sqrt{R^2 + r^2 + Z^2 - 2rR\cos\alpha} \right.
$$
$$
\left. + R\cos\alpha \, \ln\left(r - R\cos\alpha + \sqrt{R^2 + r^2 + Z^2 - 2rR\cos\alpha}\right) \right]_{r=a_{i-1}}^{a_i} d\alpha .
$$

$$(4.34)$$

The right-hand side integral in (4.34) has two parts. While the former leads to a complete elliptic function that can be calculated relatively easily, the latter needs to be calculated numerically, for example, using high-order Gaussian quadrature formulas (Appendix C).

The electric potential can be calculated analytically only in two cases: along the z-axis and in the plane of the ring. In the former case, for $R = 0$ we obtain

$$
\varphi(Z) = \frac{1}{4\pi\varepsilon_0} \sum_{i=1}^{n} \sigma_i \int_{\alpha=0}^{2\pi} \int_{r=a_{i-1}}^{a_i} \frac{r}{\sqrt{r^2 + Z^2}} \, d \, d\alpha + \varphi_0
$$
$$
= \frac{1}{2\varepsilon_0} \sum_{i=1}^{n} \sigma_i \left[\sqrt{a_i^2 + Z^2} - \sqrt{a_{i-1}^2 + Z^2} \right] + \varphi_0 .
$$

$$(4.35)$$

In the latter case, using $Z = 0$ leads to

$$
\varphi(R) = \frac{1}{4\pi\varepsilon_0} \sum_{i=1}^{n} \sigma_i \int_{\alpha=0}^{2\pi} \int_{r=a_{i-1}}^{a_i} \frac{r}{\sqrt{r^2 + R^2 - 2rR\cos\alpha}} \, dr d\alpha + \varphi_0 .
$$

$$(4.36)$$

In the following we consider a ring with external radius $R_2 = 0.2\,\mathrm{m}$ and internal radius R_1. The total charge σ on the ring is $Q = 10^{-10}$ C and we set $\varphi_0 = 0$. Let us study the role of the discretization parameter n, of the internal radius R_1, and the field map in the vicinity of the ring. Figure 4.9 depicts the nonuniform subdivision of the ring in the radial direction. Figures 4.10 and 4.11 show piecewise-constant approximations of σ/Q in the radial direction for $n = 24$ and $n = 500$, respectively. As n increases, one can see an unlimited growth of the charge density σ toward both endpoints $r = R_1$ and $r = R_2$.

Figure 4.12 depicts the distribution of the electric potential in the vicinity of the ring (internal radius of the ring is $R_1 = 0.1\,\mathrm{m}$ and its potential $\varphi = 7.217$ V). Finally, for the same parameters, Fig. 4.13 shows the distribution of the potential φ along the z-axis.

4.3.2 Current density in a harmonic current carrying massive hollow conductor

The basic arrangement for this problem is depicted in Fig. 4.14. A massive nonmagnetic hollow conductor of circular cross section carries harmonic current and its harmonic magnetic field influences the distribution of the current density in its interior. Our aim is to find this distribution.

Let us briefly recall the analytical solution. The basic equation for the current density phasor $\underline{J}_z$ along the radius r reads

$$\frac{1}{r}\frac{\partial}{\partial r}\left(r\frac{\partial \underline{J}_z(r)}{\partial r}\right) = \mathrm{j}\mu_0\omega\gamma\underline{J}_z(r)\,,\tag{4.37}$$

where γ stands for the electrical conductivity. The solution to (4.37) is given by a combination of modified zero-order Bessel functions of the first and second kinds (denoted by I_0 and K_0, respectively),

$$\underline{J}_z(r) = \underline{C}_1 I_0(\underline{k}r) + \underline{C}_2 K_0(\underline{k}r)\,,\tag{4.38}$$

where $\underline{k} = \sqrt{-\mathrm{j}\mu_0\omega\gamma}$ and the constants $\underline{C}_1, \underline{C}_2$ have to be determined from the boundary conditions. These conditions, for example, can acquire the form

$$\int_S \underline{J}_z(r)r\,\mathrm{d}r\mathrm{d}\alpha = 2\pi \int_{R_1}^{R_2} \underline{J}_z(r)r\,\mathrm{d}r = \underline{I}\,,\tag{4.39}$$

where $\underline{I}$ is the phasor of the given total current in the conductor and

$$\underline{H}_\alpha(r = R_1) = 0\,.\tag{4.40}$$

Since the tangential component of the magnetic field strength along the internal circumference of the conductor vanishes, we have

$$\left(\frac{\mathrm{d}\underline{J}_z}{\mathrm{d}r}\right)_{r=R_1} = 0\,.\tag{4.41}$$

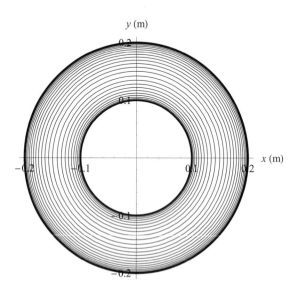

Figure 4.9.   Nonequidistant radial subdivision of the ring, $n = 24$.

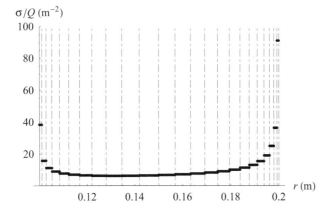

Figure 4.10.   Piecewise-constant radial distribution of σ/Q for $R_1 = 0.1\,\mathrm{m}$, $n = 24$.

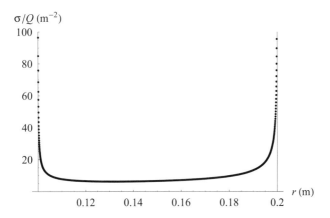

Figure 4.11.   Piecewise-constant radial distribution of σ/Q for $R_1 = 0.1\,\mathrm{m}$, $n = 500$.

After applying boundary conditions (4.39), we obtain the final dependence

$$\underline{J}_z(r) = \frac{\underline{k}I}{2\pi R_2} \cdot \frac{I_1(\underline{k}R_1)K_0(\underline{k}r) - K_1(\underline{k}R_1)I_0(\underline{k}r)}{I_1(\underline{k}R_1)K_1(\underline{k}R_2) - K_1(\underline{k}R_1)I_1(\underline{k}R_2)}, \qquad (4.42)$$

where I_1 and K_1 are the modified first-order Bessel functions of the first and second kinds.

Let us also calculate this example using the integral approach based on formula (4.21). We will take advantage of the fact that the current density J_z only depends on the radius r. The situation is depicted in Fig. 4.15.

For the phasor of the current density at any point $Q \in \langle R_1, R_2 \rangle$, equation (4.21) yields

$$- \underline{J}_z(Q) + \mathrm{j} \cdot \frac{\mu_0 \gamma \omega}{2\pi} \cdot \int_{\alpha=0}^{2\pi} \int_{R_1}^{R_2} \underline{J}_z(r) \ln(d) r \, \mathrm{d}r \, \mathrm{d}\alpha + \underline{J}_{z0} = 0. \qquad (4.43)$$

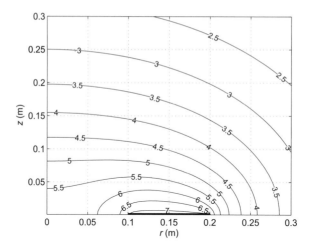

Figure 4.12.   Radial distribution of the potential φ in the vicinity of the ring.

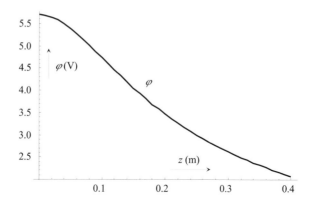

Figure 4.13.   Distribution of potential along the z axis ($R_1 = 0.1\,\mathrm{m}$, $n = 60$).

Here,

$$d^2 = R^2 + r^2 - 2Rr \cos \alpha, \qquad (4.44)$$

where d is the distance of the reference point Q from a general integration point P, and $\underline{J}_{z0}$ is an unknown complex constant. Equation (4.43) has to be supplemented with condition (4.39) for the total current.

Integrating (4.44) with respect to the angle α, we obtain

$$\int_{\alpha=0}^{2\pi} \ln(R^2 + r^2 - 2Rr \cos \alpha)\, \mathrm{d}\alpha = 2\pi \ln(b^2), \qquad (4.45)$$

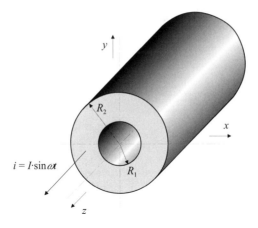

Figure 4.14.   A hollow conductor of circular shape carrying harmonic current.

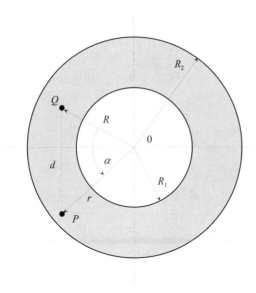

Figure 4.15.   Schematic view of a massive hollow conductor.

where $b = R$ for $R \geq r$ and $b = r$ for $R < r$. Rearranging (4.42), we obtain

$$
-\underline{J}_z(R) + \mathrm{j} \cdot \mu_0 \gamma \omega \ln(R) \cdot \int_{R_1}^{R} \underline{J}_z(r) r \, \mathrm{d}r
$$

$$
+ \mathrm{j} \cdot \mu_0 \gamma \omega \cdot \int_{R}^{R_2} \underline{J}_z(r) \ln(r) r \, \mathrm{d}r + \underline{J}_{z0} = 0 \,. \tag{4.46}
$$

Next, let us divide the cross section of the conductor into n circular rings with radii $a_0 = R_1 < a_1 < \cdots < a_n = R_2$. Each circular ring is supposed to carry a constant current density with a phasor $\underline{J}_{zi}$, $i = 1, 2, \ldots, n$. Consider, moreover, that reference points lie at the radii b_i, $i = 1, 2, \ldots, n$, where

$$b_i = \tfrac{1}{2}(a_i + a_{i-1}).$$

The discretization of (4.46) yields

$$-\underline{J}_{zi} + \mathrm{j} \cdot \mu_0 \gamma \omega \ln(b_i) \sum_{j=1}^{i-1} \underline{J}_{zj} \int_{a_{j-1}}^{a_j} r\,\mathrm{d}r + \mathrm{j} \cdot \mu_0 \gamma \omega \ln(b_i)\underline{J}_{zi} \int_{a_{i-1}}^{b_i} r\,\mathrm{d}r$$

$$+ \mathrm{j} \cdot \mu_0 \gamma \omega \underline{J}_{zi} \int_{b_i}^{a_i} \ln(r) r\,\mathrm{d}r + \mathrm{j} \cdot \mu_0 \gamma \omega \sum_{j=i+1}^{n} \underline{J}_{zj} \int_{a_{j-1}}^{a_j} \ln(r) r\,\mathrm{d}r + \underline{J}_{z0} = 0\,.$$

$$(4.47)$$

Equation (4.47) must be supplemented with discretized equation (4.39),

$$2\pi \sum_{i=1}^{n} \underline{J}_{zi} \int_{a_{i-1}}^{a_i} r\,\mathrm{d}r = \underline{I}\,. \tag{4.48}$$

In this way we obtain a system of linear algebraic equations for $\underline{J}_{zi}$, $i = 1, 2, \ldots, n$ that can be written in the matrix form

$$\boldsymbol{SL} = \boldsymbol{P}\,. \tag{4.49}$$

Here, $\boldsymbol{S}$ is a square matrix of rank $n + 1$ with entries

$$s_{ii} = -1 + \mathrm{j} \cdot \mu_0 \gamma \omega \left(\frac{a_i^2}{2} \ln(a_i) - \frac{a_i^2}{4} + \frac{b_i^2}{4} - \frac{a_{i-1}^2}{2} \ln(b_i) \right)\,, \quad i = 1, 2, \ldots, n\,,$$

$$s_{ij} = \mathrm{j} \cdot \mu_0 \gamma \omega \ln(b_i) \left(\frac{a_j^2 - a_{j-1}^2}{2} \right)\,, \quad 1 \leq j < i \leq n\,,$$

$$s_{ij} = \mathrm{j} \cdot \mu_0 \gamma \omega \left(\frac{a_i^2}{2} \ln(a_i) - \frac{a_i^2}{4} - \frac{a_{i-1}^2}{2} \ln(a_{i-1}) + \frac{a_{i-1}^2}{4} \right)\,, \quad 1 \leq i < j \leq n\,,$$

$$s_{i,n+1} = 1\,, \quad i = 1, 2, \ldots, n\,, \quad s_{n+1,j} = \pi(a_j^2 - a_{j-1}^2)\,, \quad j = 1, 2, \ldots, n\,,$$

$$s_{n+1,n+1} = 0\,. \tag{4.50}$$

The vector $\boldsymbol{L}$ contains the unknowns,

$$l_i = \underline{J}_{zi}\,, \quad i = 1, 2, \ldots, n\,, \quad l_{n+1} = \underline{J}_{z0}\,, \tag{4.51}$$

and $\boldsymbol{P}$ is the right-hand side vector,

$$p_i = 0\,, \quad i = 1, 2, \ldots, n\,, \quad p_{n+1} = \underline{I} \tag{4.52}$$

According to our experience, computations carried out in this way take practically the same time as the evaluation of complicated analytical expressions.

For an illustration, let us solve the problem for the parameters $R_1 = 0.01\,\mathrm{m}$, $R_2 = 0.02\,\mathrm{m}$, $\gamma = 57\,\mathrm{MS/m}$ (copper), $f = 50\,\mathrm{Hz}$, $I = 6000\,\mathrm{A}$. The task was calculated with $n = 20$ uniform circular rings, see also Ref. [138]. The distribution of the modulus of current density along the radius $R_1 < r < R_2$ is depicted in Fig. 4.16. A comparison of numerical and analytical results can be found in Table 4.1. The differences in the worst cases did not exceed 1 %.

4.3.3 Current density in a system consisting of a harmonic current carrying massive hollow cylindrical conductor—a coaxial shielding pipe

The arrangement to be studied is depicted in Fig. 4.17. A massive nonmagnetic hollow cylindrical conductor carrying harmonic current I_1 of frequency f is placed in a concentric electrically conductive pipe. The task is to find the distribution of the current density in both parts of the system.

This task (seemingly very simple) has no analytical solution. The basic difficulty consists in the fact that we are not able to prescribe a boundary condition on the external surface of the pipe as we do not know in advance the total current induced in it. That is why we show the solution of this problem by the integral approach and the results will be validated by a professional FEM-based code. Another aim of this example is to show how to handle the methodology in case one element (or more) in the system does not carry any source current (see the remark below (4.9)). Moreover, while the distribution of current density in the conductor affects the distribution of the same quantity in the shielding pipe, the opposite statement does not hold.

The phasors of the field current density in the conductor and shielding pipe have obviously only one nonzero component in the axial z direction that is a function of radius r. Starting from formula (4.21), we immediately obtain the system of equations describing the problem in the form

$$- \underline{J}_z(r_1) + \mathrm{j} \cdot \frac{\mu_0 \gamma_1 \omega}{2\pi} \cdot \int_{\alpha=0}^{2\pi} \int_{R_1}^{R_2} \underline{J}_{z1}(r)\ln(d_1)r\,\mathrm{d}r\,\mathrm{d}\alpha + \underline{J}_{z0} = 0\,, \qquad (4.53)$$

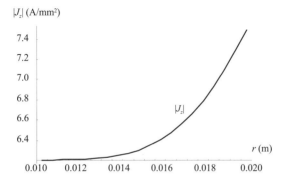

Figure 4.16.   Distribution of the modulus of current density J_z along the radius r.

Table 4.1.   Comparison of analytical and numerical results for $J_z(r)$.

radius r (m)	real part of $\underline{J}_z$ (anal.) (A/mm^2)	imag. part of $\underline{J}_z$ (anal.) (A/mm^2)	real part of $\underline{J}_z$ (num.) (A/mm^2)	imag. part of $\underline{J}_z$ (num.) (A/mm^2)
0.01025	5.80130	−2.19920	5.80240	−2.19771
0.01075	5.81334	−2.16739	5.81442	−2.16590
0.01125	5.83673	−2.10506	5.83779	−2.10355
0.01175	5.87068	−2.01331	5.87169	−2.01177
0.01225	5.91430	−1.89303	5.91525	−1.89147
0.01275	5.96658	−1.74495	5.96747	−1.74335
0.01325	6.02648	−1.56964	6.02728	−1.56799
0.01375	6.09280	−1.36754	6.09351	−1.36585
0.01425	6.16430	−1.13898	6.16490	−1.13724
0.01475	6.23961	−0.88423	6.24009	−0.88243
0.01525	6.31729	−0.60344	6.31764	−0.60159
0.01575	6.39578	−0.29674	6.39599	−0.29484
0.01625	6.47345	0.03579	6.47350	0.03774
0.01675	6.54855	0.39411	6.54844	0.39612
0.01725	6.61924	0.77820	6.61895	0.78025
0.01775	6.68357	1.18801	6.68309	1.19011
0.01825	6.73951	1.62351	6.73883	1.62565
0.01875	6.78491	2.08465	6.78401	2.08681
0.01925	6.81752	2.57131	6.81640	2.57350
0.01975	6.83500	3.08335	6.83364	3.08555

$$- \underline{J}_z(r_2) + j \cdot \frac{\mu_0 \gamma_2 \omega}{2\pi} \cdot \int_{\alpha=0}^{2\pi} \int_{R_1}^{R_2} \underline{J}_{z1}(r) \ln(d_2) r \, dr \, d\alpha$$

$$+ j \cdot \frac{\mu_0 \gamma_2 \omega}{2\pi} \cdot \int_{\alpha=0}^{2\pi} \int_{R_3}^{R_4} \underline{J}_{z2}(r) \ln(d_3) r \, dr \, d\alpha = 0 , \qquad (4.54)$$

$$2\pi \int_{R_1}^{R_2} \underline{J}_{z1}(r) r \, dr = \underline{I}_1 . \qquad (4.55)$$

Here, $\underline{J}_{z1}(r)$ is the phasor of current density in the conductor, $\underline{J}_{z2}(r)$ is the same quantity in the shielding pipe, γ_1 is the electrical conductivity of the conductor, γ_2 is the electrical conductivity of the pipe, r_1 is the radius of the reference point Q_1 in the conductor, r_2 is the radius of the reference point Q_2 in the shielding pipe, and

$$d_1 = \sqrt{r^2 + r_1^2 - 2rr_1 \cos\alpha}\,, \quad r \in \langle R_1, R_2 \rangle\,, \quad r_1 \in \langle R_1, R_2 \rangle\,,$$

$$d_2 = \sqrt{r^2 + r_2^2 - 2rr_2 \cos\alpha}\,, \quad r \in \langle R_1, R_2 \rangle\,, \quad r_2 \in \langle R_3, R_3 \rangle\,,$$

$$d_3 = \sqrt{r^2 + r_2^2 - 2rr_2 \cos\alpha}\,, \quad r \in \langle R_3, R_4 \rangle\,, \quad r_2 \in \langle R_3, R_3 \rangle\,.$$

The discretization is performed in the same way as in the previous subsection. Both conductor and pipe are divided into m and n circular rings, respectively, and in every one of them the corresponding phasor of current density ($\underline{J}_{z1}(r)$ or $\underline{J}_{z2}(r)$) is considered constant. In accordance with (4.47), (4.51), and Fig. 4.18 we can write

$$-\underline{J}_{z1,i}(r_1) + \mathrm{j}\cdot\mu_0\gamma_1\omega\ln(b_i)\sum_{j=1}^{i-1}\underline{J}_{z1,j}\int_{a_{j-1}}^{a_j} r\,\mathrm{d}r$$

$$+\mathrm{j}\cdot\mu_0\gamma_1\omega\ln(b_i)\underline{J}_{z1,i}\int_{a_{i-1}}^{b_i} r\,\mathrm{d}r$$

$$+\mathrm{j}\cdot\mu_0\gamma_1\omega\underline{J}_{z1,i}\int_{b_i}^{a_i} \ln(r)r\,\mathrm{d}r$$

$$+\mathrm{j}\cdot\mu_0\gamma_1\omega\sum_{j=i+1}^{m}\underline{J}_{z1,j}\int_{a_{j-1}}^{a_j} \ln(r)r\,\mathrm{d}r + \underline{J}_{z1,0} = 0\,,$$

$$i = 1, \dots, m\,, \tag{4.56}$$

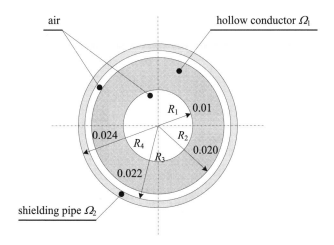

Figure 4.17. A hollow conductor of circular shape in a shielding pipe.

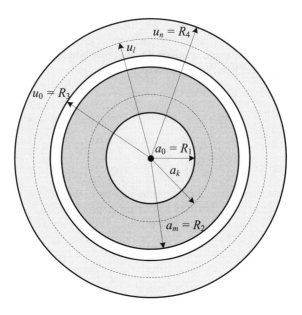

Figure 4.18.   Discretization of the system.

$$
- \underline{J}_{z2,l}(r_2) + \mathrm{j} \cdot \mu_0 \gamma_2 \omega \ln(v_l) \sum_{j=1}^{m} \underline{J}_{z1,j} \int_{a_{j-1}}^{a_j} r \, \mathrm{d}r
$$

$$
+ \mathrm{j} \cdot \mu_0 \gamma_2 \omega \ln(v_l) \sum_{j=1}^{l-1} \underline{J}_{z2,j} \int_{u_{j-1}}^{u_j} r \, \mathrm{d}r
$$

$$
+ \mathrm{j} \cdot \mu_0 \gamma_2 \omega \ln(v_l) \underline{J}_{z2,l} \int_{u_{l-1}}^{u_l} r \, \mathrm{d}r
$$

$$
+ \mathrm{j} \cdot \mu_0 \gamma_2 \omega \underline{J}_{z2,l} \int_{v_l}^{u_l} \ln(r) r \, \mathrm{d}r
$$

$$
+ \mathrm{j} \cdot \mu_0 \gamma_2 \omega \sum_{j=l+1}^{n} \underline{J}_{z2,j} \int_{u_{j-1}}^{u_j} \ln(r) r \, \mathrm{d}r = 0 , \quad l = 1, \ldots, n , \tag{4.57}
$$

$$
2\pi \sum_{i=1}^{m} \underline{J}_{z1,i} \int_{a_{i-1}}^{a_i} r \, \mathrm{d}r = \underline{I} . \tag{4.58}
$$

The above system with $m + n + 1$ unknowns $\underline{J}_{z1,i}$, $i = 1, \ldots, m$, $\underline{J}_{z2,l}$, $l = 1, \ldots, n$, and $\underline{J}_{z1,0}$ gives the distribution of current densities in particular circular rings.

We analyzed a system consisting of a copper conductor and copper shielding pipe $\gamma_1 = \gamma_2 = 57 \times 10^6$ S/m whose dimensions are given in Fig. 4.19 First, Fig. 4.19. contains the distribution of the real part of the phasor of current density along the radius of both the conductor and pipe for $|\underline{I}_1| = 6000$ A, $f = 100$ Hz, $m = 48$, and $n = 12$.

Table 4.2 shows the convergence of the results as a function of the numbers m and n. The tested quantities are the real and imaginary parts of the total current $\underline{I}_2$ induced in the shielding pipe. The difference between the corresponding components of the current for $m = 8$, $n = 2$ and $m = 64$, $n = 16$ is about 0.05%. This means that it is quite sufficient to consider only 10 elements for reaching very high accuracy of computations.

Another interesting result is the dependence of the real and imaginary components of the total current $\underline{I}_2$ induced in the shielding pipe on frequency f of the field current $\underline{I}_1$ (its amplitude being 6000 A). This dependence is depicted in Fig. 4.20.

The above results were validated by the finite element analysis of the problem by COM-SOL Multiphysics. For a series of frequencies we tested the convergence of the results depending on the position of the artificial boundary. The following two figures show the most important results for current $I_1 = 6000$ A and frequency $f = 100$ Hz. Figure 4.21 shows the convergence of the total current I_2 induced in the shielding pipe with grow-

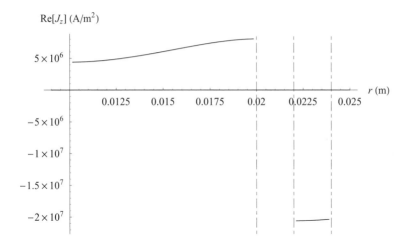

Figure 4.19. Distribution of the real part of the phasor of current density along the radius of both the conductor and pipe ($I_1 = 6000$ A, $f = 100$ Hz, $m = 48$, and $n = 12$).

Table 4.2. Real and imaginary parts of the current in the shielding pipe as functions of discretization parameters m and n.

m	4	8	16	32	64
n	1	2	4	8	16
Re[$\underline{I}_2$]	−5919.0	−5923.89	−5924.87	−5925.12	−5925.18
Im[$\underline{I}_2$]	760.265	761.294	761.146	761.196	761.209

ing radius r of the circular artificial boundary. The comparable accuracy with the results obtained by the integral approach was only achieved for $r = 1$ m, which is about forty times the outer radius of the shielding pipe. For radius $r = 1$ m of the artificial boundary, Fig. 4.22 shows the comparison of results obtained by the integral method and the FEM (COMSOL Multiphysics). The integral method in this case is unambiguously quicker and more accurate.

4.4 STATIC AND HARMONIC PROBLEMS IN TWO DIMENSIONS

In this section we are concerned with various electrostatics arrangements such as charged rectangular plates, cylindrical electrodes of finite lengths, or toroidal surfaces. Here, the integral approach may be more efficient than the differential one, particularly in cases with distant or complicated artificial boundaries. In the context of harmonic magnetic fields, one often needs to study arrangements containing long parallel conductors of various cross sections. This subject is discussed in Section 4.4.3.

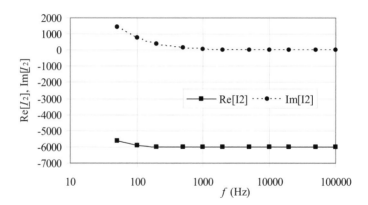

Figure 4.20. Dependence of the real and imaginary components of the total current I_2 induced in the shielding pipe on frequency f of the field current I_1 ($|I_1| = 6000$ A, $m = 32$, $n = 8$).

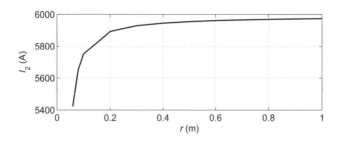

Figure 4.21. Convergence of the total current I_2 induced in the pipe on the radius r of the artificial boundary ($|I_1| = 6000$ A, $f = 100$ Hz).

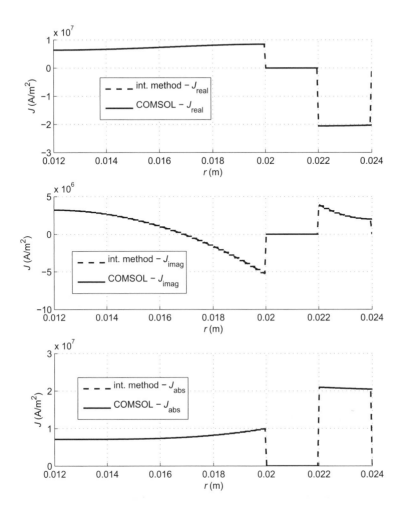

Figure 4.22.   Comparison of results obtained by the integral method and the FEM ($|I_1| = 6000$ A, $f = 100$ Hz, radius of the artificial boundary for FEM $r = 1$ m).

4.4.1   Electric field of a thin rectangular plate

Consider a perfectly electrically conductive thin rectangular plate surrounded by air and carrying a total charge Q, as illustrated in Fig. 4.23. The plate has dimensions $2a \times 2b$, lies in the xy-plane, and its center coincides with the origin of the coordinate system. Our aim is to compute the distribution of the charge density σ in the plate as well as the surrounding electric field.

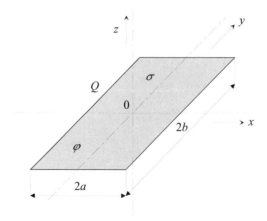

Figure 4.23.   The investigated thin rectangular plate.

Let us denote the constant potential of the plate by symbol φ. Let us choose an arbitrary point $P = (c, d)$, where $0 \leq c \leq a$ and $0 \leq d \leq b$, as illustrated in Fig. 4.24. The potential $\varphi(P) = \varphi$ can be expressed as

$$\varphi(P) = \frac{1}{4\pi\varepsilon_0} \int_S \frac{\sigma \, dS}{r} + \varphi_0 \,, \tag{4.59}$$

where r denotes the distance of the reference point P from the integration point and φ_0 is some constant. Using axial symmetries, expression (4.22) can be rewritten into a first-kind Fredholm integral equation,

$$\varphi(P) = \frac{1}{4\pi\varepsilon_0} \int_{x=0}^a \int_{y=0}^b \sigma(x, y)g(x, y, c, d) \, dy \, dx + \varphi_0 \,, \tag{4.60}$$

where

$$g(x, y, c, d) = f_1(x, y, c, d) + f_2(x, y, c, d) + f_3(x, y, c, d) + f_4(x, y, c, d)$$

and

$$f_1(x, y, c, d) = \frac{1}{\sqrt{(x - c)^2 + (y - d)^2}} \,,$$

$$f_2(x, y, c, d) = \frac{1}{\sqrt{(x - c)^2 + (y + d)^2}} \,,$$

$$f_3(x, y, c, d) = \frac{1}{\sqrt{(x + c)^2 + (y - d)^2}} \,,$$

$$f_4(x, y, c, d) = \frac{1}{\sqrt{(x + c)^2 + (y + d)^2}} \,. \tag{4.61}$$

Let us begin with a piecewise-constant approximation. We subdivide the segment $\langle 0, a \rangle \times \langle 0, b \rangle$ into n elements, which are denoted by S_i, $i = 1, 2, \ldots, n$. By $P_i = (c_i, d_i)$ we denote

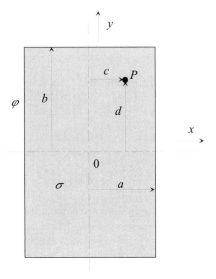

Figure 4.24. Computation of the charge density $\sigma(x, y)$ in the thin plate.

the midpoint of element S_i. For every P_i, equation (4.60) yields

$$4\pi\varepsilon_0(\varphi(P_i) - \varphi_0)/Q = \text{const}$$

$$= \sum_{j=1}^{n} \frac{\sigma_j}{Q} \cdot \int_{S_j} [f_{1i}(x, y, c_i, d_i) + f_{2i}(x, y, c_i, d_i)$$

$$+ f_{3i}(x, y, c_i, d_i) + f_{4i}(x, y, c_i, d_i)] \, dS, \tag{4.62}$$

where σ_j is the constant approximation of charge density in the element S_j. The equation for the total charge reads

$$4 \sum_{j=1}^{n} \frac{\sigma_j}{Q} S_j = 1, \tag{4.63}$$

where S_j is the area of the jth cell. In this way we obtain a system of linear algebraic equations in the form

$$\mathbf{ML} = \mathbf{P}, \tag{4.64}$$

where $\mathbf{M}$ is a square matrix of rank $n + 1$ with entries

$$m_{ij} = \int_{S_j} [f_{1i}(x, y, c_i, d_i) + f_{2i}(x, y, c_i, d_i) + f_{3i}(x, y, c_i, d_i) + f_{4i}(x, y, c_i, d_i)] \, dS,$$

$$i, j = 1, 2, \ldots, n,$$

$$m_{i,n+1} = -1, \quad i = 1, 2, \ldots, n, \quad m_{n+1,j} = 4S_j, \quad j = 1, 2, \ldots, n, \quad m_{n+1,n+1} = 0. \tag{4.65}$$

The vector $\boldsymbol{L}$ contains the unknowns,

$$l_i = \frac{\sigma_i}{Q}, \quad i = 1, 2, \ldots, n, \quad l_{n+1} = C, \tag{4.66}$$

and the vector $\boldsymbol{P}$ represents the right-hand side,

$$p_i = 0, \quad i = 1, 2, \ldots, n, \quad p_{n+1} = 1. \tag{4.67}$$

The calculation of the coefficients m_{ij}, $i, j = 1, 2, \ldots, n$ requires a nontrivial analytical integration that is different for triangles and rectangles. For both cases, the calculations are described in more detail in Appendix C.

Let us solve a sample problem with the parameters $a = 0.4\,\text{m}$, $b = 0.2\,\text{m}$, and total charge $Q = 10^{-10}\,\text{C}$. By symmetry, we only consider the first quadrant $x \geq 0, y \geq 0$ and subdivide it uniformly using 40 and 20 elements in the x- and y-directions, respectively. Figure 4.25 shows the approximate distribution of the charge density σ. It can clearly be seen that the charge density grows to infinity toward the boundary of the plate.

Figures 4.26 and 4.27 show the distribution of the electric field in the yz- and xz-planes, respectively.

4.4.2 Electric field of a charged cylinder

Next, let us study the arrangement depicted in Fig. 4.28, where a total charge Q is distributed on the surface of a finite cylinder of radius R and length $2h$.

The solution is analogous to the example discussed in the previous section. First, we subdivide the surface of the cylinder as shown in Fig. 4.29. Both the upper and lower bases are subdivided into n circular rings of radii $0 = a_1 < a_2 < \cdots < a_{n+1} = R$. Second, the upper and lower parts of its shell are divided into p cylindrical rings given by the points

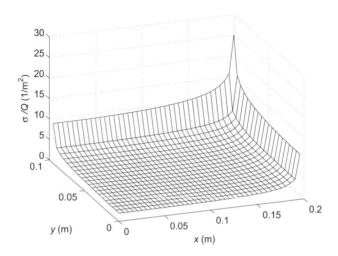

Figure 4.25.   Approximate charge density over one-fourth of the plate.

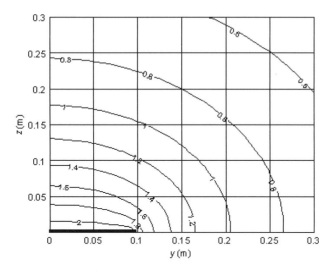

Figure 4.26. Electric field in the yz-plane.

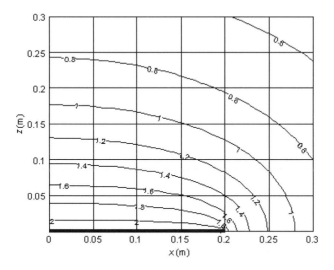

Figure 4.27. Electric field in the xz-plane.

$0 = c_1 < c_2 < \cdots < c_{p+1} = h$ (only the discretization of the upper part is depicted). The approximation of the charge density σ over these elements is assumed piecewise-constant. Let us denote $b_i = (a_i + a_{i+1})/2$, $i = 1, 2, \ldots, n$ and $d_j = (c_j + c_{j+1})/2$, $j = 1, 2, \ldots, p$. Approximate charge densities on the cylindrical rings are denoted by σ_{ir}, $i = 1, 2, \ldots, n$ and on the cylindrical rings by σ_{jz}, $j = 1, 2, \ldots, p$.

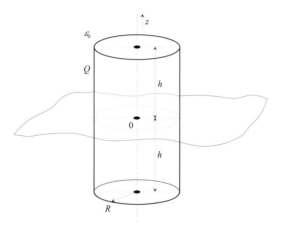

Figure 4.28. Cylindrical surface carrying a charge Q.

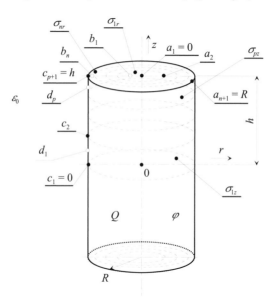

Figure 4.29. Discretization of the surface of the cylinder.

The potential corresponding to the radius b_i on the upper base can be expressed as

$$
\varphi = \varphi(b_i, h) = \frac{1}{4\pi\varepsilon_0} \sum_{k=1}^{n} \sigma_{ir} \int_{\alpha=0}^{2\pi} \int_{r=a_k}^{a_{k+1}} \frac{r\,dr\,d\alpha}{\sqrt{b_i^2 + r^2 - 2b_i r \cos\alpha}}
$$

$$
+ \frac{1}{4\pi\varepsilon_0} \sum_{k=1}^{n} \sigma_{ir} \int_{\alpha=0}^{2\pi} \int_{r=a_k}^{a_{k+1}} \frac{r\,dr\,d\alpha}{\sqrt{b_i^2 + r^2 + 4h^2 - 2b_i r \cos\alpha}}
$$

$$
+ \frac{1}{4\pi\varepsilon_0} \sum_{l=1}^{p} \sigma_{lz} \int_{\alpha=0}^{2\pi} \int_{z=c_l}^{c_{l+1}} \frac{R\,dz\,d\alpha}{\sqrt{b_i^2 + R^2 + (z-h)^2 - 2b_i R \cos\alpha}}
$$

$$
+ \frac{1}{4\pi\varepsilon_0} \sum_{l=1}^{p} \sigma_{lz} \int_{\alpha=0}^{2\pi} \int_{z=c_l}^{c_{l+1}} \frac{R\,dz\,d\alpha}{\sqrt{b_i^2 + R^2 + (z+h)^2 - 2b_i R \cos\alpha}} + \varphi_0 \,.
$$

For the potential corresponding to the position d_j on the upper half of the cylindrical shell, we obtain

$$\varphi = \varphi(d_j, h) = \frac{1}{4\pi\varepsilon_0} \sum_{k=1}^{n} \sigma_{ir} \int_{\alpha=0}^{2\pi} \int_{r=a_k}^{a_{k+1}} \frac{r \, dr \, d\alpha}{\sqrt{r^2 + R^2 + (h - d_j)^2 - 2rR\cos\alpha}}$$

$$+ \frac{1}{4\pi\varepsilon_0} \sum_{k=1}^{n} \sigma_{ir} \int_{\alpha=0}^{2\pi} \int_{r=a_k}^{a_{k+1}} \frac{r \, dr \, d\alpha}{\sqrt{r^2 + R^2 + (h + d_j)^2 - 2rR\cos\alpha}}$$

$$+ \frac{1}{4\pi\varepsilon_0} \sum_{l=1}^{p} \sigma_{lz} \int_{\alpha=0}^{2\pi} \int_{z=c_l}^{c_{l+1}} \frac{R \, dz \, d\alpha}{\sqrt{2R^2 + (z - d_j)^2 - 2R^2\cos\alpha}}$$

$$+ \frac{1}{4\pi\varepsilon_0} \sum_{l=1}^{p} \sigma_{lz} \int_{\alpha=0}^{2\pi} \int_{z=c_l}^{c_{l+1}} \frac{R \, dz \, d\alpha}{\sqrt{2R^2 + (z + d_j)^2 - 2R^2\cos\alpha}} + \varphi_0 \,.$$

$$(4.69)$$

As usual, we need to impose a supplementary condition for the total charge Q,

$$2\pi \sum_{i=1}^{n} \sigma_{ir}(a_{i+1}^2 - a_i^2) + 2 \cdot 2\pi R \sum_{j=1}^{p} \sigma_{jz}(c_{j+1} - c_j) = Q\,. \qquad (4.70)$$

Exploiting the symmetry of the problem, we obtain a system of linear equations of the form

$$\boldsymbol{SL} = \boldsymbol{P}\,. \qquad (4.71)$$

Here, $\boldsymbol{S}$ is a square matrix of rank $n + p + 1$ with elements

$$s_{ij} = \int_{\alpha=0}^{2\pi} \int_{r=a_j}^{a_{j+1}} \frac{r \, dr d\alpha}{\sqrt{r^2 + b_i^2 - 2rb_i\cos\alpha}}$$

$$+ \int_{\alpha=0}^{2\pi} \int_{r=a_j}^{a_{j+1}} \frac{r \, dr \, d\alpha}{\sqrt{r^2 + b_i^2 + 4h^2 - 2rb_i\cos\alpha}}\,, \quad i, j = 1, 2, \ldots, n\,, \quad (4.72)$$

$$s_{ij} = \int_{\alpha=0}^{2\pi} \int_{z=c_j}^{c_{j+1}} \frac{R \, dz \, d\alpha}{\sqrt{b_i^2 + R^2 + (z - h)^2 - 2b_i R\cos\alpha}}$$

$$+ \int_{\alpha=0}^{2\pi} \int_{z=c_j}^{c_{j+1}} \frac{R \, dz \, d\alpha}{\sqrt{b_i^2 + R^2 + (z + h)^2 - 2b_i R\cos\alpha}}\,,$$

$$i = 1, 2, \ldots, n\,, \quad j = n + 1, n + 2 \ldots, n + p\,, \qquad (4.73)$$

$$s_{ij} = \int_{\alpha=0}^{2\pi} \int_{r=a_j}^{a_{j+1}} \frac{r\,dr\,d\alpha}{\sqrt{r^2 + R^2 + (h - d_i)^2 - 2rR\cos\alpha}}$$
$$+ \int_{\alpha=0}^{2\pi} \int_{r=a_j}^{a_{j+1}} \frac{r\,dr\,d\alpha}{\sqrt{r^2 + R^2 + (h + d_i)^2 - 2rR\cos\alpha}},$$
$$i = n+1, n+2, \ldots, n+p, \quad j = 1, 2, \ldots, n, \tag{4.74}$$

$$s_{ij} = \int_{\alpha=0}^{2\pi} \int_{z=c_j}^{c_{j+1}} \frac{R\,dz\,d\alpha}{\sqrt{2R^2 + (z - d_i)^2 - 2R^2\cos\alpha}}$$
$$+ \int_{\alpha=0}^{2\pi} \int_{z=c_j}^{c_{j+1}} \frac{R\,dz\,d\alpha}{\sqrt{2R^2 + (z + d_i)^2 - 2R^2\cos\alpha}},$$
$$i, j = n+1, n+2, \ldots, n+p, \tag{4.75}$$

$$\begin{aligned}
s_{i,n+p+1} &= -1, \quad i = 1, 2, \ldots, n+p, \\
s_{n+p+1,j} &= 2\pi(a_{j+1}^2 - a_j^2), \quad j = 1, 2, \ldots, n, \\
s_{n+p+1,j} &= 4\pi R(c_{j+1} - c_j), \quad j = n+1, n+2, \ldots, n+p, \\
s_{n+p+1,n+p+1} &= 0.
\end{aligned} \tag{4.76}$$

The right-hand side vector $\boldsymbol{P}$ of length $n + p + 1$ is defined as

$$p_i = 0, \quad i = 1, 2, \ldots, n+p, \quad p_{n+p+1} = 1. \tag{4.77}$$

Finally, $\boldsymbol{L}$ is a vector of the same length $n + p + 1$ with entries

$$l_i = \frac{\sigma_{ir}}{Q}, \quad i = 1, 2, \ldots, n,$$

$$l_i = \frac{\sigma_{iz}}{Q}, \quad i = n+1, n+2, \ldots, n+p,$$

$$l_{n+p+1} = K, \quad K = (\varphi - \varphi_0)\frac{4\pi\varepsilon_0}{Q}. \tag{4.78}$$

The integrals occurring in (4.72)–(4.75) can be divided into two groups:

$$I_1 = \int_{\alpha=0}^{2\pi} \int_{r=a_j}^{a_{j+1}} \frac{r\,dr\,d\alpha}{\sqrt{r^2 - 2rM\cos\alpha + N^2}},$$

$$I_2 = \int_{\alpha=0}^{2\pi} \int_{z=c_j}^{c_{j+1}} \frac{R\,dz\,d\alpha}{\sqrt{(z + X)^2 - Y\cos\alpha + Z^2}}, \tag{4.79}$$

where $M, N, X, Y,$ and Z are various constants. Integrating I_1 with respect to r, we obtain

$$I_1 = \int_{\alpha=0}^{2\pi} \left[f(r,\alpha) + M\cos\alpha \ln(r - M\cos\alpha + f(r,\alpha)) \right]_{r=a_j}^{r=a_{j+1}} d\alpha, \qquad (4.80)$$

where

$$f(r,\alpha) = \sqrt{r^2 - 2rM\cos\alpha + N^2}.$$

The integration of I_2 with respect to z yields

$$I_2 = \int_{\alpha=0}^{2\pi} R \left[\ln(z + X + \sqrt{(z+X)^2 - Y\cos\alpha + Z^2}) \right]_{z=c_j}^{z=c_{j+1}} d\alpha. \qquad (4.81)$$

Most of these integrals have to be calculated numerically except for the first integral in (4.72), which can be expressed in terms of complete elliptic functions (see (4.31) and (4.32)). The numerical evaluation of both integrals in (4.75) must be carried out carefully due to the presence of singular points. Alternatively, these two integrals may be calculated as follows:

$$\begin{aligned}
I &= \int_{\alpha=0}^{2\pi} \int_{z=c_j}^{c_{j+1}} \frac{R\,dz\,d\alpha}{\sqrt{2R^2 + (z \pm d_i)^2 - 2R^2\cos\alpha}} \\
&= 2\int_{z=c_j}^{c_{j+1}} \int_{\alpha=0}^{\pi} \frac{dz\,d\alpha}{\sqrt{2 - 2\cos\alpha + \left(\frac{z \pm d_i}{R}\right)^2}} \\
&= 2\int_{z=c_j}^{c_{j+1}} \int_{\alpha=0}^{\pi/2} \frac{d\beta}{\sqrt{\sin^2\beta + (z \pm d_i)^2/(4R^2)}}\,dz \\
&= 2\int_{z=c_j}^{c_{j+1}} \int_{\alpha=0}^{\pi/2} \frac{d\beta}{\sqrt{1 + (z \pm d_i)^2/(4R^2) - \sin^2\beta}}\,dz \\
&= 2\int_{z=c_j}^{c_{j+1}} \frac{1}{\sqrt{1 + (z \pm d_i)^2/(4R^2)}} K\left(\frac{1}{1 + (z \pm d_i)^2/(4R^2)}\right)\,dz, \qquad (4.82)
\end{aligned}$$

where K denotes the complete elliptic integral of the first kind. Then the numerical integration of (4.82) does not cause problems anymore.

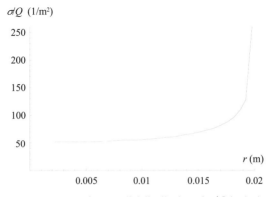

Figure 4.30.   Approximate radial distribution of σ/Q in the base.

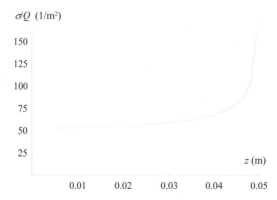

Figure 4.31. Approximate distribution of σ/Q along the shell.

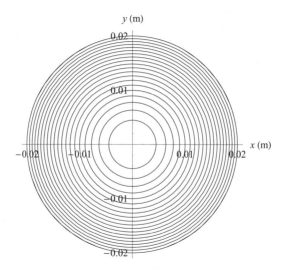

Figure 4.32. Nonuniform subdivision of the base.

Let us present the results of a sample computation with the parameters $R = 0.02\,\mathrm{m}$, $h = 0.05\,\mathrm{m}$, $n = p = 20$. Figure 4.30 shows the distribution of the quantity σ/Q along the radius of the base for $r \in \langle 0, R \rangle$. Figure 4.31 shows the distribution of the same quantity along the shell for $z \in \langle 0, h \rangle$.

Both circles at $z = \pm h$, $r = R$ represent singularities with $\sigma \to \infty$. Therefore, we used nonuniform discretization (refined as $r \to R$ and $z \to h$) that provided better results than a uniform mesh, shown in Fig. 4.32.

4.4.3 Harmonic currents in a long conductor of arbitrary cross section

A long massive nonmagnetic conductor of an arbitrary cross section carries a harmonic current i of amplitude I and frequency f. The situation is depicted in Fig. 4.33 (the conductor is oriented in the z-direction).

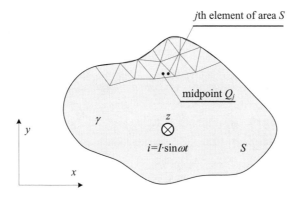

Figure 4.33. Long massive conductor of an arbitrary cross section.

Let us return to the general relation (4.21). After leaving out velocity-related terms and adjusting it for a single conductor, we obtain

$$-\underline{J}_z(Q) + \mathrm{j} \cdot \frac{\mu_0 \gamma \omega}{2\pi} \cdot \int_S \underline{J}_z(P) \cdot \ln[r_{PQ}]\,\mathrm{d}S + \underline{J}_{z0} = 0\,. \tag{4.83}$$

As usual, relation (4.83) is supplemented by an integral constraint for the total current in the form

$$\int_S \underline{J}_z(P)\,\mathrm{d}S = \underline{I}\,. \tag{4.84}$$

Let the cross section of the conductor be covered by elements $S_1, S_2, \ldots, S_n$ with midpoints denoted as $Q_1, Q_2, \ldots, Q_n$. The constant approximation of the current density $\underline{J}_z$ in every element S_i is denoted by J_{zi}. Equations (4.83) and (4.84) are approximated as follows:

$$-\underline{J}_z(Q_i) + \mathrm{j} \cdot \frac{\mu_0 \gamma \omega}{2\pi} \cdot \sum_{j=1}^n \underline{J}_{zj} \int_{S_j} \ln[r_{PQ_i}]\,\mathrm{d}S + \underline{J}_{z0} = 0, \quad i = 1, 2, \ldots, n, \tag{4.85}$$

$$\sum_{j=1}^n \underline{J}_{zj}\,\mathrm{area}(S_j) = \underline{I}\,. \tag{4.86}$$

This leads to a system of linear equations

$$\boldsymbol{SL} = \boldsymbol{P}\,, \tag{4.87}$$

where the matrix S of rank $n + 1$ contains the entries

$$s_{ii} = -1 + j \cdot \frac{\mu_0 \gamma \omega}{2\pi} \int_{S_i} \ln[r_{PQ_i}] \, dS, \quad i = 1, 2, \ldots, n,$$

$$s_{ij} = j \cdot \frac{\mu_0 \gamma \omega}{2\pi} \int_{S_j} \ln[r_{PQ_i}] \, dS, \; 1 \le i \ne j \le n,$$

$$s_{i,n+1} = 1, \quad i = 1, 2, \ldots, n,$$

$$s_{n+1,i} = \text{area}(S_i), \quad i = 1, 2, \ldots, n,$$

$$s_{n+1,n+1} = 0. \tag{4.88}$$

The right-hand side vector P has the form

$$p_i = 0, \quad i = 1, 2, \ldots, n, \quad p_{n+1} = \underline{I}, \tag{4.89}$$

and the entries of the vector L are the unknowns,

$$l_i = \underline{J}_{zi}, \quad i = 1, 2, \ldots, n, \quad l_{n+1} = \underline{J}_{z0}. \tag{4.90}$$

Analytical calculation of integrals of the form $\int_{S_j} \ln[r_{PQ_i}] \, dS$, occurring in (4.88), is described in Appendix C. for both triangular and quadrilateral elements.

The effective impedance of the conductor per unit length is defined by

$$Z'_{\text{eff}} = R'_{\text{eff}} + j \cdot \omega L'_{\text{eff}}, \tag{4.91}$$

where the effective resistance R'_{eff} can be determined from the total Joule losses in the conductor,

$$R'_{\text{eff}} = \frac{1}{\gamma |\underline{I}|^2} \sum_{i=1}^{n} |\underline{J}_{zi}|^2 \text{area}(S_i). \tag{4.92}$$

The internal inductance L'_{eff} follows from the formula

$$L'_{\text{eff}} = \frac{1}{\mu_0 |\underline{I}|^2} \sum_{i=1}^{n} |\underline{B}_{zi}|^2 \text{area}(S_i), \tag{4.93}$$

where the distribution of $\underline{B}$ over the cross-section of the conductor may be found using a standard integral expression.

In the following we are concerned with the computation of the effective impedance per unit length Z'_{eff} of massive copper conductors that are used for long-distance transmission of currents of medium and high frequencies; see Refs. 139 and 140. It is our goal to study several conductors with different cross sections of the same size 10^{-6} m², and compare the results to a reference massive copper conductor of circular cross section. The first type of the conductor, in three versions, is depicted in Fig. 4.34.

Due to symmetry of the cross sections, it is sufficient to consider the first quadrant only. For this part we use several triangular meshes with different densities – finer meshes are employed for higher frequencies of the harmonic current. The largest mesh had close to 3000 elements that produced approximately 6000 linear algebraic equations (4.87).

Figure 4.35 shows the distribution of the modulus of the current density along the curve ABCNA (see Fig. 4.34.) for a current with amplitude $I = 6$ A and frequency $f = 1$ MHz.

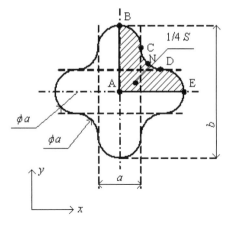

Version I: $a = 0.000437$ m, $b = 0.001372$ m
Version II: $a = 0.000384$ m, $b = 0.001536$ m
Version III: $a = 0.000337$ m, $b = 0.001686$ m

Figure 4.34.   Massive conductor of the first type.

These results are in very good agreement with a FEM computation performed using Quick-Field 5.0.

Figure 4.36 presents the frequency-dependent ratio of the effective resistance per unit length R'_{eff} for all three versions of the conductor related to their direct current resistance R'_0.

As the differences between particular curves are not big, Fig. 4.37 shows their detail for higher frequencies. It is obvious that the resistance per unit length of the profile conductors is really lower than that of the circular conductor. Moreover, the longer the arms of the cross (dimension b), the lower the resistance of the conductor.

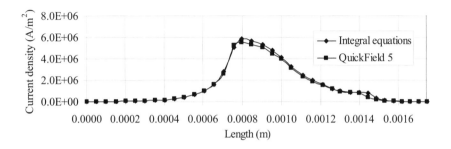

Figure 4.35.   Distribution of the modulus of eddy current density along line ABCNA (see Fig. 4.34.) for $I = 6$ A and frequency $f = 1$ MHz (version I).

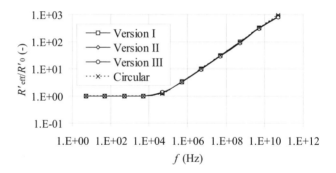

Figure 4.36.   Ratio of R'_{eff}/R'_0 versus the frequency for the conductor.

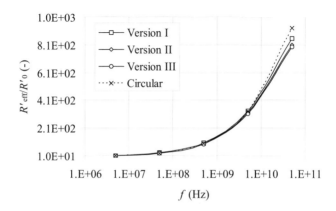

Figure 4.37.   Detail of Fig. 4.36 for higher frequencies.

Figure 4.38 shows the frequency-dependent ratio of the internal inductance per unit length L'_{eff} of the investigated conductor and circular conductor of the same cross section related to the corresponding direct current inductances L'_0. For medium and higher frequencies, the profile conductors exhibit lower values than the circular conductor of the same area. And similar to the case of the resistance, the internal inductance decreases with longer arms of the cross.

Another type of conductor (thin strip conductor) in three versions is depicted in Fig. 4.39. This is a typical flat thin conductor used to transmit high-frequency currents.

Figure 4.40 shows the distribution of the modulus of eddy current density along the curve ABCDA for the current $I = 6$ A and frequency $f = 1$ MHz. Again, these results are almost identical to results obtained by the FEM using code QuickField 5.0.

For frequencies up to 1 MHz, the values of the effective impedance of profile conductors are comparable with the impedance of the reference conductor with circular cross section. For higher frequencies, however, these impedances decrease.

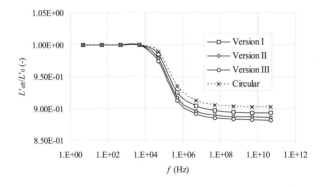

Figure 4.38. Ratio of L'_{eff}/L'_0 versus frequency of the harmonic current.

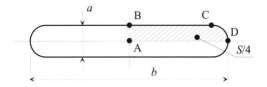

Version I: $a = 0.000437$ m, $b = 0.001372$ m
Version II: $a = 0.000384$ m, $b = 0.001536$ m
Version III: $a = 0.000337$ m, $b = 0.001686$ m

Figure 4.39. Thin strip conductor.

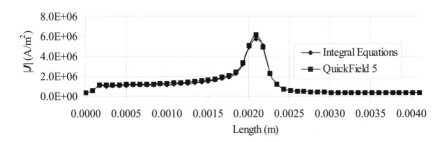

Figure 4.40. Distribution of the modulus of eddy current density along the curve ABCDA for $I = 6$ A and frequency $f = 1$ MHz (version I).

4.5 STATIC PROBLEMS IN THREE DIMENSIONS

Most electrostatic problems exhibit significant three-dimensional (3D) features. Until now we have investigated the distribution of the electric charge σ on surfaces of solitary charged bodies. In reality, these bodies usually are parts of larger electrically neutral systems. For example, we can mention the influence of the ground and other electrodes in the system. The solution of 3D problems by means of integral methods is challenging due to the large numbers of degrees of freedom and corresponding large dense matrices. Very large problems, therefore, still require the application of differential methods. In this section, we illustrate the application of the integral approach on a pair of solitary charged cubes (Section 4.5.1) and on a pair of charged plates in a general position in space (Section 4.5.2). In both cases the results have only an informative character and their accuracy is rather low.

4.5.1   Electric field of two charged cubes

The basic arrangement containing a pair of electrically conductive charged cubes is depicted in Fig. 4.41. The cubes carry potentials $\varphi_1 = 50$ V and $\varphi_1 = -50$ V, respectively, they have identical edge length $a = 0.02$ m, and the distance between their centers is $d = 0.027$ m. The system is surrounded by air (see Refs. 141 and 142).

The discretization of the problem is performed as follows: the faces S_i, $i = 1, 2, \ldots, 12$, of both cubes are covered with uniform meshes, each of them consisting of $n \times n$ square cells T_{ij}, $i = 1, 2, \ldots, 12$, $j = 1, 2, \ldots, n \times n$. By M_{ij} we denote the midpoint of the element T_{ij}. The charge density σ in each cell is approximated by a constant σ_{ij}. The approximate solution to is given by

$$\varphi(R) = \frac{1}{4\pi\varepsilon_0} \sum_{i=1}^{12} \sum_{j=1}^{n \times n} \sigma_{ij} \int_{T_j} \frac{\mathrm{d}T}{|\mathbf{r}_R - \mathbf{r}_X|} + \varphi_0 , \tag{4.94}$$

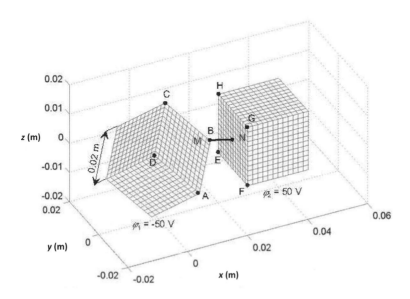

Figure 4.41.   Arrangement with two charged cubes.

where R denotes a reference point (an element midpoint) with coordinates x_R, y_R, z_R and X is an integration point with coordinates x, y, z. Their distance is given by

$$|\mathbf{r}_R - \mathbf{r}_X| = \sqrt{(x_R - x)^2 + (y_R - y)^2 + (z_R - z)^2}. \tag{4.95}$$

Finally, we set $\varphi_0 = 0$ (then the potential $\varphi(R)$ vanishes as $R \to \infty$). Putting in (4.94) $R = M_{rs}$, $r = 1, 2, \ldots, 12$, $s = 1, 2, \ldots, n \times n$ for all particular cells, we obtain a system of linear algebraic equations as usual. The integral $\int_{T_j} \frac{\mathrm{d}T}{|\mathbf{r}_R - \mathbf{r}_X|}$ occurring in (4.94) can be modified easily to the form

$$\int_S \frac{\mathrm{d}S}{r},$$

whose calculation is shown in Appendix C.

The task was solved for several values of n between 6 and 20. Fig. 4.42. depicts the approximate distribution of the charge density σ on the face ABCD. It is in good agreement with experiment that the highest values of the charge density can be found along the edges. In reality, these values tend to infinity.

Fig. 4.43., shows the approximate distribution of the charge density σ on the face EFGH, where a mild growth can be observed close to the corner B of the other cube.

The knowledge of the charge density σ allows us to calculate the distribution of the electric potential in the system by means of standard integral expressions. For illustration, the electric potential is calculated in the planes A and B which are depicted in Fig. 4.44.

The distribution of the potential in the planes A and B is shown in Figs. 4.45. and 4.46., respectively. The equipotential lines were obtained by linear interpolation of pointwise calculated values.

The components of the electric field strength at any selected point can be calculated directly from the distribution of the surface charges, which provides much more accurate results compared to their calculation from the potential. However, the former approach

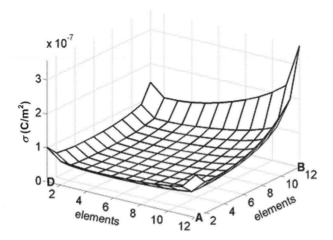

Figure 4.42.   Approximate distribution of the charge density σ on the face ABCD, $n = 12$.

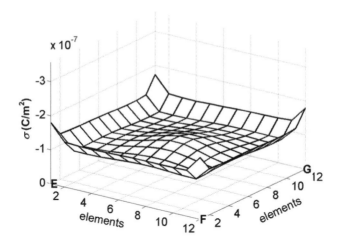

Figure 4.43. Approximate distribution of the charge density σ on the face EFGH, $n = 12$.

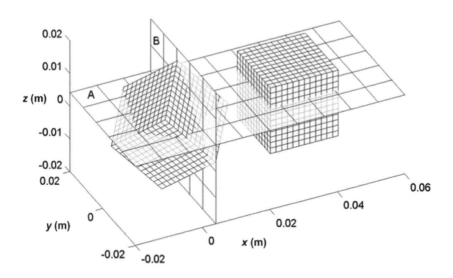

Figure 4.44. Planes A and B where the electric potential is calculated.

requires additional operations associated with necessary coordinate transforms and takes a considerable amount of time. Fig. 4.47. shows the distribution of the electric field strength E in the vicinity of both cubes.

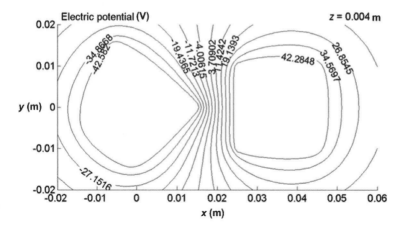

Figure 4.45. Approximate distribution of the electric potential in the plane A.

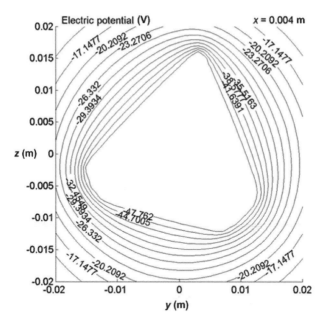

Figure 4.46. Approximate distribution of the electric potential in the plane B.

Finally we show a convergence study in Table 4.3. The capacitance of the system is determined using the formula

$$C = \frac{|Q_1| + |Q_2|}{\varphi_2 - \varphi_1} = \frac{|Q_1| + |Q_2|}{100}$$

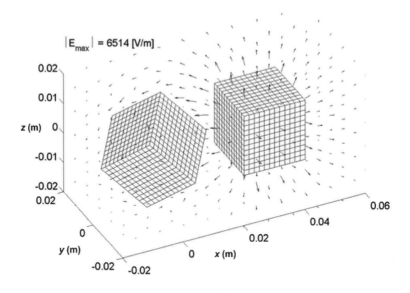

Figure 4.47. Approximate distribution of the electric field strength E in the system.

(arithmetic mean of the absolute values of the total charges on both cubes is considered).

Table 4.3. Convergence study with respect to the edge subdivision parameter n.

edge subdivision parameter n	charge Q_1 (C)	charge Q_2 (C)	capacitance C (F)	number of unknowns	CPU time (s) (Athlon XP 2000+
6	−1.2086e−10	1.2119e−10	1.2103e−12	432	8.139
7	−1.2122e−10	1.2156e−10	1.2139e−12	588	16.078
8	−1.2148e−10	1.2183e−10	1.2166e−12	768	29.359
9	−1.2168e−10	1.2203e−10	1.2186e−12	972	51.156
10	−1.2184e−10	1.2219e−10	1.2202e−12	1200	82.719
11	−1.2196e−10	1.2231e−10	1.2214e−12	1452	131.547
12	−1.2206e−10	1.2241e−10	1.2224e−12	1728	200.281
20	−1.2247e−10	1.2283e−10	1.2265e−12	4800	2736.514

4.5.2   Electric field of two charged plates

Assume an arrangement containing a pair of charged thin plates (see Refs. 141 and 143) surrounded by air, as shown in Fig. 4.48. The horizontal plate marked as ABCD carries potential $\varphi_1 = 50\,V$ and the potential of the other plate EFGH is $\varphi_2 = -50\,V$. Both plates are identical, with edge length $a = 0.02\,m$ and the distance between their centers is $d = 0.011\,m$.

The continuous mathematical model of the problem is analogous to the previous case. Each plate is covered with a uniform 12×12 quadrilateral grid and the piecewise-constant approximation yields a system of linear algebraic equations analogous to (4.59). Figure 4.49 depicts the approximate distribution of the electric charge σ in the plane ABCD. Its highest values are found along the side AD that lies closest to the vertical plate.

Figure 4.50 shows the distribution of the charge density on the surface EFGH. This distribution is quite symmetric along the horizontal axis parallel to the line AD, where its values are higher.

4.6   TIME-DEPENDENT EDDY CURRENT PROBLEMS IN ONE DIMENSION AND TWO DIMENSIONS

Many problems of this type are related to long massive conductors and their parallel systems. We can mention, for example, the heating and force effects in a three-phase system of conductors under short circuit conditions, or the computation of self- and mutual inductances in general systems of conductors carrying pulse currents.

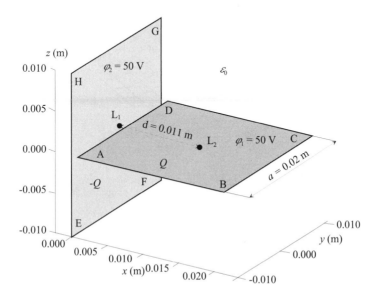

Figure 4.48.   The arrangement containing two charged thin plates.

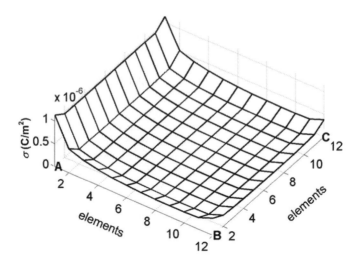

Figure 4.49.   Approximate distribution of the electric charge σ in the plane ABCD.

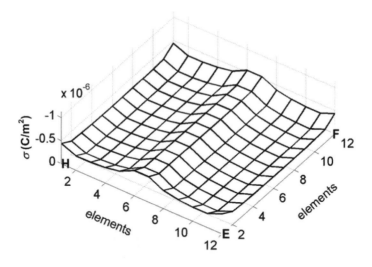

Figure 4.50.   Approximate distribution of the electric charge σ in the plane EFGH.

4.6.1   Massive conductor carrying time-dependent current

Assume a long massive nonmagnetic conductor of circular cross section with radius R_1, electrical conductivity γ, and relative magnetic permeability $\mu_r = 1$, carrying a general time-dependent current $i(t)$. Our task is to find the time distribution of the current density at selected internal points as well as the time-dependent resistance and internal inductance. The situation is depicted in Fig. 4.51.

The time-dependent distribution of the current density $J_z(R,t)$, $0 \leq R \leq R_1$ is given by formula (4.18) modified for a single conductor,

$$- J_z(R,t) + \frac{\mu_0 \gamma}{2\pi} \cdot \int_{\alpha=0}^{2\pi} \int_0^{R_1} \frac{\mathrm{d}J_z(r,t)}{\mathrm{d}t} \ln(d) r \, \mathrm{d}r \, \mathrm{d}\alpha + J_{z0}(t) = 0 . \tag{4.96}$$

Here,

$$d = \sqrt{r^2 + R^2 - 2rR\cos\alpha} \tag{4.97}$$

is the distance between the reference point Q and a general integration point $P(r,\alpha)$, as shown in Fig. 4.52.

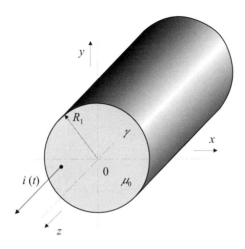

Figure 4.51. The investigated conductor.

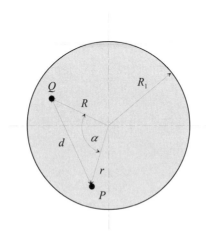

Figure 4.52. The reference and integration points.

The first integration with respect to α can be performed in the same way as in (4.46) and one obtains

$$
- J_z(R, t) + \mu_0 \gamma \ln R \cdot \int_0^R \frac{\mathrm{d}J_z(r, t)}{\mathrm{d}t} r \, \mathrm{d}r
$$

$$
+ \mu_0 \gamma \cdot \int_R^{R_1} \frac{\mathrm{d}J_z(r, t)}{\mathrm{d}t} \ln(r) r \, \mathrm{d}r + J_{z0}(t) = 0 \,. \tag{4.98}
$$

Using a discretization analogous to that in section 4.4.3 and the Euler method for the time integration, we obtain

$$
- J_{zi}(t_k) + \mu_0 \gamma \ln(b_i) \sum_{j=1}^{i-1} \frac{J_{zj}(t_k) - J_{zj}(t_{k-1})}{\Delta t_k} \int_{a_{j-1}}^{a_j} r \, \mathrm{d}r
$$

$$
+ \mu_0 \gamma \ln(b_i) \frac{J_{zi}(t_k) - J_{zi}(t_{k-1})}{\Delta t_k} \int_{a_{i-1}}^{b_i} r \, \mathrm{d}r
$$

$$
+ \mu_0 \gamma \frac{J_{zi}(t_k) - J_{zi}(t_{k-1})}{\Delta t_k} \int_{b_i}^{a_i} \ln(r) r \, \mathrm{d}r
$$

$$
+ \mu_0 \gamma \sum_{j=i+1}^{n} \frac{J_{zj}(t_k) - J_{zj}(t_{k-1})}{\Delta t_k} \int_{a_{j-1}}^{a_j} \ln(r) r \, \mathrm{d}r
$$

$$
+ J_{z0}(t_k) = 0 \,, \quad i = 1, 2, \ldots, n. \tag{4.99}
$$

Here, the index k denotes the time level ($k = 0, 1, 2, \ldots$) and Δt_k the kth time step. This system together with the condition

$$
\pi \sum_{i=1}^{n} J_{zi}(t_k)(a_i^2 - a_{i-1}^2) = i(t_k)
$$

leads to a recurrent system of equations in the matrix form

$$
\boldsymbol{V}_k \boldsymbol{J}_k = \boldsymbol{W}_k \boldsymbol{J}_{k-1}. \tag{4.100}
$$

The matrix $\boldsymbol{V}_k$ has rank $n + 1$ and its entries are given by

$$
v_{ki,i} = -1 + \frac{\mu_0 \gamma}{\Delta t_k} \left(\frac{a_i^2}{2} \ln(a_i) - \frac{a_i^2}{4} + \frac{b_i^2}{4} - \frac{a_{i-1}^2}{2} \ln(b_i) \right), \quad i = 1, 2, \ldots, n \,,
$$

$$
v_{ki,j} = \frac{\mu_0 \gamma}{\Delta t_k} \ln(b_i) \left(\frac{a_j^2 - a_{j-1}^2}{2} \right), \quad 1 \le j < i \le n \,,
$$

$$
v_{ki,j} = \frac{\mu_0 \gamma}{\Delta t_k} \left(\frac{a_i^2}{2} \ln(a_i) - \frac{a_i^2}{4} - \frac{a_{i-1}^2}{2} \ln(a_{i-1}) + \frac{a_{i-1}^2}{4} \right), \quad 1 \le i < j \le n \,,
$$

$$
v_{ki,n+1} = 1 \,, \quad i = 1, 2, \ldots, n \,, \quad v_{kn+1,j} = \pi(a_j^2 - a_{j-1}^2) \,, \quad j = 1, 2, \ldots, n \,,
$$

$$
v_{kn+1,n+1} = 0 \,. \tag{4.101}
$$

The matrix $\boldsymbol{W}_k$ has the entries

$$w_{ki,i} = \frac{\mu_0 \gamma}{\Delta t_k} \left(\frac{a_i^2}{2} \ln(a_i) - \frac{a_i^2}{4} + \frac{b_i^2}{4} - \frac{a_{i-1}^2}{2} \ln(b_i) \right), \quad i = 1, 2, \ldots, n,$$

$$w_{ki,j} = \frac{\mu_0 \gamma}{\Delta t_k} \ln(b_i) \left(\frac{a_j^2 - a_{j-1}^2}{2} \right), \quad 1 \le j < i \le n,$$

$$w_{ki,j} = \frac{\mu_0 \gamma}{\Delta t_k} \left(\frac{a_i^2}{2} \ln(a_i) - \frac{a_i^2}{4} - \frac{a_{i-1}^2}{2} \ln(a_{i-1}) + \frac{a_{i-1}^2}{4} \right), \quad 1 \le i < j \le n,$$

$$w_{ki,n+1} = 0, \quad i = 1, 2, \ldots, n, \quad w_{kn+1,j} = 0, \quad j = 1, 2, \ldots, n,$$

$$w_{kn+1,n+1} = 1. \tag{4.102}$$

Finally, the column vectors $\boldsymbol{J}_{k-1}$ and $\boldsymbol{J}_k$ have the form

$$j_{k-1,i} = J_{zi}(t_{k-1}), \quad i = 1, 2, \ldots, n, \quad j_{k-1,n+1} = i(t_k),$$
$$j_{k,i} = J_{zi}(t_k), \quad i = 1, 2, \ldots, n, \quad j_{k,n+1} = J_{z0}(t_k). \tag{4.103}$$

System (4.100) can be written

$$\boldsymbol{J}_k = \boldsymbol{M}_k \boldsymbol{J}_{k-1}, \quad \boldsymbol{M}_k = \boldsymbol{V}_k^{-1} \boldsymbol{W}_k. \tag{4.104}$$

If the time step is constant, then the matrix $\boldsymbol{M}_k$ does not depend on time.

The resistance $R'(t)$ of the conductor is assumed to be temperature independent. Its time evolution per unit length may be determined from the total losses per unit length $P'(t)$. These can be calculated approximately using the formula

$$P'(t) = \frac{\pi}{\gamma} \sum_{i=1}^{n} (a_i^2 - a_{i-1}^2) J_{zi}(t)^2. \tag{4.105}$$

This yields

$$R'(t) = \frac{P'(t)}{i(t)^2}. \tag{4.106}$$

The internal inductance per unit length $L'(t)$ can be determined from the magnetic field energy per unit length $W'(t)$. There holds

$$L'(t) = \frac{2W'(t)}{i(t)^2}, \tag{4.107}$$

where

$$2W'(t) = 2\mu_0 \pi \int_0^{R_1} H_\varphi^2(r, t) r \, dr, \tag{4.108}$$

$H_\varphi(r, t)$ being the tangential component of magnetic field strength that is a function of radius r and time t. Formula (4.108) can be written

$$2W'(t) = 2\mu_0 \pi \sum_{i=1}^{n} \int_{a_{i-1}}^{a_i} H_\varphi^2(r, t) r \, dr, \tag{4.109}$$

where the values of $H_\varphi(r,t)$ in the interval $r \in \langle a_{i-1}, a_i \rangle$ must be approximated. It follows from

$$2\pi r H_\varphi(r,t) = \int_S J_z \mathrm{d}S \doteq \pi \sum_{j=1}^{i-1} J_{zj}(t)(a_j^2 - a_{j-1}^2) + \pi J_{zi}(t)(r^2 - a_{i-1}^2)$$

that

$$H_\varphi(r,t)_{r \in \langle a_{i-1}, a_i \rangle} = \frac{\sum_{j=1}^{i-1} J_{zj}(t)(a_j^2 - a_{j-1}^2) + J_{zi}(t)(r^2 - a_{i-1}^2)}{2r}. \tag{4.110}$$

Putting

$$C_i(t) = \sum_{j=1}^{i-1} J_{zj}(t)(a_j^2 - a_{j-1}^2) - J_{zi}(t)a_{i-1}^2$$

and substituting (4.110) into (4.109), we obtain

$$2W'(t) = \frac{\mu_0 \pi}{2} \sum_{i=1}^{n} \int_{a_{i-1}}^{a_i} \left(\frac{C_i(t) + J_{zi}(t)r^2}{r} \right)^2 r \, \mathrm{d}r.$$

This finally yields

$$2W'(t) = \frac{\mu_0 \pi}{2} \sum_{i=1}^{n} \left[C_i^2(t) \ln \frac{a_i}{a_{i-1}} + C_i(t) J_{zi}(t)(a_i^2 - a_{i-1}^2) + J_{zi}^2(t) \frac{a_i^4 - a_{i-1}^4}{4} \right]. \tag{4.111}$$

Now we have to calculate three limits:

$$\lim_{t \to 0} L'(t) = \frac{\mu_0}{8\pi} = \frac{10^{-7}}{2} \text{ H/m}, \tag{4.112}$$

$$\lim_{t \to 0} R'(t) = \frac{1}{\gamma S} = \frac{1}{\pi R_1^2 \gamma}, \Omega/\text{m}, \tag{4.113}$$

and the first term in (4.111),

$$\lim_{a_0 \to 0} C_1^2(t) \ln \frac{a_1}{a_0} = 0. \tag{4.114}$$

Case 1: Harmonic current   The accuracy of this algorithm was first tested on a conductor connected to a source of harmonic current because the results may easily be checked (at least for the steady state) by the analytical method mentioned in Section 4.4.3. The radius of the conductor $R_1 = 0.005$ m, the electrical conductivity $\gamma = 57$ MS/m, the amplitude of the current is 300 A, and the current frequency $f = 5000$ Hz. The analytical distribution of the moduli of the steady-state current density along the radius is depicted in Fig. 4.53.

Numerical computations were performed using Mathematica 5.2 for $n = 25$, $i(t) = 300 \sin(10000\pi t)$, $\Delta t = 10^{-7}$ s and the first five periods. The circular rings were chosen to have equal areas. Figure 4.54 shows the time evolution of the current density corresponding to the radius $r = 0.0005$ m. This figure also shows purely sinusoidal current density calculated analytically (the thicker dotted line), described by the function $J_z(t) = 0.509001 \sin(10000\pi t + 2.25905)$ A/mm^2.

Figure 4.55 shows the same quantity for the radius $r = 0.002548$ m (closer to the axis of the conductor). Figure 4.56 corresponds to the radius $r = 0.0049$ m (near the surface of the conductor).

The reader can see differences in the evolution, amplitude, and phase shift. It is interesting that the differences between the amplitudes of current density obtained analytically and numerically in the steady state are practically negligible – after the first four periods the current density reaches the steady state and the differences between both curves at their maxima do not exceed about 0.2% (this accuracy further grows with growing number n of the circular rings and decreasing time step $\triangle t$). For example, the amplitude of the steady-state current density at radius $r = 0.002914$ m calculated analytically is 2.1674 A/mm^2, while the numerically obtained value (after five periods) is 2.165 A/mm^2.

Case 2: Pulse current Next, let us consider the same conductor as in the previous case, now connected to a source of pulse current $i(t) = 20000(e^{-100t} - e^{-1000t})$ that is depicted in Fig. 4.57.

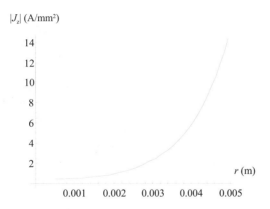

Figure 4.53. Radial distribution of the modulus of steady-state current density.

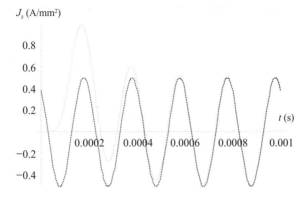

Figure 4.54. Time evolution of the current density at $r = 0.0005$ m.

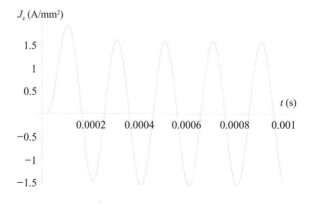

Figure 4.55. Time evolution of the current density at $r = 0.002548$ m.

This time the cross section was split into $n = 40$ circular rings with equal widths (see Fig. 4.58). The time step was chosen as $\triangle t = 0.00000005$ s and the task was solved in time interval $t \in \langle 0, T_{\max} = 0.02 \rangle$ s, thus for 400000 time steps. The computation was then stopped as the current was practically fully damped.

For higher values of n (the number of the rings) we may have problems with inverting matrix $\boldsymbol{V}_k$ (see (4.104)), which has to be carried out with high precision. This is possible when using SW Mathematica, but in other environments (MatLab) it can create difficulties. In such a case it is better to transform the solution of (4.100) into a form that works with the time increments of the current densities in two successive time steps. Then the system matrix $\boldsymbol{V}_k$ may be modified into another matrix whose elements $v_{ki,j}$ for $j > i+1$ are equal to zero. The solution is then much more accurate and the only drawback of this algorithm is that it consists of more steps.

Figure 4.59 shows the distribution of the current density along the radius of the conductor at various time instants. In the period when the pulse current rises, the current density grows

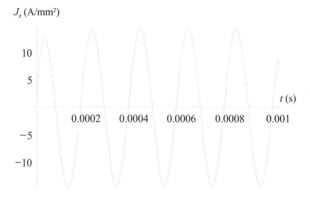

Figure 4.56. Time evolution of the current density at $r = 0.00495$ m.

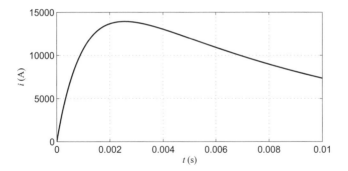

Figure 4.57.   Pulse current $i(t) = 20000(e^{-100t} - e^{-1000t})$.

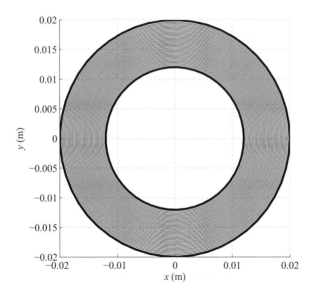

Figure 4.58.   Discretization of the ring.

with the radius, but after the current exceeds its maximum this distribution slightly decreases. On the other hand, Fig. 4.60 shows the time evolution of current densities at three radii (inner surface of the conductor, mean radius, and outer surface of the conductor). These curves are of a similar character as the considered current pulse.

Finally, Fig. 4.61 shows the space and time distributions of current densities within the conductor.

Figure 4.62 shows the equivalent resistance $R'(t)$ of the conductor per unit length during a short period of time at the very beginning of the process. The resistance rises quickly from its initial value $R'(0) = 0.0002234\,\Omega/\text{m}$ to about $0.0075\,\Omega/\text{m}$ (which is almost 35 times more); then it decays exponentially back to the initial value. The computation of

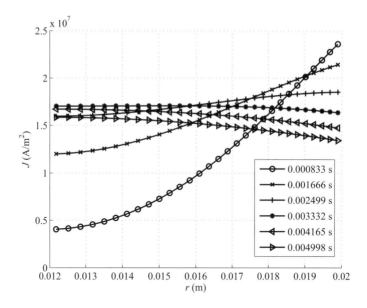

Figure 4.59. Distribution of the current density along the radius of the conductor at different time instants.

the function $R'(t)$ has to be carried out with extreme care, otherwise numerical errors may accumulate in time and cause an incorrect growth of the resistance. This is due to rapidly decreasing values of $i(t)^2$ in the denominator of (4.106), while currents passing through the individual circular rings may be substantially different from zero.

Finally, Fig. 4.63 shows the internal inductance $L'(t)$ of the conductor per unit length. Its initial value $L'(0) = 5 \cdot 10^{-8}$ H/m first drops rapidly to $L' = 2 \times 10^{-9}$ H/m but then it rises back to the original value $L'(0)$. Also, here the time integration must be performed very carefully to suppress numerical errors during integration. The computations were very fast – 10^4 time steps only took several seconds on a 3 GHz PC with 2 GB RAM.

In order to validate the methodology, some results of this example were compared with results calculated by the FEM using code COMSOL Multiphysics. For example, Fig. 4.64 shows the time evolution of current densities at the same radii as in Fig. 4.65, but for a shorter time interval. Nevertheless, the differences do not exceed about 0.5% (this is the principal reason why these curves are not depicted directly in Fig. 4.60).

Direct comparison of both methods is shown in Fig. 4.65 that contains the dependence of the current density along the radius for time 0.003 s. The differences are negligible again.

4.6.2 Pulse current in a long conductor of rectangular profile

In this section we continue with an example that no longer is solvable analytically. We are interested in the distribution of the current density in a nonmagnetic conductor of rectangular cross section carrying a time-variable current. The electrical conductivity of the conductor is γ and the dimensions of its cross section are a and b, as shown in Fig. 4.66.

For the numerical approximation, the cross section is covered with a mesh consisting of triangular or rectangular elements $S_1, S_2, \ldots, S_n$, as indicated in Fig. 4.66. We denote the element midpoints by $Q_i, i = 1, 2, \ldots, n$. Again we use a piecewise-constant approximation of the current density $J_{zi}, i = 1, 2, \ldots, n$, in the elements. The model (4.18) is discretized as follows:

$$- J_z(Q_i, t) + \frac{\mu_0 \gamma}{2\pi} \cdot \sum_{j=1}^{n} \frac{\mathrm{d} J_{zj}(t)}{\mathrm{d}t} \int_{S_j} \ln(d_{ij}) \, \mathrm{d}S + J_{z0}(t) = 0, \quad i = 1, 2, \ldots, n.$$

(4.115)

As usual we also impose an additional condition for the total current,

$$\sum_{i=1}^{n} J_{zi}(t) \mathrm{area}(S_i) = i(t).$$ (4.116)

The symbol d_{ij} stands for the distance between the reference point Q_i and a general integration point $P_j(x, y)$ of S_j, so that

$$d = \sqrt{(x - x_{Q_i})^2 + (y - y_{Q_i})^2}, \quad P_j(x, y) \in S_j.$$ (4.117)

Relation (4.115) is further manipulated in the same way as in the previous section. The Euler method with the time steps $\triangle t_1, \triangle t_2, \ldots$ leads to the matrix equation (4.100), $\mathbf{V}_k \mathbf{J}_k =$

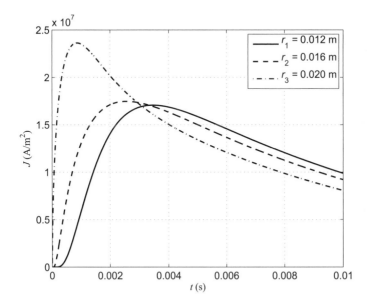

Figure 4.60. Time evolution of the current density at three different radii (integrodifferential method).

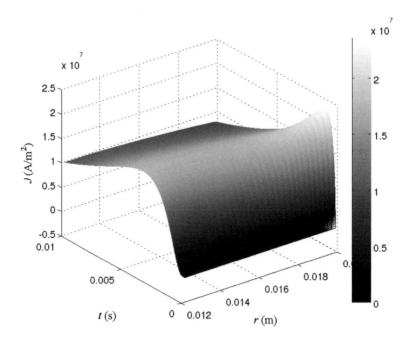

Figure 4.61. Space and time distributions of current densities within the conductor.

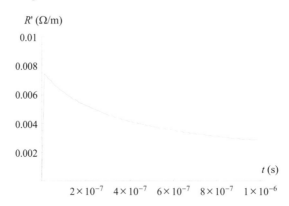

Figure 4.62. Time evolution of the equivalent resistance per unit length $R'(t)$.

$\mathbf{W}_k \mathbf{J}_{k-1}$. In this case the matrices are given by

$$v_{ki,i} = -1 + \frac{\mu_0 \gamma}{2\pi \triangle t_k} \int_{S_i} \ln(d_{ii}) \, \mathrm{d}S \,, \quad i = 1, 2, \ldots, n \,,$$

$$v_{ki,j} = \frac{\mu_0 \gamma}{2\pi \triangle t_k} \int_{S_i} \ln(d_{ij}) \, \mathrm{d}S \,, \quad 1 \leq i, j \leq n \,, \quad i \neq j \,,$$

$$v_{ki,n+1} = 1 \,, \quad i = 1, 2, \ldots, n \,, \quad v_{kn+1,j} = S_j \,, \quad j = 1, 2, \ldots, n \,,$$

$$v_{kn+1,n+1} = 0 \tag{4.118}$$

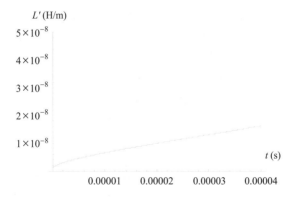

Figure 4.63.   Time evolution of the internal inductance per unit length $L'(t)$.

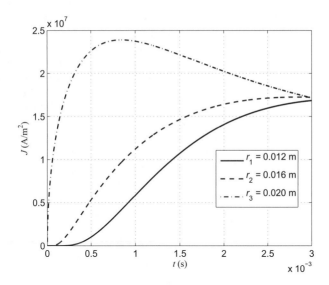

Figure 4.64.   Time evolution of the current density at three different radii (finite difference method).

and

$$w_{ki,j} = \frac{\mu_0 \gamma}{2\pi \Delta t_k} \int_{S_j} \ln(d_{ij}) \, dS \,, \quad i,j = 1, 2, \ldots, n \,,$$

$$w_{ki,n+1} = 0 \,, \quad i = 1, 2, \ldots, n \,, \quad w_{kn+1,j} = 0 \,, \quad j = 1, 2, \ldots, n \,,$$

$$w_{kn+1,n+1} = 1 \,. \tag{4.119}$$

The vectors $\boldsymbol{J}_k$ and $\boldsymbol{J}_{k-1}$ are the same as in (4.103). The integrals of the type $\int_{S_j} \ln(d_{ij})\, \mathrm{d}S$ are calculated in Appendix C. If the time step $\triangle t_k$ is constant, matrices $\boldsymbol{V}_k$ and $\boldsymbol{W}_k$ remain the same for all time steps, which makes the implementation simpler.

Numerical example   Consider a copper conductor with $\gamma = 57\,\mathrm{MS/m}$ of square cross section $0.1 \times 0.1\,\mathrm{m}^2$. At the initial time $t = 0$, the conductor is connected to a source of harmonic current with amplitude $I = 1\,\mathrm{A}$ and frequency $f = 50\,\mathrm{Hz}$. The cross section of the conductor is covered with a mesh containing 2700 elements. We define three check points $A = (0.00015, 0.00015)$, $B = (0.005, 0.00015)$, and $C = (0.005, 0.005)$, as shown in Fig. 4.67. The time step $\triangle t$ is 10^{-5} s.

Figures 4.68, 4.69, and 4.70 show the time evolution of the current density at the points A, B, and C in several periods before they reach the steady state. In order to reach the steady state, we need three periods for the points A and B, and seven periods for C.

4.6.3   Short-circuit effects in a three-phase system

Dynamic short-circuit forces acting among long massive conductors of a three-phase system represent complex time-dependent functions of time, because the short-circuit currents generally contain several time-variable components. Distribution of these currents over the cross sections of particular conductors is, moreover, not uniform due to skin and proximity effects. Nowadays, evaluation of the short-circuit forces is mostly realized by approximate formulas employing the known time evolution of the short-circuit currents and coefficients which respect the arrangement of the conductors and shapes of their cross sections.

In this section we present a method based on a numerically calculated distribution of the current densities in the conductors. Knowledge of the distribution of current densities at each time step yields the distribution of the magnetic field in the system. Consequently, we can calculate both the instantaneous values of forces as well as the specific Joule losses (internal sources of heat). We use the algorithm presented in the previous section, the only difference being we deal with three parallel conductors instead of one.

Thus, consider a symmetric three-phase system comprising conductors of the same rectangular cross section. The situation is depicted in Fig. 4.72. The conductors are made from copper whose electrical conductivity is $\gamma = 57\,\mathrm{MS/m}$, and the dimensions of their cross sections are $0.01\,\mathrm{m} \times 0.04\,\mathrm{m}$. The distance between their centers is $a = 0.3\,\mathrm{m}$.

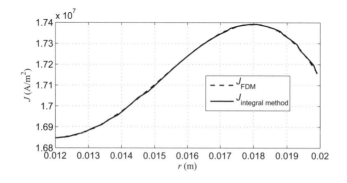

Figure 4.65.   Distribution of the current density along the radius of the conductor for $t = 0.003$ s calculated by the integrodifferential and finite difference methods.

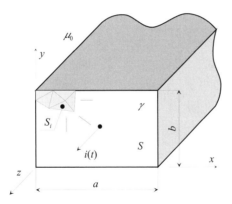

Figure 4.66.   Scheme of a conductor of rectangular profile.

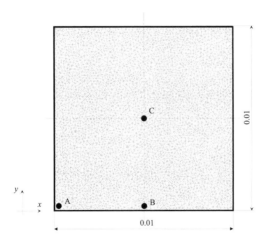

Figure 4.67.   Discretization of the profile and position of the check points.

The current amplitude in all three conductors before and after fault was 2000 A and 6400 A, respectively. Their values at the time of fault is $i_{10} = 2000$ A, $i_{20} = -1000$ A, and $i_{30} = -1000$ A. Provided that the time constant of the electric circuit after fault is $T = 0.1$ s, the phase shift $\alpha = \pi/6$ and $\arctan(\omega L/R) = \pi/3$, the particular currents are given by the following equations:

$$i_1(t) = 2000 \cdot e^{-10t} + 6400 \cdot \left[\sin\left(\omega t - \frac{\pi}{6}\right) + \frac{1}{2} \cdot e^{-10t} \right],$$

$$i_2(t) = -1000 \cdot e^{-10t} + 6400 \cdot \left[\sin\left(\omega t - \frac{5\pi}{6}\right) + \frac{1}{2} \cdot e^{-10t} \right],$$

$$i_3(t) = -1000 \cdot e^{-10t} + 6400 \cdot \left[\sin\left(\omega t - \frac{3\pi}{2}\right) - \frac{1}{2} \cdot e^{-10t} \right]. \qquad (4.120)$$

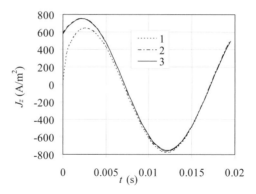

Figure 4.68.   Time evolution of the current density at the point A.

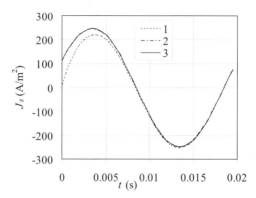

Figure 4.69.   Time evolution of the current density at the point B.

Relations (4.49) and (4.50), extended to the case of three parallel conductors, were used to obtain an approximate distribution of the initial current densities at the moment of fault. Each cross section was covered by a mesh with 326 elements, and we used a time step of $\triangle t = 10^{-4}$ s. The corresponding time evolution is shown in Fig. 4.73.

Figure 4.74 shows the time evolution of the x-components of forces (per meter of length) acting on the conductors. Figure 4.75 shows the y-components. In order to check the accuracy of the computation, we evaluate the sum of all three forces (which in the exact case is zero). Our numerical results gave values on the order of 10^{-12}. The same problem was solved using the FEM (QuickField 5), and in this case the accuracy only was about 10^{-5}.

4.7   STATIC AND 2D EDDY CURRENT PROBLEMS WITH MOTION

Static and 2D linear eddy current problems with motion are usually rather idealized cases of real situations. In this section we shall deal with several typical examples that may, nevertheless, be handled in this manner. Investigated will be two charged thin conductors

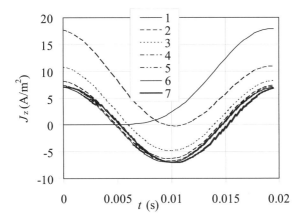

Figure 4.70. Time evolution of the current density at the point C.

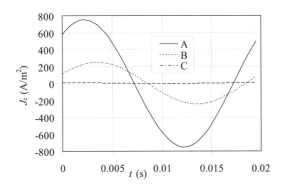

Figure 4.71. The steady-state harmonic current densities at points A, B, and C.

that move with respect to one another, a long conductor that carries periodical current and moves above a long massive electrically conductive plate, continual induction heating of a nonmagnetic cylinder by a moving inductor, and an axisymmetric electrodynamic launcher.

4.7.1 Distribution of charge in a system of two moving conductors

The example simulates the time-dependent evolution of distribution of electric charge along two straight conductors AB and CD of the same lengths $l_1 = l_2 = l = 1$ m and radii $r_1 = r_2 = 0.0005$ m. Their endpoints are defined as A $\equiv [0, 0, 0]$, B $\equiv [1, 0, 0]$, C $\equiv [0.5, -0.5, h(t)]$, and D $\equiv [0.5, 0.5, h(t)]$; see Fig. 4.76. The function $h(t)$ expresses the time-dependent position of the second conductor with respect to the first one. For this example we choose $h(t) = (25 - t)/100$ m, $t \in [0, 24]$ s, which also specifies the velocity of the second conductor. Let the potential of the first unmoving conductor AB be $\varphi_1 = 0$ V

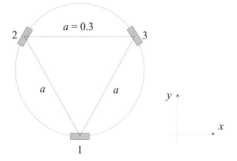

Figure 4.72. Arrangement comprising three massive conductors.

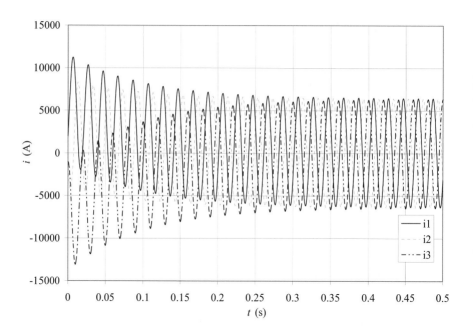

Figure 4.73. Time evolution of the short-circuit currents.

and potential of the moving conductor CD be $\varphi_2 = 1000$ V. Relative permittivity of the neighbor medium $\varepsilon_r = 1$.

The computations start from the continuous model (4.1) and its discretization is carried out analogously as in previous sections. The distances between any two cells on both conductors are functions of time. Both conductors are divided into $n = 500$ equally sized rings (see Fig. 4.77) and each of the rings is divided into 8 cells. This leads to 8000 unknowns for the computation.

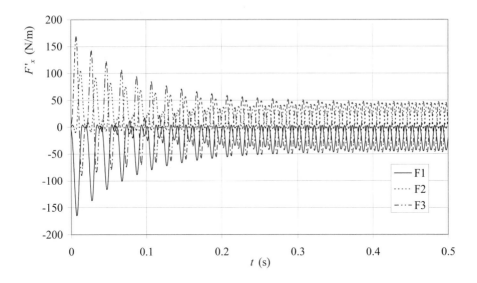

Figure 4.74.   Time evolution of the x-component of short-circuit forces.

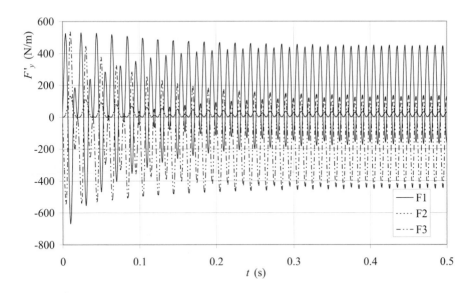

Figure 4.75.   Time evolution of the y-component of short-circuit forces.

In order to process the results we found for each ring the sum of all 8 cell values of charge density σ related to its axial length. Due to symmetry it is sufficient to plot only results corresponding to one of the conductors.

For an illustration, Fig. 4.78 shows the distribution of σ for $t = 5\,\mathrm{s}$ ($h(t) = 0.2\,\mathrm{m}$), for $t = 20\,\mathrm{s}$ ($h(t) = 0.05\,\mathrm{m}$), and finally for $t = 24\,\mathrm{s}$ ($h(t) = 0.01\,\mathrm{m}$).

A long massive conductor of rectangular cross section that carries periodical current moves above the conductive plate; see Fig. 4.79. Both parts are made of copper of electrical conductivity $\gamma = 57 \times 10^6$ S/m. The task is to map the time dependence of eddy current density at points A, B and C of the plate.

The time dependence of the periodical field current is depicted in Fig. 4.77, including its mathematical description. Its amplitude is 1 A while its frequency varies within a given interval at the level of tens of Hertz.

The algorithm of computation starts again from (4.21). Let us first separate the equations describing the behavior of both parts. Denoting the moving conductor by index 1 and the unmoving plate by index 2 and putting $\mathbf{v}_{11} = \mathbf{v}_{22} = \mathbf{0}$ while $\mathbf{v}_{21}(t) = -\mathbf{i}v$, $\mathbf{v}_{12}(t) = \mathbf{i}v$ ($\mathbf{i}$ being the unit vector in the x-direction), we can write

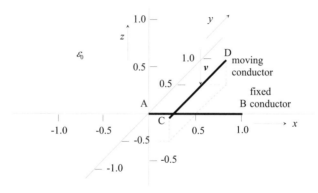

Figure 4.76.   Arrangement of two charged conductors.

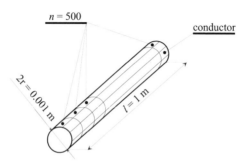

Figure 4.77.   Discretization of the conductors.

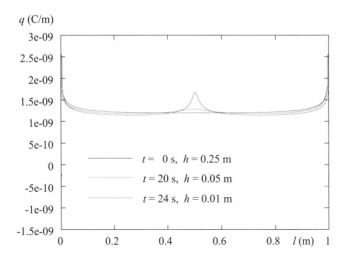

Figure 4.78.   Distribution of surface charge along each conductor at three various time-levels.

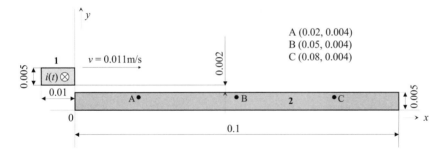

Figure 4.79.   Geometry of the investigated arrangement.

$$- J_{z1}(Q_1, t) + \frac{\mu_0 \gamma_1}{2\pi} \int_{S_1} \frac{\mathrm{d}J_{z1}(P_1, t)}{\mathrm{d}t} \ln[r_{P_1 Q_1}(t)] \,\mathrm{d}S$$

$$+ \frac{\mu_0 \gamma_1}{2\pi} \int_{S_2} \frac{\mathrm{d}J_{z2}(P_2, t)}{\mathrm{d}t} \ln[r_{P_2 Q_1}(t)] \,\mathrm{d}S$$

$$- \frac{\mu_0 \gamma_1}{2\pi} \int_{S_2} J_{z2}(P_2, t) \cdot \frac{v \cdot r_{P_2 Q_1, x}(t)}{r_{P_2 Q_1}^2(t)} \,\mathrm{d}S + J_{z10}(t) = 0,$$

$$- J_{z2}(Q_2, t) + \frac{\mu_0 \gamma_2}{2\pi} \int_{S_1} \frac{\mathrm{d}J_{z1}(P_1, t)}{\mathrm{d}t} \ln[r_{P_1 Q_2}(t)] \,\mathrm{d}S$$

$$+ \frac{\mu_0 \gamma_2}{2\pi} \int_{S_2} \frac{\mathrm{d}J_{z2}(P_2, t)}{\mathrm{d}t} \ln[r_{P_2 Q_2}(t)] \,\mathrm{d}S$$

$$+ \frac{\mu_0 \gamma_2}{2\pi} \int_{S_1} J_{z1}(P_1, t) \cdot \frac{v \cdot r_{P_1 Q_2, x}(t)}{r_{P_1 Q_2}^2(t)} \,\mathrm{d}S = 0 \qquad (4.121)$$

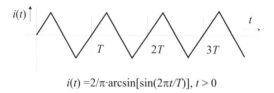

$$i(t) = 2/\pi \cdot \arcsin[\sin(2\pi t/T)],\ t > 0$$

Figure 4.80.   Time dependence of the field current.

with indirect boundary condition

$$\int_{S_1} J_{z1}(P_1, t)\,dS = i(t).\tag{4.122}$$

After the zero-order (current density in each element is considered uniform) space discretization of both cross sections and using the simplest Euler time integration, we obtain for each time level a system of linear equations in the form

$$-J_{z1}(Q_{1j}, t_k) + \frac{\mu_0 \gamma_1}{2\pi} \sum_{i=1}^{n_1} \frac{J_{z1}(P_{1i}, t_k) - J_{z1}(P_{1i}, t_{k-1})}{\triangle t_k} \int_{S_{1i}} \ln[r_{P_{1i}Q_{1j}}(t_k)]\,dS$$

$$+ \frac{\mu_0 \gamma_1}{2\pi} \sum_{l=1}^{n_2} \frac{J_{z2}(P_{2l}, t_k) - J_{z2}(P_{2l}, t_{k-1})}{\triangle t_k} \int_{S_{2l}} \ln[r_{P_{2l}Q_{1j}}(t_k)]\,dS$$

$$- \frac{\mu_0 \gamma_1 v}{2\pi} \sum_{l=1}^{n_2} J_{z2}(P_{2l}, t_k) \int_{S_{2l}} \frac{x_{P_{2l}Q_{1j}}(t_k)}{r^2_{P_{2l}Q_{1j}}(t_k)}\,dS + J_{z10}(t_k) = 0,\quad j = 1, 2, \dots, n_1,$$

$$- J_{z2}(Q_{2m}, t_k) + \frac{\mu_0 \gamma_2}{2\pi} \sum_{i=1}^{n_1} \frac{J_{z1}(P_{1i}, t_k) - J_{z1}(P_{1i}, t_{k-1})}{\triangle t_k} \int_{S_{1i}} \ln[r_{P_{1i}Q_{2m}}(t_k)]\,dS$$

$$+ \frac{\mu_0 \gamma_2 v}{2\pi} \sum_{i=1}^{n_1} J_{z1}(P_{1i}, t_k) \int_{S_{1i}} \frac{x_{P_{1i}Q_{2m}}(t_k)}{r^2_{P_{1i}Q_{2m}}(t_k)}\,dS$$

$$+ \frac{\mu_0 \gamma_2}{2\pi} \sum_{l=1}^{n_2} \frac{J_{z2}(P_{2l}, t_k) - J_{z2}(P_{2l}, t_{k-1})}{\triangle t_k} \int_{S_{2l}} \ln[r_{P_{2l}Q_{2m}}(t_k)]\,dS = 0,$$

$$m = 1, 2, \dots, n_2,$$

$$\sum_{i=1}^{n_1} J_{z1}(P_{1i}, t_k) S_{1i} = i(t_k),\tag{4.123}$$

where n_1 and n_2 are numbers of elements in cross sections 1 and 2, k denotes the time level, while Q_{1j} and Q_{2m} are the midpoints of the jth element of the first part and mth element of the second part, respectively. Thus, every time level is fully described by $n_1 + n_2 + 1$ linear equations that may be expressed in the matrix form as

$$[\boldsymbol{U}_k] \cdot [\boldsymbol{J}_k] = [\boldsymbol{W}_k] \cdot [\boldsymbol{J}_{k-1}]\tag{4.124}$$

containing the following entries:

$$u_{i,j,k} = \frac{\mu_0 \gamma_1}{2\pi \triangle t_k} \int_{S_{1j}} \ln[r_{Q_{1i}P_{1j}}(t_k)] \, \mathrm{d}S \,, \quad 1 \le i,j \le n_1 \,, \quad i \ne j \,,$$

$$u_{i,j,k} = -1 + \frac{\mu_0 \gamma_1}{2\pi \triangle t_k} \int_{S_{1j}} \ln[r_{Q_{1i}P_{1j}}(t_k)] \, \mathrm{d}S \,, \quad 1 \le i = j \le n_1 \,,$$

$$u_{i,n_1+j,k} = \frac{\mu_0 \gamma_1}{2\pi \triangle t_k} \int_{S_{2j}} \ln[r_{Q_{1i}P_{2j}}(t_k)] \, \mathrm{d}S - \frac{\mu_0 \gamma_1 v}{2\pi} \int_{S_{2j}} \frac{x_{Q_{1i}P_{2j}}(t_k)}{r_{Q_{1i}P_{2j}}^2(t_k)} \, \mathrm{d}S \,,$$
$$1 \le i \le n_1 \,, \quad 1 \le j \le n_2 \,,$$

$$u_{n_1+i,j,k} = \frac{\mu_0 \gamma_2}{2\pi \triangle t_k} \int_{S_{1j}} \ln[r_{Q_{2i}P_{1j}}(t_k)] \, \mathrm{d}S + \frac{\mu_0 \gamma_1 v}{2\pi} \int_{S_{1j}} \frac{x_{Q_{2i}P_{1j}}(t_k)}{r_{Q_{2i}P_{1j}}^2(t_k)} \, \mathrm{d}S \,,$$
$$1 \le i \le n_2 \,, \quad 1 \le j \le n_1 \,,$$

$$u_{n_1+i,n_1+j,k} = \frac{\mu_0 \gamma_2}{2\pi \triangle t_k} \int_{S_{2j}} \ln[r_{Q_{2i}P_{2j}}(t_k)] \, \mathrm{d}S \,, \quad 1 \le i,j \le n_2 \,, \quad i \ne j \,,$$

$$u_{n_1+i,n_1+j,k} = -1 + \frac{\mu_0 \gamma_2}{2\pi \triangle t_k} \int_{S_{2j}} \ln[r_{Q_{2i}P_{2j}}(t_k)] \, \mathrm{d}S \,, \quad 1 \le i = j \le n_2 \,,$$

$$u_{i,n_1+n_2+1,k} = 1 \,, \quad 1 \le i \le n_1 \,, \quad u_{i,n_1+n_2+1} = 0 \,, \quad i > n_1 \,,$$

$$u_{n_1+n_2+1,j,k} = S_{1j} \,, \quad 1 \le j \le n_1 \,, \quad u_{n_1+n_2+1,j,k} = 0 \,, \quad j > n_1 \,. \tag{4.125}$$

In a similar way

$$w_{i,j,k} = \frac{\mu_0 \gamma_1}{2\pi \triangle t_k} \int_{S_{1j}} \ln[r_{Q_{1i}P_{1j}}(t_k)] \, \mathrm{d}S \,, \quad 1 \le i,j \le n_1 \,,$$

$$w_{i,j,k} = \frac{\mu_0 \gamma_1}{2\pi \triangle t_k} \int_{S_{1j}} \ln[r_{Q_{1i}P_{1j}}(t_k)] \, \mathrm{d}S \,,$$
$$1 \le i = j \le n_1 \,, \quad 1 \le i \le n_1 \,, \quad 1 \le j \le n_2 \,,$$

$$w_{n_1+i,j,k} = \frac{\mu_0 \gamma_2}{2\pi \triangle t_k} \int_{S_{1j}} \ln[r_{Q_{2i}P_{1j}}(t_k)] \, \mathrm{d}S \,,$$
$$1 \le i \le n_2 \,, \quad 1 \le j \le n_1 \,,$$

$$w_{n_1+i,n_1+j,k} = \frac{\mu_0 \gamma_2}{2\pi \triangle t_k} \int_{S_{2j}} \ln[r_{Q_{2i}P_{2j}}(t_k)] \, \mathrm{d}S \,, \quad 1 \le i,j \le n_2 \,,$$

$$w_{i,j,k} = 0 \,, \quad 1 \le i \le n_1 + n_2 \,, \quad j > n_1 + n_2 \,,$$

$$w_{i,j,k} = 0 \,, \quad i > n_1 + n_2 \,, \quad 1 \le j \le n_1 + n_2 \,,$$

$$w_{i,j,k} = 0 \,, \quad i,j > n_1 + n_2 \,, \quad i \ne j \,,$$

$$w_{i,j,k} = 1 \,, \quad i,j > n_1 + n_2 \,, \quad i = j \,. \tag{4.126}$$

Finally, the vectors $[\boldsymbol{J}_k]$ and $[\boldsymbol{J}_{k-1}]$ contain the following elements:

$$J_{i,k} = J_{z1}(Q_{1i}, t_k), \quad 1 \leq i \leq n_1,$$

$$J_{n_1+i,k} = J_{z2}(Q_{2i}, t_k), \quad 1 \leq i \leq n_2,$$

$$J_{n_1+n_2+1,k} = J_{z10}(t_k), \tag{4.127}$$

$$J_{i,k-1} = J_{z1}(Q_{1i}, t_{k-1}), \quad 1 \leq i \leq n_1,$$

$$J_{n_1+i,k-1} = J_{z2}(Q_{2i}, t_{k-1}), \quad 1 \leq i \leq n_2,$$

$$J_{n_1+n_2+1,k-1} = i_1(t_k), \quad J_{n_1+n_2+2,k-1} = i_2(t_k) = 0 \tag{4.128}$$

(the total current in the plate is equal to zero).

Definite integrals of the type

$$I_1 = \int_S \ln[r] \, \mathrm{d}S,$$

$$I_2 = \int_S \frac{x}{r^2} \, \mathrm{d}S,$$

$$I_3 = \int_S \frac{y}{r^2} \, \mathrm{d}S$$

over the mesh elements appearing in (4.125) and (4.126) are processed and evaluated in Appendix C.

The algorithm was validated by several computations of the same arrangement without motion using well-known FEM codes (QuickField 5, FEMM 4.0). The agreement was excellent.

The example [144] considers (after careful testing of the convergence of results) the following input data: geometrical dimensions and velocity of the field conductor agree with Fig. 4.79, frequency $f = 10\,\mathrm{Hz}$ ($T = 0.1\,\mathrm{s}$), number of triangles covering the cross section of the field conductor $n_1 = 200$, plate $n_2 = 1325$, time step $\triangle t = 10^{-4}\,\mathrm{s}$.

The computations are relatively slow because at each time level it is necessary to repeatedly evaluate matrix $[\boldsymbol{J}_k]$ and calculate its inverse. Moreover, the higher the frequency, the finer the mesh has to be to achieve the same accuracy. Figure 4.81 shows the time evolution of current density at point $A \equiv (0.02, 0.004)$ of the plate, Fig. 4.82 at point $B \equiv (0.05, 0.004)$ and, Fig. 4.83 at point $C \equiv (0.08, 0.004)$.

The calculated curves exhibit perfect symmetry. The time dependence of current density at point A is opposite to that at point C, and perfectly visible also is the time symmetry at point B. Even this fact indicates the correctness of the computations.

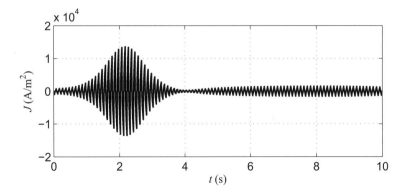

Figure 4.81. Time evolution of current density at point A.

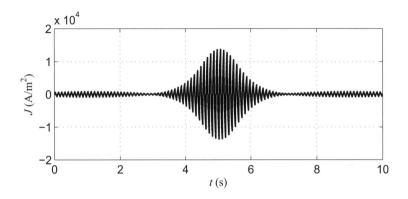

Figure 4.82. Time evolution of current density at point B.

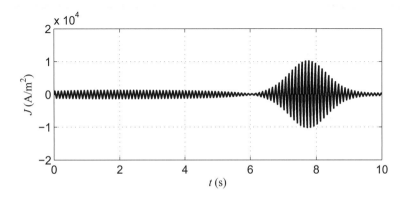

Figure 4.83. Time evolution of current density at point C.

CHAPTER 5

INDIRECT SOLUTION OF ELECTROMAGNETIC FIELDS BY THE BOUNDARY ELEMENT METHOD

5.1 INTRODUCTION

The boundary element method (BEM) is an approximate computational technique for solving linear partial differential equations (PDEs). A nice overview of historical development of this method can be found in Section 1.2 of Ref. 157. In contrast to the finite element method (FEM), BEM is an *integral method*. It departs from a boundary integral reformulation of the underlying PDE called *boundary integral equation* (BIE) and yields a system of linear algebraic equations with a full matrix, which typically is solved by means of Gauss elimination. In contrast to this, the FEM yields sparse matrices that can be solved using sparse iterative (and more recently also sparse direct) solvers. the BEM can be applied in many areas of engineering and science including electrostatics, electromagnetics, linear elasticity, fluid mechanics, and acoustics (see, e.g., Refs. 155, 157–160, and 167 and the references therein). In computational electromagnetics, the more traditional name method of moments (MoM) is often, though not always, synonymous with BEM.

Some kind of comparison of advantages and disadvantages of the BEM versus its main competitor, the FEM, is a traditional and indivisible part of every BEM text. At this time, therefore, let us express several subjective opinions as well.

There is no question that the BEM is more suitable than the FEM for certain types of engineering problems (this book demonstrates it clearly). The most frequently cited advantage of the BEM over the FEM is that the former only requires the discretization of the surface of the domain. This eliminates the necessity of volumetric meshing, which is one of the most time-consuming operations in the finite element analysis. The BEM is

Integral Methods in Low-Frequency Electromagnetics. By I. Doležel, P. Karban, and P. Šolín.

most advantageous when dealing with domains whose volumetric meshing is problematic, and whose surface-to-volume ratio is small. (Note, for example, that the surface-to-volume ratio is very large for thin shells, and thus the BEM is not the perfect method for this type of problem.) The BEM also is known to achieve good accuracy at points of stress or flux concentration, such as reentrant corners or edges. Yet another advantage of the BEM over the FEM is that it is better suited for problems involving fields that extend to infinity.

On the other hand, a major disadvantage of the BEM is that it only can be applied to PDEs whose *Green's function* (or fundamental solution) is known. The number of PDE operators whose Green's functions are known is rather limited, and no general procedure for the derivation of Green's functions is available. In practice, this places considerable restrictions on the range and generality of problems to which boundary elements are practical.

The Green's function is based on the solution of the PDE subject to a singular load (e.g., the electrical field arising from a point charge, or displacement field arising from a point load). Typically, the solution is infinite at the point of application of the singular load, and integrating such singular fields is not easy. For simple element geometries (e.g., planar triangles) analytical integration can be used. For more general elements, however, it may be necessary to design purely numerical schemes that adapt to the singularity. Such schemes come at great computational cost. Some savings in the integration cost are possible when the source point and target element lie far apart – then the local gradient surrounding the source point may be easy to approximate due to a smooth decay of the Green's function far from the singularity. This feature is used often to accelerate boundary element problem calculations. Green's functions of axisymmetric problems typically involve elliptic integrals whose evaluation is nontrivial.

Nonlinearities can be included in the formulation, but they generally introduce volume integrals, which then require the volume to be discretized, removing one of the most important advantages of the BEM. Another point where the BEM is not as flexible as the FEM is the extension to higher-order approximations (here we mean cubic and higher-degree polynomials), error control, and automatic adaptivity.

There are numerous texts on Green's functions [151–153, 156, 162]. An interesting on-line resource for Green's functions is the *Green's Function Library* at the web page of the University of Nebraska, Lincoln. Worth mentioning also is the web page created by the boundary element community (http://www.boundaryelements.com/), where lots of useful information about Green's functions and the BEM can be found.

In Section 5.1.1 we illustrate the process of converting a linear PDE into a boundary integral equation. Since the Dirac functional and consequently also the Green's function are defined very vaguely in most texts, we make an attempt to provide a safe framework for operations with these objects. We also touch on simple variational techniques, which make it possible to understand rigorously facts that most practitioners deduce from vague statements. We deliberately sacrifice some subtle details to keep the text reasonably simple. In order to understand words like "weak," "almost all," and "almost everywhere," we refer the reader to Appendix A in Ref. 166. More subtle details need to be looked up in more advanced functional analytic texts [163–165].

To make this text reasonably self-contained, we also mention basic approximation techniques for the boundary integral equations and present a concise overview of Green's functions for partial differential operators in Section 5.1.2.

5.1.1 Fundamental concepts

Let us illustrate the basic ideas of the boundary element method on the example of a 2D potential problem described by the Laplace equation

$$-\Delta\phi = 0 \quad \text{in } \Omega. \tag{5.1}$$

Here Δ is the Laplacian and Ω a 2D or 3D bounded domain. The boundary of Ω is smooth with the exception of a finite number of nonsmooth "corners." Prior to introducing the boundary element method, we need to discuss several elementary techniques, starting with Green's identities.

5.1.1.1 Green's second identity This is a basic identity of variational calculus that can be found in virtually every textbook on partial differential equations. Assume a pair of twice weakly differentiable functions ϕ and λ in the domain Ω. Then

$$\int_\Omega (\phi\Delta\lambda - \lambda\Delta\phi)\,\mathrm{d}x = \int_{\partial\Omega} \left(\phi\frac{\partial\lambda}{\partial\nu} - \lambda\frac{\partial\phi}{\partial\nu}\right)\,\mathrm{d}S. \tag{5.2}$$

Here, the symbols $\partial\Omega$ and ν stand for the boundary to Ω and the unit outer normal vector to $\partial\Omega$ (defined almost everywhere on $\partial\Omega$). This identity holds in the weak sense, that is, for functions that have singularities. In the following it is applied to singular Green's functions.

Green's second identity is an immediate consequence of Green's first identity (also called *Green's theorem* or *generalized integration by parts formula*):

$$\int_\Omega (\Delta\lambda)\phi\,\mathrm{d}x = -\int_\Omega \nabla\lambda\cdot\nabla\phi\,\mathrm{d}x + \int_{\partial\Omega} \frac{\partial\lambda}{\partial\nu}\phi\,\mathrm{d}S. \tag{5.3}$$

To deduce (5.2), apply Green's theorem to $(\Delta\phi)\lambda$ and subtract the result from (5.3).

5.1.1.2 Dirac functional and Green's function The Green's function is used heavily in many areas of physics and engineering, yet its definition in most physical and engineering texts is very vague. Consequently, many students and researchers do not feel comfortable working with it, which in turn has a negative influence on the popularity of the boundary element method. Therefore, let us try to explain what the Green's function is and what it is not.

We will take the Laplace operator as an example. Typically, the Green's function λ_z corresponding to a point $z \in \Omega$ is said to be the solution of the equation

$$-\Delta\lambda_z = \delta_z, \tag{5.4}$$

where δ_z is the singular point load corresponding to the point z. However, the Dirac functional δ_z is not a standard mathematical function, because there is no function that equals infinity at z, equals zero everywhere else, and whose integral over the entire space equals one. Equation (5.4) is an intuitive symbol, but not a rigorous equation with which one can work. The Dirac functional δ_z is a *linear form* that *takes an arbitrary function g as an argument and returns its value at the point z*. The Dirac functional is often defined in spaces of continuous functions over the domain Ω. By V let us denote one such space, and let $z \in \Omega$. Then the Dirac functional is defined as

$$\delta_z(w) = w(z) \quad \text{for all } w \in V. \tag{5.5}$$

If V is a Hilbert space (has an inner product), then the Riesz representation theorem says that every linear form φ over the space V has a unique representant $v_\varphi \in V$ (a function in the original space) such that

$$\varphi(w) = \int_\Omega v_\phi(\boldsymbol{x})w(\boldsymbol{x})\,\mathrm{d}\boldsymbol{x} \quad \text{for all } w \in V\,. \tag{5.6}$$

Note that *if $\delta_{\boldsymbol{z}}$ had a representant in the space V*, then this would be a function with the properties described above, that is, it would be zero everywhere except $\boldsymbol{z}$, it would "be equal to infinity" at $\boldsymbol{z}$, and its integral would be one. This is the natural intuition behind the Dirac functional that many physicists and engineers like. However, let us repeat that these conditions do not define a function. Moreover, note that the space of continuous functions is not a Hilbert space, and the most frequently used spaces in computational engineering such as the Lebesgue and Sobolev spaces cannot operate with pointwise function values. For details, see Appendix A in Ref. 166. As a consequence, the Riesz representant of the Dirac functional $\delta_{\boldsymbol{z}}$ does not exist in these spaces.

Still, one can work with the symbolical expression $\delta_{\boldsymbol{z}}(\boldsymbol{x})$ similarly as if it was a standard function defined in $\mathbb{R}^d$, but *only under the integral sign*, and with the meaning

$$\int_{\mathbb{R}^d} \delta_{\boldsymbol{z}}(\boldsymbol{x})w(\boldsymbol{x})\mathrm{d}\boldsymbol{x} = w(\boldsymbol{z})\,. \tag{5.7}$$

Now let us see how this translates into the definition of the Green's function. In the light of the above, it is clear that one cannot define the Green's function to be the solution of (5.4). This would include at least two further mistakes in addition to what was said previously: First, note that the Laplace operator deletes constants and linear polynomials, and thus the solution $\lambda_{\boldsymbol{z}}$ could not be unique. Second, the Green's function would have to be twice continuously differentiable, otherwise the application of the Laplace operator on it would not be permitted.

The correct way to define the Green's function is through the variational (weak) formulation. In one spatial dimension, the Green's function for the Laplace operator can be obtained easily as a piecewise-linear function that even satisfies given Dirichlet boundary conditions. Let us skip this trivial case. In two and three spatial dimensions, the geometric variability of the domain Ω does not allow us to take into account the boundary conditions, and thus we look for Green's functions defined in the entire domain $\mathbb{R}^d$.

The Green's function is defined as the solution of the variational equation

$$-\int_{\mathbb{R}^d} \Delta\lambda_{\boldsymbol{z}}(\boldsymbol{x})w(\boldsymbol{x})\,\mathrm{d}\boldsymbol{x} = w(\boldsymbol{z}) \quad \text{for all } w \in V\,, \tag{5.8}$$

where V is the standard Sobolev space. Through (5.7), the reader can make an intuitive connection between (5.8) and the symbolic equation (5.4).

It is important for the reader to see that the (weak) Laplacian of $\lambda_{\boldsymbol{z}}$ is zero for (almost all) $\boldsymbol{x} \neq \boldsymbol{z}$. Usually people conclude this from (5.4), but the same can be shown correctly using a simple variational argument. Assume that this is not true, and in that case we are able to find at least a very small open set S in Ω not containing $\boldsymbol{z}$, where $-\Delta\lambda_{\boldsymbol{z}} > 0$ (this is a deliberate choice, without loss of generality we could also say $-\Delta\lambda_{\boldsymbol{z}} < 0$). Since the function w is arbitrary in V, we can choose it to be positive in the set S and zero outside (in particular, $w(\boldsymbol{z}) = 0$). However, then we have a positive number on the left-hand side of (5.8), obtained by integrating the product of two positive functions over S, while the right-hand side of (5.8) is $w(z) = 0$, which is a contradiction.

Note that the definition of the Green's function via (5.8) eliminates all the problems encountered above: λ_z is defined in a correct way, it is unique, and nonsmooth and singular behavior is allowed.

5.1.1.3 Boundary integral equation
It is widely known (see, e.g., Refs. 152, 157, and 158) that the Green's function for the Laplace operator in two spatial dimensions is

$$\lambda_z(x) = \frac{1}{2\pi} \ln\left(\frac{1}{|x-z|}\right) \tag{5.9}$$

and that in three dimensions it has the form

$$\lambda_z(x) = \frac{1}{4\pi|x-z|}. \tag{5.10}$$

Here, $|x-z|$ is the Euclidean distance of the points x and z,

$$|x-z| = \sqrt{\sum_i (x_i - z_i)^2}.$$

Note that in both cases, the Green's function λ_z is twice weakly differentiable. We encourage the reader to calculate the Laplacian of both functions and verify that it is zero whenever $x \neq z$.

Let z be an arbitrary point in Ω, $\lambda_z(x)$ the Green's function of the Laplace operator corresponding to z, and $\phi(x)$ the unknown solution of the Laplace equation (assumed to be twice weakly differentiable as well). We insert these two functions into (5.2):

$$\int_\Omega (\phi\Delta\lambda_z - \lambda_z\Delta\phi)\,dx = \int_{\partial\Omega}\left(\phi\frac{\partial\lambda_z}{\partial\nu} - \lambda_z\frac{\partial\phi}{\partial\nu}\right)dS. \tag{5.11}$$

Using (5.8), the fact that the (weak) Laplacian of λ_z is zero outside Ω, and the fact that ϕ is a (weak) solution of the Laplace equation, (5.11) simplifies to

$$-\phi(z) = \int_{\partial\Omega}\left(\phi(x)\frac{\partial\lambda_z(x)}{\partial\nu} - \lambda_z(x)\frac{\partial\phi(x)}{\partial\nu}\right)dS. \tag{5.12}$$

Note that the application of the Green's function to (5.11) eliminated the volumetric integrals. Thus, identity (5.12) only contains integrals over the boundary $\partial\Omega$ and is called a *boundary integral equation* (BIE). Equation (5.12) is valid for points z lying in the interior of Ω only. If the point z lies on the boundary $\partial\Omega$, we obtain a slightly different equation

$$-\frac{1}{2}\phi(z) = \int_{\partial\Omega}\left(\phi(x)\frac{\partial\lambda_z(x)}{\partial\nu} - \lambda_z(x)\frac{\partial\phi(x)}{\partial\nu}\right)dS \tag{5.13}$$

(see, e.g., Section 2.2 in Ref. 158 or Section 3.6.3 in Ref. 161). Equation (5.13) is used to calculate approximate values of ϕ and $\partial\phi/\partial\nu$ along the entire boundary $\partial\Omega$. Once these functions are known, equation (5.12) is used to evaluate the value of ϕ for any interior point of the domain Ω. Let us now describe how equation (5.13) is solved.

5.1.1.4 Approximate solution of equation (5.13) In practice, equation (5.2) always is equipped with some boundary conditions. Let us assume, for example, that the boundary $\partial\Omega$ is divided into two disjoint parts Γ_D and Γ_N, where different types of boundary conditions are prescribed: Dirichlet condition

$$\phi(\boldsymbol{x}) = g_D(\boldsymbol{x}) \quad \text{for all } \boldsymbol{x} \in \Gamma_D \tag{5.14}$$

and a Neumann condition

$$\frac{\partial\phi(\boldsymbol{x})}{\partial\nu} = g_N(\boldsymbol{x}) \quad \text{for all } \boldsymbol{x} \in \Gamma_N, \tag{5.15}$$

where $\nu(\boldsymbol{x})$ is the unit outer normal vector to $\partial\Omega$ at the point $\boldsymbol{x}$. The reader does not have to worry about corners where ν is undefined, since the corners represent a zero-measure set that plays no role in the variational context. On the computational side, ν will always be defined using a boundary edge. The situation is depicted in Fig. 5.1.

For the purpose of numerical approximation, both parts of the boundary are approximated using small linear segments, as shown in Fig. 5.2.

By $K_1, K_2, \ldots, K_{M_D}$ and $K_{M_D+1}, K_{M_D+2}, \ldots, K_{M_D+M_N}$ let us denote the segments corresponding to Γ_D and Γ_N, respectively. The total number of segments is denoted by $M = M_D + M_N$. These segments are called *boundary elements*. Usually, one uses sufficiently many of them so that the geometry of the domain is captured well, and it is desirable to use an even finer division close to reentrant corners and edges where singularities are expected.

The simplest approach to the approximation of equation (5.13) is to use piecewise-constant elements. Thus, every element K_i carries one unknown parameter Y_i corresponding geometrically to its midpoint m_i. On elements corresponding to Γ_D, where the solution value $y_i = \phi(m_i)$ is known from the Dirichlet boundary condition, the unknown Y_i represents the normal derivative, $Y_i = \partial\phi/\partial\nu(m_i)$. Vice versa, on elements corresponding to Γ_N, where the normal derivative $y_i = \partial\phi/\partial\nu(m_i)$ is known, the unknown Y_i stands for the function value, $Y_i = \phi(m_i)$. Since the Green's function $\lambda_{\boldsymbol{z}}$ is known explicitly for every point $\boldsymbol{z} = m_i$, its values as well as normal derivatives are always known.

Now we can proceed to the construction of the system of linear algebraic equations. There will be M equations, one for every midpoint m_i, $i = 1, 2, \ldots, M$. Since both the known and unknown values of ϕ and $\partial\phi/\partial\nu$ on the boundary are assumed elementwise constant, the boundary integration in (5.13) reduces to

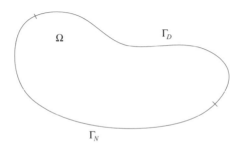

Figure 5.1. Different types of boundary conditions.

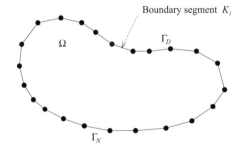

Figure 5.2. Splitting the boundary into linear segments.

$$-\frac{1}{2}\phi(m_i) = \sum_{j=1}^{M}\phi(m_j)\int_{K_j}\frac{\partial\lambda_{m_i}(m_j)}{\partial\nu_j} - \sum_{j=1}^{M}\frac{\partial\phi(m_j)}{\partial\nu_j}\int_{K_j}\lambda_{m_i}(m_j), \quad i=1,2,\ldots,M.$$
(5.16)

Here, ν_j stands for the corresponding unit outer normal vector. Let us first look at the M_D equations corresponding to the Dirichlet boundary Γ_D:

$$-\frac{1}{2}y_i = \sum_{j=1}^{M_D}y_j\int_{K_j}\frac{\partial\lambda_{m_i}(m_j)}{\partial\nu_j} + \sum_{j=M_D+1}^{M}Y_j\int_{K_j}\frac{\partial\lambda_{m_i}(m_j)}{\partial\nu_j}$$
$$-\sum_{j=1}^{M_D}Y_j\int_{K_j}\lambda_{m_i}(m_j) - \sum_{j=M_D+1}^{M}y_j\int_{K_j}\lambda_{m_i}(m_j), \quad i=1,2,\ldots,M_D.\ (5.17)$$

After rearranging terms with unknowns Y_j to the left-hand side and terms with known values y_i, y_j to the right-hand side, we obtain

$$\sum_{j=1}^{M_D}\underbrace{\int_{K_j}\lambda_{m_i}(m_j)}_{s_{ij}}Y_j - \sum_{j=M_D+1}^{M}\underbrace{\int_{K_j}\frac{\partial\lambda_{m_i}(m_j)}{\partial\nu_j}}_{s_{ij}}Y_j$$
$$= \underbrace{\frac{1}{2}y_i + \sum_{j=1}^{M_D}y_j\int_{K_j}\frac{\partial\lambda_{m_i}(m_j)}{\partial\nu_j} - \sum_{j=M_D+1}^{M}\int_{K_j}\lambda_{m_i}(m_j)y_j}_{f_i}, \quad i=1,2,\ldots,M_D.$$
(5.18)

Here, the underbraced values s_{ij} are the entries of the final system matrix $S = \{s_{ij}\}_{i,j=1}^{M}$ and the values f_i are part of the final right-hand side vector $F = \{f_i\}_{i=1}^{M}$.

The remaining M_N equations corresponding to the Neumann boundary Γ_N have the form

$$
\underbrace{-\frac{1}{2} Y_i}_{s_{ii}} - \sum_{j=1}^{M_D} \underbrace{\int_{K_j} \frac{\partial \lambda_{m_i}(m_j)}{\partial \nu_j} Y_j}_{s_{ij}} + \sum_{j=M_D+1}^{M} \underbrace{\int_{K_j} \lambda_{m_i}(m_j) Y_j}_{s_{ij}}
$$

$$
= \underbrace{\sum_{j=M_D+1}^{M} y_j \int_{K_j} \frac{\partial \lambda_{m_i}(m_j)}{\partial \nu_j} - \sum_{j=1}^{M_D} \int_{K_j} \lambda_{m_i}(m_j) y_j}_{f_i}, \quad i = M_D + 1, M_D + 2, \ldots, M .
$$

$$(5.19)$$

Actually, we have more information about ϕ on Γ_D and about $\partial \phi / \partial \nu$ on Γ_N than midpoint values $y_i = \phi(m_i), i = 1, 2, \ldots, M_D$ and $y_i = \partial \phi / \partial \nu(m_i), i = M_D+1, M_D+2, \ldots, M$. This information was not used in the above discretization scheme, but it can be taken into account: instead of working with the known midpoint values under the integral signs, we can leave there the original functions ϕ and $\partial \phi / \partial \nu$, and integrate numerically their products with the Green's function and its normal derivative.

It is easy to see that the system of linear algebraic equations can be written in the form $SY = F$, where $Y = (Y_1, Y_2, \ldots, Y_M)^T$ is the vector of unknowns and the $M \times M$ matrix S has a two-by-two block structure that needs to be taken into account in computer implementation.

5.1.1.5 Computer implementation   We assume that the reader has some experience with numerical quadrature, computer implementation of numerical methods for integral equations, and the Gauss elimination method for full matrices, so we will not dwell on these issues. The only (obvious) remark is that the evaluation of diagonal matrix entries involves singular integrals that should be computed analytically whenever possible. Integrals corresponding to off-diagonal matrix entries $s_{ij}, i \neq j$ can be approximated numerically using a suitable Gaussian quadrature rule. As a reference for Gaussian quadrature (containing points and weights in digital format) we recommend the CD-ROM accompanying Ref. 94.

As a basic data structure for an element K_i we suggest a structure comprising the following variables: y_i for the known value (of either $\phi(m_i)$ or $\partial \phi / \partial \nu_i(m_i)$), Y_i for the complementary unknown value of $\partial \phi / \partial \nu_i(m_i)$ or $\phi(m_i)$, the unit normal vector ν_i, the element length l_i, two values for the singular integrals of the Green's function and its derivative, and a flag indicating whether the element lies on the Dirichlet or Neumann boundary. In practice, the numerical integration is performed in a reference interval, not in the physical boundary elements.

Finally, let us mention that higher-order approximation of the boundary integral equation (5.13), mainly in two spatial dimensions, is discussed in numerous texts [157, 158, 167].

5.1.2   Green's functions of common differential operators

In this section we present Green's functions of several widely used linear operators. For the derivation of most of them we refer to Appendix B of Ref. 159.

5.1.2.1 Laplace operator in Cartesian coordinates   We consider the Laplace equation

$$-\Delta u = 0.$$

In two dimensions, the corresponding Green's function and the flux have the forms

$$\lambda_z(x) = -\frac{1}{2\pi}\ln(r), \quad \frac{\partial \lambda_z}{\partial \nu}(x) = -\frac{1}{2\pi r}\frac{\partial r}{\partial \nu}$$

and in three dimensions,

$$\lambda_z(x) = \frac{1}{4\pi r}, \quad \frac{\partial \lambda_z}{\partial \nu}(x) = -\frac{1}{4\pi r^2}\frac{\partial r}{\partial \nu}.$$

Here and in the following, we use the symbol $r = |z - x|$, and ν is an arbitrary unit vector in two and three dimensions, respectively.

5.1.2.2 Laplace operator in spherical coordinates   The Laplace equation $-\Delta u = 0$ in spherical coordinates has the form

$$-\frac{1}{\rho^2}\frac{\partial}{\partial\rho}\left(\rho^2\frac{\partial u}{\partial\rho}\right) - \frac{1}{\rho^2\sin\theta}\frac{\partial}{\partial\theta}\left(\sin\theta\frac{\partial u}{\partial\theta}\right) - \frac{1}{\rho^2\sin^2\theta}\frac{\partial}{\partial\theta}\left(\frac{\partial^2 u}{\partial\psi^2}\right) = 0.$$

For spherically symmetric problems, where the solution does not depend on the angles θ and ψ, this simplifies to

$$-\frac{1}{\rho^2}\frac{\partial}{\partial\rho}\left(\rho^2\frac{\partial u}{\partial\rho}\right) = 0.$$

This is a 1D problem and the corresponding Green's function has the form

$$\lambda_{\rho_*}(\rho) = -\frac{1}{4\pi\rho} \quad \text{for } \rho > \rho_*$$

and

$$\lambda_{\rho_*}(\rho) = -\frac{1}{4\pi\rho_*} \quad \text{for } \rho < \rho_*.$$

5.1.2.3 Helmholtz operator in Cartesian coordinates   The Helmholtz equation has the form

$$-\Delta u - k^2 u = 0,$$

where $k \neq 0$ is a real number. In two dimensions, the corresponding Green's function and the flux have the forms

$$\lambda_z(x) = \frac{j}{4}H_0^{(1)}(kr), \quad \frac{\partial \lambda_z}{\partial \nu}(x) = -\frac{jk}{4}H_1^{(1)}(kr)\frac{\partial r}{\partial \nu},$$

where $H_0^{(1)}$ is the Hankel function of the first kind and zero order, defined as

$$H_0^{(1)}(kr) = J_0(kr) + jY_0(kr).$$

The other Hankel function $H_1^{(1)}$ of the first kind and first order is obtained via the relation

$$\frac{\partial}{\partial r}H_0^{(1)} = -H_1^{(1)}.$$

Here, J and Y are Bessel functions of the first and second kinds, with the subscript indicating their order. In three dimensions, the Green's function and the flux look as follows:

$$\lambda_z(x) = \frac{1}{4\pi r}e^{-jkr}, \quad \frac{\partial \lambda_z}{\partial \nu}(x) = -(1+jkr)\frac{1}{4\pi r^2}e^{-jkr}\frac{\partial r}{\partial \nu}.$$

5.1.2.4   *Biharmonic operator in Cartesian coordinates*   The biharmonic equation

$$-\Delta^2 u = 0$$

plays an important role in plate bending problems. In two dimensions, the corresponding Green's function has the form

$$\lambda_z(x) = \frac{r^2}{8\pi}\left[\ln\left(\frac{1}{r}\right) + 1\right],$$

and in three dimensions it has the form

$$\lambda_z(x) = \frac{r}{8\pi}$$

(see Ref. 158, p. 127).

5.2   BEM-BASED SOLUTION OF DIFFERENTIAL EQUATIONS

This section describes in more detail the boundary element method. We will explain its particular steps, illustrate the algorithm on a 1D example, and show how the algorithm can be extended for 2D and 3D problems.

5.2.1   Particular steps of the solution

Consider an arbitrary differential equation. The standard way of its solution by the BEM is based on applying the technique of weighted residuals and consists of these steps:

- Weighting the equation with a suitable test function (this step transforms the originally differential problem on an integral equation).

- Integration of this equation by parts (this technique can be repeated several times, with respect to the order of the corresponding differential operator). The result then contains one or more boundary terms containing the boundary values of the investigated function and its derivatives. Some of these values are usually unknown, so that we typically obtain a mixed boundary-value problem.

- The weighting function is chosen as the fundamental solution of the original differential equation (but with the adjoint operator), with the Dirac function on the right-hand side.

- After inserting this fundamental solution (and known boundary conditions) into the mixed boundary-value problem, we can express the solution in terms of only the known boundary values. In this manner we obtain the remaining unknown boundary values.

- Computation of the function in the interval. This is mostly realized by evaluating integral expressions.

5.2.2 Illustrative example in one dimension

Consider an inhomogeneous 1D differential equation with constant coefficients

$$2\frac{\mathrm{d}^2 f}{\mathrm{d}x^2} + 3f = 3x^3 \tag{5.20}$$

defined in interval $\langle 0, 2\rangle$ with boundary conditions

$$f(0) = 0, \quad f(2) = 0. \tag{5.21}$$

It can be shown relatively easily (using variation of constants or another suitable technique) that solution to this equation reads

$$f = x^3 - 4x \tag{5.22}$$

and this function is depicted in Fig. 5.3.

   Now we will solve the problem by the boundary element method according to the steps indicated in the previous section. Normalize first (5.20) to the form

$$\frac{\mathrm{d}^2 f}{\mathrm{d}x^2} + \frac{3f}{2} - \frac{3x^3}{2} = 0 \tag{5.23}$$

and denote the corresponding differential operator

$$D = \frac{\mathrm{d}^2}{\mathrm{d}x^2} + \frac{3}{2}. \tag{5.24}$$

For any weighting function g we can write

$$\int_0^2 \left(\frac{\mathrm{d}^2 f}{\mathrm{d}x^2} + \frac{3f}{2} - \frac{3x^3}{2}\right) g \,\mathrm{d}x = 0. \tag{5.25}$$

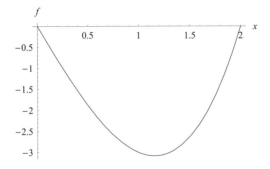

Figure 5.3. Function $f = x^3 - 4x$ in interval $\langle 0, 2\rangle$.

The term containing the derivative will be integrated by parts. The first integration yields

$$\int_0^2 \frac{d^2 f}{dx^2} g \, dx = \left[\frac{df}{dx} g \right]_0^2 - \int_0^2 \frac{df}{dx} \frac{dg}{dx} \, dx \,, \tag{5.26}$$

and, after an analogous integration of the second term in (5.26), we obtain

$$\int_0^2 \frac{d^2 f}{dx^2} g \, dx = \left[\frac{df}{dx} g \right]_0^2 - \left[\frac{dg}{dx} f \right]_0^2 + \int_0^2 \frac{d^2 g}{dx^2} f \, dx \,. \tag{5.27}$$

After substituting (5.27) into (5.25) we have

$$\int_0^2 \left(\frac{d^2 g}{dx^2} + \frac{3g}{2} \right) f \, dx - \frac{3}{2} \int_0^2 g x^3 \, dx + \left[\frac{df}{dx} g \right]_0^2 - \left[\frac{dg}{dx} f \right]_0^2 = 0 \,, \tag{5.28}$$

and as the last term on the left-hand side is equal to zero ($f(2) = f(0) = 0$), there holds

$$\int_0^2 \left(\frac{d^2 g}{dx^2} + \frac{3g}{2} \right) f \, dx - \frac{3}{2} \int_0^2 g x^3 \, dx + \left[\frac{df}{dx} g \right]_0^2 = 0 \,. \tag{5.29}$$

Here the values of df/dx at both boundary points 0 and 2 are unknown.

As we can see from the first term of (5.29), the adjoint operator acting on function g is the same as operator D; see (5.24). In such a case we speak about the self-adjoint operator. Now we have to determine the weighting function, which is represented by solution of operator equation

$$Dg = \frac{d^2 g}{dx^2} + \frac{3g}{2} = \delta(x - \xi) \,, \tag{5.30}$$

where δ is the Dirac function and ξ is the "load point" at which we apply the source. Now this definition will be used for two purposes. First, we can easily calculate the first term in (5.29),

$$\int_0^2 \left(\frac{d^2 g}{dx^2} + \frac{3g}{2} \right) f \, dx = \int_0^2 \delta(x - \xi) f \, dx = f(\xi) \,, \tag{5.31}$$

and second, we can find the function g itself. As the solution of equation

$$\frac{d^2 u}{dx^2} + \alpha^2 u = \delta(x - \xi)$$

is

$$u = \frac{\sin(\alpha|x - \xi|)}{2\alpha} \,,$$

we obtain (for $\alpha^2 = 3/2$)

$$g = \frac{\sin\left(\sqrt{\frac{3}{2}} |x - \xi| \right)}{2\sqrt{\frac{3}{2}}} \,. \tag{5.32}$$

Substitution of these results into (5.29) provides

$$f(\xi) - \frac{3}{2}\int_0^2 \frac{\sin\left(\sqrt{\frac{3}{2}}\,|x - \xi|\right)}{2\sqrt{\frac{3}{2}}}\,x^3\,dx + f'(2)\frac{\sin\left(\sqrt{\frac{3}{2}}\,|2 - \xi|\right)}{2\sqrt{\frac{3}{2}}}$$

$$-f'(0)\frac{\sin\left(\sqrt{\frac{3}{2}}\,|1 - \xi|\right)}{2\sqrt{\frac{3}{2}}} = 0. \tag{5.33}$$

Inserting here the boundary points $\xi = 0$ and $\xi = 2$, we obtain two algebraic equations for $f'(0)$ and $f'(2)$ in the form

$$f(0) - \frac{3}{2}\int_0^2 \frac{\sin\left(\sqrt{\frac{3}{2}}\,x\right)}{2\sqrt{\frac{3}{2}}}\,x^3\,dx + f'(2)\frac{\sin\left(2\sqrt{\frac{3}{2}}\right)}{2\sqrt{\frac{3}{2}}} = 0,$$

$$f(2) - \frac{3}{2}\int_0^2 \frac{\sin\left(\sqrt{\frac{3}{2}}\,|2 - x|\right)}{2\sqrt{\frac{3}{2}}}\,x^3\,dx - f'(0)\frac{\sin\left(2\sqrt{\frac{3}{2}}\right)}{2\sqrt{\frac{3}{2}}} = 0, \tag{5.34}$$

and as $f(0) = f(2) = 0$, we immediately have

$$f'(0) = -\frac{3}{2}\int_0^2 \frac{\sin\left(\sqrt{\frac{3}{2}}\,|2 - x|\right)\,x^3\,dx}{\sin\left(2\sqrt{\frac{3}{2}}\right)}$$

and

$$f'(0) = -\frac{3}{2}\int_0^2 \frac{\sin\left(\sqrt{\frac{3}{2}}\,x\right)\,x^3\,dx}{\sin\left(2\sqrt{\frac{3}{2}}\right)}. \tag{5.35}$$

A simple computation gives

$$f'(0) = -4, \quad f'(2) = 8,$$

which are the exact results. Indeed, as (see 5.22) $f(x) = x^3 - 4x \Rightarrow f'(x) = 3x^2 - 4$, we immediately get the above values.

The final step is to determine the value of function f at an arbitrary point ξ. Again we start from (5.33), where we substitute for $f'(0)$ and $f'(2)$:

$$f(\xi) = \frac{3}{2}\int_0^2 \frac{\sin\left(\sqrt{\frac{3}{2}}\,|x - \xi|\right)}{2\sqrt{\frac{3}{2}}}\,x^3\,dx - 8\frac{\sin\left(\sqrt{\frac{3}{2}}\,|2 - \xi|\right)}{2\sqrt{\frac{3}{2}}}$$

$$-4\frac{\sin\left(\sqrt{\frac{3}{2}}\,|1 - \xi|\right)}{2\sqrt{\frac{3}{2}}}. \tag{5.36}$$

The calculations provide

$$\frac{3}{2} \int_0^2 \frac{\sin\left(\sqrt{\frac{3}{2}}\,|x - \xi|\right)}{2\sqrt{\frac{3}{2}}}\, x^3 \, \mathrm{d}x$$

$$= \xi^3 - 4\xi + \sqrt{\frac{8}{3}} \left(2\sin\left[\sqrt{\frac{3}{2}}\,(2 - \xi)\right] + \sin\left[\sqrt{\frac{3}{2}}\,\xi\right] \right), \tag{5.37}$$

and after putting into (5.36), we finally have

$$f(\xi) = \xi^3 - 4\xi, \tag{5.38}$$

which exactly corresponds with the solution (5.22).

5.2.3 Multidimensional problems

The previous algorithm can easily be extended for solving multidimensional tasks. Consider a general differential equation in the form

$$Df - a = 0, \tag{5.39}$$

where f denotes the investigated function defined in region Ω, D is the differential operator (it must be linear, with constant coefficients), and b is the right-hand side representing the source function. Selecting a weighting function g we can write

$$\int_\Omega (Df - a)g \, \mathrm{d}\Omega = 0. \tag{5.40}$$

Application of the integration by parts and Gauss' theorem leads to transformation of the domain integrals into boundary integrals and we obtain

$$\int_\Omega f \cdot D^* g \, \mathrm{d}\Omega - \int_\Omega a \cdot g \, \mathrm{d}\Omega + \int_\Gamma (Bf \cdot S^* g - Su \cdot B^* g) \mathrm{d}\Gamma, \tag{5.41}$$

where B and S are boundary operators and the asterisk denotes their adjoint forms. Evidently, formula (5.40) is analogous to formula (5.28) derived for the 1D case before. The first term in (5.40) gives again $f(x, y)$, where y is the load point.

Formula (5.41) holds, however, only when the load point y is located inside domain Ω. If it lies somewhere on the boundary, equation (5.41) must be transformed (using a specific limiting process) to the so-called boundary integral equation (BIE). This equation then provides (after discretization) the values of function f or its normal derivatives at selected points on the boundary of domain Ω.

5.3 PROBLEMS WITH 1D INTEGRATION AREA

The spectrum of problems in low-frequency electromagnetics that can be solved by the boundary element method (BEM) with 1D integration area is rather narrow. Typical are some idealized 2D planar and axisymmetric problems with well-defined boundaries and boundary conditions. Nevertheless, solution of such examples is extremely useful because some of them are solvable analytically and this allows evaluating the accuracy of the applied BEM algorithms.

In this section we will solve the following tasks:

- electric field in the region of two parallel charged eccentric cylinders,

- magnetic field in the air gap of a rotating machine,

- electric field near the high-voltage conductors,

- magnetic field of a conductor above a ferromagnetic plate of constant magnetic permeability.

All these examples were solved by a BEM code developed and written by the authors of this book, with the exception of the procedure Triangle used for the discretization of the definition areas of the particular problems (by author Jonathan Richard Shewchuk, see http://www-2.cs.cmu.edu/ quake/triangle.html). The results obtained were validated analytically or by FEM-based professional codes (mostly COMSOL Multiphysics).

5.3.1 Two eccentrically placed charged cylinders

Consider the arrangement in Fig. 5.4 that is infinitely long in the direction of the z axis. The internal cylinder of radius R_1 carries potential φ_1, the external cylinder of radius R_2 potential φ_2. The eccentricity is denoted as e, the dielectrics between both cylinders has relative permittivity ε_r. The task is to map the distribution of the charge on the surface of both cylinders and electric field in the region between them and to find the capacitance per unit length of the arrangement.

The solution will be performed by the BEM and validated using the analytical results obtained from the method of conformal mapping.

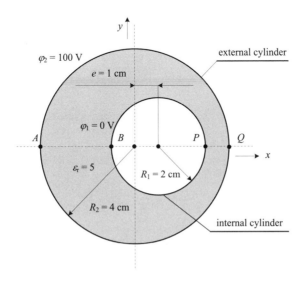

Figure 5.4.   Two infinitely long eccentric cylinders.

Let us start with the analytical computation using analytical function

$$w = p \cdot \ln \left(\frac{z - d}{z + d} \right) + q, \quad w = u + j \cdot v, \quad z = x + j \cdot y, \tag{5.42}$$

where p, q, and d are real constants. Separation of the real and imaginary parts leads to equations of two families of circles in the form

$$\left(x + d \coth \frac{u - q}{p} \right)^2 + y^2 = \left(\frac{d}{\sinh \frac{u-q}{p}} \right)^2 \tag{5.43}$$

and

$$x^2 + \left(y - d \cot \frac{v - q}{p} \right)^2 = \left(\frac{d}{\sin \frac{v-q}{p}} \right)^2. \tag{5.44}$$

Suppose now that the function u represents the electric potential φ. The unknown parameters d, q, and p can be found from the set of the following equations:

$$R_1 = \frac{d}{\sinh[(u_1 - q)/p]}$$

(cylinder of radius R_1 carries potential $u_1 = \varphi_1 = 0\,\mathrm{V}$),

$$R_2 = \frac{d}{\sinh[(u_2 - q)/p]}$$

(cylinder of radius R_2 carries potential $u_2 = \varphi_2 = 100\,\mathrm{V}$), and

$$e = d \coth \frac{u_1 - q}{p} - d \coth \frac{u_2 - q}{p}$$

(relation for the eccentricity e).

Putting

$$\frac{u_1 - q}{p} = \alpha, \quad \frac{u_2 - q}{p} = \beta \tag{5.45}$$

we have to solve a system

$$R_1 = \frac{d}{\sinh \alpha}, \quad R_2 = \frac{d}{\sinh \beta}, \quad e = d \coth \alpha - d \coth \beta$$

with results

$$\alpha = \operatorname{arg\,cosh} \frac{R_2^2 - R_1^2 - e^2}{2 e R_1} = 1.66992,$$

$$\beta = \operatorname{arg\,cosh} \frac{R_2^2 - R_1^2 + e^2}{2 e R_2} = 1.06673,$$

and

$$d = R_1 \sinh \alpha = R_2 \sinh \beta = 0.0512348.$$

From (5.45) we immediately obtain

$$p = -165.786, \quad q = 276.849.$$

At this moment we have a full description of equipotential lines $u = $ const in the system by (5.43)—the parameters d, p, and q are already known. As for the force lines, they are given by lines $v = $ const. As parameter $\beta \in \langle 0, 2\pi \rangle$, parameter v must lie in the interval $\langle v_1, v_2 \rangle$, where $v_1 = q = 276.849$ and $v_2 = 2p\pi + q = -487.966$. The equipotential and force lines in transformed plane u, v are depicted in Fig. 5.5.

The equipotentials in the real system in plane x, y are depicted in Fig. 5.6. The capacitance per unit length (1 m) follows from the formula

$$C' = \varepsilon_0 \varepsilon_r \frac{v_1 - v_2}{u_2 - u_1} = 4.60518 \times 10^{-10} \text{ F/m} . \tag{5.46}$$

The last computation provides the distribution of the potential and module of electric field strength E along the line AB (see Fig. 5.4). We will start from the real part of formula (5.42) for $y = 0$. We easily obtain

$$u = p \cdot \ln\left(\frac{x - d}{x + d}\right) + q ,$$

where $x \in \langle x_A, x_B \rangle$. Immediately we find that (see Fig. 5.6) $x_A = -0.105$ and $x_B = -0.075$. Analogously,

$$|E| = \left|\frac{du}{dx}\right| = \left|\frac{2pd}{x^2 - d^2}\right| .$$

Now the same example was calculated by the boundary element method. The boundary of the problem (represented by both cylinders) was discretized by an ever-growing number of elements in order to evaluate the convergence of the solution. Figure 5.7 shows the dependence of the capacitance C' calculated by the BEM on the number of the discretization elements. The difference is about 0.3%.

Figure 5.8 shows the distribution of potential between points A and B (see Fig. 5.4) obtained both analytically and by the BEM (the number of elements being 1000). The differences are small (both curves are practically identical) and reach a maximum of about 1% in the vicinity of point A (everywhere else the difference practically vanishes). Figure 5.9 shows the same distribution between points P and Q.

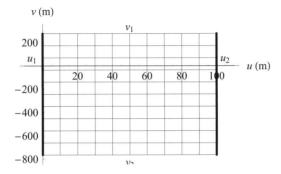

Figure 5.5.   Equipotential ($u = $ const) and force ($v = $ const) lines in transformed plane u, v.

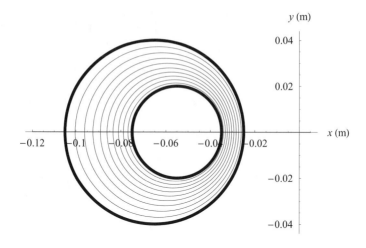

Figure 5.6.   Equipotentials in the real plane x, y.

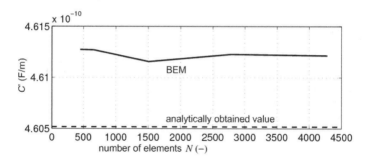

Figure 5.7.   Convergence of the capacitance C'.

Finally, Fig. 5.10 shows the distribution of the module of electric field strength between points A and B. Even in this case the differences between the analytical and numerical solutions do not exceed about 1%.

5.3.2   Magnetic field in the air gap of a rotating machine

Another problem solved in this section is the distribution of magnetic field in a rotating machine. Both rotor and stator have eight slots and their relative permeabilities μ_r are supposed to be infinitely high. It is necessary to find the distribution of magnetic scalar potential ψ in the gap and the dependence of its reluctance per unit of axial length of the motor on the angle of shifting. The basic geometrical dimensions of the cross section of the machine are shown in Fig. 5.11.

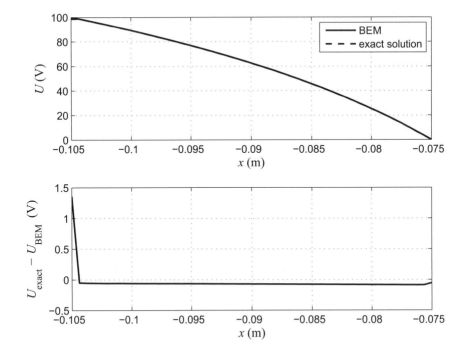

Figure 5.8. Distribution of potential between points A and B (see Fig. 5.4).

The distribution of magnetic scalar potential in the gap is described by the Laplace equation

$$\frac{\partial^2 \psi_{\mathrm{m}}}{\partial x^2} + \frac{\partial^2 \psi_{\mathrm{m}}}{\partial y^2} = 0. \tag{5.47}$$

The boundary conditions are given as

$$\psi_{\mathrm{mr}} = \psi_1, \quad \psi_{\mathrm{ms}} = \psi_2, \tag{5.48}$$

where ψ_{mr} is the value of the scalar magnetic potential along the boundary rotor–air gap (due to infinite relative permeability of the rotor it is a constant) and ψ_{ms} is its value along the boundary stator–air gap (another constant). These values can be selected quite arbitrarily.

According to the Hopkinson law we can write

$$\int_{\mathrm{r}}^{\mathrm{s}} \boldsymbol{H}\,\mathrm{d}\boldsymbol{l} = R_{\mathrm{m}}\Phi', \tag{5.49}$$

where magnetic field strength $\boldsymbol{H}$ is integrated along the force line from the rotor r to stator s, R_{m} is the magnetic reluctance, and Φ' is the magnetic flux per unit of axial length of the

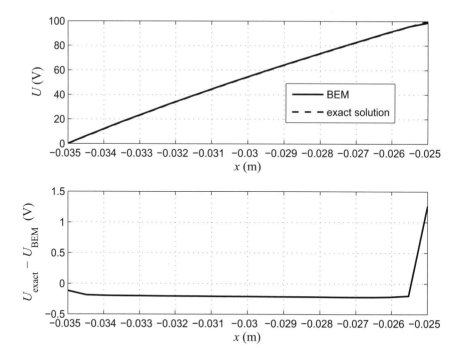

Figure 5.9.   Distribution of potential between points P and Q (see Fig. 5.4).

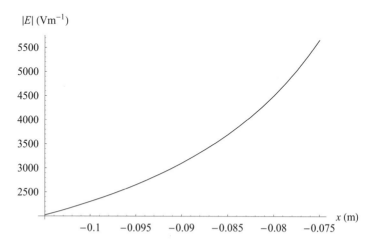

Figure 5.10.   Distribution of the module of electric field strength between points A and B (see Fig. 5.4).

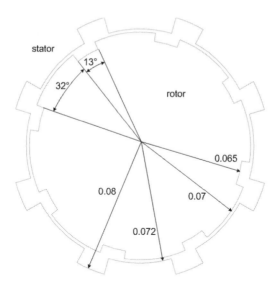

Figure 5.11.   The cross section of the investigated machine.

motor. From (1.32) we immediately obtain

$$\int_r^s - \operatorname{grad} \psi_m \, d\mathbf{l} = - \int_r^s d\psi = R_m \Phi' \tag{5.50}$$

and, hence,

$$R_m = \frac{\psi_{mr} - \psi_{ms}}{\Phi'}. \tag{5.51}$$

The magnetic flux per unit length Φ' is then calculated as

$$\Phi' = \int \mu_0 H \, d\mathbf{s}, \tag{5.52}$$

where the integration is carried out along the boundary stator–air gap (or rotor–air gap).

Based on the above formulas, the algorithm of computation consists of the following steps:

- Computation of the distribution of scalar magnetic potential in the gap between the stator and rotor using the boundary element method. Both boundaries of the rotor and stator characterized by the Dirichlet conditions (selected values of ψ_{mr} and ψ_{ms}) are discretized with the aim to find there the complementary Neumann boundary conditions representing the components of magnetic field strength H in the directions normal to these boundaries.

- Computation of distribution of the corresponding magnetic flux density B along the boundary of the rotor (or stator) and its integration.

- Computation of magnetic reluctance of the air gap.

Several positions of the rotor with respect to stator are depicted in Fig. 5.12. The computations for every position were performed with about one thousand linear elements covering the boundaries of both parts. The results (reluctance of the air gap per unit of axial length on the angle of shifting) calculated by the BEM and FEM is depicted in Fig. 5.13. The differences are brought about by different meshing and quite different method of computation (the mesh for the FEM had about 50,000 triangular elements). The times of computation were fully comparable.

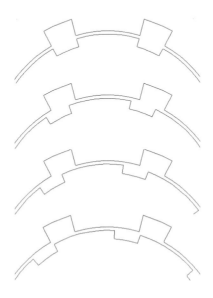

Figure 5.12. Several positions of the rotor and stator.

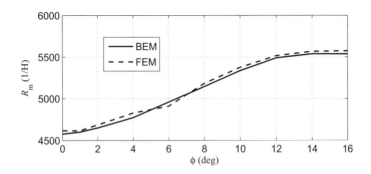

Figure 5.13. Dependence of the magnetic reluctance on the angle of shifting.

5.3.3 Electric field near a high-voltage three-phase line

Nowadays, the lines of high and very high voltages have to satisfy standards determining the maximum acceptable values of electric and magnetic fields in their vicinity. In this example we will investigate the distribution of electric field in the vicinity of a three-phase line.

In a lot of similar cases the distribution of electric field can simply be calculated analytically, using the method of images. But, for an illustration, it will be calculated by the boundary element method and the results will again be validated by the finite element method.

The investigated arrangement is depicted in Fig. 5.14. Potential of earth is supposed to be zero, voltages of the three phases of amplitude $U = 22$ kV and frequency $f = 50$ Hz are harmonic and mutually shifted by $120°$. All dimensions are given in meters.

Consider time $t = 0.006$ s. At this moment the values of voltage in particular conductors reach $U_{01} = U \cdot \sin(2\pi f t) = 20.923$ kV, $U_{02} = U \cdot \sin(2\pi f t - 2\pi/3) = -4.574$ kV, and $U_{02} = U \cdot \sin(2\pi f t + 2\pi/3) = -16.349$ kV. The artificial boundary with the Dirichlet condition ($\varphi = 0$) was placed at a sufficient distance from the conductors (the dimensions of the investigated area being 60 m×30 m, see Fig. 5.15).

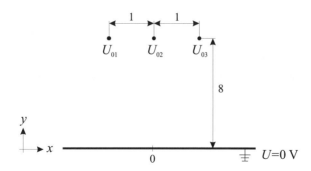

Figure 5.14. The investigated arrangement with the high-voltage three-phase line.

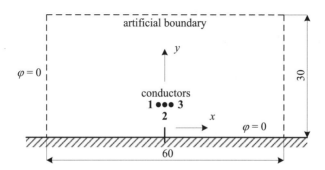

Figure 5.15. The definition area of the problem.

The electric field in the system is described by the Laplace equation for electric potential φ in the form

$$\frac{\partial^2 \varphi}{\partial x^2} + \frac{\partial^2 \varphi}{\partial y^2} = 0 \qquad (5.53)$$

with the above boundary condition. Now the algorithm of computation consists of the following steps:

- Computation of the Neumann condition along the boundary (a part of earth and the artificial boundary) using the boundary element method.

- Computation of distribution of potential within the investigated area using common integral expressions.

- Computation of the distribution of electric field.

- Visualization of the results.

For the discretization of the boundary we used 311 elements (i.e., the corresponding algebraic system providing the normal derivatives of function φ contained 311 equations). This number was enough for reaching accuracy better than 2%.

Some results are depicted in four following figures. Figure 5.16 shows the distribution of potential below the high-voltage line at the height of a person's head (1.8 m). The agreement between the BEM and FEM is obviously quite perfect.

Electric field strength E and its components cannot be calculated with such an accuracy as potential (because these quantities have to be determined by its numerical differentiation, which always leads to deterioration of accuracy). Nevertheless, even these distributions may be declared correct and their comparison with the results obtained by the FEM exhibits very good accordance.

Figure 5.17 shows the distribution of components E_x along the same line, Fig. 5.18 the distribution of component E_y, and Fig. 5.19 its module. All these curves correspond to typical maps obtained experimentally.

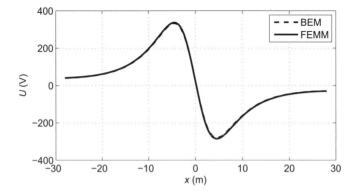

Figure 5.16. Distribution of potential below the high-voltage line.

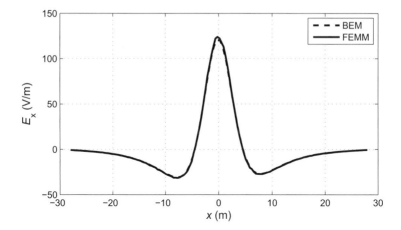

Figure 5.17. Distribution of component E_x below the high-voltage line.

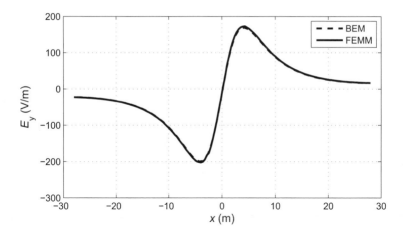

Figure 5.18. Distribution of component E_y below the high-voltage line.

5.3.4 Magnetic field of a massive conductor above a ferromagnetic plate

The geometry of the task (symmetric with respect to the y axis) is shown in Fig. 5.20. All dimensions are given in meters. The Cu conductor carries direct current of density $\mathbf{J} = \mathbf{k}J_z$ whose module $|\mathbf{J}| = 10^6$ A/m^2. Magnetic permeability μ_r of the plate is considered constant and its value is 300.

The task is described by magnetic vector potential $\mathbf{A}$ that has only one component A_z in the direction of the z axis. The governing equation reads

$$\frac{\partial^2 A_z}{\partial x^2} + \frac{\partial^2 A_z}{\partial y^2} = -\mu_0 \mu_r J_z \tag{5.54}$$

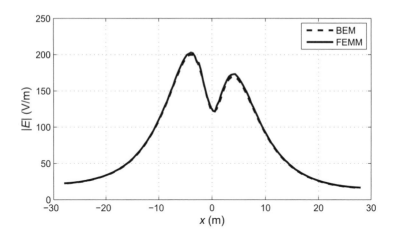

Figure 5.19.   Distribution of module $|E|$ below the high-voltage line.

with boundary conditions

$$A_z = 0 \ \text{ along line BCDA}, \qquad \frac{\partial A_z}{\partial n} = 0 \ \text{ along line AB}. \qquad (5.55)$$

where line BCD represents the artificial boundary.

In this case the computation by the BEM is somewhat complicated. The problem consists in the necessity of sufficiently fine discretization of the ferromagnetics–air interface with well-defined indices of particular triangles on both sides of the interface. Unfortunately, the program Triangle does not make it possible, so that for this purpose we had to develop a special procedure that allowed, however, only processing of a relative small number of elements. That is why some results are characterized by a lower accuracy than we

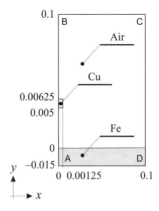

Figure 5.20.   Arrangement with a massive conductor above a ferromagnetic plate.

obtained in previous examples. This is typical not for the distribution of magnetic vector potential itself, but mainly for magnetic flux density whose components are calculated by its numerical differentiation.

For an illustration, Fig. 5.21 shows the distribution of equipotentials in the system calculated by FEM.

Figure 5.22 depicts the distribution of quantity A_z along the z axis (the interface between air and the ferromagnetic plate) and Fig. 5.23 along the y axis.

While Fig. 5.22 exhibits a very good accordance between the results obtained by both BEM and FEM, this is not the case for Fig. 5.23 (the reasons were mentioned above). The corresponding errors are much more expressed in Figs. 5.24 and 5.25, showing the distribution of the normal components of magnetic flux density along the same lines.

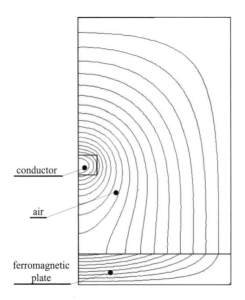

Figure 5.21.   Distribution of the force lines in the system.

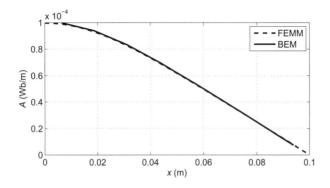

Figure 5.22.   Distribution of magnetic vector potential along the x axis.

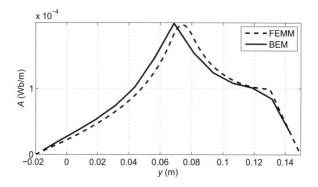

Figure 5.23. Distribution of magnetic vector potential along the y axis.

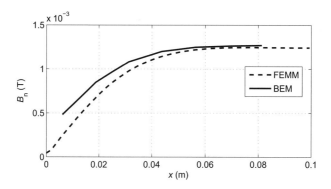

Figure 5.24. Distribution of magnetic flux density perpendicular to the x axis.

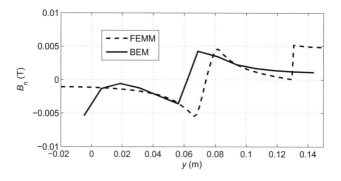

Figure 5.25. Distribution of magnetic flux density perpendicular to the y axis.

CHAPTER 6

INTEGRAL EQUATIONS IN SOLUTION OF SELECTED COUPLED PROBLEMS

An integral or integrodifferential approach may successfully be used even for solution of specific coupled problems with or without motion characterized by linearity and homogeneity. We can mention the problems of induction heating of nonferromagnetic bodies and movement as a consequence of the interaction between the time-variable primary magnetic field and eddy currents induced in electrically conductive parts of the system.

In these tasks we use the above approach for determination of the time and space distribution of eddy currents, while the temperature field (usually smooth) is calculated by the finite element method and eventual motion is processed by classical methods for solution of ordinary differential equations.

6.1 CONTINUAL INDUCTION HEATING OF NONFERROUS CYLINDRICAL BODIES

6.1.1 Introduction

Continual induction heating of nonferrous metal bodies belongs to widely spread heat-treatment techniques used for the improvement of their mechanical properties, drying of their surfaces (e.g., after their machining in order to get rid of oil or other coolants), and other similar purposes. But its numerical modeling is still a relatively complicated business due to the mutual interaction of the electromagnetic and temperature fields (the physical properties of the body and inductor are generally temperature -dependent functions) and, particularly, time-variable boundary conditions due to the movement of the inductor or the

Integral Methods in Low-Frequency Electromagnetics. By I. Doležel, P. Karban, and P. Šolín. Copyright © 2009 John Wiley & Sons, Inc.

heated body. Application of classical finite element techniques here necessitates remeshing of the definition area at every time level, which may significantly decelerate the computation of the electromagnetic field.

For heat processing of materials with linear physical properties we will use the integrodifferential approach for finding the eddy currents and corresponding Joule losses in the heated body, while the temperature will be determined using the FEM. This approach requires only discretization of the active parts of the system (i.e., the inductor and processed body). Moreover, it is not necessary to with the boundary conditions, as they are implemented directly in the kernel functions of the relevant integrals.

6.1.2 Formulation of the technical problem

Consider a long nonferrous body that is to be heated continually by induction. This may be realized by one or several inductors slowly moving along it, or, vice versa, the body itself may move in a system of appropriately arranged static inductors. Two typical simple arrangements are shown in Fig. 6.1.

Suppose that the geometry of the system and material parameters of its particular subdomains are given. Now the task is to propose such parameters (amplitudes and frequency) of the field currents and mutual velocities between the inductor and heated body that provide the required temperature profile in it.

6.1.3 Mathematical model and its solution

6.1.3.1 The continuous model   The mathematical model of the problem consists of two equations describing (1) the spatial and temporal distribution of the eddy currents and Joule losses in the body and (2) the temperature field in the system.

While the model describing the distribution of eddy currents and Joule losses is given by (4.10) and (4.9) transformed for the axisymmetric arrangement, the nonstationary temperature field T in the current carrying parts of the system is described by the heat transfer

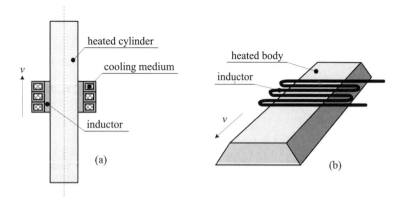

Figure 6.1.   Two basic possibilities of continual induction heating: (a) static body, moving inductor and (b) moving body, static inductor.

equation with respect to the motion [168]:

$$\operatorname{div}(\lambda \operatorname{grad} T) = \varrho c_p \frac{dT}{dt} - w_J = \varrho c_p \left(\frac{\partial T}{\partial t} + \boldsymbol{v} \operatorname{grad} T \right) - w_J, \tag{6.1}$$

where λ is the thermal conductivity, ϱ the specific mass, c_p the specific heat at the constant pressure, $\boldsymbol{v}$ the velocity, and w_J the specific Joule losses. The physical parameters λ, c_p, and the electrical conductivity γ are generally temperature-dependent functions. Equation (6.1) has to be supplemented with the boundary condition that respects the convection and radiation of heat. This condition reads

$$-\lambda \frac{dT_s}{dn} = \alpha = (T_s - T_{\text{ext}}) + \sigma C (T_s^4 - T_i^4), \tag{6.2}$$

where α is the convective heat transfer coefficient (generally a function of temperature and velocity), T_s is the local surface temperature of the body, n denotes the external normal to the surface, σ is the Stefan–Boltzmann constant ($\sigma = 5.6704 \times 10^{-8}$ kg/s$^3 \cdot$ K^4), C is a constant respecting the influences of emissivity, absorption, and configuration factors, T_i (simplified) is the temperature of the field winding, and T_{ext} is the temperature of the ambient medium (air).

6.1.4   Illustrative example

The methodology is illustrated on an example of continual induction drying of the surface of an aluminum cylindrical pipe by an inductor that moves at a given velocity along it.

6.1.4.1 *Input data*   The basic arrangement is depicted in Fig. 6.2 and may be considered axisymmetric. All dimensions are given in meters. The process of heating takes (for the inductor velocity $v_z = 0.001$ m/s) 250 s. The temperature of the pipe surface (whose initial temperature $T_0 = 20$ °C) should reach 140–200 °C, which is quite enough for its drying. Consequent intensive cooling of the pipe then takes 150 s. Other important data follow:

- electrical conductivity of Al (for $T = 20$ °C) $\gamma_1 = 33 \times 10^6$ S/m,

- thermal conductivity of Al (for $T = 20$ °C) $\lambda_1 = 237$ W/m$\cdot$ K,

- specific mass of Al (for $T = 20$ °C) $\varrho_1 = 2700$ kg/m^3,

- specific heat of Al (for $T = 20$ °C) $c_{p1} = 897$ J/kg$\cdot$ K,

- temperature of the ambient air $T_{\text{ext}} = 20$ °C.

After reaching the surface temperature $T_s = 150$ °C the pipe starts to be cooled by a big fan and the coefficient of the convective heat transfer grows from the original value $\alpha_{11} = 20$ W/m$^2 \cdot$ K to $\alpha_{12} = 100$ W/m$^2 \cdot$ K. The task is to propose the amplitude and frequency of the field current in the inductor that would satisfy the above requirements.

6.1.4.2 *Model and its discretization*   The discrete model in the axisymmetric arrangement works with two elements: pipe Ω_1 and inductor Ω_2. The pipe does not move ($\boldsymbol{v}_1 = \boldsymbol{0}$) and carries no external current, so that $i_1(t) = 0$. The inductor, connected to a source, carries harmonic external current $i_2(t)$, and moves at velocity $\boldsymbol{v}_2(t)$ in the direction of the z axis. The electrical conductivities of the pipe and inductor are γ_1 and γ_2, respectively.

The vectors of the current density in both elements Ω_1 and Ω_2 have only one nonzero component in the circumferential direction φ. Considering these specific features, the system with the indirect conditions provides three basic equations in the form

$$
J_{1\varphi}(Q_1,t) + \frac{\mu_0\gamma_1}{4\pi} \int_{\Omega_1} \frac{\frac{\mathrm{d}J_{1\varphi}(P_1,t)}{\mathrm{d}t} \cos\varphi \, \mathrm{d}V}{r_{P_1 Q_1}(t)} + \frac{\mu_0\gamma_1}{4\pi} \int_{\Omega_2} \frac{\frac{\mathrm{d}J_{2\varphi}(P_2,t)}{\mathrm{d}t} \cos\varphi \, \mathrm{d}V}{r_{P_2 Q_1}(t)}
$$

$$
- \frac{\mu_0\gamma_1}{4\pi} \int_{\Omega_2} \frac{(v_{2z}(t) z_{P_2 Q_1}(t)) J_{2\varphi}(P_2,t) \cos\varphi \, \mathrm{d}V}{r_{P_2 Q_1}^3(t)} = 0 , \tag{6.3}
$$

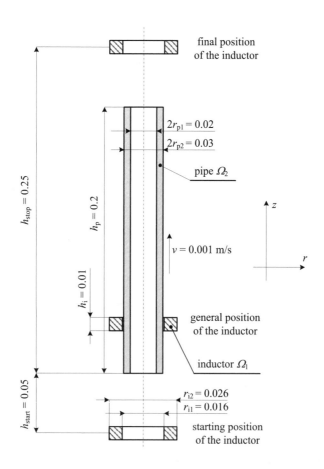

Figure 6.2.   The solved arrangement.

$$J_{2\varphi}(Q_2,t) + \frac{\mu_0\gamma_2}{4\pi}\int_{\Omega_1}\frac{\frac{\mathrm{d}J_{1\varphi}(P_1,t)}{\mathrm{d}t}\cos\varphi\,\mathrm{d}V}{r_{P_1Q_2}(t)} + \frac{\mu_0\gamma_2}{4\pi}\int_{\Omega_2}\frac{\frac{\mathrm{d}J_{2\varphi}(P_2,t)}{\mathrm{d}t}\cos\varphi\,\mathrm{d}V}{r_{P_2Q_2}(t)}$$

$$+ \frac{\mu_0\gamma_2}{4\pi}\int_{\Omega_1}\frac{(v_{2z}(t)z_{P_1Q_2}(t))J_{1\varphi}(P_1,t)\cos\varphi\,\mathrm{d}V}{r_{P_1Q_2}^3(t)} + J_{20\varphi}(t) = 0\,, \qquad (6.4)$$

$$\int_{S_2}J_{2\varphi}(P_2,t)\mathrm{d}S = N_2i_2(t)\,, \qquad (6.5)$$

where S_2 is the cross section of the inductor, N_2 the number of its turns and φ the angle between the reference and integration points.

If the current densities are harmonic, the system (6.3), (6.4), and (6.5) may be rewritten in terms of the phasors:

$$\underline{J}_{1\varphi}(Q_1) + \mathrm{j}\cdot\frac{\mu_0\omega\gamma_1}{4\pi}\int_{\Omega_1}\frac{\underline{J}_{1\varphi}(P_1)\cos\varphi\,\mathrm{d}V}{r_{P_1Q_1}(t)} + \mathrm{j}\cdot\frac{\mu_0\omega\gamma_1}{4\pi}\int_{\Omega_2}\frac{\underline{J}_{2\varphi}(P_2)\cos\varphi\,\mathrm{d}V}{r_{P_2Q_1}(t)}$$

$$- \frac{\mu_0\gamma_1}{4\pi}\int_{\Omega_2}\frac{(v_{2z}(t)z_{P_2Q_1}(t))\underline{J}_{2\varphi}(P_2)\cos\varphi\,\mathrm{d}V}{r_{P_2Q_1}^3(t)} = 0\,, \qquad (6.6)$$

$$\underline{J}_{2\varphi}(Q_2) + \mathrm{j}\cdot\frac{\mu_0\omega\gamma_2}{4\pi}\int_{\Omega_1}\frac{\underline{J}_{1\varphi}(P_1)\cos\varphi\,\mathrm{d}V}{r_{P_1Q_2}(t)} + \mathrm{j}\cdot\frac{\mu_0\omega\gamma_2}{4\pi}\int_{\Omega_2}\frac{\underline{J}_{2\varphi}(P_2)\cos\varphi\,\mathrm{d}V}{r_{P_2Q_2}(t)}$$

$$+ \frac{\mu_0\gamma_2}{4\pi}\int_{\Omega_2}\frac{(v_{2z}(t)z_{P_1Q_2}(t))\underline{J}_{1\varphi}(P_1)\cos\varphi\,\mathrm{d}V}{r_{P_1Q_2}^3(t)} + \underline{J}_{20\varphi} = 0\,, \qquad (6.7)$$

$$\int_{S_2}\underline{J}_{2\varphi}(P_2)\mathrm{d}S = N_2\underline{I}_2\,, \qquad (6.8)$$

where $\underline{I}_2$ is the phasor of the current in the inductor.

Let the number of discretization elements in the heated pipe be m_1, in the inductor m_2. Now the above system can be rewritten once more as follows:

$$\underline{J}_{1k\varphi}(Q_{1k}) + \mathrm{j}\cdot\frac{\mu_0\omega\gamma_1}{4\pi}\sum_{i=1}^{m_1}\underline{J}_{1i\varphi}(P_{1i})\int_{\Omega_{1i}}\frac{\cos\varphi\mathrm{d}V}{r_{P_{1i}Q_{1k}}(t)}$$

$$+ \mathrm{j}\cdot\frac{\mu_0\omega\gamma_1}{4\pi}\sum_{i=1}^{m_2}\frac{\underline{J}_{2i\varphi}(P_{2i})\int_{\Omega_{2i}}\cos\varphi\mathrm{d}V}{r_{P_{2i}Q_{1k}}(t)}$$

$$- \frac{\mu_0\gamma_1}{4\pi}\sum_{i=1}^{m_2}v_{2z}(t)\underline{J}_{2i\varphi}(P_{2i})\int_{\Omega_{2i}}\frac{(z_{P_{2i}Q_{1k}}(t))\cos\varphi\mathrm{d}V}{r_{P_{2i}Q_{1k}}^3(t)} = 0\,, \qquad (6.9)$$

$$\underline{J}_{2k\varphi}(Q_{2k}) + \mathrm{j}\cdot\frac{\mu_0\omega\gamma_2}{4\pi}\sum_{i=1}^{m_2}\underline{J}_{2i\varphi}(P_{2i})\int_{\Omega_{1i}}\frac{\cos\varphi\mathrm{d}V}{r_{P_{1i}Q_{2k}}(t)}$$

$$+ \, \mathrm{j} \cdot \frac{\mu_0 \omega \gamma_2}{4\pi} \sum_{i=1}^{m_2} \frac{\underline{J}_{2i\varphi}(P_{2i}) \int_{\Omega_{2i}} \cos \varphi \mathrm{d}V}{r_{P_{2i}Q_{2k}}(t)}$$

$$+ \frac{\mu_0 \gamma_2}{4\pi} \sum_{i=1}^{m_1} v_{2z}(t) \underline{J}_{1i\varphi}(P_{1i}) \int_{\Omega_{1i}} \frac{(z_{P_{1i}Q_{2k}}(t)) \cos \varphi \mathrm{d}V}{r_{P_{1i}Q_{2k}}^3(t)} = 0 \,, \qquad (6.10)$$

$$\sum_{i=1}^{m_2} \underline{J}_{2i\varphi}(P_{2i}) = N_2 \underline{I}_2 \,. \qquad (6.11)$$

Particular cells used for the discretization are mostly rings of triangular or rectangular cross sections, as shown in Fig. 6.3. Now the last operation to be done is evaluation of integrals occurring in (6.9) and (6.10). This evaluation depends on the type of element and we will show it just for the rectangular ones (integration over a general ring of triangular cross section is extremely laborious). Let us start from Fig. 6.4.

Let Q_k be the reference point in the kth cell. The integration is carried out over another element with index i. We first calculate the integral

$$I_{1ki} = \int_{\Omega_i} \frac{\cos \varphi \, \mathrm{d}V}{a} \,,$$

where a is the distance between the barycenter of the cross section of cell k and a general integration point of cell i. This integral can be rewritten in the form

$$I_{1ki} = \int_{\varphi=0}^{2\pi} \cos \varphi \left[\int_{r=R_{1i}}^{R_{2i}} \int_{z=Z_{1i}}^{Z_{2i}} \frac{r \, \mathrm{d}z \, \mathrm{d}r}{\sqrt{r^2 + R_k^2 - 2rR_k \cos \varphi + (z - Z_k)^2}} \right] \mathrm{d}\varphi, \quad (6.12)$$

where R_k and Z_k are the barycentric coordinates of the cross section of the element with index k:

$$R_k = \frac{R_{1k} + R_{2k}}{2}, \quad Z_k = \frac{Z_{1k} + Z_{2k}}{2}.$$

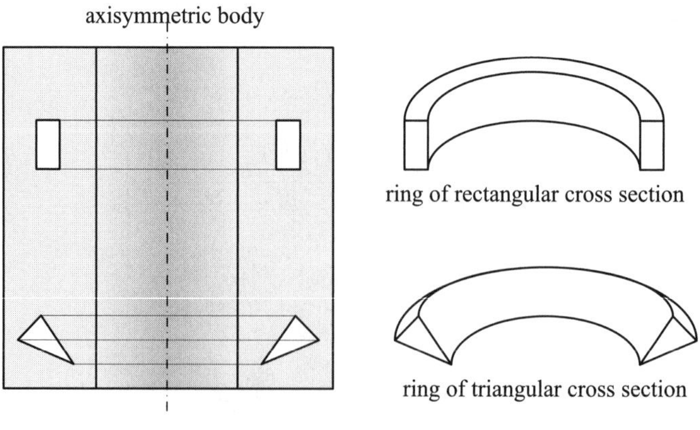

Figure 6.3.   Possible ways of discretization of axisymmetric bodies.

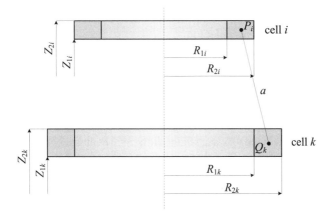

Figure 6.4.   Computation of selected integrals over a rectangular ring.

The first two integrals in (6.12) with respect to r and z can be calculated analytically. The results can be found in Appendix. C. The last definite integral with respect to φ has to be calculated numerically.

Analogously we can calculate another integral occurring in the velocity term in (6.9) and (6.10), namely,

$$I_{2ki} = \int_{\Omega_i} \frac{z_{ki} \cos \varphi \, \mathrm{d}V}{a^3} \,,$$

where $z_{ki} = Z_k - z$, $z \in \Omega_i$. The integral can be rewritten in the form

$$I_{2ki} = \int_{\varphi=0}^{2\pi} \cos \varphi \left[\int_{r=R_{1i}}^{R_{2i}} \int_{z=Z_{1i}}^{Z_{2i}} \frac{(Z_k - z)r \, \mathrm{d}z \, \mathrm{d}r}{\left(\sqrt{r^2 + R_k^2 - 2rR_k \cos \varphi + (z - Z_k)^2} \right)^3} \right] \mathrm{d}\varphi \,.$$

$$(6.13)$$

As there holds

$$
\begin{aligned}
G(r,z) &= \int_r \int_z \frac{(Z_k - z)r \, \mathrm{d}z \, \mathrm{d}r}{\left(\sqrt{r^2 + R_k^2 - 2rR_k \cos \varphi + (z - Z_k)^2} \right)^3} \\
&= -\sqrt{r^2 + R_k^2 - 2rR_k \cos \varphi + (z - Z_k)^2} \\
&\quad - R_k \cos \varphi \ln \left(r - R_k \cos \varphi + \sqrt{r^2 + R_k^2 - 2rR_k \cos \varphi + (z - Z_k)^2} \right) \,,
\end{aligned}
$$

we easily obtain

$$I_{2ki} = -\int_{\varphi=0}^{2\pi} \cos \varphi \left[G(R_{2i}, Z_{2i}) - G(R_{2i}, Z_{1i}) - G(R_{1i}, Z_{2i}) + G(R_{1i}, Z_{1i}) \right] \mathrm{d}\varphi \,.$$

Even this integral has to be calculated numerically.

The computations of the distribution of current densities in the system based on the above approach were performed by a code written in MatLab by the authors. The consequent temperature field was calculated also by our own code, based, however, on the classical finite element analysis (that is why no details are provided concerning its fundamentals).

6.1.4.3 Results of calculation

The methodology was tested for a number of the parameters of the field current. But only several of them satisfy the requirements of the task, that is, the desired temperature profile along the cylinder. Selected results for the current of the inductor $J_{ext,2} = 22 \times 10^6$ A/m^2 (effective value) and frequency $f = 5$ kHz are depicted in several of the following figures. The total number of cells covering the pipe and inductor for the computation of electromagnetic and thermal quantities was about 4000. Most of the results were validated by professional code COMSOL Multiphysics.

Figure 6.5 shows the time evolution of the effective current density at five selected points closely below the surface of the pipe (in the figure these points are described by their r and z coordinates). It is clear that significant eddy current densities in the pipe are induced just below the inductor while with growing distance from it they drop very fast.

Figure 6.6 shows the time evolution of the average value of the specific Joule losses in the pipe that gives a good idea about the evolution of the average temperature in its wall (whose value, even when it has no physical significance, is also practically uniform). Figure 6.7 shows the time evolution of the temperature at the points shown in Fig. 6.5.

Next three figures show further results that are, moreover, compared with the results obtained by the professional code COMSOL Multiphysics supplemented with our own procedures and scripts. Figure 6.8 shows the distribution of the effective value of eddy current density along the radius of the pipe with coordinate $z = 0.1$ m (center of the pipe)

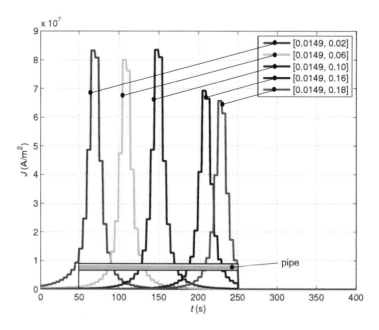

Figure 6.5.   Time evolution of eddy current densities at the selected points of the pipe.

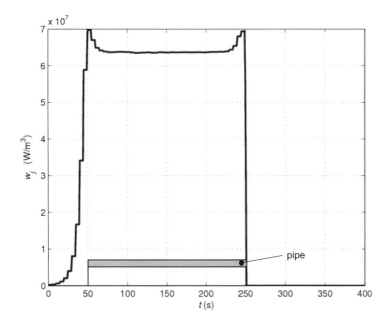

Figure 6.6. Time evolution of the average Joule losses in the pipe.

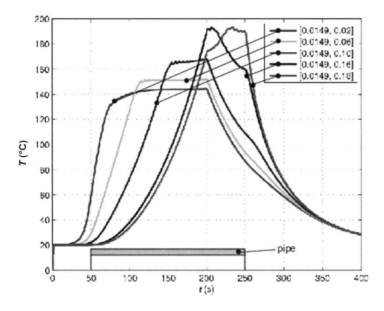

Figure 6.7. Time evolution of the temperature at the selected points of the pipe.

at the moment when the inductor is also in the center of the pipe. The differences do not exceed about 5% and are brought about by different meshing and calculation.

Figure 6.9 contains the time evolution of the effective value of eddy current density at two specified points of the pipe calculated by our own code and COMSOL Multiphysics. Finally, Fig. 6.10 shows the time evolution of the temperature at the same points calculated again by both mentioned approaches. Even with the different algorithms of calculation and strongly different meshing, the results exhibit quite good agreement.

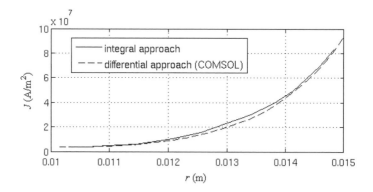

Figure 6.8.   Time evolution of the effective value of eddy current density along the radius of the pipe in its center.

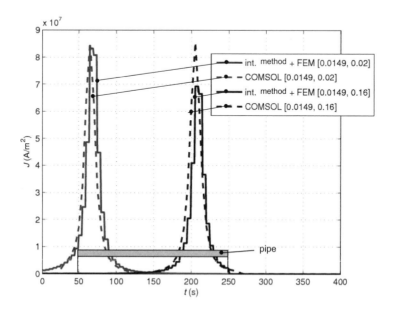

Figure 6.9.   Comparison of the distribution of the effective current density at two specified points of the pipe.

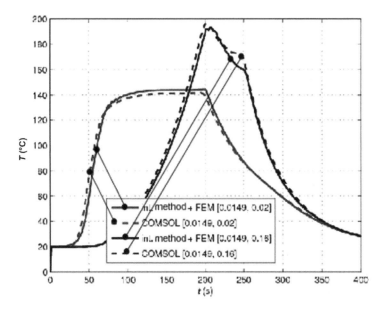

Figure 6.10. Comparison of the time evolution of temperature at two specified points of the pipe.

Unfortunately, even when the results obtained by both approaches are very similar (the differences caused by the different discretization and different method of computation are relatively low), there is no way to decide (without an experiment) which of them is more accurate.

6.1.5 Conclusion

It was confirmed that both (integrodifferential and differential) methods provide practically the same results. The time of computation is also comparable, in some cases even somewhat shorter. The power of the integrodifferential approach grows particularly in the case of field currents of general time dependencies or higher velocity of the inductor.

New research in the field will be aimed at the application of integrodifferential methods of higher orders of accuracy, which are expected to lead to a substantial decrease in the degrees of freedom of the problem (and, consequently, to shortening of computation time) at the same or higher precision of the results.

6.2 INDUCTION HEATING OF A LONG NONMAGNETIC CYLINDRICAL BILLET ROTATING IN A UNIFORM MAGNETIC FIELD

6.2.1 Introduction

Induction heating of nonmagnetic (mainly aluminum) billets is a widely spread industrial technology used for their softening before hot forming. The conventional heaters in the form of cylindrical coils made of a massive hollow conductor cooled by water (see Fig. 6.11) exhibit, however, rather low electrical efficiency (about 50–60%). This means that more than 40% of the total power is transformed into heat loss in the inductor that is dissipated in the cooling water.

Unfortunately, for induction heating of workpieces of general geometries it is not easy to propose another technique that would exhibit a substantially higher efficiency. But for cylindrical and, more generally, axisymmetric workpieces, an innovative technique was recently introduced consisting of heating a billet by its rotation in a uniform magnetic field produced by direct current or permanent magnets. Also possible are inverse techniques based on heating of stationary billets by a multiphase winding, gradually connected coils carrying direct currents or rotating magnets. It is estimated that the efficiency of some of these systems could reach even 80%.

6.2.2   Formulation of the technical problem

This example presents the integrodifferential approach to modeling of the process (several authors analyzed the process by the finite element method, e.g., Refs. 169 and 170). The arrangement of the system under investigation consisting of the inductor and billet is depicted in Fig. 6.12.

Rotation of the billet in a uniform magnetic field generates eddy currents in it that bring about the corresponding Joule losses and temperature rise of the billet. While the distribution of steady-state eddy currents and Joule losses in the heated cylinder is modeled by the method of integral equations, the nonstationary temperature field is calculated by the finite element method. Calculated are the most important characteristics of the process (Joule losses, temperature profile, etc.) as functions of the number of revolution and radius of the billet.

6.2.3   Continuous mathematical model of the problem

6.2.3.1   Eddy currents in the billet   It is necessary to find the distribution of eddy currents in the arrangement in Fig. 6.13 consisting of three electrically conductive parts

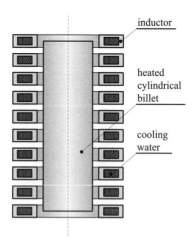

Figure 6.11.   Induction heating of static cylinder by a classical static inductor.

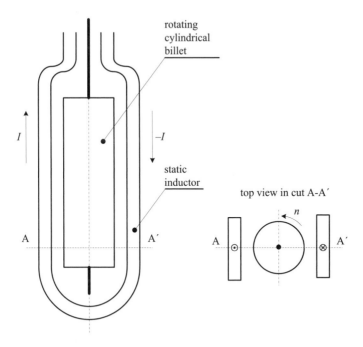

Figure 6.12.   Induction heating of rotating cylinder by static inductor.

Ω_1 (rotating billet) and Ω_2, Ω_3 (static inductors of general cross sections). The system is supposed to be infinitely long in the direction of the z axis.

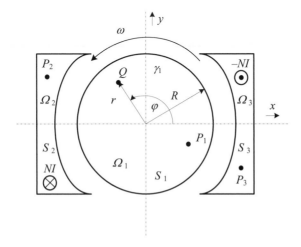

Figure 6.13.   Detailed view of the solved arrangement.

Consider a reference point Q in the cross-section of the billet. Magnetic vector potential A at this point, which has only one nonzero component A_{1z} in the z direction, may be expressed as follows

$$A_{1z}(Q) = A_{1z}(r, \varphi) = -\frac{\mu_0}{2\pi} \int_{\Omega_1} J_{1z}(P_1) \ln(s_{QP_1}) dS - \frac{\mu_0}{2\pi} \int_{\Omega_2} J_{2z}(P_2) \ln(s_{QP_2}) dS$$

$$- \frac{\mu_0}{2\pi} \int_{\Omega_3} J_{3z}(P_3) \ln(s_{QP_3}) dS, \tag{6.14}$$

where $J_{1z}(P_1)$ denotes the zth component of the current density at a general integration point P_1 of the cross section of the billet and $J_{2z}(P_2)$ and $J_{3z}(P_3)$ have similar definitions in inductors Ω_2 and Ω_3. Finally, symbols s_{QP_1}, s_{QP_2}, and s_{QP_3} denote the distances between the relevant points.

When the field coils Ω_2 and Ω_3 consist of thin conductors, we can neglect the influence of eddy currents (induced due to rotation of billet Ω_1) in them. Then $J_{2z}(P_2)$ and $J_{3z}(P_3)$ represent the source direct current densities independent of the position of points P_2 and P_3, so that

$$J_{2z} = \frac{NI}{S_2}, \quad J_{3z} = -\frac{NI}{S_3}. \tag{6.15}$$

The density of eddy currents induced at point Q is given by

$$J_{1z}(Q) = -\gamma_1 \frac{dA_{1z}(Q)}{dt} = -\gamma_1 \frac{dA_{1z}(r, \varphi)}{dt} = -\gamma_1 \left[\frac{\partial A_{1z}(Q)}{\partial r} \frac{dr}{dt} + \frac{\partial A_{1z}(Q)}{\partial \varphi} \frac{d\varphi}{dt} \right].$$

As the point Q rotates with respect to the z axis of the billet (without any change of its radius), there holds

$$J_{1z}(Q) = -\gamma_1 \frac{\partial A_{1z}(Q)}{\partial \varphi} \frac{d\varphi}{dt} = -\gamma_1 \omega \frac{\partial A_{1z}(Q)}{\partial \varphi}, \tag{6.16}$$

where ω is the angular velocity of the billet. After substituting (6.16) into (6.14) we obtain

$$J_{1z}(r, \varphi) = \frac{\mu_0 \omega \gamma_1}{2\pi} \cdot \frac{\partial}{\partial \varphi} \left[\int_{\Omega_1} J_{1z}(r, \varphi) \ln(s_{QP_1}) dS \right.$$

$$\left. + J_{2z} \int_{\Omega_2} \ln(s_{QP_2}) dS - J_{3z} \int_{\Omega_3} \ln(s_{QP_3}) dS \right]. \tag{6.17}$$

Now we have to consider that

- the distance s_{QP_1} does not depend on angle φ (it is always constant),

- the distance s_{QP_2}, $P_2 \equiv P_2(x, y) \in \Omega_2$ can be expressed as

$$s_{QP_2} = \sqrt{(r\cos\varphi - x)^2 + (r\sin\varphi - y)^2},$$

and

- the distance s_{QP_3}, $P_3 \equiv P_3(x, y) \in \Omega_3$ can be expressed as

$$s_{QP_3} = \sqrt{(r\cos\varphi - x)^2 + (r\sin\varphi - y)^2}.$$

Substituting the above relations and (6.15) into (6.17) we obtain

$$
\begin{aligned}
J_{1z}(r,\varphi) = \frac{\mu_0\omega\gamma_1}{2\pi} \cdot \left[\int_{\Omega_1} \ln(s_{QP_1}) \frac{\partial J_{1z}(r,\varphi)}{\partial \varphi} \mathrm{d}S \right.\\
\left. + \frac{NI}{S_2} \int_{\Omega_2} \frac{\partial \ln(s_{QP_2})}{\partial \varphi} - \frac{NI}{S_3} \int_{\Omega_3} \frac{\mathrm{d}\ln(s_{QP_3})}{\mathrm{d}\varphi} \right],
\end{aligned}
\tag{6.18}
$$

and putting

$$
\frac{\partial \ln(s_{QP_2})}{\partial \varphi} = \frac{r(x\sin\varphi - y\cos\varphi)}{(r\cos\varphi - x)^2 + (r\sin\varphi - y)^2}
$$

(the same holds even for s_{QP_3}), we finally obtain

$$
\begin{aligned}
J_{1z}(r,\varphi) - \frac{\mu_0\omega\gamma_1}{2\pi} \cdot \int_{\Omega_1} \ln(s_{QP_1}) \frac{\partial J_{1z}(r,\varphi)}{\partial \varphi} \mathrm{d}S \\
= \frac{\mu_0\omega\gamma_1}{2\pi} \frac{NI}{S_2} \int_{\Omega_2} \frac{r(x\sin\varphi - y\cos\varphi)\mathrm{d}S}{(r\cos\varphi - x)^2 + (r\sin\varphi - y)^2} \\
- \frac{\mu_0\omega\gamma_1}{2\pi} \frac{NI}{S_3} \int_{\Omega_3} \frac{r(x\sin\varphi - y\cos\varphi)\mathrm{d}S}{(r\cos\varphi - x)^2 + (r\sin\varphi - y)^2}.
\end{aligned}
\tag{6.19}
$$

This is the basic continuous electromagnetic model of the problem. The terms with unknown values of eddy current densities are on the left-hand side, while the right-hand side contains integrals whose analytical or numerical computation (depending on the cross section of the inductors) is relatively easy.

6.2.3.2 Joule losses The specific Joule losses w_J at the reference point Q of the billet representing the internal sources of heat are given by

$$
w_J(Q) = \frac{J_{1z}^2(Q)}{\gamma_1}.
\tag{6.20}
$$

The total Joule losses per unit length of the billet (given in W/m) are

$$
W_J' = \int_{\Omega_1} w_J(Q)\mathrm{d}S.
$$

6.2.3.3 Drag torque Another very important quantity (from the viewpoint of the total efficiency of the device) is the drag torque T_d that is produced as a consequence of the interaction between the field currents in the inductor and eddy currents in the billet. Since the billet is infinitely long, however, this quantity will be calculated per 1 meter of its axial length and we will denote it as T_d'. It is obvious that this torque also has only one nonzero component T_{dz}'.

The torque can be calculated from the formula

$$
T_d' = \int_{\Omega_1} (r_Q \times f_Q)\mathrm{d}S,
\tag{6.21}
$$

where $\boldsymbol{r}_Q$ is the position vector of point Q and $\boldsymbol{f}_Q$ is the specific Lorentz force at the same point, whose element $\mathrm{d}\boldsymbol{f}_Q$ follows from the expression

$$\mathrm{d}\boldsymbol{f}_Q = \boldsymbol{J}_1(Q) \times \mathrm{d}\boldsymbol{B}_Q .$$

Here $\boldsymbol{J}_1(Q)$ is the vector of current density at point Q (that has only one nonzero component J_{1z} in the z direction) and $\mathrm{d}\boldsymbol{B}_Q$ is the magnetic flux density produced by filaments located at points P_2 and P_3 in elements Ω_2 and Ω_3. The above vector equation may be split into two component equations:

$$\mathrm{d}f_{Qx} = -J_{1z}(Q) \cdot \mathrm{d}B_{Qy}, \ \ \mathrm{d}f_{Qy} = J_{1z}(Q) \cdot \mathrm{d}B_{Qx}$$

where the components of magnetic flux density $\mathrm{d}B_{Qx}$ and $\mathrm{d}B_{Qy}$ at point Q due to current density at point $P_2(x_2, y_2) \in \Omega_2$ are given by the formulas

$$
\begin{aligned}
\mathrm{d}B_{Qx2} &= -\frac{\mu_0 J_{2z}}{2\pi} \cdot \frac{y - y_2}{(x - x_2)^2 + (y - y_2)^2} \\
&= -\frac{\mu_0 J_{2z}}{2\pi} \cdot \frac{r\sin\varphi - y_2}{(r\cos\varphi - x_2)^2 + (r\sin\varphi - y_2)^2} ,
\end{aligned}
\tag{6.22}
$$

$$
\begin{aligned}
\mathrm{d}B_{Qy2} &= \frac{\mu_0 J_{2z}}{2\pi} \cdot \frac{x - x_2}{(x - x_2)^2 + (y - y_2)^2} \\
&= \frac{\mu_0 J_{2z}}{2\pi} \cdot \frac{r\cos\varphi - y_2}{(r\cos\varphi - x_2)^2 + (r\sin\varphi - y_2)^2} .
\end{aligned}
\tag{6.23}
$$

Analogous formulas can be obtained for the contributions $\mathrm{d}B_{Qx3}$ and $\mathrm{d}B_{Qy3}$ due to current density J_{3z} at point $P_3(x_3, y_3) \in \Omega_3$. In this way we obtain

$$
\begin{aligned}
f_{Qx} &= -\int_{\Omega_2} J_{1z}(Q)\mathrm{d}B_{Qy2}\mathrm{d}S - \int_{\Omega_3} J_{1z}(Q)\mathrm{d}B_{Qy3}\mathrm{d}S \\
&= -\frac{\mu_0 J_{2z} J_{1z}(Q)}{2\pi} \cdot \int_{\Omega_2} \frac{(x - x_2)\mathrm{d}S}{(x - x_2)^2 + (y - y_2)^2} \\
&\quad - \frac{\mu_0 J_{3z} J_{1z}(Q)}{2\pi} \cdot \int_{\Omega_3} \frac{(x - x_3)\mathrm{d}S}{(x - x_3)^2 + (y - y_3)^2} ,
\end{aligned}
\tag{6.24}
$$

$$
\begin{aligned}
f_{Qy} &= \int_{\Omega_2} J_{1z}(Q)\mathrm{d}B_{Qx2}\mathrm{d}S + \int_{\Omega_3} J_{1z}(Q)\mathrm{d}B_{Qx3}\mathrm{d}S \\
&= \frac{\mu_0 J_{2z} J_{1z}(Q)}{2\pi} \cdot \int_{\Omega_2} \frac{(y - y_2)\mathrm{d}S}{(x - x_2)^2 + (y - y_2)^2} \\
&\quad + \frac{\mu_0 J_{3z} J_{1z}(Q)}{2\pi} \cdot \int_{\Omega_3} \frac{(y - y_3)\mathrm{d}S}{(x - x_3)^2 + (y - y_3)^2} .
\end{aligned}
\tag{6.25}
$$

The elementary drag torque $\mathrm{d}T'_{\mathrm{dz}}$ is now given as

$$\mathrm{d}T'_{\mathrm{dz}} = x \cdot f_{Qy} - y \cdot f_{Qx}
\tag{6.26}$$

and full drag torque T'_{dz} is

$$T'_{dz} = \int_{\Omega_1} (x \cdot f_{Qy} - y \cdot f_{Qx}) dS. \tag{6.27}$$

From the computational viewpoint, however, it is more convenient to express the elementary torque as

$$dT'_{dz} = r \cdot f_{Q\varphi}, \tag{6.28}$$

where

$$f_{Q\varphi} = f_{Qy} \cos \varphi - f_{Qx} \sin \varphi, \tag{6.29}$$

and full drag torque T'_{dz} as

$$T'_{dz} = \int_{\Omega_1} r \cdot f_{Q\varphi} dS. \tag{6.30}$$

In most cases the integration of (6.26) has to be carried out numerically (analytical computation is possible only in (6.24) and (6.25) provided that the cross sections S_2 and S_3 of the field coils are geometrically simple areas).

6.2.3.4 *Temperature rise of the billet*
The nonstationary temperature field T in the current carrying parts of the system is described by the heat transfer equation including the influence of the motion:

$$\operatorname{div} \lambda \operatorname{grad} T = \varrho c_p \left[\frac{\partial T}{\partial t} + v \cdot \operatorname{grad} T \right] - w_{Ja}, \tag{6.31}$$

where λ is the thermal conductivity, ϱ the specific mass, c_p the specific heat at constant pressure, v the velocity of motion, and w_{Ja} the average specific Joule losses given as

$$w_{Ja}(r) = \frac{1}{2\pi} \int_{\varphi=0}^{2\pi} w_J(r, \varphi) d\varphi. \tag{6.32}$$

The physical parameters γ, λ, and c_p are generally temperature-dependent functions.

Equation (6.31) has to be supplemented by a boundary condition that respects the convection and radiation of heat from the body; see (6.2) with the explanation of the corresponding quantities.

6.2.4 Example of computation

6.2.4.1 *Input data*
A long aluminum billet of parameters $\gamma_1 = 33 \times 10^6$ S/m and $\lambda_1 = 237$ W/m· K rotates in a time-invariable magnetic field generated by a massive inductor of dimensions given in Fig. 6.14. The current density in the inductor $J_{2z} = -J_{3z} = 3 \times 10^7$ A/m². The convective heat transfer coefficient $\alpha = 100$ W/m²· K, the ambient temperature $T_{ext} = 20$ °C, and $C = 0.8$.

6.2.4.2 *Aim of the solution*
It is necessary to find the following:

- for the basic frequency of rotation $n = 6000$/min (or $f = 100$/s) the distribution of eddy current density along the cross section of the billet and time evolution of its temperature profile,

- the dependence of the total Joule losses $W'_{\rm J}$ and drag torque $T'_{\rm dz}$ on frequency of rotation,

- the dependence of the total Joule losses $W'_{\rm J}$ and drag torque $T'_{\rm dz}$ on the radius R of the billet (with remaining geometry of the inductor).

6.2.4.3   *Computation*   Let us first determine the right-hand side $I_{\rm r}(r, \varphi)$ of (6.19). For the considered shape of the inductor we have

$$
\begin{aligned}
I_{\rm r}(r, \varphi) &= \frac{\mu_0 \omega \gamma_1}{2\pi} \frac{NI}{S_2} \int_{\Omega_2} \frac{r(x \sin \varphi - y \cos \varphi) \mathrm{d}S}{(r \cos \varphi - x)^2 + (r \sin \varphi - y)^2} \\
&\quad - \frac{\mu_0 \omega \gamma_1}{2\pi} \frac{NI}{S_3} \int_{\Omega_3} \frac{r(x \sin \varphi - y \cos \varphi) \mathrm{d}S}{(r \cos \varphi - x)^2 + (r \sin \varphi - y)^2} \\
&= \frac{\mu_0 \omega \gamma_1}{2\pi} \frac{NI}{S_2} \int_{\beta=-\pi/3}^{\pi/3} \int_{q=R_1}^{R_2} \frac{r(q \cos \beta \sin \varphi - q \sin \beta \cos \varphi) q \, \mathrm{d}q \, \mathrm{d}\beta}{(r \cos \varphi - q \cos \beta)^2 + (r \sin \varphi - q \sin \beta)^2} \\
&\quad - \frac{\mu_0 \omega \gamma_1}{2\pi} \frac{NI}{S_3} \int_{\beta=2\pi/3}^{4\pi/3} \int_{q=R_1}^{R_2} \frac{r(q \cos \beta \sin \varphi - q \sin \beta \cos \varphi) q \, \mathrm{d}q \, \mathrm{d}\beta}{(r \cos \varphi - q \cos \beta)^2 + (r \sin \varphi - q \sin \beta)^2},
\end{aligned}
$$

where we put $x = q \sin \beta$ and $y = q \cos \beta$. After several rearrangements we have

$$
\begin{aligned}
I_{\rm r}(r, \varphi) &= \frac{\mu_0 \omega \gamma_1}{2\pi} \frac{NI}{S_2} \int_{\beta=-\pi/3}^{\pi/3} \int_{q=R_1}^{R_2} \frac{rq^2 \sin(\varphi - \beta) \mathrm{d}q \, \mathrm{d}\beta}{r^2 + q^2 - 2rq \cos(\varphi - \beta)} \qquad (6.33) \\
&\quad - \frac{\mu_0 \omega \gamma_1}{2\pi} \frac{NI}{S_3} \int_{\beta=2\pi/3}^{4\pi/3} \int_{q=R_1}^{R_2} \frac{rq^2 \sin(\varphi - \beta) \mathrm{d}q \, \mathrm{d}\beta}{r^2 + q^2 - 2rq \cos(\varphi - \beta)}. \qquad (6.34)
\end{aligned}
$$

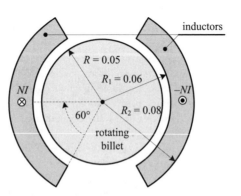

Figure 6.14.   The investigated system.

Calculating

$$G(r, \varphi, q, \beta) = \int_\beta \int_q \frac{rq^2 \sin(\varphi - \beta) \mathrm{d}q \mathrm{d}\beta}{r^2 + q^2 - 2rq\cos(\varphi - \beta)}$$

$$= \frac{qr\cos(\beta - \varphi)}{2} + \frac{r^2 \cos(2(\beta - \varphi)) - q^2}{4} \ln(q^2 + r^2 - 2qr\cos(\beta - \varphi))$$

$$+ r^2 \arctan\left[\frac{r\cos(\beta - \varphi) - q}{r\sin(\beta - \varphi)}\right] \cos(\beta - \varphi)\sin(\beta - \varphi),$$

$$(6.35)$$

we immediately have (because $S_2 = S_3 = \pi(R_2^2 - R_1^2)/3$)

$$I_r(r, \varphi) = \frac{\mu_0 \omega \gamma_1}{2\pi} \frac{3NI}{\pi(R_2^2 - R_1^2)} \cdot [G(r, \varphi, R_2, \pi/3) - G(r, \varphi, R_1, \pi/3)$$

$$- G(r, \varphi, R_3, -\pi/3 + G(r, \varphi, R_1, -\pi/3) - G(r, \varphi, R_2, 4\pi/3)$$

$$+ G(r, \varphi, R_2, 2\pi/3) + G(r, \varphi, R_1, 4\pi/3) - G(r, \varphi, R_1, 2\pi/3)].$$

$$(6.36)$$

Discretization of the cross section of the billet was performed in the classical manner (about 3000 triangular elements) and distribution of the induced eddy currents and specific Joule losses in them was determined using the algorithm mentioned in Chapter 4.

Determination of the specific Lorentz force acting at the reference point $Q \equiv Q(x, y) \equiv Q(r, \varphi)$, see (6.24)–(6.29), starts from the specific Lorentz force $f_{Q\varphi}$ that is given as

$$f_{Q\varphi} = \frac{\mu_0 J_{2z} J_{1z}(Q)}{2\pi} \cdot \left[\int_{\Omega_2} \frac{(y - y_2)\mathrm{d}S_2}{(x - x_2)^2 + (y - y_2)^2} \right.$$

$$\left. - \int_{\Omega_3} \frac{(y - y_3)\mathrm{d}S_3}{(x - x_3)^2 + (y - y_3)^2} \right] \cos\varphi$$

$$+ \left[\int_{\Omega_2} \frac{(x - x_2)\mathrm{d}S}{(x - x_2)^2 + (y - y_2)^2} - \int_{\Omega_3} \frac{(x - x_3)\mathrm{d}S}{(x - x_3)^2 + (y - y_3)^2} \right] \sin\varphi.$$

$$(6.37)$$

Its evaluation requires computation of the integrals

$$f_1 = \int_{\Omega_2} \frac{[(y - y_2)\cos\varphi - (x - x_2)\sin\varphi]\mathrm{d}S}{(x - x_2)^2 + (y - y_2)^2}$$

and

$$f_2 = \int_{\Omega_3} \frac{[(y - y_3)\cos\varphi - (x - x_3)\sin\varphi]\mathrm{d}S}{(x - x_2)^2 + (y - y_2)^2},$$

where $(x, y) \in \Omega_1$, $(x_2, y_2) \in \Omega_2$, and $(x_3, y_3) \in \Omega_3$. Putting $x = r\cos\varphi$, $x_2 = q\cos\beta$, $y = r\sin\varphi$, and $y_2 = q\sin\beta$, we can write

$$
\begin{aligned}
f_1 &= \int_{\beta=2\pi/3}^{4\pi/3} \int_{q=R_1}^{R_2} \frac{(r\sin\varphi - q\sin\beta)\cos\varphi - (r\cos\varphi - q\cos\beta)\sin\varphi}{(r\cos\varphi - q\cos\beta)^2 + (r\sin\varphi - q\sin\beta)^2} \, q \, dq \, d\beta \\
&= \int_{\beta=2\pi/3}^{4\pi/3} \int_{q=R_1}^{R_2} \frac{q^2 \sin(\varphi - \beta)}{r^2 + q^2 - 2rq\cos(\beta - \varphi)} \, dq \, d\beta .
\end{aligned}
\tag{6.38}
$$

Computation of this integral is the same as for integral (6.35). The only difference is parameter r in the numerator of its integrand.

Evaluation of the torque (6.30) has to be carried out numerically, because the current density $J_{1z}(Q)$ varies from element to element.

The time evolution of the temperature in the billet was solved by the finite element method. Its distribution over its cross section is calculated (due to its revolution) from the average specific Joule losses (6.32).

6.2.4.4 Results and their discussion
Solution of the example provided a lot of results. The most important of them are summarized in several of the following figures.

For the basic frequency of revolution ($n = 6000/\text{min}$), Fig. 6.15 shows the distribution of the values of steady-state eddy current densities in the billet along its radii for various angles indicated in the same figure. For angles $\varphi \geq 180°$, there holds (due to antisymmetry) $J_{1z}(r, \varphi) = -J_{1z}(r, \varphi - 180)$.

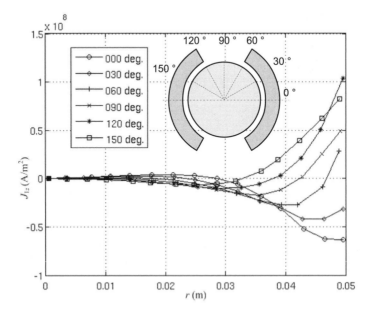

Figure 6.15. Steady-state eddy current densities along the radii of the billet ($n = 6000/\text{min}$), angles $\varphi = 0°$, $30°$, $60°$, $90°$, $120°$, $150°$.

Validation of these results was carried out by calculation of the same values by the finite element method using COMSOL Multiphysics. Figure 6.16 shows the distribution of steady-state eddy current densities along the radius characterized by angle $\varphi = 30°$. The differences are caused by using substantially different discretization and a different method of computation (and, unfortunately, it cannot be decided which way is more accurate).

Figure 6.17 shows the distribution of the steady-state specific average Joule losses W_{Ja} along the radius of the billet. This distribution does not depend on angle φ due to its rotation (see 6.32)) and the value up to radius $r = 0.03$ m is practically negligible.

For the above distribution of the steady-state specific average Joule losses, Fig 6.18 shows the distribution of the temperatures along the radius for the given time levels (revolutions $n = 6000/\text{min}$). This distribution is relatively smooth (the difference between the temperatures at the axis of the billet and at its surface is low—about 50 °C—due to the high thermal conductivity of aluminum).

Figure 6.19 shows the dependence of the total steady-state Joule losses W_J' per unit length of the billet. These losses grow with the number of revolutions, but this growth decelerates. This is because with the growing number of revolutions the eddy currents are produced in ever thinner surface layers of the billet.

Figure 6.20 depicts the dependence of the drag torque T_{dz}' on the number of revolutions. The torque has its maximum at about $n = 10$ s^{-1} and its value exceeds 800 N· m/m (while for $n = 300$ s^{-1} it is approximately four times lower). The reason is the same as in the case of the total eddy current losses; with growing value of n eddy currents are produced in thinner and thinner surface layers and their force interaction decreases.

Figures 6.21 and 6.22 show the dependence of the total steady-state Joule losses W_J' per unit length of the billet and torque T_{dz}' per unit length for basic revolutions $n = 200$ s^{-1}, but for varying radius R of the billet ranging in the interval $\langle 0.03, \ 0.57 \rangle$ m (with growing values of R there decreases the width between the billet and inductor). Both curves have strongly linear character.

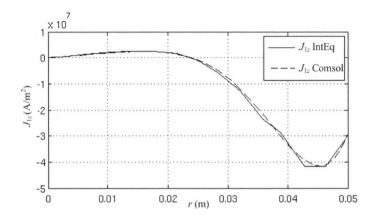

Figure 6.16.   Comparison of the distribution of eddy current density along the radius of the billet for angle $\varphi = 30°$ (integral method and FEM).

6.2.5 Conclusion

The combined integrodifferential approach provides the same results as the finite element technique. Its application, however, is easier in several respects (no artificial boundary, discretization of only active parts of the system, direct computation of eddy currents in the billet).

Future work in the domain will be aimed at the dynamical behavior of the system (time evolution of the angular velocity, eddy currents induced in the billet, and its average temperature).

6.3 PULSED INDUCTION ACCELERATOR

6.3.1 Introduction

The pulsed induction accelerator (PIA) is a device for launching small metal electrically conductive bodies with high acceleration. The device is schematically depicted in Fig. 6.23. Its principal parts are the field circuit supplied from a charged capacitor, field coil, and launched body. After it is switched on, the circuit starts carrying damped oscillatory current (its first part being similar to a pulse). The corresponding pulsed magnetic field produced by the coil then induces eddy currents (almost of the opposite phase shift) in the launched body. And the interaction between the primary magnetic field and these eddy currents gives rise to a repulsive electrodynamic force acting on the body, which is launched away from the field coil.

The principle was tested many times and used in both military and civil applications. In the military sphere we can mention the induction-based coilguns (but the possibilities of their practical use were found rather nonprospective, more effective are the railguns); in the civil sphere similar devices were installed, for instance, in DC high-speed circuit breakers in order to quickly increase the mutual distance of their contacts and accelerate their switching-off process.

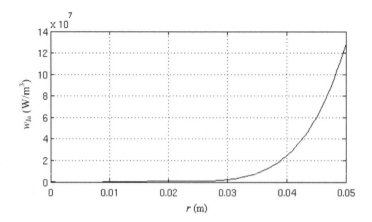

Figure 6.17. Distribution of the specific average Joule losses along the radius of the billet for $n = 6000/\text{min}$.

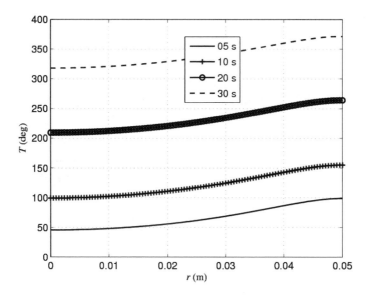

Figure 6.18.   Distribution of the temperature along the radius of the billet at various time levels ($n = 6000/\text{min}$).

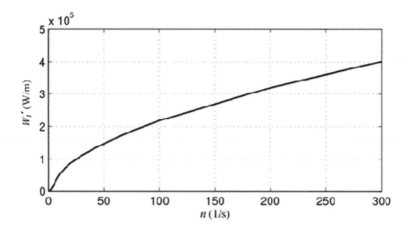

Figure 6.19.   Dependence of the total Joule losses W_J' generated in the billet on the number of revolutions n (s^{-1}).

The device was modeled by several methods, prevailingly by the FEM and also using an approach based on electric circuits. Here we will show its modeling by the integrodifferential technique and evaluate its advantages and drawbacks.

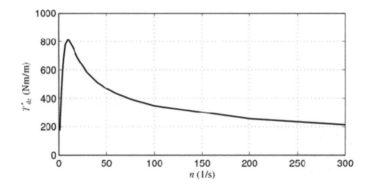

Figure 6.20. Dependence of the drag torque T'_{dz} of the billet on the number of revolutions n (s^{-1}).

6.3.2 Formulation of the problem

Let the system in Fig. 6.23 be considered axisymmetric and linear. The task is to find the time evolution of current $i(t)$ in the field circuit and velocity $v(t)$ of the projectile in common with its trajectory $s(t)$. Material properties as well as the geometry of the system are supposed to be known and at this moment they are considered independent of temperature. The problems associated with the temperature rise of the system will not be solved in this example.

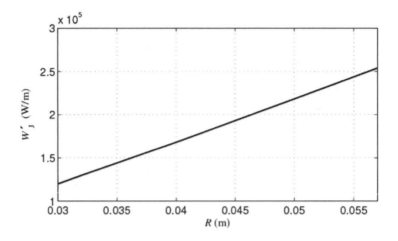

Figure 6.21. Dependence of the total Joule losses W'_J per unit length generated in the billet on its radius R ($n = 200$ s^{-1}).

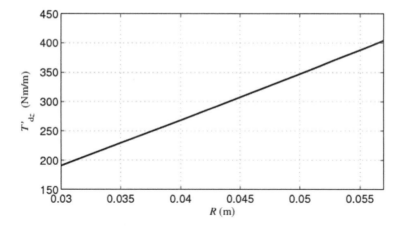

Figure 6.22.   Dependence of the drag torque T'_{dz} per unit length produced by the billet on its radius R ($n = 200$ s^{-1}).

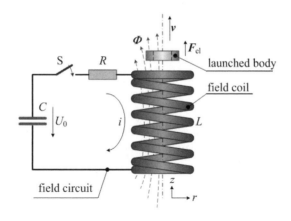

Figure 6.23.   A simplified arrangement of pulsed induction accelerator.

6.3.3 Continuous mathematical model

We first formulate the ordinary differential equations describing the electric and mechanical circuits of the system.

The time evolution of current in the field circuit is described by the equation

$$U_0 - \frac{1}{C} \int_{\tau=0}^{t} i \, d\tau = Ri + \frac{d}{dt}(Li), \tag{6.39}$$

where U_0 is the initial voltage of the capacitor, R denotes the total resistance of the considered circuit (that includes resistances of the coil, feeding conductors, and capacitor), and L inductance that is a function of instantaneous position z of the launched body and skin effect in all active parts of the system.

The initial conditions read

$$i(0) = 0, \quad \left[\frac{di}{dt}\right]_{t=0} = \frac{U_0}{L_0}, \tag{6.40}$$

where L_0 is the inductance of the system in the initial position (before the process of launching).

Provided that the movement of the projectile is realized in the z direction, the time evolution of its velocity $v_z(t)$ and trajectory $s_z(t)$ can be described by the equations

$$m\frac{dv_z}{dt} = F_{el,z} - F_{f,z} - F_{a,z}, \quad v_z = \frac{dz}{dt} \tag{6.41}$$

with initial conditions

$$v_z(0) = 0, \quad s_z(0) = s_0. \tag{6.42}$$

Here m is the mass of the projectile, $F_{el,z} = F_{el,z}(s_z)$ is the dynamic force acting on it, $F_{f,z}$ denotes possible friction (e.g., in the leading tube), and $F_{a,z} = F_{a,z}(v_z)$ is the aerodynamic resistance of the surrounding medium (air). Finally, symbol s_0 stands for the initial position of the projectile.

The instantaneous value of L can be expressed from energy of the magnetic field W_{mf} accumulated in the system using the formula

$$L = \frac{2W_{mf}}{i^2}, \tag{6.43}$$

where

$$W_{mf} = \frac{1}{2}\int_V \boldsymbol{J} \cdot \boldsymbol{A} \, dV. \tag{6.44}$$

Here $\boldsymbol{J}$ and $\boldsymbol{A}$ denote the vectors of the current density and magnetic vector potential, respectively. As these vectors only have nonzero components in the circumferential direction φ, we can write

$$W_{mf} = \frac{1}{2}\int_V J_\varphi A_\varphi dV. \tag{6.45}$$

Integration is here carried out only over the current domains (field coil and projectile).

Magnetic flux density $\boldsymbol{B}$ in the axisymmetric system has only two nonzero components, B_r and B_z. Electrodynamic force $F_{el,z}$ acting on the projectile in the axisymmetric arrangement is then expressed as

$$F_{el,z} = -\int_{V_p} J_\varphi B_r \cdot dV, \tag{6.46}$$

while effects of the radial force (or axial component of the magnetic flux density) are eliminated. Integration of (6.46) is performed just over the volume of the projectile. The principal question is how to find the time-variable distribution of eddy currents in the launched body (whose knowledge allows computing the corresponding quantities A_φ and B_r of the magnetic field).

The algorithm of the calculation is realized by the following steps, provided we know the geometry of the system, material properties, circuit elements, and coefficients of friction and aerodynamic resistance.

1. The process starts at time $t_0 = 0$ with $v_z(0) = 0$, $i(0) = 0$, $s_z(0) = s_0$, and $F_{el,z}(0) = 0$. We select time step $\triangle t$ for the time integration.

2. Determination of $L(0)$ (representing the initial inductance of the system) that is equal to the self-inductance of the field coil. Computation of this quantity is performed using the formula derived for air-core coils.

3. Initialization of the integration process.

4. $t_{l+1} = t_l + \triangle t$.

5. Numerical computation of $i_{l+1} = i(t_{l+1})$ and its first derivative.

6. Computation of current densities in the field winding and body in time t_{l+1} using the integral approach. Velocity of motion of the projectile in the first time step is considered zero, in other steps it is already nonzero.

7. Computation of vector potential and magnetic flux density in the system using classical integral expressions based on the knowledge of current densities.

8. Computation of $W_{mf,l+1} = W_{mf}(t_{l+1})$, $L_{l+1} = L(t_{l+1})$, and $F_{el,z,l+1} = F_{el,z}(t_{l+1})$.

9. Computation of $v_{z,l+1} = v_z(t_{l+1})$ and $s_{z,l+1} = s_z(t_{l+1})$ and return to step 4. Computations are stopped depending on a selected condition (prescribed time, trajectory, etc.).

The flow chart of the algorithm is given in Fig. 6.24.

Now we will deal with the steps of the algorithm concerning determination of the field and integral quantities. Let us start from Fig. 6.25, which schematically depicts the inductor with the projectile.

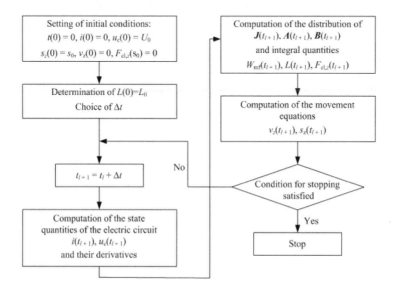

Figure 6.24. Flow chart of the algorithm.

In the domain of the inductor (Ω_1) the principal equation for the distribution of current density reads

$$-J_{\varphi 1}(Q_1, t) + \frac{\mu_0 \gamma_1}{4\pi} \int_{\Omega_1} \frac{\mathrm{d}J_{\varphi 1}(P_1, t)}{\mathrm{d}t} \cdot \frac{\mathrm{d}V}{r_{Q_1, P_1}}$$

$$+\frac{\mu_0 \gamma_1}{4\pi} \int_{\Omega_2} \frac{\mathrm{d}J_{\varphi 2}(P_2, t)}{\mathrm{d}t} \cdot \frac{\mathrm{d}V}{r_{Q_1, P_2}} + J_{\varphi 01}(t) = 0 \qquad (6.47)$$

with indirect condition

$$\int_{S_1} J_{\varphi 1}(Q_1, t)\mathrm{d}S = N_1 i_1(t). \qquad (6.48)$$

Here Q_1 is a reference point $Q_1 \in \Omega_1$, P_1 and P_2 are general integration points $P_1 \in \Omega_1$, $P_2 \in \Omega_2$, r_{Q_1, P_1} and r_{Q_1, P_2} are the distances between the relevant points, $J_{\varphi 01}(t)$ is an unknown function of time, γ_1 is the electrical conductivity of the inductor, and N_1 is the number of turns in the field coil.

Analogously, for the domain of the projectile we obtain

$$-J_{\varphi 2}(Q_2, t) + \frac{\mu_0 \gamma_2}{4\pi} \int_{\Omega_1} \frac{\mathrm{d}J_{\varphi 1}(P_1, t)}{\mathrm{d}t} \cdot \frac{\mathrm{d}V}{r_{Q_2, P_1}}$$

$$+\frac{\mu_0 \gamma_2}{4\pi} \int_{\Omega_2} \frac{\mathrm{d}J_{\varphi 2}(P_2, t)}{\mathrm{d}t} \cdot \frac{\mathrm{d}V}{r_{Q_2, P_2}} = 0. \qquad (6.49)$$

Here we do not prescribe any additional condition as the time evolution of the total current in the projectile is not known.

If the field coil is wound by a thin conductor, the current density $J_{\varphi 1}$ over its cross section can be considered homogeneous ($J_{\varphi 1} = N_1 i_1 / S_1$). In such a case the problem is

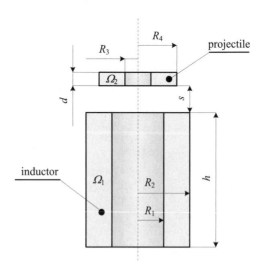

Figure 6.25. Inductor with the projectile.

described by a modification of expression (6.49) in the form

$$-J_{\varphi 2}(Q_2, t) + \frac{\mu_0 \gamma_2 N_1}{4\pi S_1} \frac{\mathrm{d}i_1}{\mathrm{d}t} \cdot \int_{\Omega_1} \frac{\mathrm{d}V}{r_{Q_2, P_1}}$$

$$+ \frac{\mu_0 \gamma_2}{4\pi} \int_{\Omega_2} \frac{\mathrm{d}J_{\varphi 2}(P_2, t)}{\mathrm{d}t} \cdot \frac{\mathrm{d}V}{r_{Q_2, P_2}} = 0. \tag{6.50}$$

Knowing the distribution of current densities, computation of the field quantities A and B at a reference point $Q = Q(R, Z)$ is realized by means of integral expressions:

$$A_\varphi(Q) = A_\varphi(R, Z) = \frac{\mu_0}{4\pi} \left[\int_{\Omega_1} \frac{J_{\varphi 1}(P_1) \cos \varphi \mathrm{d}V}{d_1} + \int_{\Omega_2} \frac{J_{\varphi 2}(P_2) \cos \varphi \mathrm{d}V}{d_2} \right],$$

$$\begin{aligned} B_r(Q) &= B_r(R, Z) \\ &= \frac{\mu_0}{4\pi} \left[\int_{\Omega_1} \frac{J_{\varphi 1}(P_1)(Z - z) \cos \varphi \mathrm{d}V}{d_1^3} + \int_{\Omega_2} \frac{J_{\varphi 2}(P_2)(Z - z) \cos \varphi \mathrm{d}V}{d_2^3} \right], \end{aligned}$$

and

$$\begin{aligned} B_z(Q) &= B_z(R, Z) \\ &= \frac{\mu_0}{4\pi R} \int_{\Omega_1} \frac{J_{\varphi 1}(P_1)[r(r - R \cos \varphi) + (Z - z)^2] \cos \varphi \mathrm{d}V}{d_1^3} \\ &\quad + \frac{\mu_0}{4\pi R} \int_{\Omega_2} \frac{J_{\varphi 2}(P_2)[r(r - R \cos \varphi) + (Z - z)^2] \cos \varphi \mathrm{d}V}{d_2^3}. \end{aligned}$$

Here $\mathrm{d}V = r \, \mathrm{d}r \, \mathrm{d}\varphi \, \mathrm{d}z$ and

$$d_1 = \sqrt{r^2 + R^2 - 2rR \cos \varphi + (Z - z)^2}, \quad (r, \varphi, z) \in \Omega_1,$$

$$d_2 = \sqrt{r^2 + R^2 - 2rR \cos \varphi + (Z - z)^2}, \quad (r, \varphi, z) \in \Omega_2.$$

After computing distribution of these quantities we can determine the energy of the magnetic field W_{mf} (6.45), inductance L of the system (6.43), and repulsive force $F_{\mathrm{el},z}$ (6.46).

6.3.4 Discretized model and its numerical solution

Both the coil and charge are divided into n_1 and n_2 elements in the form of rings with triangular cross sections of volumes V_{ij}, $i = 1, 2$, $j = 1, \ldots, n_i$. The distribution of current density $J_{\varphi, ij}$ in each cell is assumed uniform. The continuous equations (6.47), (6.48), and (6.49) are then discretized in the following way:

$$-J_{\varphi, 1j}(t) + \frac{\mu_0 \gamma_1}{4\pi} \sum_{k=1}^{2} \sum_{l=1}^{n_k} \frac{\mathrm{d}J_{\varphi, kl}(t)}{\mathrm{d}t} \int_{V_{kl}} \frac{\mathrm{d}V}{r_{1j, kl}}(t) + J_{\varphi, 10}(t) = 0, \quad j = 1, \ldots, n_1,$$

$$\tag{6.51}$$

$$\sum_{j=1}^{n_1} J_{\varphi, 1j}(t) S_{1j} = i_1(t) \tag{6.52}$$

$$-J_{\varphi,2j}(t) + \frac{\mu_0\gamma_2}{4\pi}\sum_{k=1}^{2}\sum_{l=1}^{n_k}\frac{\mathrm{d}J_{\varphi,kl}(t)}{\mathrm{d}t}\int_{V_{kl}}\frac{\mathrm{d}V}{r_{2j,kl}}(t) + J_{\varphi,10}(t) = 0, \quad j = 1,\ldots,n_2,$$

(6.53)

Here S_{1j} denotes the cross section of the ring with index $1j$. The time integration may be performed either by the Euler technique (that requires finer discretization with respect to time) or by more sophisticated techniques (such as Runge–Kutta). Application of the Euler method leads for the mth time level to

$$-J_{\varphi,1j}(t_m) + \frac{\mu_0\gamma_1}{4\pi}\sum_{k=1}^{2}\sum_{l=1}^{n_k}\frac{J_{\varphi,kl}(t_m) - J_{\varphi,kl}(t_{m-1})}{\triangle t_m}\int_{V_{kl}}\frac{\mathrm{d}V}{r_{1j,kl}(t_m)} + J_{\varphi,10}(t_m) = 0,$$

$$j = 1,\ldots,n_1,$$

(6.54)

$$\sum_{j=1}^{n_1}J_{\varphi,1j}(t_m)S_{1j} = i_1(t_m),$$

(6.55)

$$-J_{\varphi,2j}(t_m) + \frac{\mu_0\gamma_2}{4\pi}\sum_{k=1}^{2}\sum_{l=1}^{n_k}\frac{J_{\varphi,kl}(t_m) - J_{\varphi,kl}(t_{m-1})}{\triangle t_m}\int_{V_{kl}}\frac{\mathrm{d}V}{r_{2j,kl}(t_m)} + J_{\varphi,20}(t_m) = 0,$$

$$j = 1,\ldots,n_2,$$

(6.56)

where symbol $\triangle t_m$ denotes the corresponding time step. Computation of integrals over circular rings is discussed in Appendix C.3. The above equations may be rearranged into a recurrent system providing the distribution of current densities in particular cells. Its matrix form is

$$\mathbf{V}_m \cdot \mathbf{J}_m = \mathbf{W}_m \cdot \mathbf{J}_{m-1}$$

and, hence,

$$\mathbf{J}_m = \mathbf{V}_m^{-1} \cdot \mathbf{W}_m \cdot \mathbf{J}_{m-1}.$$

Matrix $\mathbf{M}_m = \mathbf{V}_m^{-1} \cdot \mathbf{W}_m$ changes from one time level to another due to the movement of the projectile.

The nonlinear ordinary differential equations (6.39) and (6.41) describing the behavior of the electric and mechanical circuits are discretized in the standard way.

6.3.5 Example of calculation

Consider the arrangement in Fig. 6.23. Geometry of the field coil and accelerated projectile (both parts are axisymmetric) is given in Fig. 6.26. The other parameters follow:

- total capacitance of the capacitor bank $C = 18.8 \times 10^{-3}$ F,

- voltage of the capacitor bank $U_0 = 35$ V,

- inductance of the field coil $L = 155 \times 10^{-9}$ H,

- number of its turns $N = 60$,

- resistance of the coil and feeding circuitry $R = 0.0072\,\Omega$,

- mass of the Al projectile $m_{\mathrm{Al}} = 0.000278\,\mathrm{kg}$,

- coefficient of the aerodynamic resistance $c = 0.9$,

- effective cross section of the projectile $S_{Al} = 1.1 \times 10^{-4}\,\text{m}^2$,

- electrical conductivity of aluminum $\gamma_{Al} = 33 \times 10^6$ S/m,

- electrical conductivity of copper $\gamma_{Cu} = 57 \times 10^6$ S/m,

- time step $\triangle t = 10^{-6}$ s.

In order to validate the calculated results, we also performed an experiment on the device schematically depicted in Fig. 6.27. With respect to the parameters of the field current we used a power thyristor as a switching device.

With respect to the velocity of launching it was very problematic to directly measure the time evolution of the current in the circuit. That is why we measured the time evolution of

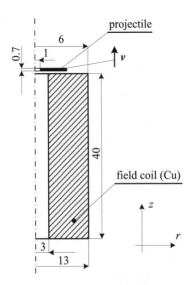

Figure 6.26. Geometry of the field coil and projectile.

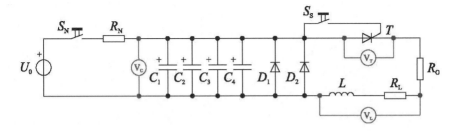

Figure 6.27. Scheme of the measuring circuit. U_0–voltage source STATRON 2225, 2×60 V, 2.5 A; V_c, V_r, V_L–oscilloscope TDS 2014B, four channels, 100 MHz; R_N–resistor 10 Ω, 10 W; S_N–push button for switching the thyristor; $C_1, \ldots, C_4$–capacitors HITANO 4.7 mF, 63 V; D_1, D_2–diodes 1N5408; T–thyristor KT708 ($U_{Max} = 700$ V), $I_{AVG} = 15$ A, case TO-48; R_0–resistance of the feeding circuitry; R_L–resistance of the field coil; L–field coil.

the voltage drop on a special resistor and from its time dependence and parameters of the circuit we calculated the evolution of the current. This current was then replaced by a pulse current in the form of the difference of two exponentials. Both currents related to their maximum value are depicted in Fig. 6.28. Their agreement is very good. As the system is linear, for higher values of the source voltage the current pulse for various maxima remains the same.

Finally, the same example was solved by COMSOL Multiphysics supplemented with our own procedures and scripts. The results abound. For example, Fig. 6.29 shows the time evolution of the Lorentz force acting on the projectile for a current pulse of maximum value 360 A. It is evident that the agreement is excellent.

Figure 6.30 shows four pulse currents that differ from one another by their peak values. Figure 6.31 depicts the corresponding evolutions of trajectories of the projectile and Fig. 6.32 shows their details from the instant of switching-on up to time $t = 10^{-4}$ s.

Figure 6.33 depicts the corresponding evolutions of velocities of the projectile and Fig. 6.34 their details from the instant of switching-on up to time $t = 10^{-4}$ s.

In fact, comparison of the depicted time evolutions with experimental data is extremely difficult. Nevertheless, the measurements were repeated several times and the measured evolution of the normalized current pulses (related to their peak values) exhibited good agreement. Moreover, the measured peak point of the trajectory changed from 0.03 to 0.04 m. This approximately corresponds to current i_3 in Fig. 6.30.

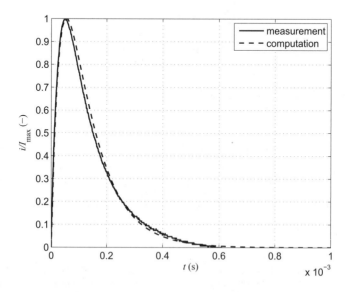

Figure 6.28.   Measured and calculated currents (related to their maximum value 360 A) in the field circuit.

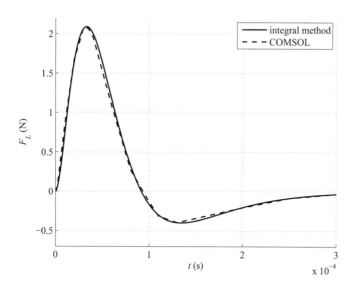

Figure 6.29.   Time evolution of the Lorentz force acting on the projectile.

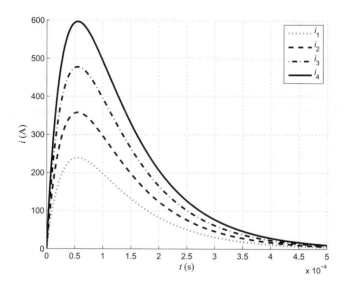

Figure 6.30.   Time evolution of the current pulses with various amplitudes.

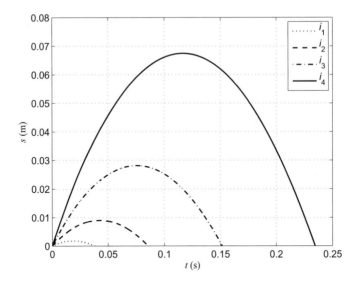

Figure 6.31. Time evolution of trajectories of the projectile for currents in Fig. 6.30.

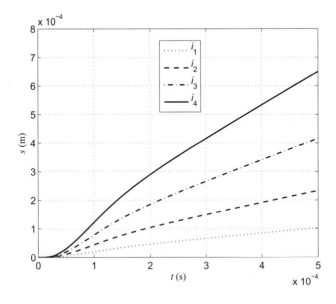

Figure 6.32. Time evolution of the beginning parts of the trajectories for currents in Fig. 6.30.

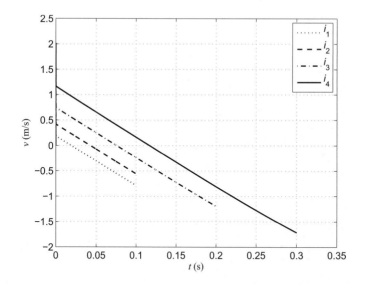

Figure 6.33. Time evolution of velocities of the projectile for currents in Fig. 6.30.

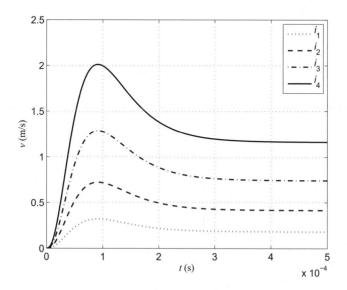

Figure 6.34. Time evolution of the beginning parts of the velocities for currents in Fig. 6.30.

CHAPTER 7

NUMERICAL METHODS FOR INTEGRAL EQUATIONS

7.1 INTRODUCTION

Numerical methods for integral equations have been discussed extensively in a large number of monographs and research papers (see, e.g., Refs. 22, 27, 203, 210, and 213 and the references therein). This chapter does not aim to substitute as a textbook on this topic. Instead, it is our goal to present a unified framework of the *projection methods* that include both the widely used collocation and Galerkin methods, with emphasis on methods using higher-order piecewise-polynomial approximations (higher-order methods). We will deal mainly with Fredholm equations of the second kind that lead to well-posed problems and thus are suitable for our purposes. Fredholm equations of the first kind were studied, for example, in Refs. 204, 209 and 215. For Volterra and other types of integral equations, as well as for nonlinear integral equations, see Refs. 23, 208, 211, and 214 and references therein.

7.1.1 Model problem

Let us consider a model second-kind Fredholm integral equation of the form

$$\lambda x(t) - \int_\Omega K(t,s) x(s)\, \mathrm{d}s = y(t) \quad \text{for all } t \in \Omega\,. \tag{7.1}$$

Integral Methods in Low-Frequency Electromagnetics. By I. Doležel, P. Karban, and P. Šolín.
Copyright © 2009 John Wiley & Sons, Inc.

Here, $\Omega \subset \mathbb{R}^d$ is the domain of interest, λ a nonzero real number, x the unknown solution defined in Ω, y a given right-hand side (data) defined in Ω, and K a given kernel function defined in $\Omega \times \Omega$. In practical applications, the kernel function K often is continuous, or weakly singular of the form

$$K(t, s) = \frac{\tilde{K}(t, s)}{|t - s|^\alpha}, \tag{7.2}$$

where $\tilde{K}$ is continuous and bounded in Ω, and $\alpha < d$ is a real exponent such that the singularity $|t - s|^\alpha$ has a finite integral in Ω.

For practical reasons, it is advantageous to reformulate problem (7.1) into an operator form: given a right-hand side $y \in X$ and $\lambda \neq 0$, find a function $x \in X$ such that

$$(\lambda - K)x = y. \tag{7.3}$$

Although we strive to keep mathematical theory on a possibly low level in this presentation, some terminology still needs to be introduced. In (7.3), the symbol X stands for a Banach space. This is a complete normed linear space. A linear space is any set that is closed under linear combination. The space is normed if it is equipped with a norm. Norm is a function defined on X that makes it possible to calculate the distance of functions in the linear space. Linear space is complete if "every convergent sequence in X has its limit in X." Not all normed linear spaces are Banach spaces. For illustration, one can construct a sequence of rational numbers whose limit is $\sqrt{2}$ (i.e., not a rational number). We work with Banach spaces in order to avoid this type of problem. More details on linear spaces, norms, convergence, Banach spaces, Hilbert spaces, and associated topics can be found in a comprehensive introductory functional analysis course in Appendix A of Ref. 59.

Typical choices for X in collocation methods are $C(\Omega)$ (functions continuous in Ω) or $L^2(\Omega)$ (functions that are square integrable in Ω). For Galerkin methods and their generalizations, one often uses Sobolev spaces $H^k(\Omega)$, consisting of functions whose all (weak) partial derivatives up to the order k are square integrable.

For simplicity, the operator $K : X \to X$ is denoted by the same symbol as the kernel function in (7.1), although these are different objects. The operator K is assumed to be compact on X. This means, roughly speaking, that a small set of functions transformed through K remains small. This technical assumption is satisfied in most cases when the kernel function in (7.1) is continuous or weakly singular, and on this level of presentation, the reader does not have to worry about it.

7.1.2 Projection methods

The main idea of projection methods is to replace the (infinite-dimensional) space X in (7.3) with a sequence of finite-dimensional subspaces $X_1 \subset X_2 \subset \cdots \subset X$. This sequence is assumed to fill X completely in the limit,

$$\lim_{n \to \infty} X_n = X.$$

By $d_n < \infty$ we denote the dimension of the space X_n. Every step of the projection method involves the solution of a discrete problem: given a right-hand side $y \in X$ and $\lambda \neq 0$, find a function $x_n \in X_n$ such that

$$(\lambda - K)x_n = y. \tag{7.4}$$

This equation does not have a solution in X_n unless by coincidence the exact solution x lies in X_n, which almost never happens in practice. Therefore, one has to make further approximations to satisfy (7.4) in some reasonable sense.

Let us explain this in more detail. Consider any basis $B = \{\phi_1, \phi_2, \ldots, \phi_{d_n}\}$ of the space X_n. The unknown approximate solution $x_n \in X_n$ can be written uniquely as a sum

$$x_n = \sum_{i=1}^{d_n} c_i \phi_i, \tag{7.5}$$

where c_i are (usually real) unknown coefficients. Substituting (7.5) into (7.4), we obtain

$$(\lambda - K) \sum_{i=1}^{d_n} c_i \phi_i = y.$$

The linearity of the integral operator yields

$$\sum_{i=1}^{d_n} c_i (\lambda - K) \phi_i = y.$$

The same can be written using the original kernel function from (7.1) as

$$\sum_{i=1}^{d_n} c_i \left(\lambda \phi_i(t) - \int_\Omega K(t, s) \phi_i(s) \, ds \right) = y(t) \quad \text{for all } t \in \Omega. \tag{7.6}$$

As we explained previously, this equation cannot be satisfied exactly in general. Therefore we introduce the residuum

$$r_n = (\lambda - K) x_n - y.$$

Written in more detail, this is

$$r_n(t) = \sum_{i=1}^{d_n} c_i \left(\lambda \phi_i(t) - \int_\Omega K(t, s) \phi_i(s) \, ds \right) - y(t). \tag{7.7}$$

Notice that $r_n \notin X_n$ in general, since $y \notin X_n$ and also $(\lambda - K) x_n \notin X_n$.

The unknown coefficients $c_1, c_2, \ldots, c_{d_n}$ of x_n are determined by forcing r_n to be close to zero in some sense. There are two basic approaches to do this: *collocation methods* and *Galerkin methods*. The former force r_n to be zero at certain nodal points, while the latter impose orthogonality of r_n to the space X_n in the variational sense (same idea as in Galerkin methods for partial differential equations [59]). These techniques are discussed in more detail in what follows.

7.2 COLLOCATION METHODS

In order to use a collocation method, one needs to choose d_n pairwise distinct (nodal) points $t_1, t_2, \ldots, t_{d_n}$ in the domain Ω. There is much freedom in the choice of these points, but not all choices are admissible. For example, the points cannot lie on the same line (if there is more than two of them). The requirement of "independence" of nodal points can be formulated exactly as follows. The determinant of the Vandermonde matrix V, $v_{ij} = \phi_i(t_j)$

must be nonzero for any basis $\phi_1, \phi_2, \ldots, \phi_{d_n}$ of the finite-dimensional space $X_n \subset X$. In the following, we will work with the space $X = C(\overline{\Omega})$ (bounded continuous functions in Ω). Optimal choice of the collocation points for one- and two-dimensional problems will be presented in Sections 7.2.1 and 7.2.4, respectively.

With a set of collocation points $t_1, t_2, \ldots, t_{d_n}$ in hand, one constructs a basis of X_n consisting of piecewise-polynomial Lagrange interpolation functions $\phi_1, \phi_2, \ldots, \phi_{d_n}$ with the property

$$\phi_i(t_j) = \delta_{ij} \quad 1 \le i, j \le d_n . \tag{7.8}$$

Here, δ_{ij} stands for the Kronecker delta symbol ($\delta_{ij} = 1$ if $i = j$ and $\delta_{ij} = 0$ otherwise).

The collocation method forces the residuum r_n to be zero at the nodal points,

$$r_n(t_i) = 0 \quad \text{for all } i = 1, 2, \ldots, d_n , \tag{7.9}$$

which translates into

$$\sum_{j=1}^{d_n} c_j \left(\lambda \underbrace{\phi_j(t_i)}_{\delta_{ij}} - \int_\Omega K(t_i, s)\phi_j(s) \, ds \right) = y(t_i), \quad 1 \le i \le d_n . \tag{7.10}$$

Thus, we obtained a system of linear algebraic equations of the form

$$SC = Y \tag{7.11}$$

for the unknown coefficient vector $C = (c_1, c_2, \ldots, c_{d_n})^T$, right-hand side vector $Y = (y(t_1), y(t_2), \ldots, y(t_{d_n}))^T$, and a $d_n \times d_n$ collocation matrix S with entries

$$s_{ij} = \lambda \delta_{ij} - \int_\Omega K(t_i, s)\phi_j(s) \, ds . \tag{7.12}$$

After solving this system for the unknown coefficients, the approximate solution x_n is calculated using (7.5).

Notice that the matrix S is *dense* (all its entries are nonzero in general). Therefore, it is difficult to solve (7.11), and even to store the matrix S in the computer memory, for very large problems. This is the main drawback of integral methods. Since the size of the matrix S drops dramatically when higher-order interpolation functions are used, the employment of higher-order methods is desirable.

Projection operator P_n   For future reference let us introduce a projection operator $P_n : X \to X_n$ that transforms any function $g \in X$ into a Lagrange interpolant $g_n \in X_n$ on the points $t_1, t_2, \ldots, t_{d_n}$. In other words, the function g_n is required to satisfy

$$g(t_i) = g_n(t_i) \quad \text{for all } i = 1, 2, \ldots, d_n . \tag{7.13}$$

The formula of the projection operator is

$$P_n(g) = \sum_{i=1}^{d_n} g(t_i)\phi_i . \tag{7.14}$$

It is left to the reader as a simple exercise to verify (7.13), linearity of P_n, and the fact that

$$P_n(P_n(g)) = P_n(g) \quad \text{for all } g \in X \tag{7.15}$$

(idempotency). With the Lagrange interpolation functions $\phi_1, \phi_2, \ldots, \phi_{d_n}$ in hand, the projection using (7.14) is fully explicit and therefore very fast. Notice that condition (7.9) can be expressed equivalently as

$$P_n r_n = 0. \tag{7.16}$$

7.2.1 Optimal collocation points in one dimension

The choice of the collocation points $t_1, t_2, \ldots, t_{d_n}$ has a crucial effect on the performance of the collocation method. Actually, these points are the only thing that matters, since they determine a unique set of basis functions $\phi_1, \phi_2, \ldots, \phi_{d_n}$ satisfying (7.8).

In one-dimensional problems, the best is to use the *Gauss–Lobatto points*. These points are usually defined in a reference interval $[-1, 1]$, there are $p+1$ of them for a polynomial of degree p, and they are mathematically proven *optimal interpolation points*. For reference, a few sets of these nodal points for polynomial degrees 2–5 are listed in Tables C.9–C.12 in Appendix C. For higher polynomial degrees see the CD-ROM accompanying Ref. 94.

7.2.2 Optimal basis functions in one dimension

Consider a one-dimensional domain $\Omega = (a, b)$ and its division

$$a = c_0 < c_1 \ldots < c_M = b.$$

This defines M elements $K_m = (c_{m-1}, c_m)$, $i = 1, 2, \cdots, M$. Each element K_m is mapped onto the reference interval $K_a = (-1, 1)$ via the linear map

$$x_{K_m}(\xi) = \frac{c_{m-1} + c_m}{2} + \frac{c_m - c_{m-1}}{2}\xi. \tag{7.17}$$

For an element K_m of polynomial degree p_m, we consider the $m+1$ Gauss–Lobatto points

$$-1 = y_1^m < y_2^m < \cdots < y_{p_m+1}^m = 1.$$

There are $p_m + 1$ basis functions $\theta_1^m, \theta_2^m, \ldots, \theta_{p_m+1}^m$ on K_a of polynomial degree p_m associated with these points via the standard Lagrange interpolation condition

$$\theta_j^m(y_k^m) = \delta_{jk} \quad \text{for all } 1 \leq j, k \leq p_m + 1. \tag{7.18}$$

Exploiting the standard Lagrange interpolation polynomial, condition (7.18) yields explicit formulas

$$\theta_i^m(\xi) = \prod_{1 \leq j \leq p_m+1, j \neq i} \frac{(\xi - y_j^m)}{(y_i^m - y_j^m)}, \quad i = 1, 2, \ldots, p_m + 1. \tag{7.19}$$

Obviously all of these shape functions are polynomials of degree p_m. In particular, for piecewise-affine approximations ($p_m = 1$) the nodal points $y_1 = -1$ and $y_2 = 1$ yield the pair of affine shape functions

$$\theta_1^1(\xi) = \frac{1 - \xi}{2}, \quad \theta_2^1(\xi) = \frac{\xi + 1}{2}. \tag{7.20}$$

A few examples of shape functions are presented for the quadratic, cubic, quartic, and quintic cases in Figures 7.1–7.4.

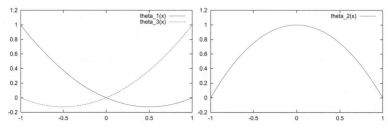

Figure 7.1. Quadratic Lagrange–Gauss–Lobatto nodal shape functions; vertex functions θ_1^2, θ_3^2 (left) and the bubble function θ_2^2 (right).

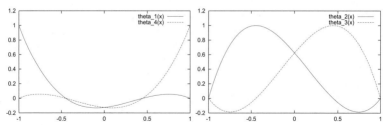

Figure 7.2. Cubic Lagrange–Gauss–Lobatto nodal shape functions; vertex functions θ_1^3, θ_4^3 (left) and bubble functions θ_2^3, θ_3^3 (right).

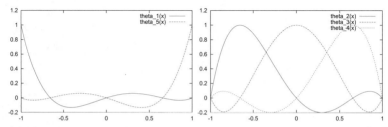

Figure 7.3. Quartic Lagrange–Gauss–Lobatto nodal shape functions; vertex functions θ_1^4, θ_5^4 (left) and bubble functions $\theta_2^4, \theta_3^4, \theta_4^4$ (right).

Shape functions associated with vertices are called *vertex functions*, and remaining shape functions (that vanish at the endpoints ± 1) are said to be *bubble functions*.

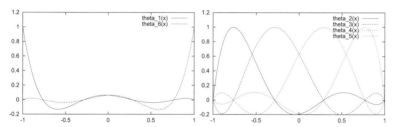

Figure 7.4. Quintic Lagrange–Gauss–Lobatto nodal shape functions; vertex functions θ_1^5, θ_6^5 (left) and bubble functions $\theta_2^5, \theta_3^5, \ldots, \theta_5^5$ (right).

The space X_n contains $M + 1$ vertex functions associated with the points $c_0, c_1, \ldots, c_M$ and $p_m - 1$ bubble functions in every element K_m. Thus, its dimension is

$$d_n = \dim(X_n) = (M + 1) + \sum_{m=1}^{M} (p_m - 1) = 1 + \sum_{m=1}^{M} p_m \,,$$

which determines the size of the matrix S from (7.12).

Next, let us construct all vertex and bubble functions in the basis of X_n using the shape functions defined above and the reference maps (7.17). We can begin with the bubble functions that are local to element interiors. On K_m, there are $p_m - 1$ bubble functions defined as

$$\phi_{K_m,j}(x) = \begin{cases} \theta_j^m(\xi) & x \in K_m \,, \\ 0 & x \notin K_m \,, \end{cases} \qquad (7.21)$$

where $x = x_{K_m}(\xi)$ and $j = 2, 3, \ldots, p_m - 1$. Intuitively, the basis functions are obtained by translating and stretching/shrinking the shape functions linearly from the reference interval K_a to the mesh element K_m, as illustrated in Fig. 7.5.

The vertex functions are constructed analogously, except that for interior mesh points $c_1, c_2, \ldots, c_{M-1}$ they extend over a pair of elements sharing the mesh point, as illustrated in Fig. 7.6.

For later reference, it is useful to notice that on every element K_m, the delta property (7.18) translates into

$$\phi_{K_m,j}\big(x_{K_m}(y_k^m)\big) = \delta_{jk} \quad \text{for all } 1 \le j, k \le p_m + 1 \,. \qquad (7.22)$$

Here, $x_{K_m}(y_k^m)$ are the Gauss–Lobatto points of degree p_m transformed from the reference interval K_a to the mesh element K_m.

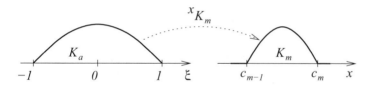

Figure 7.5. Construction of a quadratic bubble basis function in the element K_m.

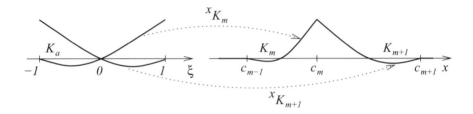

Figure 7.6.   Construction of a quadratic vertex function associated with the vertex c_m.

Going back to the original setting, the nodal points $t_1, t_2, \ldots, t_{d_n}$ are obtained as the union of the points $x_{K_m}(y_k^m)$ for all mesh elements $K_1, K_2, \ldots, K_M$ (interior mesh points $c_1, c_2, \ldots, c_{M-1}$ are counted only once). Notice that every basis function of the space X_n is nonzero at exactly one of these d_n nodal points in Ω, and zero at the remaining $d_n - 1$ of them.

7.2.3   Efficient assembly of the collocation matrix

Now we are close to constructing very efficiently the collocation matrix S. Let us first discuss the case of a continuous kernel function $K(t, s)$. The entry s_{ij} of S has the form

$$s_{ij} = \lambda \delta_{ij} - \int_\Omega K(t_i, s)\phi_j(s)\, \mathrm{d}s\,.$$

The Gauss–Lobatto points are not only optimal interpolation points, but at the same time also excellent *quadrature points*, with weights listed in the second column of Tables C.9–C.12 in Appendix C (the weights correspond to the reference interval $[-1, 1]$ and need to be scaled properly if the integration is done in another interval). The integral above is approximated numerically as follows:

$$\int_\Omega K(t_i, s)\phi_j(s)\, \mathrm{d}s \approx \sum_{k=1}^{d_n} K(t_i, t_k) \underbrace{\phi_j(t_k)}_{\delta_{jk}} w_k = K(t_i, t_j)w_j\,. \tag{7.23}$$

In other words, the value of s_{ij} is approximated using a very simple formula

$$s_{ij} = \lambda \delta_{ij} - K(t_i, t_j)w_j\,. \tag{7.24}$$

If the kernel function is weakly singular of the form (7.2),

$$K(t, s) = \frac{\tilde{K}(t, s)}{|t - s|^\alpha}\,,$$

then most off-diagonal entries in the matrix S still can be computed using the relation (7.24), provided that the points t_i and t_j belong to different elements. If they belong to the same element, then in this element we cannot perform the numerical approximation (7.23), and the integral has to be calculated by other means – for example, using adaptive numerical quadrature or analytically.

7.2.4   Optimal collocation points in two dimensions

The one-dimensional Gauss–Lobatto points have a straightforward generalization to quadrilateral elements. On a reference square $[-1, 1]^2$ they are defined using Cartesian products of the one-dimensional points. The integration weights are obtained as products of the weights of the corresponding one-dimensional points. Interestingly, these product points are mathematically proven *optimal interpolation points* on quadrilateral elements (see Refs. 205 and 206). The situation is more tricky on triangular elements, since the one-dimensional Gauss–Lobatto points do not generalize to them naturally. Instead, on triangles one has the so-called *Fekete points* [212].

The Fekete points are defined as follows. Let a bounded convex domain $K \subset \mathbb{R}^d$ be equipped with a polynomial space $P(K)$ of the dimension N_P. Given an arbitrary basis $\{\vartheta_i\}_{i=1}^{N_P}$ of the space $P(K)$, the Fekete points $\{y_i\}_{i=1}^{N_P} \subset \overline{K}$ are a point set that maximizes the determinant

$$\det L(y_1, y_2, \ldots, y_{N_P}) = \max_{\{\xi_1, \xi_2, \ldots, \xi_{N_P}\} \subset \overline{K}} \det L(\xi_1, \xi_2, \ldots, \xi_{N_P}), \qquad (7.25)$$

where L is the generalized Vandermonde matrix defined as

$$L(\xi_1, \xi_2, \ldots, \xi_{N_P}) = \{\vartheta_j(\xi_i)\}_{i,j=1}^{N_P}. \qquad (7.26)$$

Since no explicit formulas for the Fekete points are available, they have to be constructed by maximizing the determinant (7.25) numerically. This is a nonlinear optimization problem, and numerical methods may produce various solutions depending on the initial condition and other factors. The choice of the initial condition influences the result dramatically. Since the global optimality is unclear, the solutions are usually referred to as *approximate Fekete points*. A numerical algorithm for the construction of approximate Fekete points for triangles of polynomial degrees $p \leq 19$, based on a steepest ascent approach, was presented in Ref. 212.

Compared to the Gauss–Lobatto points, the advantage of the Fekete points is that they can be defined for any geometry. Numerical experiments indicate that the Lagrange interpolation functions on triangular elements built on the Fekete points have excellent approximation properties. Some known facts about the Fekete points are summarized below.

Let $p \geq 1$. The Fekete points have the following properties:

1. The Fekete points $\{y_i\}_{i=1}^{N_P} \subset \overline{K}_t$ are invariant under the choice of the basis $\{\vartheta_i\}_{i=1}^{N_P} \subset P^p(K_t)$.

2. In one-dimensional intervals and Cartesian product geometries the Fekete and Gauss–Lobatto points are the same.

3. On the edges of triangular domains the Fekete points coincide with the one-dimensional Gauss–Lobatto points.

The Fekete points for $p = 1, 2, \ldots, 15$ are shown in Fig. 7.7 and we refer to Ref. 212 for the corresponding integration weights.

7.2.5   Transformation of points from reference to physical elements

In practice, the computational domain Ω is split into nonoverlapping triangular or quadrilateral elements $K_1, K_2, \ldots, K_M$. In order to obtain the Gauss–Lobatto points in a general

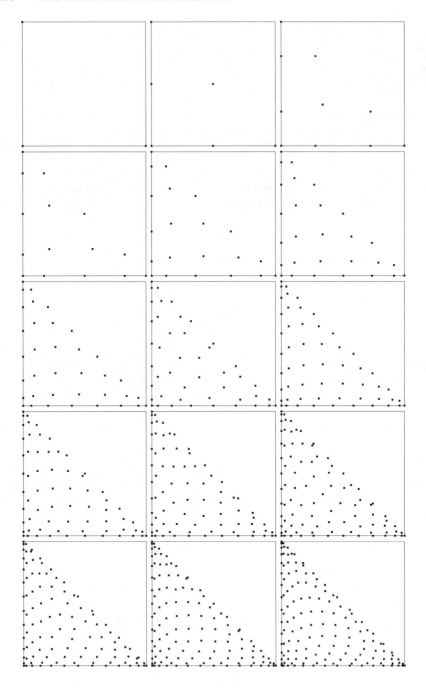

Figure 7.7. Fekete points in a reference triangle, $p = 1, 2, \ldots, 15$.

quadrilateral element, or Fekete points in a general triangular element, one has to transform the points defined on the corresponding reference domain using the *reference maps*. These maps are smooth bijections between the reference domain and the mesh elements (every element has its own map). The construction of the maps differs in the quadrilateral and triangular cases. Let us begin, for example, with the quadrilateral one.

Consider a reference quadrilateral $K_q = [-1, 1]^2$ and an arbitrary convex quadrilateral K (with straight edges), as shown in Fig. 7.8.

In order to construct the reference map $x_K : K_q \to K$, we need the following four functions:

$$
\begin{aligned}
\varphi_1(\xi_1, \xi_2) &= \tfrac{1}{4}(1 - \xi_1)(1 - \xi_2), \qquad (7.27)\\
\varphi_2(\xi_1, \xi_2) &= \tfrac{1}{4}(\xi_1 + 1)(1 - \xi_2),\\
\varphi_3(\xi_1, \xi_2) &= \tfrac{1}{4}(\xi_1 + 1)(\xi_2 + 1),\\
\varphi_4(\xi_1, \xi_2) &= \tfrac{1}{4}(1 - \xi_1)(\xi_2 + 1).
\end{aligned}
$$

Then the map x_K is defined simply as

$$
x_K(\xi_1, \xi_2) = \binom{a_1}{a_2}\varphi_1(\xi_1, \xi_2) + \binom{b_1}{b_2}\varphi_2(\xi_1, \xi_2) + \binom{c_1}{c_2}\varphi_3(\xi_1, \xi_2) + \binom{d_1}{d_2}\varphi_3(\xi_1, \xi_2).
$$
$$(7.28)$$

The reader can verify easily that

$$
x_K(-1, -1) = \binom{a_1}{a_2}, \quad x_K(1, -1) = \binom{b_1}{b_2}, \quad x_K(1, 1) = \binom{c_1}{c_2}, \quad x_K(-1, 1) = \binom{d_1}{d_2}.
$$

The map x_K is linear on the edges of the reference square K, which means that the edges of K_q are transformed onto the edges of K correctly. Since the quadrilateral K is convex, the Jacobian of the map x_K is nonzero in K, and thus the map x_K is a bijection.

In the triangular case the situation is analogous, as shown in Fig. 7.8. This time we use the functions

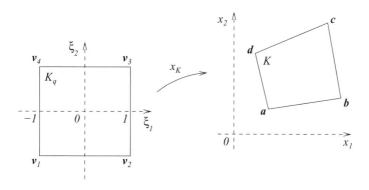

Figure 7.8. Reference map for quadrilateral elements.

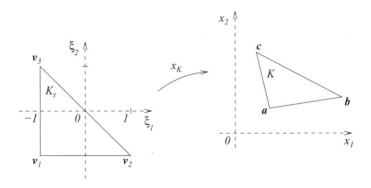

Figure 7.9.   Reference map for triangular elements.

$$\varphi_1(\xi_1, \xi_2) = \tfrac{1}{4}(1 - \xi_1)(1 - \xi_2), \qquad (7.29)$$
$$\varphi_2(\xi_1, \xi_2) = \tfrac{1}{4}(\xi_1 + 1)(1 - \xi_2),$$
$$\varphi_3(\xi_1, \xi_2) = \tfrac{1}{4}(1 - \xi_1)(\xi_2 + 1),$$

and the map x_K has the form

$$x_K(\xi_1, \xi_2) = \begin{pmatrix} a_1 \\ a_2 \end{pmatrix} \varphi_1(\xi_1, \xi_2) + \begin{pmatrix} b_1 \\ b_2 \end{pmatrix} \varphi_2(\xi_1, \xi_2) + \begin{pmatrix} c_1 \\ c_2 \end{pmatrix} \varphi_3(\xi_1, \xi_2). \qquad (7.30)$$

Again, the reader can verify easily that

$$x_K(-1, -1) = \begin{pmatrix} a_1 \\ a_2 \end{pmatrix}, \quad x_K(1, -1) = \begin{pmatrix} b_1 \\ b_2 \end{pmatrix}, \quad x_K(-1, 1) = \begin{pmatrix} c_1 \\ c_2 \end{pmatrix}.$$

In this case, the transformation x_K is *affine* (its Jacobian is constant). If the triangle K is not degenerate, then obviously the Jacobian is nonzero and the map is a bijection.

7.2.6   Optimal basis functions in two dimensions

Due to the availability of the reference map for every element K in the mesh, it is sufficient to construct the higher-order polynomial shape functions on the reference domain only. The construction is very simple for the reference square K_q, where the (two-dimensional) Gauss–Lobatto points are the Cartesian products of the one-dimensional Gauss–Lobatto points. For every (two-dimensional) Gauss–Lobatto point, the Lagrange interpolation function is the product of the corresponding one-dimensional Lagrange interpolation functions. More precisely, let t_i, t_j be a pair of one-dimensional Gauss–Lobatto points, and ϕ_i, ϕ_j the corresponding Lagrange interpolation functions. Then the corresponding Gauss–Lobatto point in the reference square K is (t_i, t_j), and the Lagrange interpolation function associated with this point has the form $\phi_{ij}(\xi_1, \xi_2) = \phi_i(\xi_1)\phi_j(\xi_2)$.

The construction of Lagrange interpolation functions for the Fekete points on the reference triangle K_t is not so straightforward and we have to resort to elementary know-how of the theory of nodal elements [59]. For an element of degree p, there are $N_P = (p+1)(p+2)/2$ Fekete points $t_1, t_2, \ldots, t_{N_P}$ in K_t. We begin by taking any basis $\vartheta_1, \vartheta_2, \ldots, \vartheta_{N_P}$ of the polynomial space of degree p on K_t. We construct the Vandermonde matrix $V = \{\vartheta_i(t_j)\}_{i,j=1}^{N_P}$. We invert this matrix (which is possible since the determinant is nonzero). Let $Z = V^{-1}$. The jth Lagrange interpolation function $\phi_j(\xi_1, \xi_2)$ is defined as

$$\phi_j(\xi_1, \xi_2) = \sum_{i=1}^{N_P} z_{ij} \vartheta_i(\xi_1, \xi_2) \,.$$

These functions satisfy the important rule (7.8),

$$\phi_j(t_i) = \delta_{ij}, \quad 1 \le i, j \le N_P$$

(see Chapter 3 in Ref. 59).

7.2.7   Efficient assembly of the collocation matrix

In both the quadrilateral and triangular cases, the resulting (two-dimensional) Lagrange interpolation functions satisfy the rule (7.8). If the kernel function $K(t, s)$ is continuous, then the integral in

$$s_{ij} = \lambda \delta_{ij} - \int_\Omega K(t_i, s) \phi_j(s) \, \mathrm{d}s$$

can be approximated again with

$$\int_\Omega K(t_i, s) \phi_j(s) \, \mathrm{d}s \approx \sum_{k=1}^{d_n} K(t_i, t_k) \underbrace{\phi_j(t_k)}_{\delta_{jk}} w_k = K(t_i, t_j) w_j \,.$$

Therefore, the approximate value of s_{ij} is

$$s_{ij} = \lambda \delta_{ij} - K(t_i, t_j) w_j \,,$$

analogous to the one-dimensional case. If the kernel function is weakly singular of the form (7.2), then the discussion at the end of Section 7.2.3 applies.

7.3   GALERKIN METHODS

It was explained in Section 7.1.2 that equation (7.6) cannot be satisfied exactly, and therefore one has to come up with some way to minimize the residual (7.7). Collocation methods do this by requiring the residual r_n to be zero at certain points in the domain (collocation points). In contrast to this, Galerkin methods minimize the residual r_n by requiring it to be orthogonal to the finite-dimensional subspace X_n. This is a variational argument that is not very intuitive. However, it can be proved easily that r_n decreases to zero as $X_n \to X$.

Let us introduce some basic terminology so that we can explain this in more detail. Hilbert space is a Banach space equipped with an inner product. Inner product is a generalization of the standard "dot product" of vectors in $\mathbb{R}^d$ to functions and even more abstract objects. The most widely used Hilbert space is $X = L^2(\Omega)$, comprising all square-integrable functions defined in Ω. This space is equipped with the inner product

$$(u, v) = \int_\Omega u(x)v(x)\,\mathrm{d}x, \quad u, v \in X\,.$$

The same inner product is inherited by any finite-dimensional subspace X_n of X.

The orthogonality of r_n to the subspace X_n is equivalent to the orthogonality of r_n to all basis functions of X_n,

$$(r_n, \phi_i) = 0 \quad \text{for all } 1 \le i \le d_n\,. \tag{7.31}$$

Using (7.7), this translates into

$$\sum_{j=1}^{d_n} c_j \int_\Omega \left(\lambda\phi_j(t) - \int_\Omega K(t, s)\phi_j(s)\,\mathrm{d}s \right) \phi_i(t)\,\mathrm{d}t = \int_\Omega y(t)\phi_i(t)\,\mathrm{d}t \quad \text{for all } 1 \le i \le d_n\,,$$

which is a system of linear algebraic equations of the form $SC = Y$. Here, the vector C comprises the unknown coefficients, the vector Y contains the right-hand side integrals, and the $d_n \times d_n$ matrix S is defined as

$$s_{ij} = \int_\Omega \left(\lambda\phi_j(t) - \int_\Omega K(t, s)\phi_j(s)\,\mathrm{d}s \right) \phi_i(t)\,\mathrm{d}t\,.$$

All integrals are evaluated numerically. This, however, is a challenging task since double integration is required.

The construction of the matrix S can be facilitated by choosing a basis in X_n that is orthonormal, that is, it satisfies

$$(\phi_i, \phi_j) = \delta_{ij}, \quad 1 \le i, j \le d_n\,.$$

Construction of orthonormal basis in X_n   The construction of orthonormal basis in $X_n \subset L^2(\Omega)$ is feasible in applications where the domain Ω is partitioned into simplices $K_1, K_2, \ldots, K_M$, and the solution x_n is sought as a piecewise-polynomial function discontinuous on element interfaces. Every simplex K_m is equipped with polynomial degree $p_m = p(K_m) \ge 0$. Every mesh cell K_m is mapped onto a reference cell $\hat{K}$ using a smooth bijective geometrical transformation $x_{K_m} : \hat{K} \to K_m$. For details on the construction of these maps see, for example, Ref. 59.

On the reference domain $\hat{K}$ we define a hierarchic orthonormal basis consisting of polynomials. By hierarchic we mean that a basis corresponding to polynomial degree $p+1$ always contains the basis corresponding to the polynomial degree p as its subset. A widely used example of such a basis are the Dubiner polynomials [207], but the reader can construct such a basis easily by using an arbitrary hierarchic polynomial basis (such as the monomial basis) and the Gram–Schmidt orthogonalization algorithm.

The key observation is that the reference maps x_{K_m} on simplices preserve L^2-orthogonality. Let the polynomials $\psi_1, \psi_2, \ldots$ form an orthonormal basis on the reference domain $\hat{K}$. Corresponding basis functions $\phi_1, \phi_2, \ldots$ on the mesh cell K_m are defined as $\phi_i(t) = \psi_i(\xi)$, $t = x_{K_m}(\xi)$. The Substitution Theorem yields that

$$\int_{K_m} \phi_i(t)\phi_j(t)\,\mathrm{d}t = \int_{\hat{K}} |J_m|\psi_i(\xi)\psi_j(\xi)\,\mathrm{d}\xi = |J_m|\delta_{ij}\,.$$

The symbol J_m stands for the Jacobian of the map x_{K_m}. For simplices, this is a constant. Unfortunately, the Jacobian is not constant for distorted quadrilateral, hexahedral, and other standard elements. If one wants to construct an orthonormal basis on such elements, one option is to perform the Gram–Schmidt process in $K_1, K_2, \ldots, K_M$ individually. This process, however, is quite CPU-time expensive.

Projection operator P_n   As in Section 7.2, let us introduce a projection operator P_n : $X \to X_n$. For the Galerkin method it is natural to choose an orthogonal projection operator satisfying

$$(g - P_n g, z) = 0 \quad \text{for all } g \in X \text{ and } z \in X_n . \tag{7.32}$$

In other words, this relation says that the projection error is normal to the subspace X_n. It can be proved that if P_n is chosen in this way, then for any $g \in X$ the projection $g_n = P_n g \in X_n$ is the best approximation of g in the subspace X_n.

Given a basis $\phi_1, \phi_2, \ldots, \phi_{d_n}$ in X_n, the projection of a function $g \in X$ is sought in the form

$$g_n = \sum_{j=1}^{d_n} a_j \phi_j .$$

After substituting this into (7.32), and using ϕ_i for z, we obtain

$$\left(g - \sum_{j=1}^{d_n} a_j \phi_j, \phi_i \right) = 0 \quad \text{for all } i = 1, 2, \ldots, d_n .$$

This can be written equivalently as

$$\sum_{j=1}^{d_n} a_j (\phi_j, \phi_i) = (g, \phi_i) \quad \text{for all } i = 1, 2, \ldots, d_n . \tag{7.33}$$

The last relation is a system of linear algebraic equations of the form $SA = G$, where the symmetric $d_n \times d_n$ matrix S contains the entries $s_{ij} = (\phi_j, \phi_i)$, $A = (a_1, a_2, \ldots, a_{d_n})^T$ is the vector of unknown coefficients, and G is the right-hand side vector containing the entries $g_i = (g, \phi_i)$.

It is left to the reader as a simple exercise to verify that the operator P_n is linear and that

$$P_n(P_n(g)) = P_n(g) \quad \text{for all } g \in X . \tag{7.34}$$

Notice that condition (7.31) can now be expressed equivalently as

$$P_n r_n = 0 ,$$

which is identical to (7.16). In this way, both projection methods are unified formally.

Linear system (7.33) has to be solved any time the projection is done. Especially with large d_n, this step can be very time consuming. The situation is simplified substantially if the basis $\phi_1, \phi_2, \ldots, \phi_{d_n}$ is orthonormal – in such a case the matrix S is just a diagonal identity matrix, and it is $A = G$. As described earlier, one can have such a basis easily when working with simplicial meshes. For practical applications, even partial orthonormality of the basis is very important and worth exploiting. In such a case, one can use the Schur complement method. Let us explain this briefly in the following.

7.3.1 Schur complement method for partially orthonormal basis

Assume that among the basis functions $\phi_1, \phi_2, \ldots, \phi_{d_n}$, the last $d_n - r$ are orthonormal. In other words,

$$(\phi_i, \phi_j) = \delta_{ij} \quad r + 1 \leq i, j \leq d_n.$$

Let us split accordingly the vectors A and G of length d_n into $A_1 = (a_1, a_2, \ldots, a_r)^T$ and $A_2 = (a_{r+1}, a_{r+2}, \ldots, a_{d_n})^T$, and $G_1 = (g_1, g_2, \ldots, g_r)^T$ and $G_2 = (g_{r+1}, g_{r+2}, \ldots, g_{d_n})^T$. The symmetric matrix S is split into four blocks S_{11}, $S_{22} = I$, and $S_{12} = S_{21}$, as shown in Fig. 7.10. Here, S_{11} has the size $r \times r$ and I is a $(d_n - r) \times (d_n - r)$ diagonal identity matrix.

With this decomposition, system (7.33) decouples into two systems,

$$S_{11} A_1 + S_{12} A_2 = G_1,$$
$$S_{21} A_1 + A_2 = G_2.$$

Expressing A_2 from the second equation, and substituting into the first one, we obtain an $r \times r$ system

$$\tilde{S}_{11} A_1 = \tilde{G}_1,$$

where $\tilde{S}_{11} = S_{11} - S_{12} S_{21}$ and $\tilde{G}_1 = G_1 - S_{12} G_2$. If $r << d_n$, then this system can be solved much faster than the full $d_n \times d_n$ system, and the solution A_1 is used to calculate the rest,

$$A_2 = G_2 - S_{21} A_1.$$

7.4 NUMERICAL EXAMPLE

This section deals with one version of the higher-order technique. While its fundamentals are discussed quite generally, particulars are shown on a simple, well understandable example.

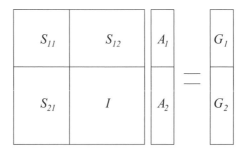

Figure 7.10.   Decomposition of the matrix S and vectors A, G for the Schur complement method.

7.4.1   Basic features of the proposed higher-order technique

The real distribution of the field current $\boldsymbol{J}$ in the jth cell of the discretization mesh is first approximated by a polynomial in the form

$$\boldsymbol{J}_j(x,y,z,t) \doteq \sum_{k=1}^{s_j} \boldsymbol{b}_{jk}(t) f_{jk}(x,y,z). \tag{7.35}$$

Here $\boldsymbol{b}_{jk}(t)$ are vectors that are generally functions of time t and $f_{jk}(x,y,z)$ are testing functions. Symbol j stands for the index of the element and s_j denotes the number of terms of the approximating polynomial in this element. With respect to building of the system matrix it is advantageous when the testing functions satisfy the condition of orthonormality, that is,

$$\int_{\Omega_j} f_{jp}(x,y,z) f_{jq}(x,y,z)\, \mathrm{d}\Omega = \delta_{pq}, \tag{7.36}$$

where Ω_j is the volume (or area) of the element and δ_{pq} stands for the Kronecker delta. If we suppose that the number of active parts in the system is n (each of them being divided into m_l, $l = 1, \ldots, n$ cells), after substituting (7.35) into (4.10) we obtain

$$\sum_{u=1}^{s_{kl}} \boldsymbol{b}_{kl,u}(t) f_{kl,u}(x,y,z) + \frac{\mu_0 \gamma_k}{4\pi} \cdot \sum_{i=1}^{n} \sum_{j=1}^{m_i} \int_{\Omega_{ij}} \frac{\sum_{u=1}^{s_{ij}} \frac{\partial \boldsymbol{b}_{ij,u}(t)}{\partial t} \cdot f_{ij,u}(x,y,z) \cdot \mathrm{d}\Omega}{r_{ij,kl}(t)}$$

$$- \frac{\mu_0 \gamma_k}{4\pi} \cdot \sum_{i=1}^{n} \sum_{j=1}^{m_i} \int_{\Omega_{ij}} \left(\frac{\boldsymbol{v}_{ki}(t) \cdot \boldsymbol{r}_{kl,ij}}{r_{ij,kl}^3(t)} \cdot \sum_{u=1}^{s_{ij}} \boldsymbol{b}_{ij,u}(t) f_{ij,u}(x,y,z) \right) \mathrm{d}\Omega + \boldsymbol{J}_{k0}(t) \doteq \boldsymbol{0},$$

$$k = 1, \ldots, n, \quad l = 1, \ldots, m_k. \tag{7.37}$$

Here $\boldsymbol{v}_{ki}(t)$ denotes the mutual velocity between the kth and ith parts and $r_{ij,kl}(t)$ is the distance between the barycenters of cells with indices ij and kl. The system must be supplemented with modified equations of the total current (4.9) (where possible) in the discretized form.

Now the equations in system (7.37) must be gradually multiplied by particular testing functions $f_{kl,u}(x,y,z)$, $u = 1, \ldots, s_{kl}$ used in the cell with index kl and integrated over the volume Ω_{kl}. This means that we solve a system of equations of the type

$$\int_{\Omega_{kl}} \left(f_{kl,q}(x,y,z) \left[\sum_{u=1}^{s_{kl}} \boldsymbol{b}_{kl,u}(t) f_{kl,u}(x,y,z) \right] \right) \mathrm{d}\Omega$$

$$+ \frac{\mu_0 \gamma_k}{4\pi} \cdot \int_{\Omega_{kl}} \left(f_{kl,q}(x,y,z) \left[\sum_{i=1}^{n} \sum_{j=1}^{m_i} \int_{\Omega_{ij}} \frac{\sum_{u=1}^{s_{ij}} \frac{\partial \boldsymbol{b}_{ij,u}(t)}{\partial t} \cdot f_{ij,u}(x,y,z) \cdot \mathrm{d}\Omega}{r_{ij,kl}(t)} \right] \right) \mathrm{d}\Omega$$

$$- \frac{\mu_0 \gamma_k}{4\pi} \cdot \int_{\Omega_{kl}} \left(f_{kl,q}(x,y,z) \left[\sum_{i=1}^{n} \sum_{j=1}^{m_i} \int_{\Omega_{ij}} \Theta \mathrm{d}\Omega \right] \right) \mathrm{d}\Omega$$

$$+ \boldsymbol{J}_{k0}(t) \int_{\Omega_{kl}} f_{kl,q}(x,y,z) \mathrm{d}\Omega \doteq \boldsymbol{0},$$

$$q = 1, \ldots s_{kl}, \quad k = 1, \ldots, n, \quad l = 1, \ldots, m_k, \tag{7.38}$$

where

$$\Theta = \frac{(\boldsymbol{v}_{ki}(t) \cdot \boldsymbol{r}_{kl,ij}) \sum_{u=1}^{s_{ij}} \boldsymbol{b}_{ij,u}(t) f_{ij,u}(x,y,z)}{r_{ij,kl}^3(t)}.$$

The solution of this system provides (at every time level $\triangle t$) the coefficients $\boldsymbol{b}_{kl,u}(t)$ in particular cells.

Even when this procedure seems to be simple, in fact, finding of the orthonormal basis of polynomial functions and the double integration in (7.38) are extremely laborious and must be done in accordance with the example solved. As there is no SW of this kind, the authors prepare their own procedures, which is, however, a long-term business. To date, we are able so solve 1D and simpler 2D arrangements. Evaluation of the volume integrals must often be carried out manually, even when one or two first integrations may be performed using SW Mathematica. Special attention has to be paid (where necessary), therefore, to numerical integration that should be as accurate as possible.

7.4.2   Illustrative example

Particular computations will be shown for a long massive tubular copper conductor that carries a pulse current. The geometry, material parameters, and time evolution of the pulse current are the same as in the example in Section 4.6.1, case 2. While the referred example was solved by the zero-order technique, in this subsection it will be solved by a higher-order approach.

Let the hollow conductor of internal and external radii $r_{\text{int}} = 0.012$ m and $r_{\text{ext}} = 0.020$ m be divided into n circular rings of radii r_j, $j = 1, \ldots, n+1$. In every layer first we will construct a system of orthonormal functions denoted as $f_{jk}(r)$, $j = 1, \ldots, n+1$, $k = 1, \ldots, s_j$, where s_j is their number in the jth element. These functions are of general shape

$$f_{jk} = \sum_{q=0}^{s_j} a_{jl,q} \cdot r^q \tag{7.39}$$

and their coefficients $a_{jl,q}$ follow from the equality

$$\langle f_{ji}(r), f_{jk}(r) \rangle = \int_{r_i}^{r_{i+1}} f_{ji}(r) \cdot f_{jk}(r) \cdot \mathrm{d}r = \delta_{ik}, \quad i, k = 1, \ldots, s_j. \tag{7.40}$$

The first five functions of this kind are

$$f_{j1}(r) = \frac{1}{r_{j+1} - r_j},$$

$$f_{j2}(r) = -\frac{\sqrt{3}(r_{j+1} + r_j)}{\sqrt{(r_{j+1} - r_j)^3}} + \frac{2\sqrt{3}r}{\sqrt{(r_{j+1} - r_j)^3}},$$

$$f_{j3}(r) = \frac{\sqrt{5}(r_{j+1}^2 + 4r_j r_{j+1} + r_j^2)}{\sqrt{(r_{j+1} - r_j)^5}} - \frac{6\sqrt{5}(r_{j+1} + r_j)r}{\sqrt{(r_{j+1} - r_j)^5}} + \frac{6\sqrt{5}r^2}{\sqrt{(r_{j+1} - r_j)^5}},$$

$$f_{j4}(r) = -\frac{\sqrt{7}(r_{j+1}^3 + 9r_j r_{j+1}^2 + 9r_j^2 r_{j+1} + r_j^3)}{\sqrt{(r_{j+1} - r_j)^7}} + \frac{12\sqrt{7}(r_{j+1}^2 + 3r_j r_{j+1} + r_j^2)r}{\sqrt{(r_{j+1} - r_j)^7}}$$

$$-\frac{30\sqrt{7}(r_{j+1}+r_j)r^2}{\sqrt{(r_{j+1}-r_j)^7}}+\frac{20\sqrt{7}r^3}{\sqrt{(r_{j+1}-r_j)^7}}, \qquad (7.41)$$

$$f_{j5}(r) = \frac{3(r_{j+1}^4 + 16r_j r_{j+1}^3 + 36r_j^2 r_{j+1}^2 + 16r_j^3 r_{j+1} + r_j^4)}{\sqrt{(r_{j+1}-r_j)^9}}$$

$$-\frac{60(r_{j+1}+r_j)(r_{j+1}^2 + 5r_j r_{j+1} + r_j^2)r}{\sqrt{(r_{j+1}-r_j)^9}}$$

$$+\frac{90(3r_{j+1}^2 + 8r_j r_{j+1} + 3r_j^2)r^2}{\sqrt{(r_{j+1}-r_j)^9}}-\frac{420(r_{j+1}+r_j)r^3}{\sqrt{(r_{j+1}-r_j)^9}}+\frac{210r^4}{\sqrt{(r_{j+1}-r_j)^9}}.$$
$$(7.42)$$

Even when determination of the analogous polynomials of higher orders is relatively easy, they exhibit more and more complicated forms. Nevertheless, they have one essential advantage: all numerical integrations necessary for processing of (7.41) (because all velocity terms are equal to zero) can be carried out analytically, with full precision. The time integration for obtaining the time evolution of coefficients (here they are of purely scalar character as the current density has only one nonzero component in the z direction) is carried out by the fourth-order Runge–Kutta technique.

For the purpose of computation the cross section of the ring was divided into two sub-rings and in each of them the real distribution of the current density was approximated by a polynomial of the third order. The coefficients of both polynomials were determined according to the presented algorithm. The number of degrees of freedom was 9 (four coefficients of two polynomials of the third order and one condition of the total current in the conductor). The results of this example obtained by the zero-order approach are summarized in Section 4.6 and provide a good idea about the time evolution of current densities in the conductor. Two following figures show, moreover, the results obtained by application of the higher-order technique.

Fig. 7.11 contains the distribution of current density along the radius of the hollow conductor for $t_1 = 0.002$ s. While the distribution of this quantity by the zero-order technique was determined for 40 circular rings (and in every ring this value is constant), now we only used two circular rings. It is obvious that the agreement is very good. But while in the first case we worked with 41 degrees of freedom (40 circular rings + condition of the total current in the conductor), now we needed just 9 degrees of freedom for obtaining the same (at least) accuracy. Similarly, Fig. 7.12 shows an analogous distribution for $t_1 = 0.003$ s.

It is easy to see that the higher-order approach allowed reducing the rank of the system matrix more than four times. Further increase of the order of the approximating polynomials leads to even higher accuracy (the same effect is achieved by an increase in the number n of the subrings). In these cases, however, testing of the convergence of results carried out for several simple 1D and 2D examples confirmed that the results differed only negligibly and the achieved accuracy was quite sufficient.

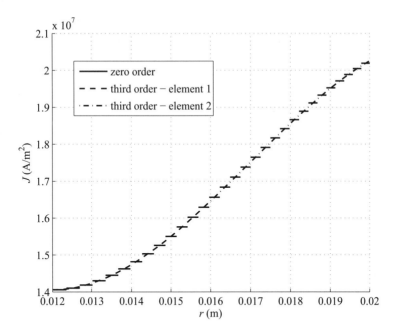

Figure 7.11.   Distribution of current density along the radius of a massive conductor for $t = 0.002$ s.

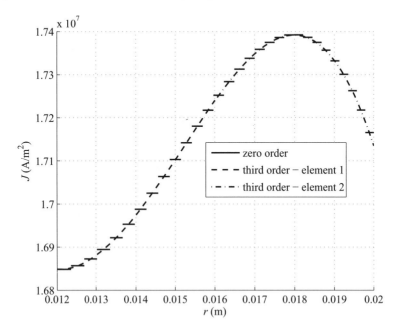

Figure 7.12.   Distribution of current density along the radius of a massive conductor for $t = 0.003$ s.

APPENDIX A

BASIC MATHEMATICAL TOOLS

A.1 VECTORS, MATRICES, AND SYSTEMS OF LINEAR EQUATIONS

Practically every numerical method discussed in this book leads to the solution of a large system of linear algebraic equations in the form

$$\boldsymbol{A} \cdot \boldsymbol{x} = \boldsymbol{b},$$

where $\boldsymbol{A}$ represents a square matrix of order n, $\boldsymbol{x}$ the vector of solutions, and $\boldsymbol{b}$ the right-side vector, both of them also being of order n. It is, therefore, vital to have sufficiently wide knowledge about these objects and operations with them. Necessary information in this respect is briefly (without details or proofs) summarized in the following sections. For more details see, for instance, Refs. 33 and 171–176.

A.1.1 Vectors

Vectors (in an n-dimensional Euclidean space) are generally objects consisting of n components. Symbol n, called the dimension of the vector, is an integer. The components of the vector are usually represented by constants or functions of the coordinates and/or time. A vector $\boldsymbol{p}$ may be written in the form

$$\boldsymbol{p} = (p_1, p_2, \ldots, p_n),$$

Integral Methods in Low-Frequency Electromagnetics. By I. Doležel, P. Karban, and P. Šolín.
Copyright © 2009 John Wiley & Sons, Inc.

where p_i, $i = 1, \ldots, n$ are the mentioned components, or in another form

$$\boldsymbol{p} = \sum_{i=1}^{n} p_i \mathbf{e}_i \,,$$

where $\mathbf{e}_i$, $i = 1, \ldots, n$ are the unit vectors in the directions of individual coordinate axes of the system. When we work with a common 3D Cartesian coordinate system, the unit vectors are denoted as $\mathbf{i}$, $\mathbf{j}$, and $\mathbf{k}$.

If α is a constant, then

$$\alpha \boldsymbol{p} = (\alpha p_1, \alpha p_2, \ldots, \alpha p_n) = \alpha \sum_{i=1}^{n} p_i \mathbf{e}_i$$

(each component p_i, $i = 1, \ldots, n$ of the vector $\boldsymbol{p}$ is multiplied by α).

A.1.1.1 Addition and subtraction of vectors

Addition and subtraction of vectors are justified just for vectors of the same dimensionality n. Let $\boldsymbol{p} = (p_1, p_2, \ldots, p_n)$ and $\boldsymbol{q} = (q_1, q_2, \ldots, q_n)$. Then

$$\boldsymbol{p} + \boldsymbol{q} = (p_1 + q_1, p_2 + q_2, \ldots, p_n + q_n)$$

and analogously

$$\boldsymbol{p} - \boldsymbol{q} = (p_1 - q_1, p_2 - q_2, \ldots, p_n - q_n) \,.$$

Let α and β be constants and $\boldsymbol{p}$ and $\boldsymbol{q}$ two vectors of dimension n. Then

$$\alpha \boldsymbol{p} + \beta \boldsymbol{q} = (\alpha p_1 + \beta q_1, \alpha p_2 + \beta q_2, \ldots, \alpha p_n + \beta q_n) = \sum_{i=1}^{n} (\alpha p_i + \beta q_i) \mathbf{e}_i \,.$$

A.1.1.2 Norm and length of a vector

The norm of a vector $\boldsymbol{p}$ is a function that assigns to the vector a scalar quantity. This function (denoted as $\|\boldsymbol{p}\|$ or, somewhat less commonly, $|\boldsymbol{p}|$) must satisfy the following rules:

- $\|\boldsymbol{p}\| \geq 0$; $\|\boldsymbol{p}\| = 0$ only when $\boldsymbol{p} = (0, 0, \ldots, 0)$ (null vector),

- $\|\alpha \boldsymbol{p}\| = |\alpha| \|\boldsymbol{p}\|$ for any constant α,

- $\|\boldsymbol{p} + \boldsymbol{q}\| \leq \|\boldsymbol{p}\| + \|\boldsymbol{q}\|$.

The most common is the Euclidean norm $\|\boldsymbol{p}\|_2$ defined as

$$\|\boldsymbol{p}\|_2 = \sqrt{\sum_{i=1}^{n} p_i^2} \,. \tag{A.1}$$

In the 3D Cartesian coordinate system the Euclidean norm of any vector $\boldsymbol{p}$ gives its length. The length of a unit vector is equal to 1.

A.1.1.3 Dot (scalar) product

The dot product is defined only for a pair of vectors of the same dimensionality n. The rule reads (the vectors being denoted by symbols $\boldsymbol{p}$ and $\boldsymbol{q}$)

$$\boldsymbol{p} \cdot \boldsymbol{q} = \sum_{i=1}^{n} p_i q_i \,.$$

Comparing this rule with (A.1), we immediately have

$$\|p\|_2 = \sqrt{p \cdot p}.$$

We say that two vectors p and q are perpendicular to one another when their dot product $p \cdot q = 0$.

A.1.1.4 Cross product   We will confine our attention to the 3D Cartesian coordinate system. Here, we can introduce the cross product of two vectors $p = (p_x, p_y, p_z)$ and $q = (q_x, q_y, q_z)$ defined as

$$p \times q = \begin{vmatrix} \mathbf{i} & \mathbf{j} & \mathbf{k} \\ p_x & p_y & p_z \\ q_x & q_y & q_z \end{vmatrix}.$$

The cross product may also be expressed as

$$p \times q = \|p\|_2 \cdot \|q\|_2 \cdot \sin\varphi \cdot \mathbf{n}_0 ,$$

where φ is the angle between the vectors p and q and $\mathbf{n}_0$ is a unit vector perpendicular to both of them; see Fig. A.1. It is clear that the length of vector $p \times q$ is equal to the parallelogram with sides of lengths p and q.

By definition, we immediately have

$$p \times q = -q \times p ,$$

$$p \times p = 0 .$$

A.1.1.5 Scalar triple product   The scalar triple product of vectors p, q, and r is defined as

$$p \cdot (q \times r) = \begin{vmatrix} p_x & p_y & p_z \\ q_x & q_y & q_z \\ r_x & r_y & r_z \end{vmatrix}$$

and its absolute value is equal to the volume of the parallelepiped with edges of lengths of the three above vectors.

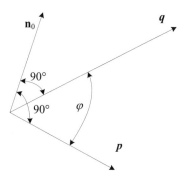

Figure A.1.   Interpretation of the cross product of vectors p and q.

A.1.1.6 Dot product in three dimensions The dot product of vectors p and q in three dimensions may also be written in the form

$$p \cdot q = \|p\|_2 \cdot \|q\|_2 \cdot \cos \varphi,$$

where φ is the angle between these vectors (see Fig. A.1).

A.1.2 Matrices

A matrix is an ordered set of numbers or expressions arranged in a rectangular form. For example, matrix A may appear as follows:

$$A = \begin{pmatrix} a_{11} & a_{12} & a_{13} & a_{14} & a_{15} \\ a_{21} & a_{22} & a_{23} & a_{24} & a_{25} \\ a_{31} & a_{32} & a_{33} & a_{34} & a_{35} \\ a_{41} & a_{42} & a_{43} & a_{44} & a_{45} \end{pmatrix}.$$

In this case the matrix A has 4 rows and 5 columns. We say that it is 4×5 matrix.

A.1.2.1 Basic types of matrices and relevant terminology This section is devoted to basic terminology in the domain of matrices.

- If a matrix A has the same number of rows and columns, say, n, we call it a square matrix of rank n. Its elements a_{ii}, $i = 1, 2, \ldots, n$ form its diagonal and are called diagonal elements.

- If all elements of matrix A are equal to zero, we call it a null matrix.

- If all elements of a square matrix A are equal to zero except for the elements in its diagonal, we call it a diagonal matrix. If all diagonal elements are equal to 1, we call it a identity matrix.

- A matrix with only one row is called a row matrix (and is identical with a row vector).

- A matrix with only one column is called a column matrix (and is identical with a column vector).

- A matrix characterized with strong predominance of zero entries is called a sparse matrix, with strong predominance of nonzero entries a dense (or, more colloquially, densely populated) matrix.

- A square matrix L is called a lower triangular matrix when its entries $l_{ij} = 0$ for $j > i$.

- A square matrix U is called an upper triangular matrix when its entries $u_{ij} = 0$ for $i > j$.

- Consider a matrix A with elements a_{ij}. Its transpose is matrix A^{T} with elements a_{ji}. For example,

$$A = \begin{pmatrix} a_{11} & a_{12} & a_{13} \\ a_{21} & a_{22} & a_{23} \end{pmatrix} \Rightarrow A^{\mathrm{T}} = \begin{pmatrix} a_{11} & a_{21} \\ a_{12} & a_{22} \\ a_{13} & a_{23} \end{pmatrix}.$$

- Consider a square matrix A with elements a_{ij}. It is called symmetric when $a_{ij} = a_{ji}$. For any symmetric matrix $A = A^{\mathrm{T}}$.

- Consider a square matrix A with elements a_{ij}. It is called skew-symmetric when $a_{ij} = -a_{ji}$.

- Consider a matrix A with elements a_{ij} and a constant α. Now αA is a matrix with elements αa_{ij}.

A.1.2.2 Addition of matrices Addition of matrices is defined only for matrices of the same kind (the numbers of their rows and columns must be the same). If we have two such matrices A and B, then matrix $A + B$ has elements $a_{ij} + b_{ij}$. Moreover, for any two constants α and β, matrix $\alpha A + \beta B$ has elements $\alpha a_{ij} + \beta b_{ij}$.

A.1.2.3 Multiplication of two matrices The product of matrices A and B is defined only if matrix A is of type $(l \times m)$ and B of type $(m \times n)$. Then the resultant matrix $C = A \cdot B$ is of type $(l \times n)$ and its elements are given by the expression

$$c_{ij} = \sum_{k=1}^{m} a_{ik} \cdot b_{kj}, \quad i = 1, \ldots, l, \quad j = 1, \ldots, n.$$

The product is generally not commutative, that is, $A \cdot B \neq B \cdot A$.

A.1.2.4 Square matrices In this section we are going to mention some useful properties of square matrices.

- Let A be an arbitrary square matrix of rank n and I an identity matrix of the same rank. Then

$$A \cdot I = I \cdot A = A.$$

- For any two square matrices A and B there holds

$$(A \cdot B)^{\mathrm{T}} = B^{\mathrm{T}} \cdot A^{\mathrm{T}}.$$

- Let D be a diagonal matrix of rank n

$$D = \begin{pmatrix} d_{11} & 0 & \ldots & 0 \\ 0 & d_{22} & \ldots & 0 \\ \ldots & \ldots & \ldots & \ldots \\ 0 & 0 & \ldots & d_{nn} \end{pmatrix}.$$

Then

$$D^k = \begin{pmatrix} d_{11}^k & 0 & \ldots & 0 \\ 0 & d_{22}^k & \ldots & 0 \\ \ldots & \ldots & \ldots & \ldots \\ 0 & 0 & \ldots & d_{nn}^k \end{pmatrix}.$$

- Determinant of a square matrix $|A|$ is a scalar quantity that plays an important role in solving systems of linear equations. If matrix A is of rank n, it can be defined using the recurrent formula

$$|A| = \begin{vmatrix} a_{11} & a_{12} & \ldots & a_{1n} \\ a_{21} & a_{22} & \ldots & a_{2n} \\ \ldots & \ldots & \ldots & \ldots \\ a_{n1} & a_{n2} & \ldots & a_{nn} \end{vmatrix} = \sum_{i=1}^{n} a_{1i} \cdot (-1)^{i+1} S_{1i} ,$$

where $S_{1i}, i = 1, \ldots, n$ is the determinant of the matrix of rank $n - 1$ obtained by deleting row 1 and column i from the original matrix A. For matrix A of rank $n = 1$ we have $|A| = a_{11}$ and for $n = 2$ analogously $|A| = a_{11}a_{22} - a_{12}a_{21}$.

- A square matrix A whose determinant $|A| \neq 0$ is called regular. As far as $|A| = 0$, the matrix A is called singular.

- A nonzero matrix A is called positively definite if for any nonzero vector p

$$p^{\mathsf{T}} A p > 0 .$$

A.1.2.5 *Inverse of a square matrix*   Consider a square matrix A of rank n. If its determinant $|A| \neq 0$, then there exists another square matrix B of rank n such that

$$A \cdot B = B \cdot A = I, \tag{A.2}$$

where I is the identity matrix of rank n. The matrix B is called the inverse to the matrix A and we denote it by the symbol A^{-1}.

Generally, the inverse matrix A^{-1} may be determined the using equation

$$A^{-1} = \frac{\mathrm{adj}(A)}{|A|} .$$

Here the symbol $\mathrm{adj}(A)$ stands for the matrix adjoint to A. The entries of $\mathrm{adj}(A)$ are given by the rule

$$a_{ij}^{\mathrm{adj}} = (-1)^{i+j} b_{ji} ,$$

where b_{ji} is the determinant of matrix B of rank $n - 1$ obtained from the original matrix A by deleting the jth row and ith column.

Even when the above algorithm for finding the elements of the inverse matrix is very simple, repeated computations of the determinants of lower and lower orders take a lot of time. That is why other (not so simple, but very efficient) procedures were developed in the past for solving this task.

A.1.3   Systems of linear equations

We will focus our attention only on linear systems described by n equations with n unknowns. Such a system is usually of the form

$$a_{11}x_1 + a_{12}x_2 + \cdots + a_{1n}x_n = b_1 ,$$

$$a_{21}x_1 + a_{22}x_2 + \cdots + a_{2n}x_n = b_2 ,$$

$$\vdots$$

$$a_{n1}x_1 + a_{n2}x_2 + \cdots + a_{nn}x_n = b_n \,. \tag{A.3}$$

The coefficients $a_{ij}, 1 \leq i, j \leq n$ and the right sides $b_1, \ldots, b_n$ are supposed to be given. Values $x_1, \ldots, x_n$ are called unknowns and have to be calculated using an appropriate method.

The system (A.3) may formally be written also in matrix form,

$$\begin{pmatrix} a_{11} & a_{12} & \ldots & a_{1n} \\ a_{21} & a_{22} & \ldots & a_{2n} \\ \ldots & \ldots & \ldots & \ldots \\ a_{n1} & a_{n2} & \ldots & a_{nn} \end{pmatrix} \cdot \begin{pmatrix} x_1 \\ x_2 \\ \ldots \\ x_n \end{pmatrix} = \begin{pmatrix} b_1 \\ b_2 \\ \ldots \\ b_n \end{pmatrix}, \tag{A.4}$$

or, in a more formal manner,

$$A \cdot x = b \,. \tag{A.5}$$

The coefficients in (A.3) are usually constants, but it is not a necessary condition. For example, when the unknowns x_i are of spatial character, the coefficients may be functions of time and vice versa. In further sections we will discuss only such systems where $|A| \neq 0$ (they are characterized by a regular matrix A).

A.1.3.1 Fundamental methods of solution

Numerous methods were developed for solving linear systems in the course of years. The selection of the most suitable method, however, is often a complicated task that depends on a lot of various conditions (rank n of the matrix A, its sparsity or density, value of its determinant $|A|$, etc.). That is why we will mention just the most fundamental procedures while for details we must refer to the common sources, such as Refs. 177–181.

In this section we will describe the following direct algorithms:

- method of inverse matrix,

- Gauss' elimination,

- LU decomposition,

and the principal iterative algorithms.

A.1.3.2 Method of the inverse matrix

Consider a system of equations with regular matrix A in the form (A.3) and multiply it from the left side by the inverse matrix ($|A|$). Now

$$A^{-1}Ax = A^{-1}b \,.$$

Taking into account (A.2), we have

$$Ix = x = A^{-1}b \,.$$

Now what we need to do is to multiply the matrix A^{-1} by the vector b.

A.1.3.3 Gauss' elimination

The algorithm is based on elementary row operations. It consists of two steps called forward elimination and back substitution, respectively. The purpose of the first step is to reduce the original matrix A to a triangular (or echelon) form. If the processed matrix A is singular, the procedure leads to a degenerate matrix, with one or more rows with only zeros (but such cases will not be discussed here). The second step is an easy algorithm that provides the solution of the system.

The first step will be illustrated for the first row of the system (A.3). Suppose that the element a_{11} is nonzero (if not, the first column of matrix A must be interchanged with another column, in which the corresponding element is nonzero). Now every row of the system has to be divided by its element in the first column unless this element is equal to zero (in such a case we do nothing). In this way we obtain another system whose first column contains only ones (at least in the first row) and/or zeros, for example,

$$x_1 + \frac{a_{12}}{a_{11}} x_2 + \cdots + \frac{a_{1n}}{a_{11}} x_n = \frac{b_1}{a_{11}} ,$$

$$x_1 + \frac{a_{22}}{a_{21}} x_2 + \cdots + \frac{a_{2n}}{a_{21}} x_n = \frac{b_2}{a_{21}} ,$$

$$\vdots$$

$$x_1 + \frac{a_{n2}}{a_{n1}} x_2 + \cdots + \frac{a_{nn}}{a_{n1}} x_n = \frac{b_n}{a_{n1}} . \tag{A.6}$$

And finally we subtract the first row from all other rows that are lead by coefficient 1, so that the first column of the new system contains only zeros with the exception of the upper element whose value is one.

$$x_1 + \frac{a_{12}}{a_{11}} x_2 + \cdots + \frac{a_{1n}}{a_{11}} x_n = \frac{b_1}{a_{11}} ,$$

$$0 + \left(\frac{a_{22}}{a_{21}} - \frac{a_{12}}{a_{11}} \right) x_2 + \cdots + \left(\frac{a_{2n}}{a_{21}} - \frac{a_{1n}}{a_{11}} \right) x_n = \frac{b_2}{a_{21}} - \frac{b_1}{a_{11}} ,$$

$$\vdots$$

$$0 + \left(\frac{a_{n2}}{a_{n1}} - \frac{a_{12}}{a_{11}} \right) x_2 + \cdots + \left(\frac{a_{nn}}{a_{n1}} - \frac{a_{1n}}{a_{11}} \right) x_n = \frac{b_n}{a_{n1}} - \frac{b_1}{a_{11}} . \tag{A.7}$$

The same algorithm is then applied to the above matrix without the first row and first column and the process is repeated until we obtain the system

$$\begin{pmatrix} 1 & c_{12} & \cdots & c_{1n} \\ 0 & 1 & \cdots & c_{2n} \\ \cdots & \cdots & \cdots & \cdots \\ 0 & 0 & \cdots & 1 \end{pmatrix} \cdot \begin{pmatrix} x_1 \\ x_2 \\ \cdots \\ x_n \end{pmatrix} = \begin{pmatrix} d_1 \\ d_2 \\ \cdots \\ d_n \end{pmatrix} .$$

During the back substitution the above system is solved by a simple algorithm in the form

$$x_n = d_n ,$$

$$x_{n-1} = d_{n-1} - c_{n-1\,n} x_n ,$$

$$\vdots$$

$$x_i = d_i - \sum_{k=i}^{n} c_{ik} x_i .$$

A.1.3.4 LU decomposition
Consider a system described by (A.4). If all principal minors of matrix A are nonzero (a principal minor of matrix A is the determinant of a

submatrix of matrix A that is formed by removing k $(0 \leq k \leq n - 1)$ rows and the corresponding columns of A), it is possible to write matrix A as a product of matrices L and U,

$$\begin{pmatrix} a_{11} & a_{12} & \ldots & a_{1n} \\ a_{21} & a_{22} & \ldots & a_{2n} \\ \ldots & \ldots & \ldots & \ldots \\ a_{n1} & a_{n2} & \ldots & a_{nn} \end{pmatrix} = \begin{pmatrix} l_{11} & 0 & \ldots & 0 \\ l_{21} & l_{22} & \ldots & 0 \\ \ldots & \ldots & \ldots & \ldots \\ l_{n1} & l_{n2} & \ldots & l_{nn} \end{pmatrix} \cdot \begin{pmatrix} u_{11} & u_{12} & \ldots & u_{1n} \\ 0 & u_{22} & \ldots & u_{2n} \\ \ldots & \ldots & \ldots & \ldots \\ 0 & 0 & \ldots & u_{nn} \end{pmatrix}.$$

We can then write

$$Ax = b \quad \Rightarrow \quad LUx = b.$$

Putting

$$Ux = y,$$

we obtain

$$Ly = b \quad \Rightarrow \quad y = L^{-1}b$$

and, hence,

$$x = U^{-1}L^{-1}b.$$

Finding the inverses to matrices L and U is easy and fast (or, after a small modification we can use the back substitution algorithm for successive computation of y and then x).

It remains to mention the basic methods for finding the matrices L and U. For example, Doolitle's algorithm, Cormen's LUP algorithm, and several others for specific types of matrices are efficient.

A.1.3.5 Iterative methods of solution

Consider again a system described by (A.4). Select the first approximation x_0 of the solution and put

$$x_{k+1} = B_k x_k + C_k b, \quad k = 0, 1, \ldots,$$

where B_k and C_k are square matrices derived (in some manner) from the matrix A. As far as the algorithm converges and is consistent (i.e., there holds $C_k A + B_k = I$), then

$$\lim_{k \to \infty} x_k = x,$$

where x is the exact solution. Nevertheless, as we do not know it, we finish the iterative process after reaching the condition

$$\|x_{k+1} - x_k\| < \varepsilon,$$

where ε denotes the selected tolerance and the symbol $\|.\|$ stands for some norm of the vector.

The simplest iterative method is used for matrices B and C, which do not vary in the course of the solution, so that

$$x_{k+1} = Bx_k + Cb, \quad k = 0, 1, \ldots.$$

If we put, moreover, $C = I$, then from the condition of the consistence $B = I - A$ we obtain

$$x_{k+1} = (I - A)x_k + b, \quad k = 0, 1, \ldots$$

or

$$\mathbf{x}_{k+1} = \mathbf{x}_k + (\mathbf{b} - \mathbf{A}\mathbf{x}_k), \quad k = 0, 1, \ldots.$$

This simplest iterative method can be improved by preconditioning, that is, multiplying the term $\mathbf{b} - \mathbf{A}\mathbf{x}_k$ by a suitable matrix from the left. This is the basis for more sophisticated iterative processes.

A.1.4 Eigenvalues and eigenvectors of matrices

Various linear transformations in vector spaces (we can mention shifting, rotation, stretching, compression, reflection and also their various combinations) are vector functions that can be expressed as

$$\mathbf{y} = \mathbf{A}\mathbf{x},$$

where $\mathbf{x}$ and $\mathbf{y}$ are the original and transformed vectors, respectively, and $\mathbf{A}$ is the vector function. As this function is linear, it must satisfy the following rules:

$$\mathbf{A}(\mathbf{x}_1 + \mathbf{x}_2) = \mathbf{A}\mathbf{x}_1 + \mathbf{A}\mathbf{x}_2$$

and

$$\mathbf{A}(\alpha\mathbf{x}) = \alpha\mathbf{A}\mathbf{x}.$$

where α is an arbitrary constant. Furthermore, we will suppose that the vector function $\mathbf{A}$ is a square matrix of rank n.

Consider, thus, a matrix $\mathbf{A}$ of rank n. If there exists a nonzero vector $\mathbf{x}$ such that

$$\mathbf{A}\mathbf{x} = \lambda\mathbf{x},$$

where λ is a scalar, then λ is called an eigenvalue of $\mathbf{A}$ and $\mathbf{x}$ a corresponding eigenvector of $\mathbf{A}$.

When $\mathbf{A}$ is the identity matrix $\mathbf{I}$, then every nonzero vector is an eigenvector. But when $\mathbf{A}$ is a general matrix, just a few vectors satisfy this condition (and the same holds for the eigenvalues). But if a vector $\mathbf{x}$ is an eigenvector of $\mathbf{A}$, then a vector $\mathbf{y} = \beta\mathbf{x}$ (β being a scalar) is also an eigenvector of $\mathbf{A}$, because

$$\mathbf{A}\mathbf{y} = \mathbf{A}(\beta\mathbf{x}) = \beta\mathbf{A}\mathbf{x} = \beta\lambda\mathbf{x} = \lambda\beta\mathbf{x} = \lambda\mathbf{y}.$$

The eigenvectors and eigenvalues are of high importance in a lot of disciplines of physics and engineering (mechanics, elasticity, oscillations). Their determination represents the first step for finding various invariants, optimization, analysis of linear systems, and other applications. One of the principal methods of finding the above quantities follows.

$$\mathbf{A}\mathbf{x} = \lambda\mathbf{x} = \lambda\mathbf{I}\mathbf{x},$$

so that

$$(\mathbf{A} - \lambda\mathbf{I})\mathbf{x} = 0.$$

This equation can be written in the form

$$
\begin{pmatrix}
a_{11} - \lambda & a_{12} & \ldots & a_{1n} \\
a_{21} & a_{22} - \lambda & \ldots & a_{2n} \\
\ldots & \ldots & \ldots & \ldots \\
a_{n1} & a_{n2} & \ldots & a_{nn} - \lambda
\end{pmatrix}
\cdot
\begin{pmatrix}
x_1 \\
x_2 \\
\ldots \\
x_n
\end{pmatrix}
=
\begin{pmatrix}
0 \\
0 \\
\ldots \\
0
\end{pmatrix}.
$$

If the matrix of the system $A - \lambda I$ is regular, the system has only the trivial solution $x_1 = x_2 = \ldots, x_n = 0$. In order to get a nonzero eigenvector, the matrix has to be singular, so that its determinant

$$
\begin{vmatrix}
a_{11} - \lambda & a_{12} & \ldots & a_{1n} \\
a_{21} & a_{22} - \lambda & \ldots & a_{2n} \\
\ldots & \ldots & \ldots & \ldots \\
a_{n1} & a_{n2} & \ldots & a_{nn} - \lambda
\end{vmatrix}
$$

has to be equal to zero.

The determinant can be expanded into a polynomial of order n. This polynomial is called the characteristic polynomial of matrix A and its roots provide the eigenvalues (whose multiplicity can be 1 or more). Generally, the number of different eigenvalues (and corresponding eigenvectors) cannot be higher than n.

A.2 VECTOR ANALYSIS

Vector analysis is one of the domains of mathematics that deals with the differential and integral operations of vectors, generally in multidimensional spaces. It contains a lot of rules and techniques that are very useful for solving a wide spectrum of physical and engineering problems. Vector analysis also provides efficient tools for the treatment of different physical fields of both scalar and vector character.

This section contains a brief summary of the terminology, definitions, and fundamental rules in the domain. The most important formulas are expressed in both the Cartesian and cylindrical coordinate systems that are mostly used for solving technical tasks discussed throughout this book.

A.2.1 Differential and integral operations with vectors in Cartesian coordinates

As was mentioned in the previous section, the components of any vector may generally be functions of time and/or space (in the simplest case, however, they are constants). We start with the relevant vector operations in the Cartesian coordinate system x, y, z with unit vectors $\mathbf{i}, \mathbf{j}$, and $\mathbf{k}$.

Let us first introduce a formal vector operator ∇ called "nabla" (or "del") that is defined as follows:

$$
\nabla = \mathbf{i}\frac{\partial}{\partial x} + \mathbf{j}\frac{\partial}{\partial y} + \mathbf{k}\frac{\partial}{\partial z}.
$$

This operator is of great importance for defining three fundamental differential operators–grad, div, and curl.

A.2.1.1 Gradient The *gradient* of a scalar function $\varphi(x, y, z)$ is a vector defined as

$$\operatorname{grad} \varphi = \mathbf{i}\,\frac{\partial \varphi}{\partial x} + \mathbf{j}\,\frac{\partial \varphi}{\partial y} + \mathbf{k}\,\frac{\partial \varphi}{\partial z}\,.$$

At a given point this vector shows the direction of the maximum change in a scalar field. The operator grad can evidently also be written in terms of the operator "nabla"

$$\operatorname{grad} \varphi = \nabla \varphi\,.$$

A.2.1.2 Divergence The *divergence* of a vector function $\mathbf{p}(x, y, z)$ is a scalar defined as

$$\operatorname{div} \mathbf{p} = \frac{\partial p_x}{\partial x} + \frac{\partial p_y}{\partial y} + \frac{\partial p_z}{\partial z}\,,$$

where p_x, p_y, and p_z are individual components of the vector $\mathbf{p}$. At a given point it provides the magnitude of the source or sink of the vector field. The operator div can similarly be written in terms of the operator "nabla,"

$$\operatorname{div} \mathbf{p} = \nabla \cdot \mathbf{p}\,.$$

A.2.1.3 Circulation The *circulation* of a vector function $\mathbf{p}(x, y, z)$ is a vector defined as

$$\operatorname{curl} \mathbf{p} = \begin{vmatrix} \mathbf{i} & \mathbf{j} & \mathbf{k} \\ \partial/\partial x & \partial/\partial y & \partial/\partial z \\ p_x & p_y & p_z \end{vmatrix}\,.$$

At a given point of a vector field this operator shows the tendency of the vector $\mathbf{p}$ to rotate about it. Even here we can use the operator "nabla" for definition:

$$\operatorname{curl} \mathbf{p} = \nabla \times \mathbf{p}\,.$$

A.2.1.4 Connectedness Connectedness is an important topological property used for distinguishing topological spaces. A topological space is called connected (or simply-connected) if it cannot be represented by a disjoint union of two and more nonempty open subsets. It is clear from Fig. A.2, which shows a connected subset (part (a)) and an unconnected subset (part (b)).

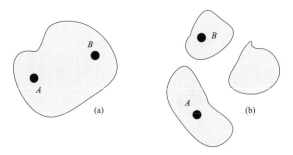

Figure A.2. Connectedness of a domain.

A stronger requirement is on a path-connected space, which is a domain where any two points A and B can be connected by a path lying in this domain (part (a)), which is impossible in part (b).

A.2.1.5 *Conservative vector fields*

Every vector field that is given by the gradient of a scalar function is called conservative. So that the vector field p defined by

$$p = \operatorname{grad} \varphi$$

is conservative.

Consider now the integral

$$I = \int_A^B p \cdot dr \,,$$

where $r = (x, y, z)$ is the position vector, so that $dr = (dx, dy, dz)$ and A and B are two arbitrary points. The expression can be rewritten as

$$I = \int_A^B \operatorname{grad} \varphi \cdot dr = \int_A^B \left(\frac{\partial \varphi}{\partial x}, \frac{\partial \varphi}{\partial y}, \frac{\partial \varphi}{\partial z} \right) (dx, dy, dz)$$

$$= \int_A^B \left(\frac{\partial \varphi}{\partial x} dx + \frac{\partial \varphi}{\partial y} dy + \frac{\partial \varphi}{\partial z} dz \right) = \int_A^B d\varphi = \varphi(B) - \varphi(A).$$

It is clear that the integral is absolutely independent of the path: it just depends on its endpoints. Hence, for any closed loop c

$$\oint_c p \cdot dr = 0 \,.$$

The converse is true, however, only when the domain containing the path c is a connected region.

A.2.1.6 *Irrotational vector fields*

A vector field p is called irrotational (or curl-free) if

$$\nabla p = 0 \,.$$

It may easily be shown that for any scalar function φ

$$\nabla \times \nabla \varphi = 0 \,,$$

which leads to the conclusion that any conservative field is also an irrotational field. The converse of this statement is true if the domain is again simply-connected.

A.2.1.7 *Solenoidal vector fields*

Every vector field p whose divergence is equal to zero is called solenoidal. This condition is satisfied if

$$p = \operatorname{curl} A \qquad\qquad (A.8)$$

(it can easily be shown that for any vector function A div$(\operatorname{curl} A) = 0$). The converse also holds: if a vector field p is solenoidal, there always exist a vector function A satisfying (A.8).

A.2.1.8 Laplacian vector fields Every vector field p that is irrotational and solenoidal is called the Laplacian vector field. This field also satisfies the conditions

$$\text{curl}\,p = 0\,,$$

$$\text{div}\,p = 0\,.$$

Thus, the vector field p may be expressed as grad φ and the last equation can be rewritten
as

$$\nabla \cdot \nabla \varphi = \nabla^2 \varphi = \triangle\varphi = 0\,.$$

The operator ∇^2 is called the Laplacian operator and we denote it also by the symbol $\triangle$.
Normally we write it in the form

$$\triangle = \frac{\partial^2}{\partial x^2} + \frac{\partial^2}{\partial y^2} + \frac{\partial^2}{\partial z^2}$$

and it may act on both scalar and vector functions, so that

$$\triangle\varphi = \frac{\partial^2 \varphi}{\partial x^2} + \frac{\partial^2 \varphi}{\partial y^2} + \frac{\partial^2 \varphi}{\partial z^2}\,,$$

$$\triangle p = \frac{\partial^2 p}{\partial x^2} + \frac{\partial^2 p}{\partial y^2} + \frac{\partial^2 p}{\partial z^2}\,.$$

The Laplacian operator satisfies Laplace's equation.

A.2.1.9 Operator curl curl One of the frequently used operators is curl curl. In the
Cartesian coordinate system it can easily be shown that

$$\text{curl}\,\text{curl}\,p = \text{grad}\,\text{div}\,p - \triangle p\,.$$

A.2.1.10 Gauss' theorem (or divergence theorem) This theorem provides a relation between a flow of a vector field through a closed surface and its behavior in the
volume inside it. Consider a 3D compact domain V with a piecewise smooth boundary
∂V. If p is a vector field continuously differentiable in $V \cup \partial V$, then

$$\int_V (\nabla \cdot p)\mathrm{d}V = \oint_{\partial V} (p \cdot n_0)\mathrm{d}S\,,$$

where n_0 denotes the outward unit normal to the boundary ∂V. While the left-hand side
of the above equation represents the total source of vector p in volume V, the right-hand
side gives the total flow from the volume V through its boundary ∂V.

A.2.1.11 Stokes' theorem This theorem provides a relation between the circulation
of a vector field along a piecewise smooth simple closed path and its behavior on the area
bounded by this path. Consider a 2D domain S with a piecewise smooth path ∂S. If p is a
vector field continuously differentiable in $S \cup \partial S$, then

$$\int_S (\nabla \times p)\mathrm{d}S = \oint_{\partial S} p \cdot \mathrm{d}l\,,$$

where $\mathrm{d}l$ is the elementary vector in the tangential direction to the path ∂S.

A.2.1.12 Green's theorem This theorem represents Stokes' theorem in two dimensions. Consider a positively oriented simple closed curve C in plane x, y that is piecewise smooth. Let S be the domain bounded by C. If $f(x, y)$ and $g(x, y)$ are continuously differentiable functions defined on S, then

$$\oint_C (f(x, y)\mathrm{d}x + g(x, y)\mathrm{d}y) = \int_S \left(\frac{\partial g(x, y)}{\partial x} - \frac{\partial f(x, y)}{\partial y} \right) \mathrm{d}S .$$

A.2.2 Other orthogonal coordinate systems

The versatility of the vector calculus is based on the fact that the form of vector equations does not depend on the coordinate system. But particular computations are mostly realized using the component equations, in such a system that allows for their easiest solution. Therefore, it is very useful to know the transformation rules for the components of various vectors in different systems and also for various vector operators.

Consider a Cartesian coordinate system (x, y, z) and continuous functions $u(x, y, z)$, $v(x, y, z)$, and $w(x, y, z)$ that are also continuously differentiable except for a finite number of points. These functions may be called curvilinear coordinates.

Let P be an arbitrary point and $\mathbf{r}$ its position vector. In the curvilinear system u, v, w its elementary change is described by the vector

$$\mathrm{d}\mathbf{r} = \frac{\partial \mathbf{r}}{\partial u} \mathrm{d}u + \frac{\partial \mathbf{r}}{\partial v} \mathrm{d}v + \frac{\partial \mathbf{r}}{\partial w} \mathrm{d}w .$$

Vectors

$$\mathbf{a}_1 = \frac{\partial \mathbf{r}}{\partial u} , \quad \mathbf{a}_2 = \frac{\partial \mathbf{r}}{\partial v} , \quad \mathbf{a}_3 = \frac{\partial \mathbf{r}}{\partial w}$$

are called the basic vectors (but not necessarily of unit magnitude) at point P and the only condition they should satisfy is their linear independence. In such a case, at point P they form the fundamental coordinate system. If the curvilinear system is orthogonal, the basic vectors are perpendicular to each other.

A.2.2.1 Metric coefficients in orthogonal systems In the Cartesian coordinate system the elementary shift is given by the relation

$$\mathrm{d}s = \sqrt{(\mathrm{d}x)^2 + (\mathrm{d}y)^2 + (\mathrm{d}z)^2} ,$$

where, for instance, $\mathrm{d}x$ may be expressed (using the curvilinear coordinates) as

$$\mathrm{d}x = \frac{\partial x}{\partial u} \mathrm{d}u + \frac{\partial x}{\partial v} \mathrm{d}v + \frac{\partial x}{\partial w} \mathrm{d}w ,$$

and analogously we can express $\mathrm{d}y$ and $\mathrm{d}z$. Now we can write

$$\mathrm{d}s = \sqrt{(\mathrm{d}u, \mathrm{d}v, \mathrm{d}w) \cdot \begin{pmatrix} g_{11} & g_{12} & g_{13} \\ g_{21} & g_{22} & g_{23} \\ g_{31} & g_{32} & g_{33} \end{pmatrix} \cdot \begin{pmatrix} \mathrm{d}u \\ \mathrm{d}v \\ \mathrm{d}w \end{pmatrix}} ,$$

where elements $g_{11}, \ldots, g_{33}$ are called metric coefficients defined by the relations

$$
\begin{aligned}
g_{11} &= \frac{\partial x}{\partial u} \cdot \frac{\partial x}{\partial u} + \frac{\partial y}{\partial u} \cdot \frac{\partial y}{\partial u} + \frac{\partial z}{\partial u} \cdot \frac{\partial z}{\partial u}, \\
g_{12} = g_{21} &= \frac{\partial x}{\partial u} \cdot \frac{\partial x}{\partial v} + \frac{\partial y}{\partial u} \cdot \frac{\partial y}{\partial v} + \frac{\partial z}{\partial u} \cdot \frac{\partial z}{\partial v}, \\
g_{13} = g_{31} &= \frac{\partial x}{\partial u} \cdot \frac{\partial x}{\partial w} + \frac{\partial y}{\partial u} \cdot \frac{\partial y}{\partial w} + \frac{\partial z}{\partial u} \cdot \frac{\partial z}{\partial w}, \\
g_{22} &= \frac{\partial x}{\partial v} \cdot \frac{\partial x}{\partial v} + \frac{\partial y}{\partial v} \cdot \frac{\partial y}{\partial v} + \frac{\partial z}{\partial v} \cdot \frac{\partial z}{\partial v}, \\
g_{23} = g_{32} &= \frac{\partial x}{\partial v} \cdot \frac{\partial x}{\partial w} + \frac{\partial y}{\partial v} \cdot \frac{\partial y}{\partial w} + \frac{\partial z}{\partial v} \cdot \frac{\partial z}{\partial w}, \\
g_{33} &= \frac{\partial x}{\partial w} \cdot \frac{\partial x}{\partial w} + \frac{\partial y}{\partial w} \cdot \frac{\partial y}{\partial w} + \frac{\partial z}{\partial w} \cdot \frac{\partial z}{\partial w}.
\end{aligned}
$$

If the curvilinear coordinate system is orthogonal, the elements

$$
g_{12} = g_{21} = g_{13} = g_{31} = g_{23} = g_{32} = 0,
$$

so that

$$
ds = \sqrt{g_{11}(du)^2 + g_{22}(dv)^2 + g_{33}(dw)^2}. \tag{A.9}
$$

Putting

$$
h_1 = \sqrt{g_{11}}, \quad h_2 = \sqrt{g_{22}}, \quad h_3 = \sqrt{g_{33}}, \tag{A.10}
$$

we can rewrite (A.9) into the form

$$
ds = \sqrt{(h_1 du)^2 + (h_2 dv)^2 + (h_3 dw)^2}.
$$

The quantities h_1, h_2, and h_3 are called Lamé coefficients.

A.2.2.2 *Vector operators in orthogonal systems*   The gradient of a scalar function φ is given by the formula

$$
\operatorname{grad} \varphi = \mathbf{u}_1 \frac{1}{h_1} \frac{\partial \varphi}{\partial u} + \mathbf{u}_2 \frac{1}{h_2} \frac{\partial \varphi}{\partial v} + \mathbf{u}_3 \frac{1}{h_3} \frac{\partial \varphi}{\partial w}.
$$

where $\mathbf{u}_1$, $\mathbf{u}_2$, and $\mathbf{u}_3$ are the unit vectors in the directions specified by the individual orthogonal directions.

The divergence of a vector function $\boldsymbol{p}$ has the form

$$
\operatorname{div} \boldsymbol{p} = \frac{1}{h_1 h_2 h_3} \left[\frac{\partial(h_2 h_3 p_1)}{\partial u} + \frac{\partial(h_1 h_3 p_2)}{\partial v} + \frac{\partial(h_1 h_2 p_3)}{\partial w} \right],
$$

where p_1, p_2, and p_3 are the components of the vector $\boldsymbol{p}$ in the orthogonal directions.

The circulation of a vector function $\boldsymbol{p}$ is

$$
\operatorname{curl} \boldsymbol{p} = \frac{1}{h_1 h_2 h_3} \cdot \begin{vmatrix} h_1 \mathbf{u}_1 & h_2 \mathbf{u}_2 & h_3 \mathbf{u}_3 \\ \partial/\partial u & \partial/\partial v & \partial/\partial w \\ h_1 p_1 & h_2 p_2 & h_3 p_3 \end{vmatrix}
$$

and finally Laplace's operator

$$\triangle = \frac{1}{h_1 h_2 h_3} \cdot \left[\frac{\partial}{\partial u} \left(\frac{h_2 h_3}{h_1} \frac{\partial}{\partial u} \right) + \frac{\partial}{\partial v} \left(\frac{h_3 h_1}{h_2} \frac{\partial}{\partial v} \right) + \frac{\partial}{\partial w} \left(\frac{h_1 h_2}{h_3} \frac{\partial}{\partial w} \right) \right] .$$

A.2.2.3 *Cylindrical coordinates* The cylindrical coordinates are defined by the relations

$$x = r \cos \alpha , \quad y = r \sin \alpha , \quad z = z , \quad \alpha \in \langle 0, 2\pi \rangle .$$

From (A.10) we immediately obtain

$$h_1 = 1 , \quad h_2 = r , \quad h_3 = 1 .$$

Denoting the unit vectors (see Fig. A.3) in the directions of the particular orthogonal axes as $\mathbf{r}_0$, $\mathbf{a}_0$, and $\mathbf{z}_0$, we get

$$\operatorname{grad} \varphi = \mathbf{r}_0 \frac{\partial \varphi}{\partial r} + \mathbf{a}_0 \frac{1}{r} \frac{\partial \varphi}{\partial \alpha} + \mathbf{z}_0 \frac{\partial \varphi}{\partial z} ,$$

$$\operatorname{div} \boldsymbol{p} = \frac{1}{r} \frac{\partial (r p_r)}{\partial r} + \frac{1}{r} \frac{\partial p_\alpha}{\partial \alpha} + \frac{\partial p_z}{\partial z} ,$$

$$\operatorname{curl} \boldsymbol{p} = \frac{1}{r} \cdot \begin{vmatrix} \mathbf{r}_0 & r\mathbf{a}_0 & \mathbf{z}_0 \\ \partial/\partial r & \partial/\partial \alpha & \partial/\partial z \\ p_r & r p_\alpha & p_z \end{vmatrix} ,$$

and

$$\triangle = \frac{1}{r} \frac{\partial}{\partial r} \left(r \frac{\partial}{\partial r} \right) + \frac{1}{r^2} \frac{\partial^2}{\partial \alpha^2} + \frac{\partial^2}{\partial z^2} .$$

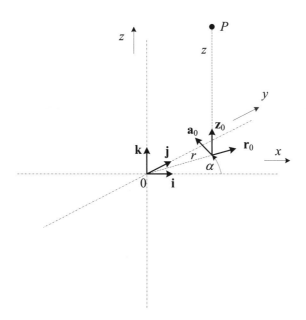

Figure A.3. Determination of the cylindrical coordinates of point P.

Of a more complicated form (unlike the Cartesian coordinate system) is the operator curl curl. After some manipulation we obtain

$$
\begin{aligned}
\text{curl curl } \boldsymbol{p} = \ & \mathbf{r}_0 \left[-\frac{1}{r^2}\frac{\partial^2 p_r}{\partial \alpha^2} - \frac{\partial^2 p_r}{\partial z^2} + \frac{1}{r^2}\frac{\partial p_\alpha}{\partial \alpha} + \frac{1}{r}\frac{\partial^2 p_\alpha}{\partial r\partial \alpha} + \frac{\partial^2 p_z}{\partial r\partial z} \right] \\
& + \mathbf{a}_0 \left[\frac{1}{r}\frac{\partial^2 p_r}{\partial r\partial \alpha} - \frac{1}{r^2}\frac{\partial p_r}{\partial \alpha} - \frac{\partial^2 p_\alpha}{\partial z^2} + \frac{p_\alpha}{r^2} - \frac{1}{r}\frac{\partial p_\alpha}{\partial r} - \frac{\partial^2 p_\alpha}{\partial r^2} + \frac{1}{r}\frac{\partial^2 p_z}{\partial \alpha\partial z} \right] \\
& + \mathbf{z}_0 \left[\frac{\partial^2 p_r}{\partial r\partial z} + \frac{1}{r}\frac{\partial p_r}{\partial z} + \frac{1}{r}\frac{\partial^2 p_\alpha}{\partial \alpha\partial z} - \frac{1}{r^2}\frac{\partial p_z}{\partial \alpha^2} - \frac{\partial^2 p_z}{\partial r^2} - \frac{1}{r}\frac{\partial p_z}{\partial r} \right].
\end{aligned}
$$

In axisymmetric arrangements we usually work with the following two cases:

- The vector $\boldsymbol{p}$ has only one nonzero component p_α in the circumferential direction α and this component depends only on coordinates r and z. In this case the resultant vector has only one component in direction α that is given by the relation

$$
\text{curl curl } \boldsymbol{p}_\alpha = \frac{p_\alpha}{r^2} - \frac{1}{r}\frac{\partial p_\alpha}{\partial r} - \frac{\partial^2 p_\alpha}{\partial r^2} - \frac{\partial^2 p_\alpha}{\partial z^2}.
$$

- The vector $\boldsymbol{p}$ has only one nonzero component p_z in the axial direction z and this component depends only on the coordinate r. In this case the resultant vector has only one component in the z direction that is given by the relation

$$
\text{curl curl } \boldsymbol{p}_z = -\frac{\partial^2 p_z}{\partial r^2} - \frac{1}{r}\frac{\partial p_z}{\partial r}.
$$

APPENDIX B

SPECIAL FUNCTIONS

This appendix summarizes the basic properties of special functions that can appear in computation of examples solved by integral and integrodifferential methods and also in algorithms for the numerical integration of functions that are not integrable analytically. Attention is particularly paid to the Bessel functions, elliptic functions, and several systems of orthogonal polynomials.

B.1 BESSEL FUNCTIONS

Occurrence of Bessel functions is characteristic for analytical solutions of electromagnetic fields in cylindrical or spherical arrangements described by Poisson's, Laplace's, or Helmholtz' partial differential equations that are solved by the separation of variables. In fact, these functions represent canonical solutions of Bessel's ordinary differential equation

$$x^2 \frac{\mathrm{d}^2 y}{\mathrm{d}x^2} + x \frac{\mathrm{d}y}{\mathrm{d}x} + (x^2 - a^2)y = 0 \,, \tag{B.1}$$

where a is an arbitrary real or complex constant. Often (e.g., in electromagnetism) we can meet another form of this equation:

$$\frac{\mathrm{d}^2 y}{\mathrm{d}x^2} + \frac{1}{x}\frac{\mathrm{d}y}{\mathrm{d}x} + (1 - \frac{a^2}{x^2})y = 0 \,.$$

Integral Methods in Low-Frequency Electromagnetics. By I. Doležel, P. Karban, and P. Šolín.
Copyright © 2009 John Wiley & Sons, Inc.

Typical tasks that lead to Bessel functions are the following:

- magnetic field produced by a cylindrical coil and similar problems,

- electromagnetic waves in cylindrical waveguides,

- conduction of heat in cylindrical objects,

- mechanical problems associated with thin circular membranes (e.g., modes of vibration).

Various problems of this kind are distinguished from one another by the constant a in (B.1). In the cylindrical problems a is usually a low integer, so that we often write n instead of a and say that the corresponding Bessel function is of the n th order.

Even when Bessel differential equations are the same for a positive and a negative value of a, it is a convention to define different Bessel functions for these values.

As the general theory of Bessel is very comprehensive, in the next section we will deal only with the basic properties of Bessel functions of integer parameter n.

B.1.1 Bessel functions of the first kind

Under Bessel functions of the first kind we understand functions that reach for $x = 0$ finite values when $n \geq 0$ and diverge there when $n < 0$. These functions, generally denoted by the letter J, can be well defined using their Taylor expansions around the point $x = 0$ in the form

$$J_a(x) = \sum_{k=0}^{\infty} \frac{(-1)^k}{k!\,\Gamma(k + a + 1)} \left(\frac{x}{2}\right)^{2k+a},$$

where Γ is the gamma function. If a is an integer ($a = n$), we immediately have

$$J_n(x) = \sum_{k=0}^{\infty} \frac{(-1)^k}{k!\,(k + n)!} \left(\frac{x}{2}\right)^{2k+n}.$$

While $J_0(0) = 1$, for $n > 0$ $J_0(n) = 0$ (see Fig. B.1).

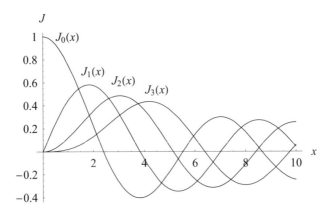

Figure B.1. Evolution of Bessel functions J for $n = 0, 1, 2, 3$.

Another way to define Bessel functions of integer order $J_n(x)$ is

$$J_n(x) = \frac{1}{\pi} \int_0^\pi \cos(nz - x\sin z)dz.$$

B.1.2 Bessel functions of the second kind

Unlike functions $J_n(x)$, Bessel functions of the second kind denoted by the letter Y, are singular at point $x = 0$. For a general parameter a these functions are defined by the formula

$$Y_a(x) = \frac{J_a(x)\cos(a\pi) - J_{-a}(x)}{\cos(a\pi)}$$

and for integer n

$$Y_n(x) = \lim_{a\to n} Y_a(x).$$

Several Bessel functions of the second kind for low values of n are depicted in Fig. B.2.
    Another way to define Bessel functions of integer order $Y_n(x)$ using an integral expression is

$$Y_n(x) = \frac{1}{\pi} \int_0^\pi \sin(x\sin z - nz)dz - \frac{1}{\pi} \int_0^\infty \left[e^{nz} + (-1)^n e^{-nz} \right] e^{-x\sinh z}dz.$$

B.1.3 Hankel functions

Hankel functions (also called Bessel functions of the third kind) for any value of a are defined by the formulas

$$H_a^1(x) = J_a(x) + j \cdot Y_a(x),$$
$$H_a^2(x) = J_a(x) - j \cdot Y_a(x),$$

where j represents the imaginary unit.

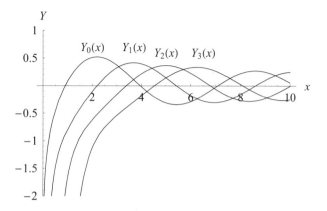

Figure B.2.   Evolution of Bessel functions Y for $n = 0, 1, 2, 3$.

B.1.4   Modified Bessel functions

Bessel functions may be defined not only for a real argument x, but also for a complex argument z. If the argument is purely imaginary, say, jx, we obtain so-called modified Bessel functions (or hyperbolic Bessel functions) of the first and second kinds. These functions are denoted as $I_a(x)$ and $K_a(x)$ and may easily be expressed in terms of functions $J_a(x)$, $Y_a(x)$, or $H_a^1(x)$, for example, as

$$I_a(x) = j^{-a} J_a(jx),$$

$$K_a(x) = \frac{\pi}{2} \frac{I_{-a}(x) - I_{-a}(x)}{\sin(a\pi)} = \frac{\pi}{2} j^{a+1} H_a^1(jx).$$

It can also be shown that both these functions are solutions to the modified Bessel equation in the form

$$x^2 \frac{d^2 y}{dx^2} + x \frac{dy}{dx} + (x^2 + a^2) y = 0.$$

For an illustration, Figs. B.3 and B.4 show the evolution of the modified Bessel functions $I_n(x)$ and $K_n(x)$ for $n = 0, 1, 2,$ and 3.

B.1.5   Asymptotic forms of Bessel functions

Bessel functions are normally expressed by infinite series. But for positive values of a and certain values of variable x they can be approximated with very good accuracy by much simpler functions. For example, the function $J_a(x)$ may be replaced by the following functions

$$J_a(x) \approx \frac{1}{\Gamma(a+1)} \left(\frac{x}{2}\right)^a \quad \text{for } 0 < x \ll \sqrt{a+1}$$

and

$$J_a(x) \approx \sqrt{\frac{2}{\pi x}} \cos\left(x - \frac{a\pi}{2} - \frac{\pi}{4}\right) \quad \text{for } x \gg \left|a^2 - \frac{1}{4}\right|,$$

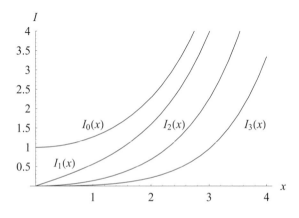

Figure B.3.   Evolution of modified Bessel functions I for $n = 0, 1, 2, 3$.

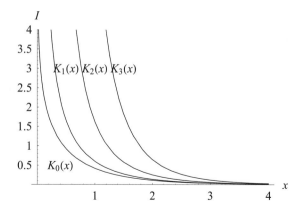

Figure B.4. Evolution of modified Bessel functions K for $n = 0, 1, 2, 3$.

while $Y_a(x)$ may be replaced by

$$Y_a(x) \approx -\frac{\Gamma(a)}{\pi}\left(\frac{2}{x}\right)^a \quad \text{for } 0 < x \ll \sqrt{a+1} \text{ and } a > 0, \qquad (\text{B.2})$$

$$Y_a(x) \approx \frac{2}{\pi}\left(\ln\left(\frac{x}{2}\right) + \gamma_E\right) \quad \text{for } 0 < x \ll 1 \text{ and } a = 0 \qquad (\text{B.3})$$

($\gamma_E = 0.577215664901532...$ being the Euler–Mascheroni constant) and finally

$$Y_a(x) \approx \sqrt{\frac{2}{\pi x}}\sin\left(x - \frac{a\pi}{2} - \frac{\pi}{4}\right) \quad \text{for } x \gg \left|a^2 - \frac{1}{4}\right|.$$

In an analogous manner we obtain approximative formulas for the functions $I_n(x)$ and $K_n(x)$:

$$I_a(x) \approx \frac{1}{\Gamma(a+1)}\left(\frac{x}{2}\right)^a \quad \text{for } 0 < x \ll \sqrt{a+1}$$

and

$$I_a(x) \approx \frac{1}{\sqrt{2\pi x}}\,e^x \quad \text{for } x \gg \left|a^2 - \frac{1}{4}\right|,$$

while

$$K_a(x) \approx \frac{\Gamma(a)}{\pi}\left(\frac{2}{x}\right)^a \quad \text{for } 0 < x \ll \sqrt{a+1} \text{ and } a > 0, \qquad (\text{B.4})$$

$$K_a(x) \approx -\ln\left(\frac{x}{2}\right) - \gamma_E \quad \text{for } 0 < x \ll 1 \text{ and } a = 0 \qquad (\text{B.5})$$

and

$$K_a(x) \approx \sqrt{\frac{\pi}{2x}}\,e^{-x} \quad \text{for } x \gg \left|a^2 - \frac{1}{4}\right|.$$

B.1.6 Some other useful relations

Bessel functions satisfy a lot of useful relations that link them with other kinds of functions, their derivatives, integrals, and so on. In this section we present the most frequent formulas used in problems associated with electromagnetic fields.

For example, functions $J_a(x)$, $Y_a(x)$, $H_a^1(x)$, and $H_a^2(x)$ satisfy the relations

$$f_{a-1}(x) + f_{a+1}(x) = \frac{2a}{x} f_a(x)$$

and

$$f_{a-1}(x) - f_{a+1}(x) = 2\frac{\mathrm{d}f_a(x)}{x} \,,$$

where $f_a(x)$ stands for any of the above functions. Combinations of these formulas provide other useful equalities, such as

$$\left(\frac{\mathrm{d}}{x\,\mathrm{d}x}\right)^p [x^a f_a(x)] = x^{a-p} f_{a-p}(x)$$

or

$$\left(\frac{\mathrm{d}}{x\,\mathrm{d}x}\right)^p \left[\frac{f_a(x)}{x^a}\right] = (-1)^p \frac{f_{a+p}(x)}{x^{a+p}} \,,$$

where p is an integer.

Analogous formulas can be obtained even for $I_a(x)$ and $K_a(x)$. For example,

$$f_{a-1}(x) - f_{a+1}(x) = \frac{2a}{x} f_a(x)$$

and

$$f_{a-1}(x) + f_{a+1}(x) = 2\frac{\mathrm{d}f_a(x)}{x} \,,$$

where $f_a(x)$ stands for any of these two functions.

Another important relation is the multiplication theorem for function $J_a(x)$ that reads

$$\beta^{-a} J_a(\beta x) = \sum_{k=0}^{\infty} \frac{1}{k!} \left(\frac{(1-\beta^2)x}{2}\right)^k J_{k+a}(x) \,,$$

where a and β are arbitrary complex numbers.

B.1.7 Computation of Bessel and other related functions

Nowadays, Bessel and other related functions are mostly calculated using their expansion into fast converging series. The relevant efficient procedures are implemented in every good mathematical code such as Mathematica, Maple, and MathCad.

For more information about Bessel functions and their practical evaluation see, for example, Refs. 182–184.

B.2 ELLIPTIC INTEGRALS

Elliptic integrals originally appeared in connection with determining the length of an arc of an ellipse. Nowadays, we say that the elliptic integral is any integral of the type

$$E(x) = \int_a^x f(t, \sqrt{P(t)}) dt \,,$$

where f is a rational function, a a constant, and $P(x)$ a polynomial of degree 3 or 4 with single roots (but some exceptions from this general rule are possible). Every elliptic integral, however, can be modified into a form containing integrals of a rational function. We distinguish the elliptic integrals of the first, second, and third kinds. But none of them can be evaluated analytically.

B.2.1 Incomplete and complete elliptic integrals of the first kind

The incomplete elliptic integral of the first kind is usually denoted by the letter F and has the following form:

$$F(x, k) = \int_{t=0}^x \frac{dt}{\sqrt{(1 - t^2)(1 - k^2 t^2)}} \,.$$

Its complete version is given by the formula

$$K(k) = F(1, k) = \int_{t=0}^1 \frac{dt}{\sqrt{(1 - t^2)(1 - k^2 t^2)}}$$

and can easily be modified as

$$K(k) = \int_{\varphi=0}^{\pi/2} \frac{d\varphi}{\sqrt{1 - k^2 \sin^2 \varphi}} \,.$$

The integral $K(k)$ can be expressed using an infinite series

$$K(k) = \frac{\pi}{2} \left[1 + \left(\frac{1}{2}\right)^2 k^2 + \left(\frac{1 \cdot 3}{2 \cdot 4}\right)^2 k^4 + \cdots + \left(\frac{(2m-1)!!}{(2m)!!}\right)^2 k^{2m} + \cdots \right] \,,$$

and for specific values of the parameter k we obtain

$$K(0) = \frac{\pi}{2} \,,$$

$$K(1) \to \infty \,.$$

The function $K(k)$ is depicted in Fig. B.5.

B.2.2 Incomplete and complete elliptic integrals of the second kind

The incomplete elliptic integral of the second kind is usually denoted by the letter E and has the following form:

$$E(x, k) = \int_{t=0}^x \frac{\sqrt{1 - k^2 t^2}}{\sqrt{1 - t^2}} dt \,.$$

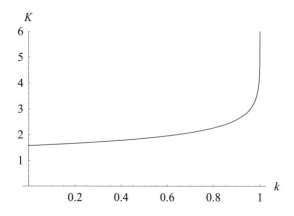

Figure B.5. Dependence of the complete elliptic integral $K(k)$ on parameter k.

Its complete version is given by the formula

$$E(k) = E(1, k) = \int_{t=0}^{1} \frac{\sqrt{1 - k^2 t^2}}{\sqrt{1 - t^2}}\, dt$$

and can easily be modified as

$$E(k) = \int_{\varphi=0}^{\pi/2} \sqrt{1 - k^2 \sin^2 \varphi}\, d\varphi \,.$$

The complete integral $E(k)$ can be expressed using an infinite series

$$E(k) = \frac{\pi}{2}\left[1 - \left(\frac{1}{2}\right)^2 \frac{k^2}{1} - \left(\frac{1 \cdot 3}{2 \cdot 4}\right)^2 \frac{k^4}{3} - \cdots - \left(\frac{(2m-1)!!}{(2m)!!}\right)^2 \frac{k^{2m}}{2m - 1} - \cdots \right],$$

and for specific values of the parameter k we obtain

$$E(0) = \frac{\pi}{2},$$

$$E(1) = 1.$$

The function $E(k)$ is depicted in Fig. B.6.

B.2.3   Incomplete and complete elliptic integrals of the third kind

These integrals are somewhat more complicated. An incomplete integral of this kind is given as

$$\Pi(n, x, k) = \int_{t=0}^{x} \frac{dt}{(1 - nt^2)\sqrt{(1 - t^2)(1 - k^2 t^2)}}\,.$$

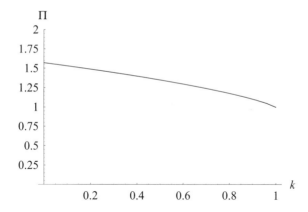

Figure B.6.   Dependence of the complete elliptic integral $E(k)$ on parameter k.

Its complete version is given by the formula

$$\Pi(n, k) = \Pi(n, 1, k) = \int_{t=0}^{x} \frac{dt}{(1 - nt^2)\sqrt{(1 - t^2)(1 - k^2 t^2)}}$$

and can easily be modified as

$$\Pi(n, k) = \int_{\varphi=0}^{\pi/2} \frac{d\varphi}{(1 - n\sin^2 \varphi)\sqrt{1 - k^2 \sin^2 \varphi}}.$$

Figure B.7 shows a family of functions $\Pi(n, k)$ for several parameters of n, $0 \le k < 1$.

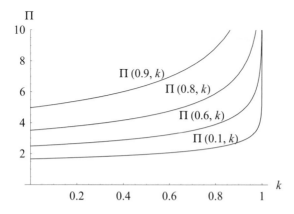

Figure B.7.   Dependence of the complete elliptic integral $\Pi(n, k)$ on k for selected parameters n.

B.2.4   Some other useful formulas

For the sake of completeness we present some more useful formulas and relations between particular elliptic integrals.

$$\int_{\varphi=0}^{\pi/2} \frac{\sin^2 \varphi \, d\varphi}{\sqrt{1-k^2 \sin^2 \varphi}} = \frac{K(k)-E(k)}{k^2},$$

$$\int_{\varphi=0}^{\pi/2} \frac{\cos^2 \varphi \, d\varphi}{\sqrt{1-k^2 \sin^2 \varphi}} = \frac{E(k)}{k^2} - \frac{1-k^2}{k^2} K(k),$$

$$\int_{\varphi=0}^{\pi/2} \frac{\sin^2 \varphi \, d\varphi}{(\sqrt{1-k^2 \sin^2 \varphi})^{3/2}} = \frac{E(k)}{k^2(1-k^2)} - \frac{K(k)}{k^2},$$

$$\int_{\varphi=0}^{\pi/2} \frac{d\varphi}{(\sqrt{1-k^2 \sin^2 \varphi})^{3/2}} = \frac{E(k)}{1-k^2},$$

$$\int_{\varphi=0}^{\pi/2} \frac{\cos^2 \varphi \, d\varphi}{(\sqrt{1-k^2 \sin^2 \varphi})^{3/2}} = \frac{K(k)-E(k)}{k^2},$$

$$\int_{\varphi=0}^{\pi/2} (\sqrt{1-k^2 \sin^2 \varphi})^{3/2} d\varphi = \frac{4-2k^2}{3} E(k) - \frac{1-m}{3} K(k),$$

$$\int_{\varphi=0}^{\pi/2} \sin^2 \varphi (\sqrt{1-k^2 \sin^2 \varphi}) \, d\varphi = \frac{2k^2-1}{3k^2} E(k) + \frac{1+k^2}{3k^2} K(k),$$

$$\int_{\varphi=0}^{\pi/2} \cos^2 \varphi (\sqrt{1-k^2 \sin^2 \varphi}) d\varphi = \frac{k^2+1}{3k^2} E(k) - \frac{1-k^2}{3k^2} K(k),$$

$$\frac{dK(k)}{dk} = \frac{(1-k^2)E(k)-K(k)}{k(1-k^2)},$$

$$\frac{dE(k)}{dk} = \frac{E(k)-K(k)}{k},$$

$$\int_{\varphi=0}^{\pi} \sqrt{a+\cos \varphi} \cdot d\varphi = \int_{\varphi=0}^{\pi} \sqrt{a-\cos \varphi} \cdot d\varphi = 2\sqrt{1+a} \cdot E\left(\sqrt{\frac{2}{1+a}}\right),$$

$$\int_{\varphi=0}^{\pi} \frac{d\varphi}{\sqrt{a+\cos \varphi}} = \int_{\varphi=0}^{\pi} \frac{d\varphi}{\sqrt{a-\cos \varphi}} = \frac{2}{\sqrt{1+a}} \cdot K\left(\sqrt{\frac{2}{1+a}}\right),$$

$$\int_{\varphi=0}^{\pi} \frac{\cos \varphi \, d\varphi}{\sqrt{a+\cos \varphi}} = -\int_{\varphi=0}^{\pi} \frac{\cos \varphi \, d\varphi}{\sqrt{a-\cos \varphi}}$$

$$= 2\sqrt{1+a} \cdot E\left(\sqrt{\frac{2}{1+a}}\right) - \frac{2a}{\sqrt{1+a}} \cdot K\left(\sqrt{\frac{2}{1+a}}\right),$$

$$\int_{\varphi=0}^{\pi} \frac{d\varphi}{(\sqrt{a + \cos\varphi})^{3/2}} = \int_{\varphi=0}^{\pi} \frac{d\varphi}{(\sqrt{a - \cos\varphi})^{3/2}} = \frac{2}{(a-1)\sqrt{1+a}} \cdot E\left(\sqrt{\frac{2}{1+a}}\right),$$

$$\int_{\varphi=0}^{\pi} \frac{\cos\varphi\,d\varphi}{(\sqrt{a + \cos\varphi})^{3/2}} = -\int_{\varphi=0}^{\pi} \frac{\cos\varphi\,d\varphi}{(\sqrt{a - \cos\varphi})^{3/2}}$$

$$= \frac{2}{\sqrt{1+a}} \cdot K\left(\sqrt{\frac{2}{1+a}}\right) - \frac{2a}{(a-1)\sqrt{1+a}} \cdot E\left(\sqrt{\frac{2}{1+a}}\right).$$

Complete elliptic integrals of the first and second kinds as well as the above formulas often occur in the evaluation of electric and magnetic fields produced by thin or massive circular rings or turns.

For more detailed information about the elliptic integrals see, for instance, Refs. 185–188.

B.3 SPECIAL POLYNOMIALS

The numerical integration is often based on techniques working with special types of polynomials creating orthogonal systems of functions on given intervals. This section is devoted to fundamental information about these systems and their properties. Special attention will particularly be paid to Legendre and Chebyshev polynomials of the first kind.

B.3.1 Legendre polynomials of the first kind

Legendre polynomials denoted by $P_n(x)$ represent the first-kind solution of the Legendre ordinary second-order differential equation in the form

$$(1 - x^2)\frac{d^2 y}{dx^2} - 2x\frac{dy}{dx} + n(n+1)y = 0,$$

where n is a nonnegative integer $n = 0, 1, 2, 3, \ldots$. Of course, as the basic equation is of the second order, we have to introduce other Legendre polynomials of the second kind $Q_n(x)$, so that

$$y(x) = C \cdot P_n(x) + D \cdot Q_n(x).$$

The Legendre polynomials may also be expressed by the formula

$$P_n(x) = \frac{1}{2^n n!} \frac{d^n (x^2 - 1)^n}{dx^n}$$

and the first six of them are given by the expressions

$$P_0(x) = 1,$$

$$P_1(x) = x,$$

$$P_2(x) = \tfrac{1}{2}(3x^2 - 1),$$

$$P_3(x) = \tfrac{1}{2}(5x^3 - 3x),$$

$$P_4(x) = \tfrac{1}{8}(35x^4 - 30x^2 + 3),$$

$$P_5(x) = \tfrac{1}{8}(63x^5 - 70x^3 + 15x).$$

Their shape in the interval $\langle -1 \le x \le 1 \rangle$ is shown in Fig. B.8..

It can easily be shown that the Legendre polynomials $P_n(x)$ form a complete orthogonal set in the interval $\langle -1 \le x \le 1 \rangle$; there holds

$$\int_{-1}^{1} P_i(x)P_j(x)\mathrm{d}x = \frac{2}{2i+1}\delta_{ij},$$

where the symbol δ_{ij} stands for the Kronecker delta.

B.3.2 Chebyshev polynomials of the first kind

Chebyshev polynomials denoted by $T_n(x)$ represent the first-kind solution of the Chebyshev ordinary second-order differential equation in the form

$$(1-x^2)\frac{\mathrm{d}^2 y}{\mathrm{d}x^2} - x\frac{\mathrm{d}y}{\mathrm{d}x} + n^2 y = 0,$$

where n is a nonnegative integer. These polynomials may also be calculated from the formula

$$T_n(x) = \cos(n\arccos(x))$$

and for the first six of them we obtain

$$T_0(x) = 1,$$

$$T_1(x) = x,$$

$$T_2(x) = 2x^2 - 1,$$

$$T_3(x) = 4x^3 - 3x,$$

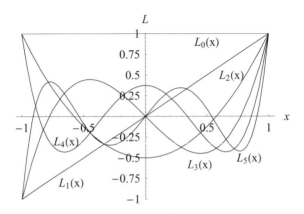

Figure B.8.   Legendre polynomials up to the fifth order in interval $\langle -1 \le x \le 1 \rangle$.

$$T_4(x) = 8x^4 - 8x^2 + 1 \,,$$

$$T_5(x) = 16x^5 - 20x^3 + 5x \,.$$

Their shape in interval $\langle -1 \le x \le 1 \rangle$ is depicted in Fig. B.9.

The Chebyshev polynomials $T_n(x)$ are orthogonal with respect to the weight

$$w = \frac{1}{\sqrt{1 - x^2}}$$

in the interval $\langle -1 \le x \le 1 \rangle$; there holds

$$\int_{-1}^{1} \frac{T_i(x)T_j(x)}{\sqrt{1 - x^2}} \, \mathrm{d}x = \frac{\pi}{2} \delta_{ij}$$

when i and j are not simultaneously zero. If $i = j = 0$, then

$$\int_{-1}^{1} \frac{T_0(x)T_0(x)}{\sqrt{1 - x^2}} \, \mathrm{d}x = \pi \,.$$

More information concerning the systems of orthogonal polynomial functions can be found in specialized books and other literature, see Refs. 189–191.

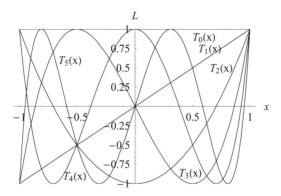

Figure B.9. Chebyshev polynomials up to the fifth order in interval $\langle -1 \le x \le 1 \rangle$.

APPENDIX C

INTEGRATION TECHNIQUES

C.1 ANALYTICAL CALCULATIONS OF SOME INTEGRALS OVER TYPICAL ELEMENTS

Many procedures associated with integral methods require evaluation of expressions containing integrals of the type $\int_S \mathrm{d}S/l$, $\int_S \ln l \, \mathrm{d}S$, or $\int_V \mathrm{d}V/l$ and others where S and V denote an element of surface or volume, respectively, and l the distance from the given reference point to a general integration point of element $\mathrm{d}S$ or $\mathrm{d}V$. The most usual surface elements in Cartesian coordinate systems are rectangles and triangles, while the most common volume elements are hexahedra and tetrahedra. Analogous elements (but with curvilinear edges or faces) could also be introduced in cylindrical or spherical coordinate systems but handling them, of course, is much more difficult.

The mentioned integrals may be proper (when the reference point lies outside the element) or improper (when the reference point lies inside it or on its boundary). Even when they reach finite values, their analytical computation is very complicated, particularly in the case of triangles or tetrahedra. On the other hand, numerical techniques (in the case of improper integrals) may often fail.

The next sections contain several useful results obtained analytically for the basic types of elements.

Integral Methods in Low-Frequency Electromagnetics. By I. Doležel, P. Karban, and P. Šolín. Copyright © 2009 John Wiley & Sons, Inc.

C.1.1 Rectangle

C.1.1.1 Integral $I_{\text{rec1}} = \int_S \mathrm{d}S/l$ Consider an arrangement in the Cartesian coordinate system (see Fig. C.1) containing a rectangular element of dimensions $2a, 2b$ in plane x, y, whose center is identical with the origin of this system. Consider also a reference point $P(u, v, w)$. This point is quite arbitrary so that $l = \sqrt{(x - u)^2 + (y - v)^2 + w^2}$. In this case we have

$$
\begin{aligned}
I_{\text{rec1}} &= \int_S \frac{\mathrm{d}S}{l} = \int_{x=-a}^{a} \int_{y=-b}^{b} \frac{\mathrm{d}y\,\mathrm{d}x}{\sqrt{(x - u)^2 + (y - v)^2 + w^2}} \\
&= \int_{x=-a}^{a} \ln \left[\frac{\sqrt{(x - u)^2 + (b - v)^2 + w^2} + b - v}{\sqrt{(x - u)^2 + (b + v)^2 + w^2} - b - v} \right] \mathrm{d}x \\
&= w \cdot \arctan \left[\frac{(u + a)(v - b)}{w\sqrt{(u + a)^2 + (v - b)^2 + w^2}} \right] \\
&\quad - w \cdot \arctan \left[\frac{(u - a)(v - b)}{w\sqrt{(u - a)^2 + (v - b)^2 + w^2}} \right] \\
&\quad - w \cdot \arctan \left[\frac{(u + a)(v + b)}{w\sqrt{(u + a)^2 + (v + b)^2 + w^2}} \right] \\
&\quad + w \cdot \arctan \left[\frac{(u - a)(v + b)}{w\sqrt{(u - a)^2 + (v + b)^2 + w^2}} \right] \\
&\quad + (v - b) \cdot \ln[\sqrt{(u + a)^2 + (v - b)^2 + w^2} - u - a] \\
&\quad + (u + a) \cdot \ln[\sqrt{(u + a)^2 + (v - b)^2 + w^2} - v + b] \\
&\quad - (v - b) \cdot \ln[\sqrt{(u - a)^2 + (v - b)^2 + w^2} - u + a] \\
&\quad - (u - a) \cdot \ln[\sqrt{(u - a)^2 + (v - b)^2 + w^2} - v + b] \\
&\quad - (v + b) \cdot \ln[\sqrt{(u + a)^2 + (v + b)^2 + w^2} - u - a] \\
&\quad - (u + a) \cdot \ln[\sqrt{(u + a)^2 + (v + b)^2 + w^2} - v - b] \\
&\quad + (v + b) \cdot \ln[\sqrt{(u - a)^2 + (v + b)^2 + w^2} - u + a] \\
&\quad + (u - a) \cdot \ln[\sqrt{(u - a)^2 + (v + b)^2 + w^2} - v - b] \,.
\end{aligned}
\tag{C.1}
$$

When $w = 0$ (the reference point lies in plane $z = 0$) we obtain

$$
\begin{aligned}
I_{\text{rec1}} &= (v - b) \cdot \ln[\sqrt{(u + a)^2 + (v - b)^2} - u - a] \\
&\quad + (u + a) \cdot \ln[\sqrt{(u + a)^2 + (v - b)^2} - v + b] \\
&\quad - (v - b) \cdot \ln[\sqrt{(u - a)^2 + (v - b)^2} - u + a] \\
&\quad - (u - a) \cdot \ln[\sqrt{(u - a)^2 + (v - b)^2} - v + b] \\
&\quad - (v + b) \cdot \ln[\sqrt{(u + a)^2 + (v + b)^2} - u - a] \\
&\quad - (u + a) \cdot \ln[\sqrt{(u + a)^2 + (v + b)^2} - v - b] \\
&\quad + (v + b) \cdot \ln[\sqrt{(u - a)^2 + (v + b)^2} - u + a] \\
&\quad + (u - a) \cdot \ln[\sqrt{(u - a)^2 + (v + b)^2} - v - b] \,,
\end{aligned}
\tag{C.2}
$$

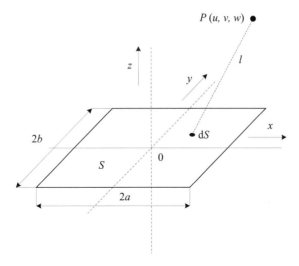

Figure C.1.   Calculation of $\int_S dS/l$ over a rectangle.

and, finally, for $u = 0$ and $v = 0$ (which is perhaps the most frequent case),

$$I_{rec1} = 2b \cdot \ln \left[\frac{\sqrt{a^2 + b^2} + a}{\sqrt{a^2 + b^2} - a} \right] + 2a \cdot \ln \left[\frac{\sqrt{a^2 + b^2} + b}{\sqrt{a^2 + b^2} - b} \right]. \tag{C.3}$$

C.1.1.2   Integral $I_{recln} = \int_S \ln l \, dS$ This integral often occurs in computations of 2D fields and we will suppose that their properties are independent of the z axis. The reference point (see Fig. C.1) now always lies in plane $z = 0$ ($w = 0$) so that $l = \sqrt{(x - u)^2 + (y - v)^2}$.

$$
\begin{aligned}
I_{\text{recln}} &= \int_S \ln l \, \mathrm{d}S = \int_{x=-a}^{a} \int_{y=-b}^{b} \ln[\sqrt{(x-u)^2 + (y-v)^2}] \, \mathrm{d}y \, \mathrm{d}x \\
&= \int_{x=-a}^{a} \left((x-u) \arctan\left[\frac{b+v}{x-u}\right] + (x-u) \arctan\left[\frac{b-v}{x-u}\right] - 2b \right) \mathrm{d}x \\
&\quad + \frac{1}{2} \int_{x=-a}^{a} \left((b-v) \ln[(b-v)^2 + (x-u)^2] \right. \\
&\quad + (b+v) \ln[(b+v)^2 + (x-u)^2] \big) \, \mathrm{d}x \\
&= \frac{1}{2}(a-u)(b-v) \ln[(a-u)^2 + (b-v)^2] \\
&\quad + \frac{1}{2}(a+u)(b-v) \ln[(a+u)^2 + (b-v)^2] \\
&\quad + \frac{1}{2}(a-u)(b+v) \ln[(a-u)^2 + (b+v)^2] \\
&\quad + \frac{1}{2}(a+u)(b+v) \ln[(a+u)^2 + (b+v)^2] \\
&\quad - 6ab + \frac{1}{2}[(b+v)^2 - (a+u)^2] \arctan\left[\frac{a+u}{b+v}\right] \\
&\quad + \frac{1}{2}[(b-v)^2 - (a-u)^2] \arctan\left[\frac{a-u}{b-v}\right] \\
&\quad + \frac{1}{2}[(b-v)^2 - (a+u)^2] \arctan\left[\frac{a+u}{b-v}\right] \\
&\quad + \frac{1}{2}[(b+v)^2 - (a-u)^2] \arctan\left[\frac{a-u}{b+v}\right].
\end{aligned}
\tag{C.4}
$$

For $u = 0$ and $v = 0$ (frequent case) we obtain

$$
I_{\text{recln}} = 2b^2 \arctan\left[\frac{a}{b}\right] + 2a^2 \arctan\left[\frac{b}{a}\right] - 6ab + 2ab \ln[a^2 + b^2].
\tag{C.5}
$$

The same result holds for reference points (a, b), $(-a, b)$, $(a, -b)$, and $(-a, -b)$ representing the vertices of the rectangle. The remaining limit cases (a, v), $(-a, v)$, $(u, -b)$, and $(-u, -b)$ (points lying on straight lines prolonging the sides of the rectangle) can easily be calculated from (C.4).

C.1.1.3 Integral $I_{recxr2} = \int_S (r_x/r^2)dS$ The integral occurs in 2D examples with motion. Starting from Fig. C.1 we have

$$I_{recxr2} = \int_{x=-a}^{x=a} \int_{y=-b}^{y=b} \frac{x-u}{(x-u)^2+(y-v)^2}\, dy\, dx$$

$$= \frac{1}{2} \int_{y=-b}^{y=b} \ln[(x-u)^2+(y-v)^2]_{x=-a}^{x=a}\, dy$$

$$= \frac{1}{2} \int_{y=-b}^{y=b} \left(\ln[(a-u)^2+(y-v)^2] - \ln[(a+u)^2+(y-v)^2]\right)\, dy$$

$$= (a-u)\left(\arctan\left[\frac{b-v}{a-u}\right] + \arctan\left[\frac{b+v}{a-u}\right]\right)$$

$$-(a+u)\left(\arctan\left[\frac{b-v}{a+u}\right] + \arctan\left[\frac{b+v}{a+u}\right]\right)$$

$$+\frac{b-v}{2}\ln[(a-u)^2+(b-v)^2] - \frac{b-v}{2}\ln[(a+u)^2+(b-v)^2]$$

$$+\frac{b+v}{2}\ln[(a-u)^2+(b+v)^2] - \frac{b+v}{2}\ln[(a+u)^2+(b-v)^2]. \quad \text{(C.6)}$$

The limit cases follow. For $a = u$

$$I_{recxr2} = -2u\left(\arctan\left[\frac{b-v}{2u}\right] + \arctan\left[\frac{b+v}{2u}\right]\right)$$

$$+\frac{b-v}{2}\ln[(b-v)^2] - \frac{b-v}{2}\ln[4u^2+(b-v)^2]$$

$$+\frac{b+v}{2}\ln[(b+v)^2] - \frac{b+v}{2}\ln[4u^2+(b-v)^2]. \quad \text{(C.7)}$$

For $a = -u$ we have

$$I_{recxr2} = 2u\left(\arctan\left[\frac{b-v}{2u}\right] + \arctan\left[\frac{b+v}{2u}\right]\right)$$

$$+\frac{b-v}{2}\ln[4u^2+(b-v)^2] - \frac{b-v}{2}\ln[(b-v)^2]$$

$$+\frac{b+v}{2}\ln[4u^2+(b+v)^2] - \frac{b+v}{2}\ln[(b-v)^2]. \quad \text{(C.8)}$$

For $b = v$

$$I_{recxr2} = (a-u)\arctan\left[\frac{2v}{a-u}\right] - (a+u)\arctan\left[\frac{2v}{a+u}\right]$$

$$+ v\ln[(a-u)^2+4v^2] - v\ln[(a+u)^2+4v^2] \quad \text{(C.9)}$$

and for $b = -v$

$$I_{\text{recxr2}} = (a - u)\arctan\left[\frac{-2v}{a - u}\right] + (a + u)\arctan\left[\frac{2v}{a + u}\right]$$
$$- v\ln[(a - u)^2 + 4v^2] + v\ln[(a + u)^2 + 4v^2].\qquad\text{(C.10)}$$

Computation of possible double limits (e.g., $a = u, b = v$) is easy and may be left to the reader.

C.1.1.4   Integral $I_{\text{recyr2}} = \int_S (r_y/r^2 \mathrm{d}S$ This is an analogous integral to I_{recxr2}:

$$
\begin{aligned}
I_{\text{recyr2}} &= \int_{x=-a}^{x=a}\int_{y=-b}^{y=b}\frac{y - v}{(x - u)^2 + (y - v)^2}\,\mathrm{d}y\,\mathrm{d}x\\
&= \frac{1}{2}\int_{x=-a}^{x=a}\ln[(x - u)^2 + (y - v)^2]_{y=-b}^{y=b}\,\mathrm{d}x\\
&= \frac{1}{2}\int_{x=-a}^{x=a}\left(\ln[(x - u)^2 + (b - v)^2] - \ln[(x - u)^2 + (b + v)^2]\right)\,\mathrm{d}x\\
&= (b - v)\left(\arctan\left[\frac{a - u}{b - v}\right] + \arctan\left[\frac{a + u}{b - v}\right]\right)\\
&\quad - (b + v)\left(\arctan\left[\frac{a - u}{b + v}\right] + \arctan\left[\frac{a + u}{b + v}\right]\right)\\
&\quad + \frac{a - u}{2}\ln[(a - u)^2 + (b - v)^2] - \frac{a - u}{2}\ln[(a - u)^2 + (b + v)^2]\\
&\quad + \frac{a + u}{2}\ln[(a + u)^2 + (b - v)^2] - \frac{a + u}{2}\ln[(a + u)^2 + (b + v)^2].
\end{aligned}
$$
$$\text{(C.11)}$$

Evaluation of the limit cases is trivial.

C.1.2   Triangle

C.1.2.1   Integral $I_{\text{trian1}} = \int_S (\mathrm{d}S/1)$ Consider a general triangle in plane x, y, in the arrangement shown in Fig. C.2 ($x_1 > 0, y_2 > 0$) and a reference point $P(u, v, w)$ whose position is quite arbitrary.

The integral is given as

$$I_{\text{trian1}} = \int_S \frac{\mathrm{d}y\,\mathrm{d}x}{\sqrt{(x - u)^2 + (y - v)^2 + w^2}}$$

and integration is performed over triangle 1231. It is now advantageous to introduce new coordinates p, q by the relations

$$x = x_1 p + x_2 q,\quad y = y_1 p + y_2 q = y_2 q,$$

$$p \in \langle 0, 1 - q\rangle,\quad q \in \langle 0, 1\rangle\qquad\text{(C.12)}$$

with Jacobian

$$J = x_1 y_2 - x_2 y_1 = x_1 y_2 = 2S,\qquad\text{(C.13)}$$

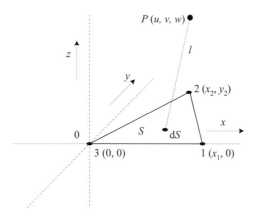

Figure C.2. Calculation of $\int_S dS/l$ over a triangle.

where S denotes the area of the triangle. Integral I_{trian1} then reads

$$I_{\text{trian1}} = 2S \cdot \int_{q=0}^{1} \int_{p=0}^{1-q} \frac{dp\, dq}{\sqrt{(x_1 p + x_2 q - u)^2 + (y_2 q - v)^2 + w^2}} \, . \tag{C.14}$$

The first integration with respect to p yields

$$I_{\text{trian1}} = y_2 \int_{q=0}^{1} \ln[aq - b + \sqrt{(y_2 q - v)^2 + (aq - b)^2 + w^2}]\, dq$$

$$-y_2 \int_{q=0}^{1} \ln[x_2 q - u + \sqrt{(y_2 q - v)^2 + (x_2 q - u)^2 + w^2}]\, dq\,, \tag{C.15}$$

where $a = x_2 - x_1$ and $b = u - x_1$. Analytical integration of (C.15) is much more complicated. It was carried out by a combination of SW Mathematica and a lot of manual work. Evidently, it is sufficient to evaluate the first integral in (C.15) because it differs from the second one only by coefficients. Let us introduce

$$A = a,\ B = -b,\ C = A^2 + y_2^2,\ D = 2AB - 2vy_2,\ G = \frac{(vA + y_2 B)^2}{A^2 + y_2^2} + w^2\,,$$

so that we can write

$$y_2 \int_{q=0}^{1} \ln[aq - b + \sqrt{(y_2 q - v)^2 + (aq - b)^2 + w^2}]\, dq$$

$$= y_2 \int_{q=0}^{1} \ln\left[Aq + B + \sqrt{C\left(q + \frac{D}{2C}\right)^2 + G}\right] dq\,. \tag{C.16}$$

Let us introduce a new variable, $s = \sqrt{C}(q + D/2C)$, so that

$$q = \frac{s}{\sqrt{C}} - \frac{D}{2C}, \ \mathrm{d}q = \frac{\mathrm{d}s}{\sqrt{C}}, \ s \in \left\langle s_1 = \frac{D}{2\sqrt{C}}, s_2 = \frac{2C+D}{2\sqrt{C}} \right\rangle,$$

and two new coefficients

$$P = \frac{A}{\sqrt{C}}, \ Q = B - \frac{AD}{2C}. \tag{C.17}$$

Now we obtain

$$y_2 \int_{q=0}^{1} \ln\left[Aq + B + \sqrt{C\left(q + \frac{D}{2C}\right)^2 + G} \right] \mathrm{d}q$$

$$= \frac{y_2}{\sqrt{C}} \int_{s=s_1}^{s_2} \ln\left[Ps + Q + \sqrt{s^2 + G} \right] \mathrm{d}s. \tag{C.18}$$

The last substitution,

$$s = \sqrt{G}\sinh[z], \ \mathrm{d}s = \sqrt{G}\cosh[z]\mathrm{d}z,$$

leading to the equality (the integrals are without limits)

$$\frac{y_2}{\sqrt{C}} \int \ln\left[Ps + Q + \sqrt{s^2 + G} \right] \mathrm{d}s$$

$$= y_2\sqrt{\frac{G}{C}} \int \cosh[z] \ln\left[P\sqrt{G}\sinh[z] + Q + \sqrt{G}\cosh[z] \right] \mathrm{d}z,$$

gives

$$\frac{y_2}{\sqrt{C}} \int \ln\left[Ps + Q + \sqrt{s^2 + G} \right] \mathrm{d}s$$

$$= \frac{y_2}{\sqrt{C}} \left(\sqrt{G}\sinh[z] + \frac{PQ}{P^2 - 1} \right) \ln\left[P\sqrt{G}\sinh[z] + Q + \sqrt{G}\cosh[z] \right]$$

$$- \sqrt{\frac{G}{C}}\sinh[z]y_2 - \frac{Qzy_2}{(P^2 - 1)\sqrt{C}}$$

$$+ \frac{2y_2\sqrt{G(1 - P^2) - Q^2}}{(P^2 - 1)\sqrt{C}} \arctan\left[\frac{(Q - \sqrt{G})\tanh[z/2] - \sqrt{G}P}{\sqrt{G(1 - P^2) - Q^2}} \right]$$

and after the back substitution for z we have

$$\frac{y_2}{\sqrt{C}} \int \ln[Ps + Q + \sqrt{s^2 + G}] \, ds$$

$$= \frac{y_2}{\sqrt{C}} \left(s + \frac{PQ}{P^2 - 1} \right) \ln[Ps + Q + \sqrt{s^2 + G}] - \frac{s}{\sqrt{C}} y_2$$

$$- \frac{Qy_2}{(P^2 - 1)\sqrt{C}} \ln \left[\frac{s + \sqrt{s^2 + G}}{\sqrt{G}} \right]$$

$$+ \frac{2y_2\sqrt{G(1 - P^2) - Q^2}}{(P^2 - 1)\sqrt{C}} \arctan \left[\frac{(Q - \sqrt{G})(\sqrt{s^2 + G} - \sqrt{G}) - s\sqrt{G}P}{s\sqrt{G(1 - P^2) - Q^2}} \right].$$

$$\text{(C.19)}$$

When $w = 0$ the formula reads

$$\frac{y_2}{\sqrt{C}} \int \ln[Ps + Q + \sqrt{s^2 + G}] \, ds$$

$$= \frac{y_2}{\sqrt{C}} \left(s + \frac{PQ}{P^2 - 1} \right) \ln[Ps + Q + \sqrt{s^2 + G}] - \frac{s}{\sqrt{C}} y_2$$

$$- \frac{Qy_2}{(P^2 - 1)\sqrt{C}} \ln \left[\frac{s + \sqrt{s^2 + G}}{\sqrt{G}} \right]. \qquad \text{(C.20)}$$

The final result is obtained after substituting upper and lower limits s_2 and s_1 given in (C.17).

C.1.2.2 Integral $I_{\text{trian ln}} = \int_S \ln l \, dS$ In the same way as in the previous case, we get (the reference point always lies in plane xy so that $w = 0$)

$$I_{\text{trian ln}} = \int_S \ln \sqrt{(x - u)^2 + (y - v)^2} \, dS, \qquad \text{(C.21)}$$

where S is the area of the triangle. After introducing new variables p and q according to (C.12), we can write

$$I_{\text{trian ln}} = \frac{x_1 y_2}{2} \cdot \int_{q=0}^{1} \int_{p=0}^{1-q} \ln[(x_1 p + x_2 q - u)^2 + (y_2 q - v)^2] \, dp \, dq. \qquad \text{(C.22)}$$

The first integration with respect to p yields

$$I_{\text{trianln}} = y_2 \int_{q=0}^{1} [T_1(q) + T_2(q) - T_3(q) - T_4(q) - T_5(q) + T_6(q)] \, dq,$$

where

$$T_1(q) = (y_2 q - v) \arctan\left[\frac{A_1 q + B_1}{y_2 q - v}\right],$$

$$T_2(q) = \tfrac{1}{2}(A_1 q + B_1) \ln[(A_1 q + B_1)^2 + (y_2 q - v)^2],$$

$$T_3(q) = -(A_1 q + B_1),$$

$$T_4(q) = (y_2 q - v) \arctan\left[\frac{A_2 q + B_2}{y_2 q - v}\right],$$

$$T_5(q) = \tfrac{1}{2}(A_2 q + B_2) \ln[(A_2 q + B_2)^2 + (y_2 q - v)^2],$$

$$T_6(q) = -(A_2 q + B_2),$$

$$A_1 = x_2 - x_1, \; B_1 = -(u - x_1), \; A_2 = x_2, \; B_2 = -u. \qquad (C.23)$$

As can easily be seen, it is enough to calculate the integral

$$y_2 \int_{q=0}^{1} [T_1(q) + T_2(q) - T_3(q)] \, dq$$

and subtract integral

$$y_2 \int_{q=0}^{1} [T_4(q) + T_5(q) - T_6(q)] \, dq$$

that differs just by coefficients A_2, B_2. The result of the first operation provides

$$y_2 \int_{q=0}^{1} [T_1(q) + T_2(q) - T_3(q)] \, dq$$

$$= \frac{y_2}{4(A_1^2 + y_2^2)}(A_1 v^2 - A_1 B_1^2 + 2vy_2 B_1) \ln[v^2 + B_1^2]$$

$$+ \frac{y_2}{4}\left(A_1 + 2B_1 - \frac{A_1 v^2 - A_1 B_1^2 + 2vy_2 B_1}{A_1^2 + y_2^2}\right) \ln[(v - y_2)^2 + (A_1 + B_1)^2]$$

$$+ \frac{y_2(2v - y_2)}{2} \arctan\left[\frac{A_1 + B_1}{v - y_2}\right]$$

$$+ \frac{y_2(v^2 y_2 - B_1^2 y_2 - 2vA_1 B_1)}{2(A_1^2 + y_2^2)} \arctan\left[\frac{A_1 B_1 - vy_2}{vA_1 + B_1 y_2}\right]$$

$$- \frac{y_2(v^2 y_2 - B_1^2 y_2 - 2vA_1 B_1)}{2(A_1^2 + y_2^2)} \arctan\left[\frac{A_1^2 + A_1 B_1 - vy_2 + y_2^2}{vA_1 + B_1 y_2}\right]$$

$$- \frac{3}{4}y_2(A_1 + 2B_1). \qquad (C.24)$$

C.1.2.3 *Integral* $I_{\text{trian xr2}} = \int_S (r_x/r^2) dS$ *for* $w = 0$ After introducing new variables p and q (see (C.12)) the integral for the triangle in Fig. C.2 reads

$$
\begin{aligned}
I_{\text{trian xr2}} &= x_1 y_2 \int_{q=0}^{1} \int_{p=0}^{1-q} \frac{(x_1 p + x_2 q - u) dp \, dq}{\sqrt{(x_1 p + x_2 q - u)^2 + (y_2 q - v)^2}} \\
&= \frac{y_2}{2} \int_{q=0}^{1} \ln[(x_1 p + x_2 q - u)^2 + (y_2 q - v)^2]_{p=0}^{p=1-q} dq \\
&= \frac{y_2}{2} \int_{q=0}^{1} \left(\ln[(y_2 q - v)^2 + (q A_1 + B_1)^2] \right. \\
&\qquad \left. - \ln[(y_2 q - v)^2 + (q A_2 + B_2)^2] \right) dq ,
\end{aligned}
\tag{C.25}
$$

where

$$
A_1 = x_2 - x_1, \; B_1 = -(u - x_1), \; A_2 = x_2, \; B_2 = -u .
\tag{C.26}
$$

Now it is sufficient to calculate the integral of the first term (with coefficients A_1, B_1) and subtract the same expression with coefficients A_2, B_2. In this way (after putting $C = y_2 - v$), we gradually obtain

$$
\begin{aligned}
&\frac{y_2}{2} \int_{q=0}^{1} \ln[(y_2 q - v)^2 + (q A_1 + B_1)^2] dq \\
&= -y_2 + \frac{y_2(A_1 v + B_1 y_2)}{A_1^2 + y_2^2} \left(\arctan\left[\frac{A_1^2 + A_1 B_1 + C y_2}{A_1 v + B_1 y_2} \right] - \arctan\left[\frac{A_1 B_1 - v y_2}{A_1 v + B_1 y_2} \right] \right) \\
&\quad + \frac{y_2(A_1 B_1 - v y_2)}{2(A_1^2 + y_2^2)} \left(\ln[(A_1 + B_1)^2 + C^2] - \ln[B_1^2 + v^2] \right) \\
&\quad + \frac{y_2}{2} \ln[(A_1 + B_1)^2 + C^2] .
\end{aligned}
\tag{C.27}
$$

C.1.2.4 *Integral* $I_{\text{trian yr2}} = \int_S (r_y/r^2) dS$ *for* $w = 0$ After introducing new variables p and q (see (C.12)) the integral for the triangle in Fig. C.2 reads

$$
\begin{aligned}
I_{\text{trian xr2}} &= x_1 y_2 \int_{q=0}^{1} \int_{p=0}^{1-q} \frac{(y_2 q - v) dp \, dq}{\sqrt{(x_1 p + x_2 q - u)^2 + (y_2 q - v)^2}} \\
&= y_2 \int_{q=0}^{1} \left(\arctan\left[\frac{q A_1 + B_1}{q y_2 - v} \right] - \arctan\left[\frac{q A_2 + B_2}{q y_2 - v} \right] \right) dq ,
\end{aligned}
\tag{C.28}
$$

where A_1, B_1, A_2, B_2 are given by (C.26). Again we can calculate only the first part of the integral with coefficients A_1, B_1 and subtract the second part with coefficients A_2, B_2. We obtain (putting $C = y_2 - v$)

$$
y_2 \int_{q=0}^{1} \arctan \frac{qA_1 + B_1}{qy_2 - v} \, dq
$$

$$
= y_2 \arctan \frac{A_1 + B_1}{C}
$$

$$
+ \frac{y_2(A_1 B_1 - v y_2)}{A_1^2 + y_2^2} \left(\arctan \left[\frac{A_1 B_1 - v y_2}{A_1 v + B_1 y_2} \right] \right.
$$

$$
\left. - \arctan \left[\frac{A_1(A_1 + B_1) + y_2 C}{A_1 v + B_1 y_2} \right] \right)
$$

$$
+ \frac{y_2(A_1 v + B_1 y_2)}{2(A_1^2 + y_2^2)} \left(\ln[(A_1 + B_1)^2 + C^2] - \ln[B_1^2 + v^2] \right) . \qquad \text{(C.29)}
$$

C.1.3   A ring of rectangular cross section

Elements of this type occur in discrete computations of axisymmetric arrangements (see Fig. C.3).

Here, it is necessary to calculate the integral

$$
I = \int_V \frac{\cos \varphi \, dV}{l} ,
$$

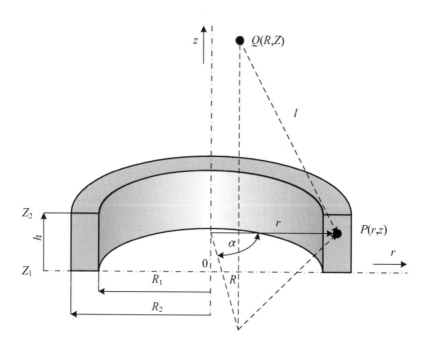

Figure C.3.   Calculation of $\int_V [(\cos \varphi dV)/l]$. over a ring of rectangular cross-section

where V is the volume of the element and l is the distance between the reference point Q and a general integration point P of the element. This integral may be rewritten as

$$I = \int_{\varphi=0}^{2\pi} \cos\varphi \left[\int_{r=R_1}^{R_2} \int_{z=Z_1}^{Z_2} \frac{r\,dr\,dz}{\sqrt{r^2 + R^2 + (z-Z)^2 - 2rR\cos\varphi}} \right] d\varphi .$$

After two analytical integrations (not quite trivial) we obtain

$$I = \int_{\varphi=0}^{2\pi} \cos\varphi \left[G(R_2, Z_2) - G(R_1, Z_2) - G(R_2, Z_1) + G(R_1, Z_1) \right] d\varphi , \qquad (C.30)$$

where

$$
\begin{aligned}
G(r,z) = {}& R(z-Z)\cos\varphi \ln(r - R\cos\varphi + \sqrt{r^2+R^2+(z-Z)^2 - 2rR\cos\varphi}) \\
&+ \frac{z-Z}{2}\sqrt{r^2+R^2+(z-Z)^2 - 2rR\cos\varphi} \\
&+ \frac{(r^2 - R^2\cos(2\varphi))}{2}\ln(z - Z + \sqrt{r^2+R^2+(z-Z)^2 - 2rR\cos\varphi}) \\
&- R^2\cos\varphi\sin\varphi \arctan\frac{(z-Z)(r - R\cos\varphi)}{R\sin\varphi\sqrt{r^2+R^2+(z-Z)^2 - 2rR\cos\varphi}} .
\end{aligned}
$$

Integral (C.30) has to be calculated numerically, using, for example, Gauss' quadrature formulas.

C.1.4 A brick

In this section we evaluate the integral

$$I = \int_V \frac{dV}{l} ,$$

where V is a brick having the dimensions given in Fig. C.4 and l is the distance between the reference point Q and a general integration point of the brick.

The integral can be rewritten as

$$I = \int_{x=X_1}^{X_2} \int_{y=Y_1}^{Y_2} \int_{z=Z_1}^{Z_2} \frac{dz\,dy\,dx}{\sqrt{(x-X)^2 + (y-Y)^2 + (z-Z)^2}} ,$$

which gives

$$
\begin{aligned}
I = {}& G(X_2, Y_2, Z_2) - G(X_2, Y_2, Z_1) + G(X_2, Y_1, Z_1) - G(X_2, Y_1, Z_2) \\
&- G(X_1, Y_2, Z_2) + G(X_1, Y_2, Z_1) - G(X_1, Y_1, Z_1) + G(X_1, Y_1, Z_2) .
\end{aligned}
$$

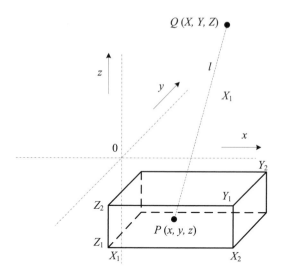

Figure C.4. Calculation of $\int_V (\mathrm{d}V/l)$ over a brick.

Here,

$$
\begin{aligned}
G(x, y, z) = {} & (x - X)(y - Y) \ln(z - Z + \sqrt{(x - X)^2 + (y - Y)^2 + (z - Z)^2}) \\
& + (x - X)(z - Z) \ln(y - Y + \sqrt{(x - X)^2 + (y - Y)^2 + (z - Z)^2}) \\
& + (y - Y)(z - Z) \ln(x - X + \sqrt{(x - X)^2 + (y - Y)^2 + (z - Z)^2}) \\
& - \frac{(x - X)^2}{2} \arctan\left[\frac{(y - Y)(z - Z)}{(x - X)\sqrt{(x - X)^2 + (y - Y)^2 + (z - Z)^2}}\right] \\
& - \frac{(y - Y)^2}{2} \arctan\left[\frac{(x - X)(z - Z)}{(y - Y)\sqrt{(x - X)^2 + (y - Y)^2 + (z - Z)^2}}\right] \\
& - \frac{(z - Z)^2}{2} \arctan\left[\frac{(x - X)(y - Y)}{(z - Z)\sqrt{(x - X)^2 + (y - Y)^2 + (z - Z)^2}}\right].
\end{aligned}
$$

C.2 TECHNIQUES OF NUMERICAL INTEGRATION

Evaluation of numerous integrals occurring in the numerical schemes and algorithms discussed in this book cannot be performed analytically. But even when it is possible, application of numerical techniques may substantially be faster, because the analytical integration often leads to very complicated resultant formulas. Let us mention, for instance, integrals of the type

$$
I(x_0, y_0, z_0) = \int_\Omega \frac{f(x, y, z)}{r} \mathrm{d}\Omega,
$$

where $f(x, y, z)$ is a polynomial function generally in three variables,

$$r = \sqrt{(x - x_0)^2 + (y - y_0)^2 + (z - z_0)^2},$$

the distance between the reference point (x_0, y_0, z_0) and the integration point (x, y, z), and Ω the domain of integration. In such a case the order of the numerical integration should correspond to the order of the polynomial. If the integrated function contains nonpolynomial terms, one has to be very careful and choose the order of accuracy of the quadrature rather a little higher than a little lower.

This section summarizes the principal schemes used for the numerical quadrature and discusses their advantages and drawbacks. In our implementations we usually prefer the Gauss quadrature because it mostly requires less computer time than the other schemes and so far we have always been satisfied with the quality of its results.

On the other hand, it can hardly be said that one of the quadrature rules is better than the others. Obviously, results obtained from various quadrature schemes of the same order of accuracy are exactly the same (or identical up to the precision of the finite computer arithmetic) for polynomials up to the same order — this is the definition. But dramatically different results can be obtained by applying the same rules to polynomials of higher-order, nonpolynomial functions or, in the worst case, oscillating functions. A limited order of the numerical integration of oscillating functions may give quite arbitrary results. It is the responsibility of each one to choose quadrature rules that fit the nature of the problem to be solved.

The fundamentals of numerical integration are dealt with in a number of references where we can find more detailed information about application of these techniques (at least in the case of simpler examples); see Refs. 192–196.

In the following we say that a quadrature rule is of nth order of accuracy if it integrates exactly all polynomials of the order n or lower (no matter whether in one or more dimensions).

C.2.1   Numerical integration in one dimension

The basic ideas of the numerical quadrature will be illustrated on 1D schemes. Let $g(y)$ be a function continuous in interval $< a, b >$, where $a < b$. Its polynomial quadrature of order n on this interval is defined as

$$\int_a^b g(y)\mathrm{d}y \approx \sum_{k=0}^n A_{n,k} g(y_{n,k}), \tag{C.31}$$

where the symbols $A_{n,k}$ and $y_{n,k}$, $k = 0, 1, \ldots, n$ denote the quadrature coefficients and nodes, respectively. The nodes $y_{n,k}$, $k = 0, 1, \ldots, n$ are supposed distinct.

Putting

$$y = cx + d, \quad c = \frac{b - a}{2}, \quad d = \frac{b + a}{2}, \tag{C.32}$$

and substituting into (C.31), we get another formula where the integration is carried out along the reference abscissa $< -1, 1 >$:

$$\int_a^b g(y)\mathrm{d}y = \int_{-1}^1 f(x)\mathrm{d}x \approx \sum_{k=0}^n w_{n,k} f(x_{n,k}), \tag{C.33}$$

where $f(x) = g(cx + d)$ and $w_{n,k} = A_{n,k}/c$. Coefficients $w_{n,k}$ are called weights.

There exist a number of possibilities in choosing suitable weights $w_{n,k}$ and nodes $x_{n,k}$ for the numerical quadrature of function $f(x)$. The selection is always based on the requirement that for certain functions the numerical quadrature provides exact results. The best way is to use polynomials of general forms. However, we can use other types of functions whose integrals can be determined analytically. The choice of such functions (monomials, goniometric functions, etc.) usually does not represent any serious problem as long as the order of accuracy is reasonably small. But in the case of higher orders one has to be very careful, because the results may be burdened by unacceptable round-off and other errors.

C.2.1.1   Newton–Cotes quadrature

The Newton–Cotes type quadrature rules are generally based on the summation of weighted function values at equidistantly distributed integration points. The $(n+1)$st point Newton–Cotes closed quadrature formula of accuracy n for polynomials of the nth order is characterized by points

$$x_{n,k} = -1 + k \cdot h_n, \quad k = 0, 1, \ldots, n, \tag{C.34}$$

where

$$h_n = 2/n, \quad n > 0.$$

The integration weights $w_{n,k}, \quad k = 0, 1, \ldots, n$ can be determined by several methods. Widely known are techniques based on the Taylor expansion of $f(x)$, Lagrange polynomials or Vandermonde matrix, for example. We will use the last way to illustrate their computation.

Let $p(x)$ be a polynomial of order n expressed as

$$p(x) = \sum_{k=0}^{n} p_{n,k} x^k \tag{C.35}$$

and let us put

$$\int_{-1}^{1} p(x)\,dx = \sum_{k=0}^{n} \frac{p_{n,k}}{k+1}[1 - (-1)^{k+1}] = \sum_{k=0}^{n} w_{n,k} p(x_{n,k}). \tag{C.36}$$

The comparison of terms on both sides of (C.36) containing the individual coefficients $p_{n,k}$ leads to a system of linear algebraic equations in the form

$$
\begin{aligned}
w_{n,0} + w_{n,1} + \cdots + w_{n,n} &= [1 - (-1)^1]/1 = 2, \\
w_{n,0}x_{n,0} + w_{n,1}x_{n,1} + \cdots + w_{n,n}x_{n,n} &= [1 - (-1)^2]/2 = 0, \\
&\vdots \\
w_{n,0}x_{n,0}^k + w_{n,1}x_{n,1}^k + \cdots + w_{n,n}x_{n,n}^k &= [1 - (-1)^{k+1}]/(k+1), \\
&\vdots \\
w_{n,0}x_{n,0}^n + w_{n,1}x_{n,1}^n + \cdots + w_{n,n}x_{n,n}^n &= [1 - (-1)^{n+1}]/(n+1).
\end{aligned}
\tag{C.37}
$$

After rearranging and substituting for h_n from (C.34) we obtain

$$
\begin{pmatrix}
1 & 1^0 & 2^0 & \cdots & n^0 \\
0 & 1^1 & 2^1 & \cdots & n^1 \\
0 & 1^2 & 2^2 & \cdots & n^2 \\
\cdots & \cdots & \cdots & \cdots & \cdots \\
0 & 1^n & 2^n & \cdots & n^n
\end{pmatrix}
\cdot
\begin{pmatrix}
w_{n,0} \\
w_{n,1} \\
w_{n,2} \\
\cdots \\
w_{n,n}
\end{pmatrix}
=
\begin{pmatrix}
2n^0/1 \\
2n^1/2 \\
2n^2/3 \\
\cdots \\
2n^n/(n+1)
\end{pmatrix}. \tag{C.38}
$$

The system is characterized by the Vandermonde matrix that is always regular and, thus, invertible. Moreover, the weights $w_{n,k}$, $k = 0, \ldots, n$ depend only on parameter n. On the other hand, the Vandermonde matrix is not well conditioned and for $n > 7$ some weights are negative, which can lead to round-off problems during the evaluation of the right-hand side of (C.38). Therefore, the closed Newton–Cotes formulas are mostly used just for low values of n.

Tables C.1–C.4 contain selected integration points and weights for low values of n. Notice that in one dimension the $(n+1)$st point closed Newton–Cotes quadrature rule has an order of accuracy n. In general, every closed Newton–Cotes formula is exact for all polynomials whose order is by one degree less than the order of the derivative in its error term. For even values of n the integration is exact for all polynomials of order $n+1$.

Particular weights for $n = 5$, $n = 6$, and $n = 7$ can be found in a number of references. But their application is not frequent.

In a similar way we can obtain the open Newton–Cotes quadrature formulas approximating the integral only by means of function values at internal points of interval $< a, b >$ (i.e., points $x_{n,1}, x_{n,2}, \ldots, x_{n,n-1}$), while points $x_{n,0} = a$ and $x_{n,n} = b$ are omitted. These formulas can be used, for example, when values $f(a)$ and $f(b)$ are unavailable. But in this case the error of the quadrature is much higher than errors of the closed Newton–Cotes formulas and for this reason they are used only very rarely.

C.2.1.2 Chebyshev quadrature
The Chebyshev type quadrature rules are based on the summation of equally weighted values of the integrated functions at non-equidistantly

Table C.1. Closed Newton–Cotes quadrature constants, order $n = 1$ (trapezoidal rule).

point No.	x-coordinate	weight
1	−1	1
2	1	1

Table C.2. Closed Newton-Cotes quadrature constants, order $n = 2$ (Simpson's 1/3 rule).

point No.	x-coordinate	weight
1	−1	$\frac{1}{3}$
2	0	$\frac{4}{3}$
3	1	$\frac{1}{3}$

Table C.3.   Closed Newton–Cotes quadrature constants, order $n = 3$ (Simpson's 3/8 rule).

point No.	x-coordinate	weight
1	-1	$\frac{1}{4}$
2	$-1/3$	$\frac{3}{4}$
3	$1/3$	$\frac{3}{4}$
4	1	$\frac{1}{4}$

Table C.4.   Closed Newton–Cotes quadrature constants, order $n = 4$ (Bode's rule).

point No.	x-coordinate	weight
1	-1	$\frac{7}{45}$
2	$-1/2$	$\frac{32}{45}$
3	0	$\frac{4}{15}$
4	$1/2$	$\frac{32}{45}$
5	1	$\frac{7}{45}$

distributed integration points. The $(n + 1)$st point Chebyshev quadrature rule for the reference interval $< -1, 1 >$ reads

$$\int_{-1}^{1} f(x)\mathrm{d}x \approx \frac{2}{n} \sum_{k=1}^{n} f(x_{n,k}) \, . \tag{C.39}$$

Notice that the uniform weight $2/n$ is determined from the integration of constant functions. The integration points (abscissas) are obtained after inserting sufficiently many linearly independent functions with known integrals (e.g., various orthogonal functions) into (C.39) and resolving the arising system of nonlinear algebraic equations. It can be shown that these abscissas may be obtained by using terms up to y^n in the Maclaurin series of the function

$$s_n(z) = \exp\left\{ \frac{n}{2} \left[-2 + \ln[(1 - z^2)(1 - z^{-2})] \right] \right\} \, . \tag{C.40}$$

Then the abscissas are the roots of function

$$C_n(x) = x^n \cdot s_n\left(\frac{1}{x}\right) \, . \tag{C.41}$$

The roots are all real only for $n < 8$ and $n = 9$. These values of n represent the only permissible orders for the Chebyshev quadrature. The polynomials $C_n(x)$ are given (C.40) by the formulas

$$C_2(x) = \tfrac{1}{3}(3x^2 - 1) \, ,$$

$$C_3(x) = \tfrac{1}{2}(2x^3 - x),$$

$$C_4(x) = \tfrac{1}{45}(45x^4 - 30x^2 + 1),$$

$$C_5(x) = \tfrac{1}{72}(72x^5 - 60x^3 + 7x),$$

$$C_6(x) = \tfrac{1}{105}(105x^6 - 105x^4 + 21x^2 - 1),$$

$$C_7(x) = \tfrac{1}{6480}(6480x^7 - 7560x^5 + 2142x^3 - 149x),$$

$$C_9(x) = \tfrac{1}{22400}(22400x^9 - 33600x^7 + 15120x^5 - 2280x^3 + 53x).$$

In the 1D case the n-point Chebyshev quadrature rules achieve $(n+1)$st order of accuracy. In Tables C.5–C.8 we shall list the integration points for $n = 2, 3, 4$, and 5 computed in SW Mathematica. For higher (and allowed) values of n the points can be found in numerous references.

Let us mention one specific case. If we numerically integrate expressions of the type

$$\frac{f(x)}{\sqrt{1 - x^2}}, \tag{C.42}$$

the corresponding Gauss–Chebyshev explicit formula reads

$$\int_{-1}^{1} \frac{f(x)}{\sqrt{1 - x^2}} \mathrm{d}x \approx \frac{\pi}{n} \sum_{i=1}^{n} f\left[\cos \frac{(2i - 1) \cdot \pi}{2n} \right]. \tag{C.43}$$

C.2.1.3 *Lobatto (Radau) quadrature* The Lobatto (Radau) type quadrature rules are based on the summation of weighted function values at nonequidistantly distributed integration points containing the endpoints of the interval of integration.

Table C.5. Chebyshev quadrature constants, $n = 2$.

point No.	x-coordinate	weight
1	$-\frac{1}{\sqrt{3}}$	1
2	$\frac{1}{\sqrt{3}}$	1

Table C.6. Chebyshev quadrature constants, $n = 3$.

point No.	x-coordinate	weight
1	$-\frac{1}{\sqrt{2}}$	$\frac{2}{3}$
2	0	$\frac{2}{3}$
3	$\frac{1}{\sqrt{2}}$	$\frac{2}{3}$

Table C.7.   Chebyshev quadrature constants, $n = 4$.

point No.	x-coordinate	weight
1	$-\sqrt{\frac{5+2\sqrt{5}}{15}}$	$\frac{1}{2}$
2	$-\sqrt{\frac{5-2\sqrt{5}}{15}}$	$\frac{1}{2}$
3	$\sqrt{\frac{5-2\sqrt{5}}{15}}$	$\frac{1}{2}$
4	$\sqrt{\frac{5+2\sqrt{5}}{15}}$	$\frac{1}{2}$

Table C.8.   Chebyshev quadrature constants, $n = 5$.

point No.	x-coordinate	weight
1	$-\sqrt{\frac{5+\sqrt{11}}{12}}$	$\frac{2}{5}$
2	$-\sqrt{\frac{5-\sqrt{11}}{12}}$	$\frac{2}{5}$
3	0	$\frac{2}{5}$
4	$\sqrt{\frac{5-\sqrt{11}}{12}}$	$\frac{2}{5}$
5	$\sqrt{\frac{5+\sqrt{11}}{12}}$	$\frac{2}{5}$

The n-point Lobatto (Radau) formula for interval $< -1, 1 >$ reads

$$\int_{-1}^{1} f(x)\mathrm{d}x \approx w_{n,1}f(-1) + \sum_{i=2}^{n-1} w_{n,i}f(x_{n,i}) + w_{n,n}f(1). \tag{C.44}$$

Analogously as for Chebyshev's rules, the integration points and weights are obtained after inserting sufficiently many linearly independent functions with known integrals into (C.44) and resolving the arising system of nonlinear algebraic equations. Notice that for the n-point rule we have $n - 2$ unknown points and n weights. Thus, we need $2n - 2$ equations, so that this quadrature rule achieves $(2n - 3)$th order of accuracy.

The unknown points $x_{n,i}$ are the roots of polynomial $L'_{n-1}(x)$, where $L_{n-1}(x)$ is Legendre's polynomial of order $n - 1$. The corresponding weights are expressed by formulas

$$w_{n,k} = \frac{2}{n \cdot (n-1) \cdot L^2_{n-1}(x_i)}, \quad k = 2, \ldots, n-1 \tag{C.45}$$

while the weights at the endpoints are

$$w_{n,1} = w_{n,n} = \frac{2}{n \cdot (n-1)}. \tag{C.46}$$

Legendre's polynomial of the nth order may be determined, for example, by computation from Rodrigues' formula

$$L_n(x) = \frac{1}{2^n n!} \cdot \frac{d^n}{dx^n}[(x^2 - 1)^n]$$

and from the second to the eighth order they acquire (together with their derivatives) the following forms:

$$L_2(x) = \tfrac{1}{2}(3x^2 - 1), \quad L_2'(x) = 3x,$$

$$L_3(x) = \tfrac{1}{2}(5x^3 - 3x), \quad L_3'(x) = \tfrac{1}{2}(15x^2 - 3),$$

$$L_4(x) = \tfrac{1}{8}(35x^4 - 30x^2 + 3), \quad L_4'(x) = \tfrac{1}{2}(35x^3 - 15x),$$

$$L_5(x) = \tfrac{1}{8}(63x^5 - 70x^3 + 15x), \quad L_5'(x) = \tfrac{1}{8}(315x^4 - 210x^2 + 15),$$

$$L_6(x) = \tfrac{1}{16}(231x^6 - 315x^4 + 105x^2 - 5), \quad L_6'(x) = \tfrac{1}{8}(693x^5 - 630x^3 + 105x),$$

$$L_7(x) = \tfrac{1}{16}(429x^7 - 693x^5 + 315x^3 - 35x),$$

$$L_7'(x) = \tfrac{1}{16}(3003x^6 - 3465x^4 + 945x^2 - 35),$$

$$L_8(x) = \tfrac{1}{128}(6435x^8 - 12012x^6 + 6930x^4 - 1260x^2 + 35),$$

$$L_8'(x) = \tfrac{1}{16}(6435x^7 - 9009x^5 + 3465x^3 - 315x). \tag{C.47}$$

Let us list the integration points and weights for a few low orders of accuracy computed in SW Mathematica (Tables C.9–C.12).

The tables of integration points (abscissas) and corresponding coefficients for higher values of n can be found in numerous references.

C.2.1.4 *Gaussian quadrature*
The Gauss type quadrature rules are based on the summation of weighted function values at nonequidistantly distributed integration points. The n-point Gauss quadrature rule for the reference abscissa $< -1, 1 >$ reads

$$\int_{-1}^{1} f(x)dx \approx \sum_{k=1}^{n} w_{n,k} f(x_{n,k}). \tag{C.48}$$

Similarly as for the Chebyshev and Lobatto (Radau) rules, the integration points and weights are obtained after inserting sufficiently many linearly independent functions with known integrals into (C.48) and resolving the arising system of nonlinear algebraic equations.

Table C.9. Lobatto (Radau) quadrature constants, $n = 3$.

point No.	x-coordinate	weight
1	-1	$\frac{1}{3}$
2	0	$\frac{4}{3}$
3	1	$\frac{1}{3}$

Table C.10. Lobatto (Radau) quadrature constants, $n = 4$.

point No.	x-coordinate	weight
1	-1	$\frac{1}{6}$
2	$-\frac{1}{\sqrt{5}}$	$\frac{5}{6}$
3	$\frac{1}{\sqrt{5}}$	$\frac{5}{6}$
4	1	$\frac{1}{6}$

Table C.11. Lobatto (Radau) quadrature constants, $n = 5$.

point No.	x-coordinate	weight
1	-1	$\frac{1}{10}$
2	$-\sqrt{\frac{3}{7}}$	$\frac{49}{90}$
3	0	$\frac{32}{45}$
4	$\sqrt{\frac{3}{7}}$	$\frac{49}{90}$
5	1	$\frac{1}{10}$

Table C.12. Lobatto (Radau) quadrature constants, $n = 6$.

point No.	x-coordinate	weight
1	-1	$\frac{1}{15}$
2	$-\sqrt{\frac{7+2\sqrt{7}}{21}}$	$\frac{14-\sqrt{7}}{30}$
3	$-\sqrt{\frac{7-2\sqrt{7}}{21}}$	$\frac{14+\sqrt{7}}{30}$
4	$\sqrt{\frac{7-2\sqrt{7}}{21}}$	$\frac{14+\sqrt{7}}{30}$
5	$\sqrt{\frac{7+2\sqrt{7}}{21}}$	$\frac{14-\sqrt{7}}{30}$
6	1	$\frac{1}{15}$

Since we have $2n$ unknown parameters at our disposal (n integration points $x_{n,k}$ and n weights $w_{n,k}$), the resultant formula will be accurate for all polynomials of order $2n - 1$ and lower.

Fortunately it can be shown that the integration points are the roots of the Legendre polynomials. Their computation is not quite trivial, but their values are tabulated in a lot of references. With the integration points $x_{n,k}$ that are known the nonlinear system reduces to a system of linear algebraic equations.

As the integration points (abscissas) are the roots of the Legendre polynomials $L_n(x)$ (see (C.46)), it can be shown that the corresponding weights are given by formulas

$$w_{n,k} = \frac{2}{(1 - x_{n,k}^2)[L_n'(x_{n,k})]^2},$$

where $x_{n,k}$ is the relevant integration point.

Let us list the integration points and weights for a few lower n-point rules calculated by the SW Mathematica (see Tables C.13–C.16).

Tables for higher values of n can be found in specialized references.

C.2.2 Numerical integration in two dimensions

Numerical integration in two dimensions represents a much more complicated business because

- the domain of integration may generally be a 2D domain of arbitrary shape,

- algorithms for finding the integration points and corresponding weights are not as simple as in the 1D case.

Nevertheless, much attention is currently paid to further development of the relevant techniques whose application is highly promising, particularly in modern numerical methods of higher orders of accuracy. In this chapter the fundamentals of the methodology will be illustrated on quadrilateral and triangular elements widely used for the numerical solution of many engineering problems.

Table C.13. Gauss quadrature constants, $n = 2$.

point No.	x-coordinate	weight
1	$-\dfrac{1}{\sqrt{3}}$	1
2	$\dfrac{1}{\sqrt{3}}$	1

Table C.14. Gauss quadrature constants, $n = 3$.

point No.	x-coordinate	weight
1	$-\dfrac{\sqrt{15}}{5}$	$\dfrac{5}{9}$
2	0	$\dfrac{8}{9}$
3	$\dfrac{\sqrt{15}}{5}$	$\dfrac{5}{9}$

Table C.15. Gauss quadrature constants, $n = 4$.

point No.	x-coordinate	weight
1	$-\sqrt{\frac{525+70\sqrt{30}}{35}}$	$\frac{18-\sqrt{30}}{36}$
2	$-\sqrt{\frac{525-70\sqrt{30}}{35}}$	$\frac{18+\sqrt{30}}{36}$
3	$\sqrt{\frac{525-70\sqrt{30}}{35}}$	$\frac{18+\sqrt{30}}{36}$
4	$\sqrt{\frac{525+70\sqrt{30}}{35}}$	$\frac{18-\sqrt{30}}{36}$

Table C.16. Gauss quadrature constants, $n = 5$.

point No.	x-coordinate	weight
1	$-\sqrt{\frac{245+14\sqrt{70}}{21}}$	$\frac{322-13\sqrt{70}}{900}$
2	$-\sqrt{\frac{245-14\sqrt{70}}{21}}$	$\frac{322+13\sqrt{70}}{900}$
3	0	$\frac{128}{225}$
4	$\sqrt{\frac{245-14\sqrt{70}}{21}}$	$\frac{322+13\sqrt{70}}{900}$
5	$\sqrt{\frac{245+14\sqrt{70}}{21}}$	$\frac{322-13\sqrt{70}}{900}$

C.2.2.1 *Numerical integration over a quadrilateral* Consider a quadrilateral Ω in plane u, v (see Fig. C.5) and a function $f(u, v)$ defined at every point of this domain. The function is supposed continuous on Ω.

The task is to find the integral

$$I_\Omega = \int_\Omega f(u, v) d\Omega = \int_{u=a}^{b} \int_{v=c}^{d} f(u, v) dv \, du \,.$$

Introducing the substitution

$$u = p_1 x + q_1, \quad v = p_2 y + q_2, \quad du = p_1 \, dx, \quad dv = p_2 \, dy \,,$$

where

$$p_1 = \frac{b-a}{2}, \quad q_1 = \frac{b+a}{2}, \quad p_2 = \frac{d-c}{2}, \quad q_2 = \frac{d+c}{2} \,,$$

we immediately obtain

$$I_\Omega = p_1 p_2 \int_{x=-1}^{1} \int_{y=-1}^{1} g(x, y) \, dy \, dx \,,$$

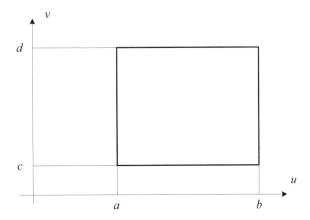

Figure C.5.   A quadrilateral.

where
$$g(x,y) = f(p_1 x + q_1, p_2 y + q_2).$$

Now the integration is performed over the reference quadrilateral $\langle -1, 1 \rangle \times \langle -1, 1 \rangle$.

It is clear that the easiest way of finding I_Ω is to use the quadrature formulas based on the Cartesian product of two 1D quadrature rules in the directions x and y. If we consider the 1D formula

$$\int_{-1}^{1} h(x)\,\mathrm{d}x = \sum_{i=1}^{n_x} w_{n_x,i} h(x_{n_x,i}),$$

where n_x is the number of integration points (see (C.33)), we can analogously write

$$\int_{x=-1}^{1} \int_{y=-1}^{1} g(x,y)\,\mathrm{d}y\,\mathrm{d}x = \sum_{i=1}^{n_x} \sum_{j=1}^{n_y} w_{n_x,i}\, w_{n_y,j}\, g(x_{n_x,i}, y_{n_y,j}).$$

This formula integrates exactly all polynomials in two variables x and y of the orders n_x and n_y, respectively.

Nevertheless, despite its simplicity the formula works with a lot of integration points (their number being $n_x n_y$). And this is the principal drawback of this algorithm. For complete polynomials of order n with $(n+1)(n+2)/2$ nonzero terms, there exist much more efficient formulas as will be shown in the next paragraph.

The most economical are the Gauss quadrature rules requiring fewer integration points than their product counterparts discussed earlier. Some of them are even known to require the minimum number of integration points. These points will be determined for complete polynomials only, starting from the symmetry of the reference quadrilateral.

Consider an integral of the type

$$\int_{u=-1}^{1} \int_{v=-1}^{1} u^j v^k \,\mathrm{d}v\,\mathrm{d}u = \frac{1-(-1)^{j+1}}{j+1} \cdot \frac{1-(-1)^{k+1}}{k+1}, \qquad (\text{C.49})$$

where j and k are nonnegative integers. If j or k is odd, the integral is equal to zero, so that such terms need not be taken into account for the computations. If both values of j and k

are odd, the value of the integral is equal to $4/(j+1)(k+1)$. And due to the equality of integrals

$$\int_{u=-1}^{1}\int_{v=-1}^{1} u^j v^k dv\, du = \int_{u=-1}^{1}\int_{v=-1}^{1} u^k v^j dv\, du\,,$$

we can work just with integrals of type (C.49) in which $j \geq k$.

Let us illustrate this fact on an example of a polynomial of variables u and v of an even order n. Now we can consider only its terms containing

$$1, u^2, u^4, \ldots, u^n\,,$$

$$u^2 v^2, u^4 v^2, \ldots, u^{n-2} v^2\,,$$

$$u^4 v^4, u^6 v^4, \ldots, u^{n-4} v^4\,,$$

$$u^6 v^6, u^8 v^6, \ldots, u^{n-6} v^6, \ldots\,.$$

The total number m of such terms is

$$m = \frac{(n+6)(n+2)}{16} \text{ for } n=4k+2 \text{ and } m = \frac{(n+4)^2}{16} \text{ for } n=4k\,,$$

while the number of all terms l of the polynomial is

$$l = \frac{(n+2)(n+1)}{2}\,.$$

We immediately see that consideration of symmetry is essential.

The problem of finding the minimum number of integration points was dealt with by Dunavant [197]. He assembled an overview of the minimum numbers of Gauss' quadrature points for both their symmetric and nonsymmetric selections. His results for the polynomials of the order up to 12 are listed in Table. C.17 (more detailed information can be found in Ref. 94).

Dunavant divided the integration points into four groups with different numbers of unknowns and tested their best choices. The algorithm leads to the solution of a strongly nonlinear number of equations. The optimal points for several low-order polynomials are listed in Tables C.18–C.20.

C.2.2.2 Numerical integration over a triangle

Consider a triangle Ω_1 in plane u, v (see Fig. C.6) and a function $f(u,v)$ defined over this triangle. The function is supposed continuous on Ω_1.

Now the task is to find the integral

$$I = \int_{\Omega_1} f(u,v) dS\,.$$

We first introduce the transform

$$u = a_1 x + b_1 y + c_1, \quad v = a_2 x + b_2 y + c_2$$

that maps the triangle Ω_1 to a reference triangle Ω_2 according to Fig. C.7.

Table C.17. Minimum numbers of quadrature points for Gauss quadrature points over a quadrilateral.

order of the polynomial	minimum number of nonsymmetric points	minimum number of symmetric points	achieved number of symmetric points
1	1	1	1
2	3	4	4
3	4	4	4
4	6	8	8
5	7	8	8
6	10	12	12
7	12	12	12
8	15	20	20
9	17	20	20
10	21	25	25
11	24	25	25
12	28	36	36

Table C.18. Gauss quadrature on the quadrilateral, $n = 0, 1$.

point No.	coordinate x	coordinate y	weight
1	0	0	4

Table C.19. Gauss quadrature on the quadrilateral, $n = 2, 3$.

point No.	coordinate x	coordinate y	weight
1	0.577350269189626	0.577350269189626	1
2	0.577350269189626	-0.577350269189626	1
3	-0.577350269189626	0.577350269189626	1
4	-0.577350269189626	-0.577350269189626	1

The unknown coefficients $a_1, b_1, c_1, a_2, b_2, c_2$ follow from the system of equations

$$u_1 = -a_1 - b_1 + c_1 ,$$
$$u_2 = a_1 - b_1 + c_1 ,$$
$$u_3 = -a_1 + b_1 + c_1 ,$$
$$v_1 = -a_2 - b_2 + c_2 ,$$
$$v_2 = a_2 - b_2 + c_2 ,$$
$$v_3 = -a_2 + b_2 + c_2 ,$$

Table C.20. Gauss quadrature on the quadrilateral, $n = 4, 5$.

point No.	coordinate x	coordinate y	weight
1	0.683130051063973	0	0.816326530612245
2	−0.683130051063973	0	0.816326530612245
3	0	0.683130051063973	0.816326530612245
4	0	−0.683130051063973	0.816326530612245
5	0.881917103688197	0.881917103688197	0.183673469387755
6	0.881917103688197	−0.881917103688197	0.183673469387755
7	−0.881917103688197	0.881917103688197	0.183673469387755
8	−0.881917103688197	−0.881917103688197	0.183673469387755

assigning the individual vertices of the triangle Ω to the new reference triangle. The solution of this system is

$$a_1 = \frac{u_2 - u_1}{2}, \quad b_1 = \frac{u_3 - u_1}{2}, \quad c_1 = \frac{u_3 + u_2}{2},$$

$$a_2 = \frac{v_2 - v_1}{2}, \quad b_2 = \frac{v_3 - v_1}{2}, \quad c_2 = \frac{v_3 + v_2}{2}.$$

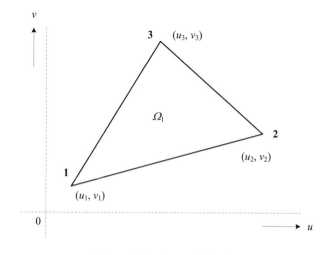

Figure C.6. A general triangle.

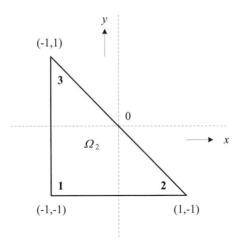

Figure C.7.   The reference triangle.

The Jacobian of the mapping is

$$J = \left| \begin{pmatrix} \partial u/\partial x & \partial u/\partial y \\ \partial v/\partial x & \partial v/\partial y \end{pmatrix} \right| = a_1 b_2 - a_2 b_1 = \frac{1}{4}[(u_2 - u_1)(v_3 - v_1) - (u_3 - u_1)(v_2 - v_1)]$$

$$= \frac{1}{4} \left| \begin{pmatrix} 1 & 1 & 1 \\ u_1 & u_2 & u_3 \\ v_1 & v_2 & v_3 \end{pmatrix} \right| = \frac{S}{2},$$

where S is the area of the original triangle. Now there holds

$$I_{\Omega_1} = \int_{\Omega_1} f(u,v)\,\mathrm{d}S = \int_{\Omega_2} g(x,y)\cdot J\,\mathrm{d}S = J \int_{\Omega_2} g(x,y)\cdot \mathrm{d}S = \frac{S}{2} \int_{\Omega_2} g(x,y)\cdot \mathrm{d}S$$

$$= \frac{S}{2} \int_{x=-1}^{1} \int_{y=-1}^{-x} g(x,y)\,\mathrm{d}y\,\mathrm{d}x , \tag{C.50}$$

where

$$g(x,y) = f(a_1 x + b_1 y + c_1, a_2 x + b_2 y + c_2).$$

Now we will show the possibilities of the numerical computation of integral (C.50).

We first extend the *Newton–Cotes quadrature* rules on the reference triangle. Let us consider an integer $n \geq 2$. Now we cover the area of the reference triangle by $m = n(n+1)/2$ points (of coordinates x_i, y_i, $i = 1, 2, \ldots, m$) forming schemes depicted for $n = 2$, $n = 3$, and $n = 4$ in Fig. C.8. The distance between the neighboring points in both directions x and y is equal to $2/(n-1)$.

Now we suppose that

$$\int_{x=-1}^{1} \int_{y=-1}^{-x} g(x,y)\,\mathrm{d}y\,\mathrm{d}x \approx \sum_{i=1}^{m} g(x_i, y_i)w_i ,$$

where w_i, $i = 1, 2, \ldots, m$ are the corresponding weights. The above relation has to become exact for any polynomial in two variables x and y of order $n - 1$. We shall illustrate it on a polynomial of order $n - 1 = 2$ in the form

$$g(x, y) = a + bx + cy + dx^2 + exy + fy^2.$$

Now

$$\int_{x=-1}^{1} \int_{y=-1}^{-x} g(x, y)\, dy\, dx = \frac{2}{3}(3a - b - c + d + f) \tag{C.51}$$

and (as $m = 6$)

$$\sum_{i=1}^{6} g(x_i, y_i)w_i = (a - b + c + d - e + f)w_1 + (a - b + d)w_2$$
$$+ (a - b - c + d + e + f)w_2 + aw_4 + (a - c + f)w_5 + (a + b - c + d - e + f)w_6 \tag{C.52}$$

The comparison of both results (C.51) and (C.52) provides

$$w_1 = 0, \; w_2 = \frac{10}{9}, \; w_3 = -\frac{2}{9}, \; w_4 = \frac{2}{9}, \; w_5 = \frac{10}{9}, \; w_6 = -\frac{2}{9}.$$

Evidently, $w_1 + w_2 + w_3 + w_4 + w_5 + w_6 = 2$, which is the area of the reference triangle.

The Newton–Cotes method is obviously simple. Nevertheless, the choice of the nodal points is far from optimal. It is better to use the points satisfying the Gauss–Lobatto quadrature rules and, particularly, Gauss' integration.

Gauss' quadrature rules in two dimensions follow the same principles as in one spatial dimension. Finding their coordinates and corresponding weights, however, is much more complicated.

We start again from the approximation

$$\int_{x=-1}^{1} \int_{y=-1}^{-x} g(x, y)\, dy\, dx \approx \sum_{i=1}^{m} g(x_i, y_i)w_i, \tag{C.53}$$

where m is the number of integration points (and here m is not equal to the number of terms of the polynomial as in the previous case). Quantities x_i, y_i, and w_i, $i = 1, 2, \ldots n$, are unknown. We shall illustrate their computation (and also some associated difficulties) on two examples, for polynomials of the first and second orders.

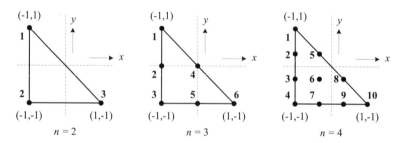

Figure C.8. Distribution of the points in the reference triangle for $n = 2$, $n = 3$, and $n = 4$.

Let the first-order polynomial be given as

$$g(x, y) = a + bx + cy.$$

Now

$$\int_{x=-1}^{1} \int_{y=-1}^{-x} g(x, y) = \frac{2}{3}(3a - b - c).$$

Considering $m = 1$, we immediately have

$$\tfrac{2}{3}(3a - b - c) = w_1(a + bx_1 + cy_1).$$

The comparison of terms corresponding to coefficients a, b, and c provides

$$w_1 = 2, \quad w_1 x_1 = -\tfrac{2}{3}, \quad w_1 y_1 = -\tfrac{2}{3}$$

and hence

$$w_1 = 2, \quad x_1 = -\tfrac{1}{3}, \quad y_1 = -\tfrac{1}{3}.$$

A complete second-order polynomial may be written in the form

$$g(x, y] = a + bx + cy + dx^2 + exy + fy^2.$$

In this case

$$\int_{x=-1}^{1} \int_{y=-1}^{-x} g(x, y) = \frac{2}{3}(3a - b - c + d + f).$$

Let us first try $m = 2$. We immediately have

$$\tfrac{2}{3}(3a - b - c + d + f) = w_1(a + bx_1 + cy_1 + dx_1^2 + ex_1 y_1 + fy_1^2)$$
$$+ w_2(a + bx_2 + cy_2 + dx_2^2 + ex_2 y_2 + fy_2^2).$$

The comparison of terms corresponding to coefficients a, b, c, d, e and f provides six nonlinear equations in the form

$$w_1 + w_2 = 2,$$
$$w_1 x_1 + w_2 x_2 = -\tfrac{2}{3},$$
$$w_1 y_1 + w_2 y_2 = -\tfrac{2}{3},$$
$$w_1 x_1 y_1 + w_2 x_2 y_2 = 0,$$
$$w_1 x_1^2 + w_2 x_2^2 = \tfrac{2}{3},$$
$$w_1 y_1^2 + w_2 y_2^2 = \tfrac{2}{3}.$$

But it can easily be shown that these equations are not independent, so that they do not provide any unambiguous solution. We must, therefore, select at least three points to satisfy (C.53). In this way we obtain nine nonlinear equations for six unknowns, which means that we can choose among them.

The same holds for polynomials of higher degrees. Moreover, the number of terms of many complete polynomials is not divisible by 3 (e.g., the complete polynomial of the order of $n = 3$ has 10 terms, so that the minimum number of integration points is 4). Nevertheless, the fundamental difficulties connected with finding these points and their weights for higher orders n consist in the necessity of solving relatively large systems of highly nonlinear algebraic equations. Lyness ad Jespersen [198] and later Dunavant [200] gradually worked out algorithms providing the integration points and their weights up to the order of the polynomial $n = 20$. But some of these points lie outside the triangle and some weights are negative, which can substantially deteriorate the accuracy of integration in the case of oscillatory functions or functions with steep changes. When integrating functions with such features, it is possible to apply adaptive formulas that compare results obtained from several different refinement levels.

Table C.21 lists the minimum predicted numbers and existing numbers of integration points over the reference triangle up to $n = 15$. More information can be found in Ref. 199.

Finally, Tables C.22–C.26 contain particular integration points and weights for the reference triangle up to $n = 5$.

Table C.21. Minimum and achieved numbers of integration points over the reference triangle.

order of the polynomial	known minimum number of points	predicted minimum number of points	achieved number of points
1	1		1
2	3		3
3	4		4
4	6		6
5	7		7
6	12		12
7	13		13
8	16		16
9	19		19
10	24		25
11		17	27
12		33	33
13		36	37
14		40	42
15		45	48

Table C.22. Integration points for the reference triangle, $n = 1$.

point No.	coordinate x	coordinate y	weight
1	−0.333333333333333	−0.333333333333333	2

Table C.23. Integration points for the reference triangle, $n = 2$.

point No.	coordinate x	coordinate y	weight
1	−0.666666666666667	−0.666666666666667	0.666666666666667
2	−0.666666666666667	0.333333333333333	0.666666666666667
3	0.333333333333333	−0.666666666666667	0.666666666666667

Table C.24. Integration points for the reference triangle, $n = 3$.

point No.	coordinate x	coordinate y	weight
1	−0.333333333333333	−0.333333333333333	−1.125000000000000
2	−0.600000000000000	−0.600000000000000	1.041666666666667
3	−0.600000000000000	0.200000000000000	1.041666666666667
4	200000000000000	−0.600000000000000	1.041666666666667

Table C.25. Integration points for the reference triangle, $n = 4$.

point No.	coordinate x	coordinate y	weight
1	−0.108103018168070	−0.108103018168070	0.446763179356022
2	−0.108103018168070	−0.783793963663860	0.446763179356022
3	−0.783793963663860	−0.108103018168070	0.446763179356022
4	−0.816847572980458	−0.816847572980458	0.219903487310644
5	−0.816847572980458	0.633695145960918	0.219903487310644
6	0.633695145960918	−0.816847572980458	0.219903487310644

C.2.3 Numerical integration in three dimensions

Numerical integration in three dimensions is generally a big complication. The number of integration points is usually very high and more economical integration is still a challenge (except for the reference cube) because it is difficult to find the Gaussian points and cor-

Table C.26. Integration points for the reference triangle, $n = 5$.

point No.	coordinate x	coordinate y	weight
1	−0.333333333333333	−0.333333333333333	0.450000000000000
2	−0.059715871789770	−0.059715871789770	0.264788305577012
3	−0.059715871789770	−0.880568256420460	0.264788305577012
4	−0.880568256420460	−0.059715871789770	0.264788305577012
5	−0.797426985353088	−0.797426985353088	0.251878361089654
6	−0.797426985353088	0.594853970706174	0.251878361089654
7	0.594853970706174	−0.797426985353088	0.251878361089654

responding weights. Nevertheless, we will mention at least numerical integration over a brick and tetrahedron.

C.2.3.1 *Integration over a brick*   Consider a brick Ω in plane u, v, w (see Fig. C.9) and a function $f(u, v, w)$ defined at every point of this domain. The function is supposed continuous on Ω.

It is necessary to calculate the integral

$$I_\Omega = \int_\Omega f(u, v, w)\mathrm{d}\Omega = \int_{u=a}^{b} \int_{v=c}^{d} \int_{w=e}^{f} f(u, v, w)\ \mathrm{d}w\ \mathrm{d}v\ \mathrm{d}u \,.$$

Introducing the substitution

$$u = p_1 x + q_1 \,, \quad v = p_2 y + q_2 \,, \quad w = p_3 z + q_3 \,,$$

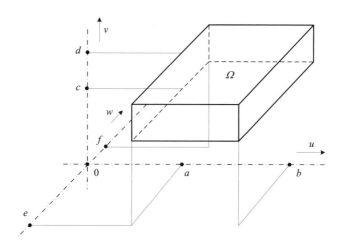

Figure C.9.   A general brick.

$$kdu = p_1\,\mathrm{d}x\,,\quad \mathrm{d}v = p_2\,\mathrm{d}y\,,\quad \mathrm{d}w = p_3\,\mathrm{d}z\,,$$

where

$$p_1 = \frac{b-a}{2}\,,\quad q_1 = \frac{b+a}{2}\,,\quad p_2 = \frac{d-c}{2}\,,$$

$$q_2 = \frac{d+c}{2}\,,\quad p_3 = \frac{f-e}{2}\,,\quad q_3 = \frac{f+e}{2}\,,$$

we obtain

$$I_\Omega = p_1 p_2 p_3 \int_{x=-1}^{1}\int_{y=-1}^{1}\int_{z=-1}^{1} g(x,y,z)\,\mathrm{d}z\,\mathrm{d}y\,\mathrm{d}x\,,$$

where

$$g(x,y,z) = f(p_1 x + q_1, p_2 y + q_2, p_3 z + q_3)\,.$$

Now the integration is performed over the reference cube $\langle -1,1\rangle \times \langle -1,1\rangle \times \langle -1,1\rangle$.

It is clear that the easiest way of finding I_Ω is to use the quadrature formulas based on the triple Cartesian product of three 1D quadrature rules in the directions x, y, and z. If we consider the 1D formula

$$\int_{-1}^{1} h(x)\,\mathrm{d}x = \sum_{i=1}^{n_x} w_{n_x,i}h(x_{n_x,i})\,,$$

where n_x is the number of integration points (see (C.33)), we can analogously write

$$\int_{x=-1}^{1}\int_{y=-1}^{1}\int_{z=-1}^{1} g\ (x,y,z)\,\mathrm{d}z\,\mathrm{d}y\,\mathrm{d}x$$

$$= \sum_{i=1}^{n_x}\sum_{j=1}^{n_y}\sum_{k=1}^{n_z} w_{n_x,i}\,w_{n_y,j}\,w_{n_z,k}\,g(x_{n_x,i},y_{n_y,j},y_{n_z,k})\ \text{(C.54)}$$

This formula integrates exactly all polynomials in three variables x, y, and z of the orders n_x, n_y, and n_z, respectively.

Nevertheless, analogous to the case of a quadrilateral, the formula works with a lot of integration points (their number being $n_x n_y n_z$), which is the principal drawback of this algorithm. For complete polynomials of order n with $(n+1)(n+2)(n+3)/6$ nonzero terms, there exist much more efficient formulas as will be shown in the next section.

C.2.3.2 *Economical integration over the reference cube*   Similar to the case of the reference square, the economical quadrature rules are derived from the manifold symmetry of the reference cube (in which we can construct 9 planes of symmetry).

Consider the integral

$$I = \int_{x=-1}^{1}\int_{y=-1}^{1}\int_{z=-1}^{1} x^j y^k z^l\,\mathrm{d}z\,\mathrm{d}y\,\mathrm{d}x\,,\qquad\text{(C.55)}$$

where j, k, and l are positive integers. If j, k, or l is odd, the integral vanishes. The symmetry with respect to various planes also allows considering only terms in which $j \geq k$ and $k \geq l$.

Dunavant [201] provides the minimum numbers of integration points for odd polynomial orders. These numbers are listed in Table C.27.

Dunavant [201] recommends dividing the integration points into seven groups with different numbers of unknowns. Then he tests the best choice of points. The results for polynomials up to the order $n = 5$ are listed in Tables C.28–C.30.

C.2.3.3 *Integration over a tetrahedron* Consider a tetrahedron Ω_1 (see Fig. C.10) and a function $f(u, v, w)$ defined over it. The function is supposed continuous on Ω_1.
Now the task is to find the integral

$$I = \int_{\Omega_1} f(u, v, w) dV .$$

We first introduce the transform

$$u = a_1 x + b_1 y + c_1 z + d_1 , \quad v = a_2 x + b_2 y + c_2 z + d_2 , \quad w = a_3 x + b_3 y + c_3 z + d_3$$

that maps the tetrahedron Ω_1 to a reference tetrahedron Ω_2 according to Fig. C.11.

Table C.27.   Minimum numbers of integration points over the Gaussian quadrature for the reference cube.

order of the polynomial	known minimum number of nonsymmetric points	known minimum number of symmetric points	achieved number of symmetric points
1	1	1	1
3	4	6	6
5	10	14	14
7	20	27	27
9	35	52	53
11	56	77	89
13	84	127	151
15	120	175	235
17	165	253	307
19	220	333	435

Table C.28.   Integration points for the reference cube, $n = 1$.

point No.	coordinate x	coordinate y	coordinate z	weight
1	0	0	0	8

Table C.29.   Integration points for the reference cube, $n = 2, 3$.

point No.	coordinate x	coordinate y	coordinate z	weight
1	1	0	0	1.3333333333
2	−1	0	0	1.3333333333
3	0	1	0	1.3333333333
4	0	−1	0	1.3333333333
5	0	0	1	1.3333333333
6	0	0	−1	1.3333333333

Table C.30.   Integration points for the reference cube, $n = 4, 5$.

point No.	coordinate x	coordinate y	coordinate z	weight
1	0.7958224257	0	0	0.8864265927
2	−0.7958224257	0	0	0.8864265927
3	0	0.7958224257	0	0.8864265927
4	0	−0.7958224257	0	0.8864265927
5	0	0	0.7958224257	0.8864265927
6	0	0	−0.7958224257	0.8864265927
7	0.7587869106	0.7587869106	0.7587869106	0.3351800554
8	0.7587869106	−0.7587869106	0.7587869106	0.3351800554
9	0.7587869106	0.7587869106	−0.7587869106	0.3351800554
10	0.7587869106	−0.7587869106	−0.7587869106	0.3351800554
11	−0.7587869106	0.7587869106	0.7587869106	0.3351800554
12	−0.7587869106	−0.7587869106	0.7587869106	0.3351800554
13	−0.7587869106	0.7587869106	−0.7587869106	0.3351800554
14	−0.7587869106	−0.7587869106	−0.7587869106	0.3351800554

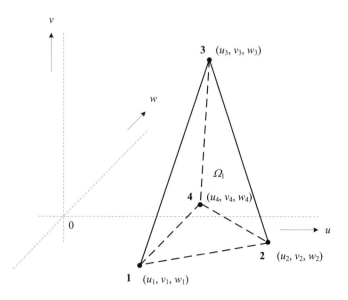

Figure C.10. A general tetrahedron.

The unknown coefficients $a_1, b_1, c_1, d_1, a_2, b_2, c_2, d_2, a_3, b_3, c_3, d_3$ follow from the system of equations

$$
\begin{aligned}
u_1 &= -a_1 - b_1 - c_1 + d_1, \\
u_2 &= a_1 - b_1 - c_1 + d_1, \\
u_3 &= -a_1 + b_1 - c_1 + d_1, \\
u_4 &= -a_1 - b_1 + c_1 + d_1, \\
v_1 &= -a_2 - b_2 - c_2 + d_2, \\
v_2 &= a_2 - b_2 - c_2 + d_2, \\
v_3 &= -a_2 + b_2 - c_2 + d_2, \\
v_4 &= -a_2 - b_2 + c_2 + d_2, \\
w_1 &= -a_3 - b_3 - c_3 + d_3, \\
w_2 &= a_3 - b_3 - c_3 + d_3, \\
w_3 &= -a_3 + b_3 - c_3 + d_3, \\
w_4 &= -a_3 - b_3 + c_3 + d_3,
\end{aligned}
$$

assigning the individual vertices of the general tetrahedron Ω_1 to the new reference tetrahedron Ω_2. The solution of this system is

$$
a_1 = \frac{u_2 - u_1}{2}, \quad b_1 = \frac{u_3 - u_1}{2}, \quad c_1 = \frac{u_4 - u_1}{2}, \quad d_1 = \frac{-u_1 + u_2 + u_3 + u_4}{2},
$$

$$
a_2 = \frac{v_2 - v_1}{2}, \quad b_2 = \frac{v_3 - v_1}{2}, \quad c_2 = \frac{v_4 - v_1}{2}, \quad d_2 = \frac{-v_1 + v_2 + v_3 + v_4}{2},
$$

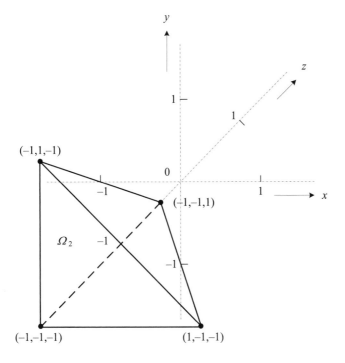

Figure C.11.   The reference triangle.

$$a_3 = \frac{w_2 - w_1}{2}, \quad b_3 = \frac{w_3 - w_1}{2}, \quad c_3 = \frac{w_4 - w_1}{2}, \quad d_3 = \frac{-w_1 + w_2 + w_3 + w_4}{2}.$$

The Jacobian of the mapping is

$$
\begin{aligned}
J &= \left| \begin{pmatrix} \partial u/\partial x & \partial u/\partial y & \partial u/\partial z \\ \partial v/\partial x & \partial v/\partial y & \partial v/\partial z \\ \partial w/\partial x & \partial w/\partial y & \partial w/\partial z \end{pmatrix} \right| \\
&= \left| \begin{pmatrix} (u_2 - u_1)/2 & (u_3 - u_1)/2 & (u_4 - u_1)/2 \\ (v_2 - v_1)/2 & (v_3 - v_1)/2 & (v_4 - v_1)/2 \\ (w_2 - w_1)/2 & (w_3 - w_1)/2 & (w_4 - w_1)/2 \end{pmatrix} \right| = \frac{3V_1}{4},
\end{aligned}
$$

where V_1 is the volume of the original tetrahedron. Now there holds

$$
\begin{aligned}
I_{\Omega_1} &= \int_{\Omega_1} f(u, v, w) \mathrm{d}V = \int_{\Omega_2} g(x, y, z) \cdot J \, \mathrm{d}V \\
&= J \int_{\Omega_2} g(x, y, z) \cdot \mathrm{d}V = \frac{3V_1}{4} \int_{\Omega_2} g(x, y, z) \cdot \mathrm{d}V \\
&= \frac{3V_1}{4} \int_{x=-1}^{1} \int_{y=-1}^{-x} \int_{z=-1}^{-1-x-y} g(x, y, z) \, \mathrm{d}z \, \mathrm{d}y \, \mathrm{d}x, \quad (\text{C.56})
\end{aligned}
$$

where

$$g(x, y, z) = f(a_1x + b_1y + c_1z + d_1, a_2x + b_2y + c_2z + d_2, a_3x + b_3y + c_3z + d_3).$$

Now we will show the possibilities of the numerical computation of integral (C.56).

Similar to the case of the reference cube we can assemble Table C.31 containing the known minimum numbers of integration points and also their achieved numbers. In fact, the integration points were found for even higher orders of the polynomial, but nothing is known about their minimum number. More details can be found in Ref. 202.

The integration points for polynomials up to the order $n = 5$ are listed in Tables C32–C36.

C.2.3.4 *Composite Gauss quadrature*   Consider the 1D quadrature rule in the form

$$\int_{x=-1}^{1} f(x)\mathrm{d}x \approx \sum_{i=1}^{n} w_i f(x_i), \quad i = 1, \ldots n,$$

Table C.31.   Minimum numbers of integration points over the Gaussian quadrature for the reference tetrahedron.

order of the polynomial	known minimum number of points	achieved number of points
1	1	1
2	4	4
3	5	5
4	11	11
5	14	14
6	24	24
7	28	31
8	40	43
9	52	53
10	68	
11		126

Table C.32.   Integration points for the reference tetrahedron, $n = 1$.

point No.	coordinate x	coordinate y	coordinate z	weight
1	–0.5	–0.5	–0.5	1.3333333333

Table C.33. Integration points for the reference tetrahedron, $n = 2$.

point No.	coordinate x	coordinate y	coordinate z	weight
1	–0.7236067977	–0.7236067977	–0.7236067977	0.3333333333
2	0.1708203932	–0.7236067977	–0.7236067977	0.3333333333
3	–0.7236067977	0.1708203932	–0.7236067977	0.3333333333
4	–0.7236067977	–0.7236067977	0.1708203932	0.3333333333

Table C.34. Integration points for the reference tetrahedron, $n = 3$.

point No.	coordinate x	coordinate y	coordinate z	weight
1	–0.5	–0.5	–0.5	–1.0666666666
2	–0.6666666666	–0.6666666666	–0.6666666666	0.6
3	–0.6666666666	–0.6666666666	0	0.6
4	–0.6666666666	0	–0.6666666666	0.6
5	0	–0.6666666666	–0.6666666666	0.6

Table C.35. Integration points for the reference tetrahedron, $n = 4$.

point No.	coordinate x	coordinate y	coordinate z	weight
1	–0.5	–0.5	–0.5	-0.1052444444
2	–0.8571428571	–0.8571428571	–0.8571428571	0.0609777777
3	–0.8571428571	–0.8571428571	0.5714285714	0.0609777777
4	–0.8571428571	0.5714285714	–0.8571428571	0.0609777777
5	0.5714285714	–0.8571428571	–0.8571428571	0.0609777777
6	–0.2011928476	–0.2011928476	–0.7988071523	0.1991111111
7	–0.2011928476	–0.7988071523	–0.2011928476	0.1991111111
8	–0.7988071523	–0.2011928476	–0.2011928476	0.1991111111
9	–0.2011928476	–0.7988071523	–0.7988071523	0.1991111111
10	–0.7988071523	–0.2011928476	–0.7988071523	0.1991111111
11	–0.7988071523	–0.7988071523	–0.2011928476	0.1991111111

where n is the number of Gauss' points in the direction of x, x_i are their coordinates, and $w_{n,i}$ are the corresponding weights. This rule integrates exactly all polynomials of the order n and lower.

Table C.36. Integration points for the reference tetrahedron, $n = 5$.

point No.	coordinate x	coordinate y	coordinate z	weight
1	−0.8145294993	−0.8145294993	−0.8145294993	0.0979907241
2	0.4435884981	−0.8145294993	−0.8145294993	0.0979907241
3	−0.8145294993	0.4435884981	−0.8145294993	0.0979907241
4	−0.8145294993	−0.8145294993	0.4435884981	0.0979907241
5	−0.3782281614	−0.3782281614	−0.3782281614	0.1502505676
6	−0.8653155155	−0.3782281614	−0.3782281614	0.1502505676
7	−0.3782281614	−0.8653155155	−0.3782281614	0.1502505676
8	−0.3782281614	−0.3782281614	−0.8653155155	0.1502505676
9	−0.0910074082	−0.0910074082	−0.9089925917	0.0567280277
10	−0.0910074082	−0.9089925917	−0.0910074082	0.0567280277
11	−0.9089925917	−0.0910074082	−0.0910074082	0.0567280277
12	−0.0910074082	−0.9089925917	−0.9089925917	0.0567280277
13	−0.9089925917	−0.0910074082	−0.9089925917	0.0567280277
14	−0.9089925917	−0.9089925917	−0.0910074082	0.0567280277

Consider another quadrature rule,

$$\int_S g(y, z)\mathrm{d}z\mathrm{d}y \approx \sum_{j=1}^{t} w_j g(y_j, z_j), \quad j = 1, \ldots t,$$

where S denotes the reference triangle, t the number of Gauss' points of coordinates y_j, z_j, and w_j their weights. This rule integrates exactly all polynomials of the order p and lower. Consider finally the formula

$$\int_S h(x, y, z)\mathrm{d}z\mathrm{d}y\mathrm{d}x \approx \sum_{i=1}^{n}\sum_{j=1}^{t} w_i w_j h(x_i, y_j, z_j),$$

$$i = 1, \ldots n, j = 1, \ldots t.$$

This formula integrates exactly all polynomials (of three independent variables x, y, z) of the order $\min(n, p)$ on a reference prism. The reason for using these formulas is that we do not know economical quadrature rules for prismas in the case of the reference cube or the tetrahedron.

REFERENCES

1. J. A. Stratton, *Electromagnetic Theory*, McGraw-Hill, New York, 1941.

2. J. D. Jackson, *Classical Electrodynamics*, 2nd edition, Wiley, Hoboken, NJ, 1975.

3. J. Van Bladel, *Electromagnetic Fields*, McGraw-Hill, New York, 1964.

4. C. A. Balanis, *Advanced Engineering Electromagnetics*, Wiley, Hoboken, NJ, 1989.

5. J. D. Kraus, *Electromagnetics*, 4th edition, McGraw-Hill, New York, 1973.

6. K. J. Binns and P. J. Lawrenson, *Analysis and Computation of Electric and Magnetic Field Problems*, Pergamon Press, Oxford, 1963.

7. K. J. Binns, P. J. Lawrenson, and C. W. Trowbridge, *The Analytical and Numerical Solution of Electric and Magnetic Fields*, Wiley, Hoboken, NJ, 1992.

8. J. W. Duffin, *Advanced Electricity and Magnetism*, McGraw-Hill, London, 1968.

9. P. Silvester, *Modern Electromagnetic Fields*, Prentice Hall, Englewood Cliffs, NJ. 1968.

10. R. M. Fano, L. J. Chu, and R. B. Adler, *Electromagnetic Fields, Energy and Forces*, Wiley, Hoboken, NJ, 1960.

11. W. Smythe. *Static and Dynamic Electricity*, McGraw-Hill, New York, 1950.

12. N. Ida, *Engineering Electromagnetics*, Springer, New York, 2000.

13. M. A. Pinsky, *Introduction to Partial Differential Equations with Applications*, McGraw-Hill, New York, 1984.

14. M. Taylor, *Partial Differential Equations*, Springer-Verlag, New York, 1996.

15. E. Zauderer, *Partial Differential Equations of Applied Mathematics*, Wiley–Interscience, Hoboken, NJ, 1989.

16. V. I. Arnold, *Lectures on Partial Differential Equations*, Springer-Verlag, Berlin, 2004.

17. C. Constanda, *Solution Techniques for Elementary Partial Differential Equations*, Chapman & Hall/CRC, Boca Raton, FL, 2002.

18. S. J. Farlow, *Partial Differential Equations for Scientists and Engineers*, Wiley, Hoboken, NJ, 1982.

19. F. John, *Partial Differential Equations*, Springer-Verlag, New York, 1982.

20. A. D. Polyanin, *Handbook of Linear Partial Differential Equations for Engineers and Scientists*, Chapman & Hall/CRC, Boca Raton, FL, 2002.

21. A. D. Polyanin and V. F. Zaitsev, *Handbook of Nonlinear Partial Differential Equations*, Chapman & Hall/CRC, Boca Raton, FL, 2004.

22. W. Hackbusch, *Integral Equations, Theory and Numerical Treatment*, Birkhäuser Verlag, Boston, 1995.

23. R. Precup, *Methods in Nonlinear Integral Equations*, Kluwer Academic Publisher, Dordrecht, 2002.

24. E. G. Ladopoulos, *Singular Integral Equations: Linear and Non-Linear Theory and its Applications in Science and Engineering*, Springer-Verlag, Berlin, 2000.

25. A. D. Polyanin and A. V. Manzhirov, *Handbook of Integral Equations*, 2nd Edition, Chapman & Hall/CRC, Boca Raton, FL, 2008.

26. H. W. Engl, *Integralgleichungen.* Springer-Verlag, Wien, 1997 (in German).

27. R. Kress, *Linear Integral Equations*, 2nd edition, Springer-Verlag, New York, 1999

28. L. V. Ahlfors, *Complex Analysis*, 3rd edition, McGraw-Hill, New York, 1979.

29. P. Henrici, *Applied and Computational Complex Analysis*, 3 vols., Wiley, Hoboken, NJ, 1993.

30. L. Bieberbach, *Conformal Mapping*, Chelsea, New York, 1964.

31. P. K. Kythe, *Computational Conformal Mapping*, Birkhäuser, Boston, 1998.

32. E. Weber, *Electromagnetic Fields: Theory and Applicstions*, Wiley, Hoboken, NJ, 1950.

33. A. Angot, *Compléments de Mathématiques à l'Usage des Ingénieurs de l'Electrotechnique et des Télécommunications*, Masson et Cie, Editions de la Revue d'Optique, Paris, 1952 (in French).

34. D. Zarko, D. Ban, and T. A. Lipo, "Analytical Solution for Cogging Torque in Surface Permanent-Magnet Motors Using Conformal Mapping," *IEEE Trans. Mag.*, **Vol. 44**, No. 1, pp. 52–65, 2008.

35. A. Ahmad and P. Auriol, "Conformal Mapping Method for Calculation of Rectangular Winding Parameters," *IEEE Trans. Mag.*, **Vol. 28**, No. 5, pp. 2823–2825, 1992.

36. T. A. Driscoll and L. N. Trefethen, *Schwarz-Christoffel Mapping*, Cambridge University Press, Cambridge, 2002.

37. E. Costamagna, "On the Numerical Inversion of the Schwarz-Christoffel Conformal Transformation," *IEEE Trans. Microwave Theory Tech.*, **Vol. 12**, No. 2, pp. 124–127, 1969.

38. E. Costamagna and A. Fanni, "Computing Capacitances via the Schwarz-Christoffel Transformation in Structures with Rotational Symmetry. Part 1," *IEEE Trans. Mag.*, **Vol. 34**, No. 5, pp. 2497–2500, 1998.

39. E. Costamagna and A. Fanni, "Analysis of Rectangular Coaxial Structures by Numerical Inversion of the Schwarz-Christoffel Transformation," *IEEE Trans. Mag.*, **Vol. 28**, No. 2, pp. 1454–1457, 1992.

40. D. C. J. Krop, E. A. Lomonova, and A. J. A. Vandenput, "Application of Schwarz-Christoffel Mapping to Permanent-Magnet Linear Motor Analysis," *IEEE Trans. Mag.*, **Vol. 44**, No. 3, pp. 352–359, 2008.

41. A. Nussbaum, "A Comparison of Exact and Finite Difference Methods for Two-Dimensional Potential Problems," *IEEE Trans. Educ.*, **Vol. 35**, No. 6, pp. 35–40, 1988.

42. K. Lee and K. Park, "Modeling Eddy Currents with Boundary Conditions by Using Coulomb's Law and the Method of Images," *IEEE Trans. Mag.*, **Vol. 38**, No. 2, pp. 1333–1340, 2002.

43. S. H. Lee, S. B. Park, S. O. Kwon, J. Y. Lee, J. J. Lee, J. P. Hong, and J. Hur, "Characteristic Analysis of the Slotless Axial-Flux Type Brushless DC Motors Using Image Method," *IEEE Trans. Mag.*, **Vol. 42**, No. 4, pp. 1327–1330, 2006.

44. F. Broyde and E. Clavelier, "The Basis of a Theory for the Shielding by Cylindrical Generalized Screens," *IEEE Trans. EMC*, **Vol. 42**, No. 4, pp. 414–426, 2000.

45. D. W. O. Heddle, *Electrostatic Lens Systems*, Adam Hilger, Bristol, 1991.

46. A. K. Gasiorski, "Finite Element Method for Power Losses Calculation in Long Rectangular Conductors Located in Transverse Harmonic Magnetic Field," *IEEE Trans. Mag.*, **Vol. 24**, No. 4, pp. 2140–2145, 1988.

47. B. Rulf, "Scattering by a Class of Composite Bodies Using Generalized Separation of Variables," *IEEE Trans. Antenna Propag.*, **Vol. 40**, No. 7, pp. 843–848, 1992.

48. A. Canova and B. Vusini, "Analytical Modeling of Rotating Eddy Current Couplers," *IEEE Trans. Mag.*, **Vol. 41**, No. 1, pp. 24–35, 2005.

49. D. Yaping, T. C. Cheng, and A. S. Faraq, "Principles of Power-Frequency Magnetic Field Shielding with Flat Sheets in a Source of Long Conductors," *IEEE Trans. EMC*, **Vol. 38**, No. 3, pp. 450–459, 1996.

50. G. D. Smith, *Numerical Solution of Partial Differential Equations: Finite Difference Methods*, Oxford University Press, New York, 1985.

51. J. W. Thomas, *Numerical Partial Differential Equations: Finite Difference Methods*, Springer, New York, 1998.

52. J. Strikwerda, *Finite Difference Schemes and Partial Differential Equations*, Wadsworth Publishing Co., Belmont, CA, 1989.

53. H. Levy and F. Lessman, *Finite Difference Equations*, Dover Science, New York, 1992.

54. M. N. Ozisik, *Finite Difference Methods in Heat Transfer*, Chapman & Hall/CRC, Boca Raton, FL, 1994.

55. K. W. Morton and D. F. Mayers, *Numerical Solution of Partial Differential Equations: An Introduction*, Cambridge University Press, Cambridge, 2002.

56. G. Sewell, *The Numerical Solution of Ordinary and Partial Differential Equations (Pure and Applied Mathematics)*, Wiley-Interscience, Hoboken, NJ, 2005.

57. W. F. Ames, *Numerical Methods for Partial Differential Equations*, 3rd edition, Scademic Press, Boston, 1992.

58. H. P. Langtangen, *Computational Partial Differential Equations: Numerical Methods and Diffpack Programming*, 2nd edition, Springer, Berlin, 2003.

59. P. Solin, *Partial Differential Equations and the Finite Element Method*, Wiley-Interscience, Hoboken, NJ, 2005.

60. D. R. Smith, *Variational Methods in Optimization*, Dover Books, New York, 1998.

61. I. M. Gelfand, *Calculus of Variation*, Dover Publications, New York, 2000.

62. C. Lanczos, *The Variational Principles of Mechanics*, Dover Books, New York, 1986.

63. O. C. Zienkiewicz, *The Finite Element Method in Engineering Science*, McGraw-Hill, London, 1971.

64. H. C. Martin and G. F. Carey, *Introduction to Finite Element Analysis— Theory and Applications*, McGraw-Hill, New York, 1973.

65. K. Huebner, E. A. Thornton, and T. G. Byrom, *The Finite Element Method for Engineers*, 3rd edition, Wiley, Hoboken, NJ, 1995.

66. R. H. Gallacher, *Finite Element Analysis Fundamentals*, Prentice Hall, Englewood Cliffs, NJ, 1975.

67. P. Silvester and R. L. Ferrari, *Finite Elements for Electrical Engineers*, 3rd edition, Cambridge University Press, Cambridge, UK, 1996.

68. T. J. R. Hughes, *The Finite Element Method*, Prentice Hall, Englewood Cliffs, NJ, 1987.

69. M. V. K. Chari and S. J. Salon, *Numerical Methods in Electromagnetism*, Academic Press, New York, 2000.

70. M. N. O. Sadiku, *Numerical Techniques in Electromagnetics*, CRC Press, Boca Raton, FL, 2000.

71. W. C. Chew, J. M. Jin, E. Michielssen, and J. Song, *Fast and Efficient Algorithms in Computational Electromagnetics*, ARTECH House, Noewood, MA, 2001.

72. J. M. Jin, *The Finite Element Method in Electromagnetics*, Wiley, Hoboken, NJ, 2002.

73. R. D. Cook, *Concepts and Applications of Finite Element Analysis*, Wiley, Hoboken, NJ, 1981.

74. K. J. Bethe, *Finite Element Procedures in Engineering Analysis*, Prentice Hall, Englewood Cliffs, NJ, 1982.

75. R. K. Livesley, *Finite Elements: An Introduction for Engineers*, Cambridge University Press, Cambridge, 1983.

76. J. N. Reddy, *An Introduction to the Finite Element Method*, McGraw-Hill, New York, 1984.

77. J.-C. Sabonndierre and J. L. Coulomb, *Finite Element Methods in CAD: Electrical and Magnetic Fields*, Springer Verlag, New York, 1987.

78. S. R. H. Hoole, *Finite Elements, Electromagnetics and Design*, Elsevier, Amsterdam, 1995.

79. B. N. Jiang, *The Least-Squares Finite Element Method: Theory and Applications in Fluid Dynamics and Electromagnetics*, Springer Verlag, Berlin, 1998.

80. N. Bianchi, *Electrical Machine Analysis Using Finite Elements*, CRC Press, Boca Raton, FL, 2005.

81. J. Bastos, *Electromagnetic Modeling by Finite Element Methods*, Marcel Dekker, New York, 2003.

82. S. Humphries, *Field Solutions on Computers*, CRC Press, Boca Raton, FL, 1997.

83. S. J. Salon, *Finite Element Analysis of Electrical Machines*, Kluwer Academic Publishers, Boston, 1995.

84. J. L. Volakis, A. Chatterjee, and L. C. Kempel, *Finite Element Method for Electromagnetics: Antennas, Microwave Circuits, and Scattering Applications*, IEEE Press and Oxford University Press, New York, 1998.

85. A. Monti, F. Ponci, and M. Riva, *Electrical Machine Theory Through Finite Element Analysis*, World Scientific, Singapore, 2001.

86. A. F. Peterson, S. L. Ray and R. Mittra, *Computational Methods for Electromagnetics*, IEEE Press, Piscataway, NJ, 1998.

87. P. Monk, *Finite Element Methods for Maxwell's Equations*, Oxford University Press, Oxford, 2003.

88. C. W. Steele, *Numerical Computation of Electric and Magnetic Fields*, 2nd edition, Chapman & Hall, New York, 1997.

89. P. B. Zhou, *Numerical Analysis of Electromagnetic Fields*, Springer Verlag, Berlin, 1993.

90. N. Ida and J. P. A. Bastos, *Electromagnetics and Calculation of Fields*, 2nd edition, Springer Verlag, New York, 1997.

91. M. Salazar-Parma, T. K. Sarkar, L. E. Garcia-Castillo, T. Roy, and A. R. Djordjevic, *Iterative and Self-Adaptive Finite Elements in Electromagnetic Modeling*, Artech House, Norwood, MA, 1998.

92. A. B. J. de Reece and T. W. Preston, *Finite Element Methods in Electrical Power Engineering*, Oxford University Press, Oxford, 2000.

93. I. E. Lager, *Finite Element Modeling of Static and Stationary Electric and Magnetic Fields*, Delft University Press, Delft, 1996.

94. P. Solin, K. Segeth, and I. Dolezel, *Higher-Order Finite Element Methods*, CRC Press, Boca Raton, FL, 2003.

95. M. Zitka, K. Segeth, and P. Solin, *Higher-Order FEM for Systems of Nonlinear Parabolic PDEs with A-Posteriori Error Estimates, Num. Math. Adv. Applic.*, **Vol. 5**, Springer, Berlin, 2004, pp. 854–863.

96. T. Vejchodsky, P. Solin, and M. Zitka, "Modular hp-FEM System HERMES and its Application to the Maxwell Equations," *Math. Comput. Simul.*, **Vol. 76**, pp. 223–228, 2007.

97. P. Solin, J. Cerveny, and I. Dolezel, "Arbitrary-Level Hanging Nodes and Automatic Adaptivity in the hp-FEM," *Math. Comput. Simul.*, **Vol. 77**, pp. 117–132, 2008.

98. P. Kus, P. Solin, and I. Dolezel, "Solution of 3D Singular Electrostatics Problems Using Adaptive hp-FEM," *COMPEL*, **Vol. 27**, No. 4, pp. 939–945, 2008.

99. E. Süli and D. F. Mayers, *An Introduction to Numerical Analysis*, Cambridge University Press, Cambridge, 2003.

100. B. Engquist and A. Majda, "Absorbing Boundary Conditions for the Numerical Simulation of Waves," *Math. Comput.*, **Vol. 31**, pp. 629–651, 1977.

101. M. W. Ali, T. H. Hubing, and J. L. Drewniak, "A Hybrid FEM/MoM Technique for Electromagnetic Scattering and Radiation from Dielectric Objects with Attached Wires," *IEEE Trans. EMC*, **Vol. 39**, No. 4, pp. 304–314, 1997.

102. J. P. Berenger, "A Perfectly Matched Layer for the Absorption of Electromagnetic Waves," *J. Comp. Phys.*, **Vol. 114**, pp. 185–200, 1994.

103. Z. S. Sacks, D. M. Kingsland, R. Lee, and J.-F. Lee, "Performance of an Anisotropic Artificial Absorber for Truncating Finite Element Meshes," *IEEE Trans. Antennas Propag.*, **Vol. 43**, pp. 1460–1463, 1995.

104. V. P. Pasko, U. S. Inan, T. F. Bell, and Y. N. Taranenko, "Sprites Produced by Quasi-Electrostatic Heating and Ionization in the Lower Ionosphere," *J. Geophys. Res.*, **Vol. 102**, pp. 4529–4561, 1997.

105. L. Tong, K. Nanbu, and H. Fukunishi, "Numerical Analysis of Initiation of Gigantic Jets Connecting Thunderclouds to the Ionosphere," *Earth Planets Space*, **Vol. 56**, pp. 1059–1065, 2004.

106. I. Dolezel, "Magnetic Field of an Ideal Circular Turn with the Rectangular Cross-Section," *Acta Technica CSAV*, **Vol. 34**, No. 1, pp. 9–34, 1989.

107. I. Dolezel, "Self-Inductance of an Air Cylindrical Coil," *Acta Technica CSAV*, **Vol. 34**, No. 5, pp. 443–473, 1989.

108. I. Dolezel, D. Verdyck, R. Belmans, and W. Geysen, "Analytical and FE Open Boundary Calculations of the Self and Mutual Inductances in a System of Concentric Cylindrical Air-Core Coils," *Acta Technica CSAV*, **Vol. 35**, No. 6, pp. 509–531, 1990.

109. I. Dolezel, "Forces in an Air Cylindrical Coil with Homogeneously Distributed Current Density in the Conductors," *Acta Technica CSAV*, **Vol. 35**, No. 2, pp. 187–222, 1990.

110. I. Dolezel, "Contribution to the Calculation of Forces Acting in a Cylindrical Air-Core Coil," *Acta Technica CSAV*, **36**, No. 5, pp. 467–478, 1991.

111. I. Dolezel, "Magnetic Field Around an Air-Core Helicoidal Coil," *Acta Technica CSAV*, **37**, No. 1, pp. 49–68, 1992.

112. R. F. Harrington, *Field Computation by Moment Methods*, Macmillan, New York, 1968.

113. L. R. Turner, "An Integral Approach to Eddy Current Calculation," *IEEE Trans. Mag.*, **Vol. 13**, pp. 1119–1121, 1977.

114. J. H. McWhirter, "Computation of Three-Dimensional Eddy Currents in Thin Conductors," *IEEE Trans. Mag.*, **Vol. 18**, pp. 456–460, 1982.

115. J. H. McWhirter, R. J. Duffin, and P. J. Brehm, "Computational Methods for Solving Static Field and Eddy Current Problems via Fredholm Integral Equations," *IEEE Trans. Mag.*, **Vol. 15**, pp. 1075–1084, 1979.

116. C. A. Antonopoulos, T. D. Tsiboukis, and E. E. Kriezis, "Field Calculation in Single- and Multilayer Coaxial Cylindrical Shells of Infinite Length by Using a Coupled and Boundary Element Method," *IEEE Trans. Mag.*, **Vol. 28**, No. 1, pp. 61–66, 1992.

117. E. E. Kriezis and J. A. Tegopoulos, "Transient Eddy Current Distribution in Cylindrical Shells," *IEEE Trans. Mag.*, **Vol. 11**, No. 5, pp. 1977–1979, 1975.

118. E. E. Kriezis and C. A. Antonopoulos, "Low-Frequency Electromagnetic Shielding in a System of Two Coaxial Cylindrical Shells," *IEEE Trans. EMC*, **Vol. 26**, No. 4, pp. 193–201, 1984.

119. E. E. Kriezis and M. N. Zervas, "Calculation of the Forces and the Field in a Cylindrical Shell with a General Excitation by Using an Integral Formulation," *IEEE Trans. Mag.*, **Vol. 20**, No. 5, pp. 1977–1979, 1984.

120. J. A. Tegopoulos and E. E. Kriezis, "Eddy Current Distribution in Cylindrical Shells of Infinite Length due to Axial Currents, Part II: Shells of Finite Thickness," *IEEE Trans. PAS*, **Vol. 90**, No. 3, pp. 1287–1294, 1971.

121. E. K. Miller, L. Medgyesi-Mitschang, and E. H. Newman, Eds., *Computational Electromagnetics: Frequency-Domain Method of Moments*, IEEE Press, New York, 1992.

122. D. Poljak and C. Y. Tham, *Integral Equation Techniques in Transient Electromagnetics*, WIT Press, Southampton, 2003.

123. J. J. H. Wang, *Generalized Moment Methods in Electromagnetics*, Wiley, Hoboken, NJ, 1991.

124. R. C. Hansen, Ed., *Moment Methods in Antennas and Scattering*, Artech House, Norwood, MA, 1990.

125. V. Rokhlin, "Rapid Solution of Integral Equations of Scattering Theory in Two Dimensions," *J. Comput. Phys.*, **Vol. 36**, No. 2, pp. 414–439, 1990.

126. C. C. Lu and W. C. Chew, "A Fast Algorithm for Solving Hybrid Integral Equations," *IEE Proc. H*, **Vol. 140**, No. 6, pp. 455–460, 1993.

127. W. M. Rucker and K. R. Richter, "Calculation of Two-Dimensional Eddy Current Problems with the Boundary Element Method," *IEEE Trans. Mag.*, **Vol. 19**, No. 6, pp. 2429–2432, 1983.

128. N. Morita, N. Kumagai, and J. R. Mautz, *Integral Equation Methods for Electromagnetics*, Artech House Inc., Norwood, 1990.

129. R. Albanese, G. Rubinacci, M. Canali, S. Stangherlin, A. Musolino, and M. Raugi, "Analysis of a Transient Nonlinear 3D Eddy Current Problem with Differential and Integral Methods," *IEEE Trans. Mag.*, **Vol. 32**, No. 3, pp. 776–779, 1996.

130. I. Tsukerman, "Stability of the Moment Method in Electromagnetic Problems," *IEEE Trans. Mag.*, **Vol. 33**, No. 2, pp. 1402–1405, 1997.

131. B. Maouche and M. Féliachi, "A Discretized Integral Method for Eddy Current Computation in Moving Objects with the Coexistence of the Velocity and Time Terms," *IEEE Trans. Mag.*, **Vol. 34**, No. 5, pp. 2567–2569, 1998.

132. G. Rubinacci, A. Tamburrino, S. Ventre, and F. Villone, "A Fast Algorithm for Solving 3D Eddy Current Problems with Integral Formulations," *IEEE Trans. Mag.*, **Vol. 37**, No. 5, pp. 3099–3103, 2001.

133. M. H. Lean and A. Wexler, "Accurate Numerical Integration of Singular Boundary Element Kernels over Boundaries with Curvature," *Int. J. Num. Math. Eng.*, **Vol. 21**, pp. 211–228, 1985.

134. H. Lei, L. Z. Wang, and Z. N. Wu, "Integral Analysis of a Magnetic Field for an Arbitrary Geometry Coil with Rectangular Cross-Section," *IEEE Trans. Mag.*, **Vol. 38**, No. 6, pp. 3589–3593, 2002.

135. O. M. Kwon, M. V. K. Chari, S. J. Salon, and K. Sivasubramanian, "Development of Integral Equation Solution for 3D Eddy Current Distribution in a Conducting Body," *IEEE Trans. Mag.*, **Vol. 39**, No. 5, pp. 2612–2614, 2003.

136. I. R. Ciric and R. Curiac, "A Single-Source Surface Integral Formulation for Eddy Current Problems," *IEEE Trans. Mag.*, **Vol. 40**, No. 2, pp. 1346–1349, 2004.

137. A. Gagnoud, "Three-Dimensional Integral Method for Modelling Electromagnetic Inductive Process," *IEEE Trans. Mag.*, **Vol. 40**, No. 1, pp. 29–36, 2004.

138. I. Dolezel and P. Karban, "Integral Model of Eddy Currents in Nonmagnetic Structures," *Acta Electrotech. Informatica*, **Vol. 4**, No. 3, pp. 5–12, 2004.

139. I. Dolezel, P. Karban, M. Mach, and B. Ulrych, "Integral Model of Skin Effect and Associated Phenomena in Long Massive Conductors," *Tech. Electrodynamics Nat. Acad. Sci. Ukraine*, **Vol. 4**, pp. 3–6, 2004.

140. I. Dolezel, P. Dvorak, P. Karban, and B. Ulrych, "Determination of Circuit Parameters of High-Frequency Profile Conductors," *Vesn. Lviv Polytech. Ukraine*, **Vol. 508**, pp. 226–234, 2004.

141. R. Hamar, I. Dolezel, and B. Ulrych, "Solution of 3D Electrostatic Problems in Homogeneous Media by Means of Integral Equations," *Proc. SPETO'2003*, May 2003, Niedzyca, Poland, pp. 35–38.

142. R. Hamar and I. Dolezel, "Convergence Problems of Integral Modeling of 3D ElectroStatic Fields with Singularities," *Proc. AMTEE'2007*, September 2007, Plzen, Czech Republic, CD-ROM.

143. R. Hamar, I. Dolezel, and B. Ulrych, "Integral Solution of Electrostatic Fields in 3D Arrangements," *Proc. AMTEE'2003*, September 2003, Plzen, Czech Republic, pp. A37–A42.

144. P. Karban, I. Dolezel, and P. Solin, "Computation of General Nonstationary 2D Eddy Currents in Linear Moving Arrangements Using Integrodifferential Approach," *COMPEL*, **Vol. 25**, No. 3, pp. 635–641, 2006.

145. C. A. Brebbia, J. Telles, and L. Wrobel, *Boundary Element Techniques. Theory and Applications in Engineering*, Springer Verlag, Berlin, 1984.

146. C. A. Brebbia, *The Boundary Element Method for Engineers*, Pentech Press, London, 1978.

147. G. Chen and J. Zhou, *Boundary Element Methods*, Academic Press, New York, 1992.

148. W. S. Hall, *The Boundary Element Method*, Kluwer Academic Publishers, The Netherlands, 1994.

149. P. K. Banerjee and R. Butterfield, *Boundary Element Methods in Engineering Science*, McGraw-Hill, New York, 1981.

150. K. Kythe, Ed., *An Introduction to Boundary Element Method*, CRC Press, Boca Raton, FL, 1995.

151. G. F. Roach, *Green's Functions*, 2nd edition, Cambridge University Press, Cambridge, UK, 1982.

152. I. Stakgold, *Green's Functions and Boundary Value Problems*, Wiley-Interscience, Hoboken, NJ, USA, 1979.

153. Y. Melnikov, *Green's Functions in Applied Mechanics*, Computational Mechanics Publications, Southampton, UK, 1994.

154. D. G. Duffy, *Green's Functions with Applications*, CRC Press, Boca Raton, FL, 2001.

155. P. K. Banerjee, *The Boundary Element Methods in Engineering*, McGraw-Hill, New York, 1994.

156. G. Barton, *Elements of Green's Functions and Propagation*, Oxford University Press, New York, 1989.

157. A. A. Becker, *The Boundary Element Method in Engineering: A Complete Course*, McGraw-Hill, New York, 1992.

158. C. A. Brebbia and J. Dominguez, *Boundary Elements, an Introductory Course*, WIT Press, Boston, 1992.

159. L. Gaul, M. Koegl, and M. Wagner, *Boundary Element Methods for Engineers and Scientists*, Springer, New York, 2003.

160. W. C. Gibson, *The Method of Moments in Electromagnetics*. Chapman & Hall/CRC, Boca Raton, FL, 2008.

161. J. T. Katsikadelis, *Boundary Elements, Theory and Applications*, Elsevier, New York, 2002.

162. O. D. Kellog, *Foundations of Potential Theory*, Dover Science Publications, New York, 1969.

163. F. Riesz and B. Sz. Nagy, *Functional Analysis*, Dover Publications, New York, 1990.

164. W. Rudin, *Functional Analysis*, McGraw-Hill, New York, 1991.

165. M. Schechter, *Principles of Functional Analysis*, 2nd edition, American Mathematical Society, Providence, RI, 2001.

166. P. Solin, *Partial Differential Equations and the Finite Element Method*, Wiley, Hoboken, NJ, 2005.

167. L. C. Wrobel and M. H. Aliabadi, *The Boundary Element Method*, Wiley, Hoboken, NJ, 2002.

168. J. P. Holman, *Heat Transfer*, McGraw-Hill, New York, 2002.

169. M. Zlobina, B. Nacke, and A. Nikonarov, "Electromagnetic and Thermal Analysis of Induction Heating of Billets by Rotation in DC Magnetic Field," *Proc. UIE Krakow*, Poland, May 2008, pp. 21–22.

170. S. Lupi and M. Forzan, "A Promising High Efficiency Technology for the Induction Heating of Aluminium Billets," *Proc. UIE Krakow*, Poland, May 2008, pp. 19–20.

171. M. D. Greenberg, *Advanced Engineering Mathematics*, 2nd edition, Prentice Hall, Englewood Cliffs, NJ, 1998.

172. E. Kreyszig, *Advanced Engineering Mathematics*, 9th edition, Wiley, Hoboken, NJ, 2005.

173. M. R. Spiegel, *Schaum's Mathematical Handbook of Formulas and Tables*, McGraw-Hill, 1998.

174. K. Janich, *Vector Analysis*, Springer, New York, 2001.

175. P. C. Mathews, *Vector Calculus*, Springer, New York, 2000.

176. M. Rahman, *Advanced Vector Analysis for Scientists and Engineers*, WIT Press, Southampton, UK, 2007.

177. R. Bellman, *Introduction to Matrix Analysis*, Society for Industrial & Applied Mathematics, Philadelphia, 1997.

178. T. S. Shores, *Applied Linear Algebra and Matrix Analysis*, Springer, New York, 2007.

179. R. A. Horn and Ch. R. Johnson, *Matrix Analysis*, Cambridge University Press, Cambridge, 1990.

180. G. H. Golub and Ch. F. van Loan, *Matrix Computations*, 3rd edition, John Hopkins University Press, Baltimore, 1996.

181. R. S. Varga, *Matrix Iterative Analysis*, Prentice Hall, Englewood Cliffs, NJ, 1962.

182. B. G. Korenev, M. Saigo, H.-J. Glaeske, and E. Moiseev, *Bessel Functions and Their Applications*, CRC Press, Boca Raton, FL, 2002.

183. F. Bowman, *Introduction to Bessel Functions*, Dover Publications, New York, 1958.

184. L. C. Andrews, *Special Functions of Mathematics for Engineers*, 2nd edition, SPIE Press, Bellingham, 1998.

185. F. Bowman, *Introduction to Elliptic Functions*, Wiley, Hoboken, NJ, 1953.

186. H. Hancock, *Elliptic Integrals*, Dover Publications, New York, 1958.

187. P. F. Byrd and M. Friedman, *Handbook of Elliptic Integrals for Engineers and Scientists*, 2nd edition, Springer, Berlin, 1971.

188. V. Prasolov and Y. Solovyev, *Elliptic Functions and Elliptic Integrals*, American Mathematical Society, Providence, RI, 1997.

189. T. J. Rivlin, *Chebyshev Polynomials: From Approximation Theory to Algebra and Number Theory*, 2nd edition, Wiley-Interscience, Hoboken, NJ, 1990.

190. J. C. Mason and D. C. Handscomb, *Chebyshev Polynomials*, Chapman & Hall/CRC Press, Boca Raton, FL, 2002.

191. D. Jackson, *Fourier Series and Orthogonal Polynomials*, Dover Books, New York, 2004.

192. D. Zwillinger, *Handbook of Integration*, Jones and Bartlett, Boston, 1992.

193. A. Stroud, *Approximate Calculation of Multiple Integrals*, Prentice Hall, Englewood Cliffs, NJ, 1971.

194. A. Stroud and D. Secrest, *Gaussian Quadrature Formulas*, Prentice Hall, Englewood Cliffs, NJ, 1966.

195. H. Engels, *Numerical Quadrature and Cubature*, Academic Press, London, 1980.

196. G. Evans, *Practical Numerical Integration*, Wiley, Chichester, UK, 1993.

197. D. A. Dunavant, "Economical Symmetrical Quadrature Rules for Complete Polynomials over a Square Domain," *Int. J. Numer. Methods Eng.*, **Vol. 21**, pp. 1777–1784, 1985.

198. J. N. Lyness and D. Jespersen, "Moderate Degree Symmetric Quadrature Rules for the Triangle," *J. Inst. Math. Appl.*, **Vol. 15**, pp. 15–32, 1975.

199. J. N. Lyness and R. Cools, "A Survey of Numerical Cubature over Triangles," *in Mathematics in Computations: A Half-Century of Computational Mathematics* (W. Gautschi, Ed.), Proc. Symposia in Applied Mathematics, Vol. 48, pp. 127–150, American Mathematical Society, Providence, RI, 1994.

200. D. A. Dunavant, "High Degree Efficient Symmetrical Gaussian Quadrature Rules for the Triangle," *Int. J. Numer. Methods Eng.*, **Vol. 21**, pp. 1129–1148, 1985.

201. D. A. Dunavant, "Efficient Symmetrical Cubature Rules for Complete Polynomials of High Degree over a Unit Cube," *Int. J. Numer. Methods Eng.*, **Vol. 23**, pp. 397–407, 1986.

202. P. Keast, "Moderate-Degree Tetrahedral Quadrature Formulas," *Comput. Methods Appl. Mech. Eng.*, **Vol. 55**, pp. 339–348, 1986.

203. K. E. Atkinson, *Numerical Solution of Integral Equations of the Second Kind*, Cambridge University Press, Cambridge, 1997.

204. A. V. Bitsadze, *Integral Equation of the First Kind*, World Scientific, Singapore, 1995.

205. L. Bos, "On Certain Configurations of Points in $\mathbb{R}^n$ Which Are Uniresolvant for Polynomial Interpolation," *J. Approx. Theory*, **Vol. 64**, pp. 271–280, 1991.

206. L. Bos, M. A. Taylor, and B. A. Wingate, "Tensor Product Gauss–Lobatto Points Are Fekete Points for the Cube," *Math. Comp.*, **Vol. 70**, pp. 1543–1547, 2001.

207. M. Dubiner, "Spectral Element Methods on Triangles and other Domains", *J. Sci. Comput.*, **Vol. 6**, pp. 345–390, 1991.

208. G. Gripenberg, S.-O. Londen, and O. Staffans, *Volterra Integral and Functional Equations*, Cambridge University Press, Cambridge, 1990.

209. C. W. Groetsch, *The Theory of Tikhonov Regularization for Fredholm Equations of the First Kind*, Pitman Publishing, Boston, 1984.

210. J. Kondo, *Integral Equations*, Clarendon Press, Oxford, 1997.

211. I. K. Lifanov, L .N. Poltavskii, and G. Vainikko, *Hypersingular Integral Equations and Their Applications*, Chapman & Hall / CRC Press, Boca Raton, FL, 2004.

212. M. A. Taylor, B. A. Wingate, and R. E. Vincent, "An Algorithm for Computing Fekete Points in the Triangle," *SIAM J. Numer. Anal.*, **Vol. 38**, pp. 1707–1720, 2000.

213. F. G. Tricomi, *Integral Equations*, Dover Publications, New York, 1985.

214. V. Volterra, *Theory of Functionals and of Integral and Integro-Differential Equations*, Dover Publications, New York, 1959.

215. G. M. Wing, *A Primer on Integral Equations of the First Kind*, SIAM, Philadelphia, 1991.

INDEX

INDEX